TESTIMONIALS HONORIN
Extraordinary Leadership During Ex

"Extraordinary Leadership during Extraordinary Times is packed with visionary insight and lucid practical guidance. On every page the reader feels Joyce Anastasia's compassionate intelligence offering the wisdom so urgently needed by leaders everywhere."

~JAMES O'DEA
Global Peace Activist, Author *Cultivating Peace, The Conscious Activist*

"At a time when dire circumstances call for true leaders rather than rulers, and real solutions must be based on natural principles rather than polarity politics, Joyce Anastasia offers a vital vision of the attributes each of us can develop to guide us in creating a thriving civilization."

~FOSTER GAMBLE
Co-creator, globally-acclaimed documentary "**Thrive**" and its movement

"Extraordinary Leadership during Extraordinary Times by Joyce Anastasia is a masterful guide for reinventing leadership using the immense power of our hearts. Through the use of evocative stories, quotes and practices, it helps illuminate what's not working in our current paradigm, teaching us to share power equitably and respectfully rather than hierarchically, to honor and value diversity, to distribute authority more wisely and justly, and to speak truth to power. In alignment with the ancient maxim "As above, so below," this book offers astute and accessible guidance for achieving the inner transformations that result in more effective, productive and joyful leadership in our relationships, companies, communities and the world."

~NINA SIMONS
Co-Founder and President, **Bioneers**, Founder, **Everywoman's Leadership**

"What is that quality that allows someone to challenge the status quo and bring up controversial subjects while assuring people all the while that something promising lives on the other side? Leadership — the sort that Joyce describes with deft elucidation. I love that she is willing to demonstrate her own bold leadership in the course of unpacking what it entails."

~KIMBERLY CARTER GAMBLE
Producer, Director, Co-Writer, globally-acclaimed documentary "**Thrive**"
CEO, **Clear Compass Media**

"Extraordinary Leadership during Extraordinary Times is indeed a truly extraordinary book. Joyce Anastasia dives deeply into the questions we all need to ask ourselves: how do we honor and express our Connection with Life, our Power, Deepest Truth, Morality, Integrity, Balance, Spirit and Inspiration? For Leaders, and that means all of us from Heads of State to parents to every individual, asking these questions for ourselves is the only real issue facing us in these times. These are the essential questions our hearts and minds need to ask to bring the world we all desire into being for our children, grandchildren and all generations that will follow. This is truly a no B.S. book!"

~DAVID MEGGYESY
Author, *Out of Their League*
Former Linebacker, NFL St. Louis Cardinals – now the Arizona Cardinals

"Gentle and yet powerful, the healing messages in this book speak with eloquence and wisdom to the raging personal and collective dysfunction of our time. Its essential message is one of hope and faith, with beautiful teachings drawn from the life experience of the author and many of the talented, creative people from all over the world who have shared her journey."

~DR. STEVE BORISH
Author, *The Land of the Living*
Associate Professor of Human Development, California State University, East Bay

"In her book, Joyce Anastasia offers us a refreshing and vital recontextualization of Leadership, by immersing readers into the interiority of it through her 7 Vital Keys. Joyce reminds us that social change is inextricably tied to personal change, and that our ability to be consciously in touch with our body, mind, emotions, spirit and soul, provides the best form of in-the-moment leadership."

~BARRY ROBBINS
Vice President, **ITP International**

"These are exceptional, extraordinary times, times of great transitions, personally and globally. In times of great changes, we have an opportunity to chart a course different from the one we have been on, so what do we want to become personally and collectively? If we open our eyes and hearts, and see and feel, we will know that We are One, not just humanity, but All is One. This book can point the direction for a change in our world from competitive individualism to recognition of the relatedness and interdependence of ourselves and everything else. As Joyce Anastasia says: "It begins with each of us." Seven "Vital Keys" to address our greatest leadership and life challenges are identified and discussed. I found the book very compelling and recommend it."

~MICHAEL TWO BEARS ANDREWS
Former Major Oil Executive, Leader and Participant in Spiritual Ceremonies

"Joyce Anastasia's book goes boldly where no man has gone before, but perhaps that's the point: what the world needs now is feminine leadership. After all, we have given masculine leadership more than its fair share of time and what have been the results? From Machiavelli to the modern day Koch brothers, the manipulation of power through money and influence has contributed to the decline of our natural world, and with it, much of the sustenance we depend upon. Anastasia's ambitious book seeks to redirect power from "Power Over" to "Power With," and while she doesn't use the phrase, she is also advocating "Power Within," because, in essence, she is reaching into our own hearts and asking us to reawaken to the real power, beauty, and wholeness of Nature already surging through us — and then to realign ourselves with that larger Self. It is that higher moral and spiritual self that wants to do the right thing; and it is this voice that needs to be spoken even in the midst of these turbulent times. In short, this is a rare book that seeks to connect the inner with the outer in deep and profound ways. Anastasia makes effective and evocative use of personal stories, her own and others', in a way that challenges us to boldly face the truth of what is happening in society and within our own hearts. Pure-hearted and honest, this book deserves to be read widely and take its place in the emerging dialogue of transformative leadership."

~GLENN APARICIO PARRY
Author, *Original Thinking: A Radical Revisioning of Time, Humanity, and Nature*

Extraordinary Leadership During Extraordinary Times

Transforming World Systems through the Hearts of Its Leaders

Joyce Anastasia

Joyce Anastasia

10/23/2016

Printed and bound in the United States of America

A CIP record for this book is available at the Library of Congress

Library of Congress Control Number: 2015906825

Lead By Wisdom, Mill Valley, CA

Paperback Book ISBN: 978-0-9908881-0-9
Hardback Book ISBN: 978-0-9908881-2-3
Ebook ISBN: 978-0-9908881-1-6

Lead By Wisdom
Mill Valley, CA 94941

www.leadbywisdom.com

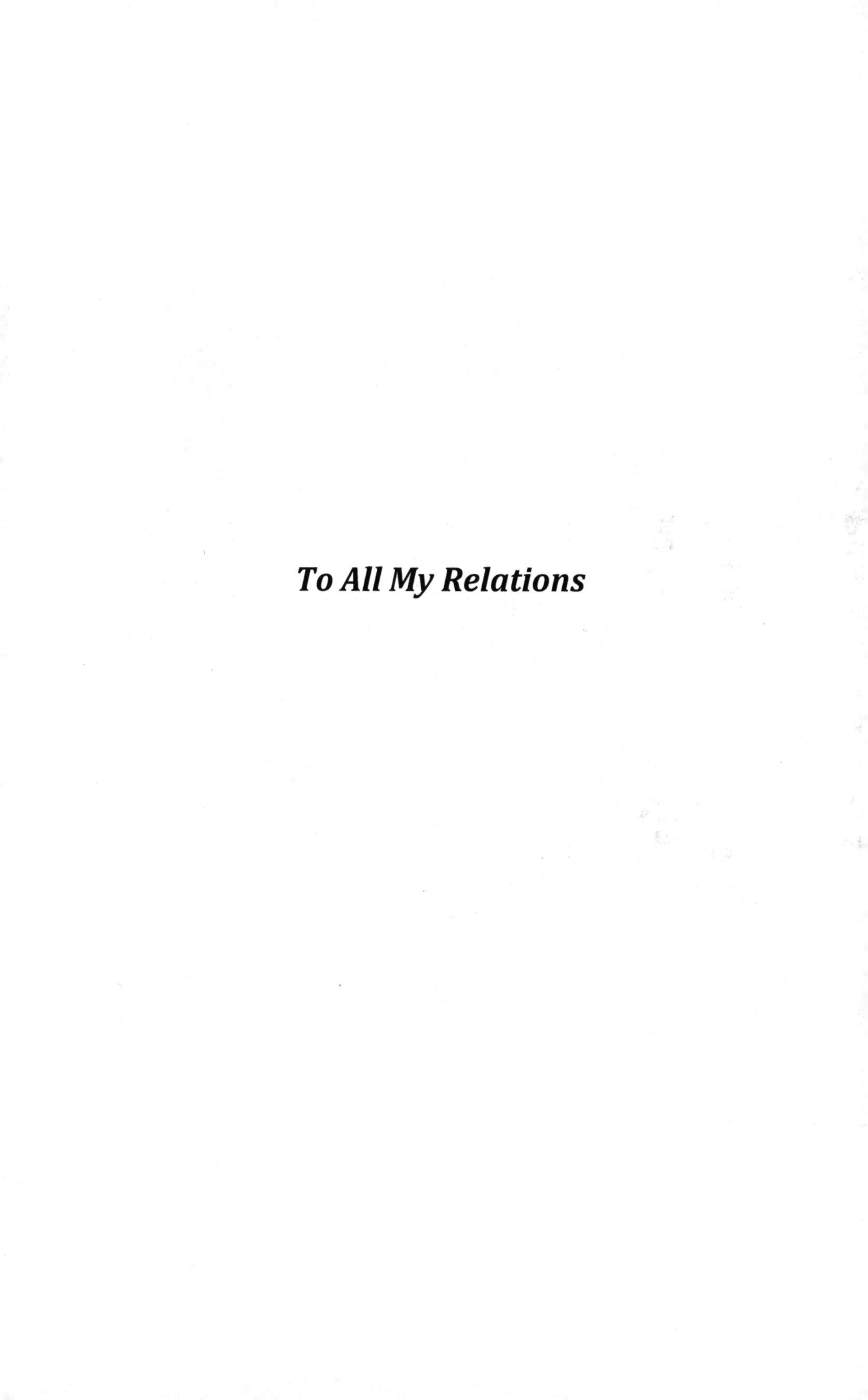

To All My Relations

Opening Prayer

Great Spirit, God-Source, All That Is ~ Thank you for opening the portals to the wisdom you have guided me to share with my fellow brothers and sisters on this planet. May we each be open to the vibration of the purest love from spirit into our world. As we prepare our bodies, minds, hearts and souls to receive this energy, may we be open to these new ways to lead and be, in our daily walk of life.

My heart is filled with gratitude for the gifts offered by Great Spirit in the messages I received for the creation of this book. May they serve as the most loving interventions, guiding our navigation through the challenges and joys of daily life, and bridging our connection with the Whole.

May we have the courage to step into the highest expression of our humanity ~ as we are a species blessed with extraordinary capacities for compassion, forgiveness and love for all beings, our sacred planet Earth and the Universe itself.

May we also take courage in listening to that deep Calling to shine light on our miraculous nature and to heed the call to Lead By Wisdom during these Extraordinary Times.

Contents

Acknowledgements

There is a higher wisdom that has served as the foundation for the evolution and creation of this book and for that, I am truly grateful. Many people say, "It takes a village," and in this case, that village extends from the seen to the unseen realms. I recognize those "helping hands" in the form of supportive vibrations from ancestors and friends who have passed — from my dear friend Chris Carey to my grandparents, great grandparents and other extended family members, then to my spiritual mentors Edgar Cayce, Jane Roberts, as well as leaders I admire, like President Lincoln, President John F. Kennedy, Gandhi, Martin Luther King, Jr., and others. I am especially moved by the consistent, clear and loving support from Master Teachers: Christ, Buddha, Krishna, the Dalai Lama, Mahavatar Babaji, Paramahansa Yogananda and his lineage, St. Francis, and all of the Angelic and Nature Spirits. To all my past and present spiritual teachers and wise mentors, some of whom I have mentioned in these writings and others who remain hidden: I am so appreciative.

This book would not have been possible without the developmental guidance of my wonderful parents: Harry and Arlene Howansky and my four siblings (and their families) who share unique gifts and are supportive of each other and fellow beings on this planet. I especially would like to thank my younger brother, Andy Howansky, whose mutually creative dialogues helped to bring about a greater ease of expression for some of the more challenging topics presented in this book. His visionary, witty and loving approach resonates so deeply with my work in the world, while his concrete expression through his three-dimensional graphics helped imbue the words with sacred geometry, setting the tone I envisioned for each of the Vital Keys. His ability to create the book cover that I saw in my dreams was miraculous — Words cannot express the gratitude I feel for him! Similarly, I'd like to thank my extended family, my cousin Chris who helped me in my early years to navigate school by teaching me how to read with greater aptitude and confidence, and another cousin, Adora, my first spiritual mentor, who helped me to be

open to all possibilities, seen and unseen, for teaching me to walk a path of love and light.

As with my supportive family, I have also been blessed with incredible teachers throughout my life and I would love for them to know how much their insights, kind words and gestures made a difference for me, even though some may have had no idea of their impact. In the same vein, I'd like to honor all my clients, my life-work experiences, the companies I've worked for and the people, places and cultures I have encountered: thank you so much for your guidance, helping me to lead with greater wisdom. Thanks especially to Shayne Mitchell for his amazing support during my trip to Egypt, one of the more pivotal experiences inspiring this book. And a very special thanks to the Foundation for Global Humanity (FGH) — Connie, Matt and Mary and all the people we met: for the depth of our encounters and engagement in service to healing all cultures and our planet. Thanks especially to the generosity of Connie Cummings, FGH Founder, colleague and friend, for supporting the creation of my book even before I began to write.

As the creative process evolved, with many twists and turns early on, I solicited the assistance of the following generous and beautiful souls: Paul Elder, Ahraiyanna Della Tone, Nancy Forbes, Harry Howansky, Mary Eileen Mueller, Kalibri Anne, Russell Munsell, Mark Small, Marla Martin and others. I feel so much gratitude for their thoughtful input, which found its way into the fabric of this book, whether seen or unseen.

Another turning point in the evolution of this book was my facilitation of the Extraordinary Leadership Telesummit I held in 2013. The contributions of each person that I interviewed were visionary and insightful. What amazing gifts these extraordinary leaders shared! Deep gratitude to: James O'Dea, Glenn A. Parry, JoAnne O'Brien-Levin, Foster Gamble, Sequoyah Trueblood, Pat McCabe ("Woman Stands Shining"), Lynne McTaggart, Stephen Dinan, Nina Simons and Kimberly Carter Gamble. Thanks to many of those same individuals who served as readers for the manuscript prior to publication, sharing their thoughtful feedback with me. Other readers and contributors included Lynnea Celestine (generous hours of transcribing), Susan Isaacs (early sacred witness),

Michael Gaza, Denis Nayangau, Marilyn Lindsay, Crissa Florentino (transcripts and tech support), Ryan and Neal Botteron (my nephews, whose lives already reflect the integration of what resonated for them; what a gift to me that they took the time!), colleagues and friends David Meggyesy, Suzanne Eugster, Michael Two Bears Andrews, Jahsiah Jacobs, Polly Higgins, Byron Belitsos and Dr. Steve Borish: their comments and suggestions were extremely helpful.

From early on in the process and each step along the way, I was blessed with a wonderful editor and thought partner, JoAnne O'Brien-Levin, who served as a beacon to help distill my work, ensuring consistency and authenticity in both the narrative and stories. I have such respect and gratitude for her wisdom, generosity and loving support. Then in the final stages of the book, my cousin and friend Judith Swota, served as an important reader and divine collaborator. She helped me to review and edit the manuscript with a fresh pair of eyes, contributing valuable insights and ideas, tapping into a unified voice that was unexpected and delightful. In addition, she meticulously worked on the final line-by-line editing. I appreciate her presence in my life and tremendously value her contributions. A special thanks to Judith and my brother Andy for their perseverance in creating a workable Index – a Herculean task!

There are so many people in my daily encounters that I wish to thank: a special honoring and gratitude for my beloved partner, J.T. Brown III, for understanding the long hours of research and writing, supporting me with feedback, technological repairs, infusion of playfulness and words of encouragement; a deep appreciation for my wonderful friend Sarah Dawson, for all the love and energetic support long-distance; and dear friends like John Caputo, Carol Hornibrook, Charles Smith, Barry Robbins, Julian Isaacs, Pat Fields, Eve Rubenstein, Lauren Harkrader, Martin Chesler, Scott Mills, Devaa H. Mitchell, Elayne Kalila Doughty and more. Thank you to the communities of Thrive (Sharla Jacobs, Jesse Koren and their team), The Big Shift (Bill Baran and all), John Eggen and Tom Bird for book publishing expertise, and the amazing staff and patrons at La Boulange Café. Please forgive me if I neglected to mention anyone directly, as I appreciate so many people I have met on my journey.

Foreword

I thank my beloved, gracious and audacious friend, Joyce Anastasia, for blessing me in this most benevolent way, by asking me to prepare the Foreword on her masterpiece of a book, "Extraordinary Leadership During Extraordinary Times." The words that Spirit has chosen to flow through her being are the Creator's stamp of approval on the magnificence of her contribution to a great shift in planetary consciousness.

At this most required time in the history of Mother Earth, Joyce has written a book that will be acknowledged as the greatest "divine appointment" to reach the centers of all hearts, of all beings, in a way that is deeply healing, and manifests this healing in clearly visible ways. Her heart-felt power has now entered the great circle of the atomic field, and has flared forth into Infinity and Eternity, where the love of the being that she is, is now recorded in the cellular structure of all sentient and non-sentient beings for the purpose of arousing the awareness that there is only one body of spirit with many faces. We are all infinite and eternal beings: we never die; we just transform into other faces of spirit, and we are all going to the same place together.

The guidance system is referred to as the "Path of Peace" — "Great Thanks, Great Peace, Great Love." When we are capable of becoming thankful for all beings, we become aware that we are all already forgiven. The most loving Mother and Father are always watching over each one of us.

There was a time, eons ago, when the word "Man" encompassed both the feminine and the masculine. Our DNA still registers that relationship in its original form. Every man has a woman inside, and every woman has a man inside. The woman was sent to this Earth with a moderating nature, and man was sent with an aggressive nature. Expressing thankfulness is the process to once again merge the feminine and masculine spirit into one balanced word. For the first step in the Path of Peace to be fully

available, this moderating-aggressive nature must come into balance. As this dichotomy of spirit becomes fully realized, Great Love and Great Thanks flow naturally into the Great Peace that fills creation.

We are now able to comprehend for the first time the fullness of love. Living love is the great gift that emerges from the joining of thankfulness, forgiveness, acceptance and peace. God promised: "I will lead you forth from the wilderness! I will lead you forth from the pain and suffering!" Joyce Anastasia has been passed the keys to fully unlock this ancient guidance!

Sequoyah Trueblood
Choctaw Elder
January 23, 2015

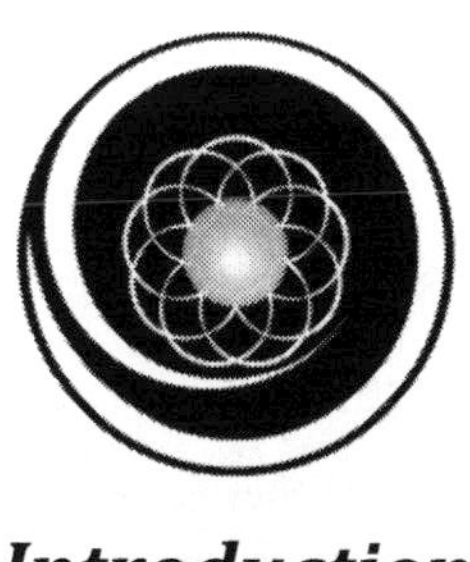

Introduction

"What you are, the world is. And without your transformation, there can be no transformation in the world."

~KRISHNAMURTI
(Visionary Philosopher)

We are living in an incredibly dynamic time of vast transition, both in our lives and in our world. For leaders this is nothing less than a call to transform in ways beyond anything we have previously envisioned, to evolve both ourselves and our systems, and to lead by greater wisdom.

Everywhere we look, foundational systems are collapsing before our eyes — from our financial system to our educational, social, political, medical, environmental systems — and beyond. These events can have a devastating effect on our psyches, sapping the exuberance of our life force, igniting physical and emotional illness, triggering both aggression and depression, and at times, increasing self-promoting behaviors when collaboration is most needed. Mainstream media further exacerbates these issues by either presenting us with mindless distractions or by sensationalizing the truth so we feel even more overwhelmed, uncertain where to look for solutions or the hope we know is needed.

At the same time that we are experiencing this whole-scale dismantlement, we are also witnessing contradictory and damaging practices in leadership — perhaps even in our own. This is characterized by the continued use of authoritarian "Power Over" approaches, a disheartening lack of integrity, ineffective means to address the pervasive social-cultural-economic imbalances and inequality, and a demoralizing sense of alienation as wars continue to rage from one side of the globe to the other.

People around the world are working diligently to help shift these trends. Yet, many in leadership positions have privately expressed to me, with tangible frustration, that they feel their hands are tied, sensing the entrenched nature of the systems currently in place. They are ready for significant change, both inside and out, but feel trapped, or uncertain where to start. It is because of their Herculean efforts and shared dream for a better world that I have been moved to create this book.

As a transformational leadership consultant and multicultural counselor, I have been trained as a fierce empath and bridge builder, seeking the root causes of complex issues and carefully slicing through that which does not serve. It is through this work that I have come to believe that the disharmonies in our world are symptomatic of the ***disharmonies that reside in our own hearts*** — the hearts of leaders, including myself. At times, we may not even be aware that we:

1. Misunderstand and misuse power.
2. Fail to speak or seek the truth.
3. Lose sight of our moral compass and fail to walk our deepest talk.
4. Believe we are separate from each other and from Nature.
5. Act in ways that are out of balance, sometimes in the extreme.
6. Forget our true nature and our connection to spirit, both of which are miraculous.
7. Lose sight of our ability to manifest our dreams and to positively transform our lives, our systems and our world.

These crucial blind spots seem to lie at the root of our global traumas. Most people wish to lead happy, meaningful and impacting lives, yet we so often make choices that inadvertently lead to harm and destruction — banishing our dreams instead of nurturing them. Let's ask ourselves: Did I once feel inspired to positively impact the world? Has something happened to my original vision? Have I been thwarted, and if so, why? What has derailed me from my sacred path?

I am encouraging everyone to ask these questions, even those who do not see themselves as "leaders" in the traditional sense of the word. We are *all* leaders — of organizations, of our families, or of our own lives — it is only a matter of scale. Whether or not we are currently in positions of

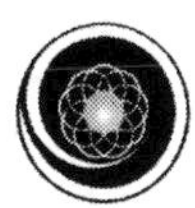

leveraged power, every change we make in our lives ripples out into the world, and influences others to do the same. That's the miraculous way in which change works: it's an energetic shift that moves in all directions, "trickling-up" to leaders at the very top, as well as down and around to touch all beings.

"Transformational leaders don't start by denying the world around them. Instead they describe a future they'd like to create."

~**SETH GODIN**
(Author, Leadership Consultant)

I'd like to share a personal story that reflects some of my inquiries into these questions regarding leaders and powerful visions. It was this experience and its aftermath that inspired me to write this book:

Several years ago, while working as a management consultant and photographer, I was asked to document a political convention. It was early morning as I walked into a small banquet hall where a delegation breakfast was about to begin. A little-known, recently-elected senator was about to deliver a speech during our meal. When my press pass was spotted, I was directed to a seat right in the front, about ten feet from the speaker's podium. Surrounding me at the table were some of our government's "movers and shakers," people who were drafting the laws of our country. I was excited to dialogue with these legislators because a large part of my consulting work involved finding innovative solutions to monumental business issues, and here were people involved with discovering solutions to even greater challenges.

When the speaker entered the room, the din of conversation fell to a whisper. He stepped to the podium and began to speak. His words seemed to galvanize the entire assembly. This man had a ***dream****. The dream was of a world that thrived on every level, where each individual was valued and respected, and allowed to contribute their gifts without fear. He spoke about the need to remove American troops from lands where we no longer belonged, and to apologize to the indigenous nations we had already harmed. He spoke of honoring all peoples and* *cultures, instead of pitting one against another. His dream included memories of his grandmother teaching him to be a man of integrity, wisdom and discernment. He also alluded to ways in which the U.S. had gone astray, succumbing to corruption so pervasive that it was now embedded in the very fabric of many of our systems. It was clear to me that the words he spoke came directly from his heart. He was speaking his truth — and that truth resonated with the deepest core of my being. As he spoke, tears welled up in my eyes and, for the first time in my long experience as a photographer, I was frozen in my tracks, barely able to snap a picture.*

My momentary paralysis was perfect, because what was most important at that moment was not a snapshot of the man, but the recognition of the dream he was presenting. If fulfilled, that dream would shake our nation loose from complacency and move it toward a more generative worldview, one of hope, peace, and sustainable, collaborative interaction. I truly believe that, in that moment, a new seed was planted within me, a luminous seed of a new kind of leadership — Extraordinary Leadership. It shone like a beacon, lighting the way toward the future.

The man who spoke that vision went on to run for President of the United States. As he campaigned, his words resonated with millions of people around the country — and, indeed, around the entire world — as they had with me. His dream was ***our*** *dream; it was humanity's dream, irrespective of nation or race. It was a* ***transpolitical*** *dream, representing the best of the American spirit, and the spirit of the world. It was so inspiring that many people began to work toward its attainment — independent of whether or not that candidate got elected into his desired office. This is the essence of divine leadership, inspiring hope, empowerment and transformation in others.*

Over a decade has passed since that profound experience. That little-known senator succeeded in becoming our president, and, while he is still respected and admired at times, many people have observed that the dreams he spoke of seem to have become lost or buried. Too many actions taken and policies created since that speech seem to be in direct

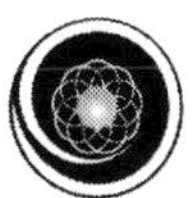

contradiction to the heart-felt beliefs and values conveyed. As a concerned citizen of the world, I ask, with love, compassion, and genuine curiosity: "What happened to those dreams?" Have those foundational beliefs really changed, or have they been co-opted? Can they re-emerge? I have found myself asking these questions about many world leaders and others in positions of power.

Please do not misunderstand my questioning as criticizing. I'm aware that I don't know the whole story. Although we can try to imagine what it's like, no one can claim to walk in another's unique shoes. We have no idea what threats or severe tactics may be present that may cause powerful leaders to relinquish their dreams.

I also want to make it clear that the point of my story is not about President Obama and whether we like or dislike him. Rather, it's about the ***collective dream*** he reminded us of — the dream that I believe millions of people on Earth share.

I found myself asking: What happened to that dream?

In my experience, the loss of a dream can happen to anyone and can significantly contribute to lost faith and hope, both in ourselves and in humanity as a whole. Maybe our dream was huge — a dream to put an end to war, or poverty, or to the environmental damage on the Earth. Maybe our dream was so big we didn't know where to start, or felt it was impossible. Or maybe our dream was more modest — like having a job that helped others, or creating a work of art that would change people's hearts, or being the first in our family to graduate from college. Or maybe our dream was simply to provide food and shelter for our loved ones and to live a peaceful life.

Sometimes even our more accessible dreams get shattered. Why does this happen? What gets in the way? We constantly see organizations that call individuals to high ideals, but fall short in their own practices. Is this just "human nature"? Or is there something deeper at work, something that, if we uncovered it, would give us the keys to unlock more of our potential and develop the wisdom to create the world we truly want?

"We must not, in trying to think about how we can make a big difference, ignore the small daily difference we can make which, over time, add up to big differences that we often cannot foresee."

~MARIAN WRIGHT EDELMAN
(Social Activist)

"Hope is being able to see that there is light despite all the darkness."

~DESMOND TUTU
(Archbishop, Spiritual Leader)

As a transformational leadership consultant, global peace ambassador, and concerned citizen of the world, I spent many months reflecting on how I could support others in their desire to make a difference — small or large — and to pursue our collective dream in spite of the challenges. What emerged was deep internal guidance to write this book. I am called to offer hope. I believe that we can reverse these pervasive trends — together.

I believe we are currently living in a "house of cards." The foundation upon which the majority of our systems has been built is no longer serving us or our planet as we had originally intended and were led to believe. So therefore it may be completely fitting that these systems shift, and in some cases crumble, so we can create something better. I believe that we already possess the keys to that creation, and that those keys lie *within us.* The systems we've created that have become so unmanageable, unwieldy, complicated, manipulative and ineffectual, are reflections of belief systems that we have collectively "bought into" — squelching our collective dream in the process.

As I continue to grow as a leader, I have come to believe that we will change our entrenched world systems only *by changing ourselves*. We need to find the courage to go *towards* our inner disharmonies, for they will be our greatest teachers. It is my belief that if we are committed to working through the ruptures and disjunctions in our own hearts and

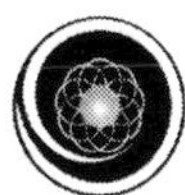

lives, we will be gifted with great healing and wisdom. In fact, such wisdom is already emerging, both within our individual hearts and in the heart of the collective. It is arising in order to serve as a new foundation for everything we do — the foundation of a more beautiful world. With that understanding, one way to look at the chaos we are experiencing is as a signal to *pay attention to what is wanting to be born.*

The feeling of resonance that surges inside us when we hear an inspired leader's words is an energetic reminder of the collective dreams that our hearts still long for. Our hearts connect, and we feel the long-forgotten desire to fully express our spirits. Knowing the strength of this inner dynamic, it becomes clear that ***to re-create the world outside of us, we must re-create the world within.*** This is the "Master Key," the key to the gridlock we feel within and without. It will take a profound retooling, a re-learning from the inside out, but pursuing this, we can shift our entire world.

To help foster this evolution of leadership, I have been guided to present what I call seven Vital Keys that make up the "Master Key." Think of these keys as guideposts to help each of us address our greatest leadership and life challenges. Through exploration of these keys, we can be led out of our internal contradictions and disharmonies, integrating new practices into our lives, and contributing instrumentally to the creation of a new and vital future. The seven Vital Keys are:

1. Consciously Choosing "Power With" versus "Power Over."
2. Seeking and Speaking Truth.
3. Honoring Integrity by Walking our Deeper Talk.
4. Dissolving Unhealthy Separation, Honoring Uniqueness Within the Whole.
5. Dancing with Dynamic Balance.
6. Remembering our Miraculous Nature.
7. Manifesting Dreams and Transforming World Systems through the Heart.

I believe these keys can serve as a foundation to internal and external transformation, and also as a source of inspiration. Here's why:

Key #1: "Consciously Choosing Power With versus Power Over" is vital because when leaders live and work without a healthy relationship to power, it undermines all the other vital keys and systems in our world. This key encourages people to explore their own relationship with power and how they have used or abused it. When our relationship to power is unhealthy, we tend to manipulate and harm others. This leads to violence. Violence begets more violence, and history has shown that the widespread misuse of power can destroy entire civilizations. When our relationship with power is healthy, we create environments of trust, and naturally motivate others to do the same, empowering positive change in the world.

Key #2: "Seeking and Speaking Truth" is vital because lying destroys trust and compromises wise decision-making. I believe we must speak aloud the deep truths of our time. While this may initially be intimidating, it is only by acknowledging what *is*, that we can begin to move through to the other side. Without a commitment to seeking and speaking the truth, systems get co-opted by those who want to control and destroy. When the pursuit of truth is upheld, people and organizations can thrive in an atmosphere of trust and confidence.

Key #3: "Honoring Integrity by Walking our Deeper Talk" is vital because it, too, fosters trust — not the least of which is trust in ourselves. Without integrity, we become fragmented and incongruent. Standing in integrity and walking our deeper talk fosters a profound sense of inner peace, which helps us feel more at ease in our responsibilities. We're able to make decisions with more clarity and to walk through conflict in healthier ways.

Key #4: "Dissolving Unhealthy Separation, Honoring Uniqueness Within the Whole" is vital because we must heal the devastating effects caused by the myth of separation. The legacy of our culture's assumption of separation leads each of us to feel that we are alone, abandoned, or not good enough, and to hide our gifts. Learning to honor each individual's uniqueness within the context of the whole helps to dissolve unhealthy separation while building trust and rapport. This is the key to creating "dream teams" that utilize as many of the talents and abilities of each individual as possible, fostering innovation and collaboration.

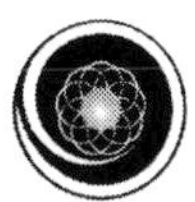

Key #5: "Dancing with Dynamic Balance" is vital because when we are out of balance, we become unstable, and much less likely to make clear and sound decisions. When the masculine and feminine principles in leadership get out of balance, we can lead with our head but not our heart, or vice versa. We can lean on logic without calling in intuition, or the opposite. We can become obsessed with action, and lose perspective due to a lack of rest and reflection. All of our many aspects are here for a reason; we need them all to become fully-realized human beings, and if we hope to resolve our global crises. Because we have embraced separation for so long, it's critical that we bring more wholeness into our lives and our work — and learning how to balance is key to this.

Key #6: "Remembering our Miraculous Nature" reminds us to look for what is possible, even under seemingly impossible circumstances, and to recognize that we are surrounded by positive forces, often unseen, that are ever-present and always supporting us. This key is vital because it reminds us that we have the opportunity, through our intention, to not only change ourselves, but also to evolve and transform the world beyond our current paradigms and into the world of our collective dream. When we really understand our miraculous nature, we will know that virtually anything is possible.

Key #7: "Manifesting Dreams and Transforming World Systems through the Heart" is vital to help identify ways to align our own sacred purpose to our greater vision, and to better understand how to manifest our personal and collective dreams. When we work with the concepts of this key, we discover that there is a "sweet spot" where our individual needs and desires intersect with those of the collective, magnifying transformative effects at all levels. We are being called to create new structures, systems and organizations, including new forms of governance, that reflect the essence of our collective dream. These new constructs can support us to not merely survive, but to thrive.

The overall intention of this book is to inspire hope by showing how these vital keys can help leaders address the many challenges and crises we currently face. One by one — and together — these vital keys can help us each unlock our potential for extraordinary leadership. To that end, each chapter provides:

- An overview of each Vital Key, its related challenges and crises, and an exploration of the link between how it is showing up in the lives of leaders and how it manifests in the world.
- True stories that give concrete examples of these crises — what they look and feel like — and how transformation can and does occur. Many of these stories are from my own life or my clients' lives, and most are archetypal in nature. (Unless otherwise indicated, the names and places in these stories have been changed to protect the identity and privacy of each individual.)
- A sacred call to action for each of us to consider. Each call is an invitation to activate our hearts, minds, bodies and spirits in powerful synergy towards global transformation.
- Innovative solutions and suggestions for transformational practices, including skill-building exercises, that each of us can follow to deepen our capacity for Extraordinary Leadership.

I am advocating that we each take responsibility to become aware of our disharmonies, and to make different choices. I say this because I believe we each have access to a powerful source of wisdom that will help us lead in new and healthier ways. This includes people who may not feel they are in positions powerful enough to be called "leaders." Whether we are rich or poor, strong or weak, high-level executives or at the bottom of the org chart, we all have the opportunity to make better choices in our own lives. And these choices *do* matter. Each individual action and decision ripples outward, building one upon another, inspiring synergies and synchronicities. This means that, in spite of current problems, we do have the potential to create the world we truly want.

The seven Vital Keys are treated separately in this book, but in reality, they are all interconnected — as is all of life. This is an integrative model of change, and part of such a model involves the understanding that energy, although invisible, radiates outward into everything, so that our thoughts and motivations have as much importance as our actions — and sometimes more. When each of us clarifies our relationship with our inner selves, we shift the existing paradigms of our societies — however

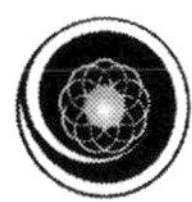

minutely — and make it a little easier for others to do the same. This is part of being an "extraordinary leader": even if we are not in positions of great public power, we can still have a great influence on what happens in our world. This is why I remain optimistic about the possibilities of this "extraordinary time" on planet Earth.

This work is an ongoing and interactive project, so all readers are encouraged to contribute their leadership challenges and best solutions into this collaborative effort at www.leadbywisdom.com.

As I've said, my overall intention is to plant seeds of hope. Despite the reality of world systems collapsing, we are not subject only to those ineffective systems; we have the innate capacity to create new, more life-affirming systems in their place. My hope is that this book will help awaken the heart of the leader in each of us. I hope it will inspire us to reach out and reconnect with others and with Nature, and to listen deeply for guidance so that we might act from a foundation of moral wholeness.

I am convinced that many leaders — both established and emerging — are longing to make a real difference in the world, just like Martin Luther King, Jr., John F. Kennedy, Mahatma Gandhi and, more currently, the Dalai Lama, indigenous wisdom keepers, Deepak Chopra, Oprah Winfrey, and others. I believe we have also been inspired by great teachers such as Christ, Krishna, Buddha, Paramahansa Yogananda, Lao Tse, Grandfather Leon Secatero, Madame Blavatsky, Mother Teresa, Amma, and more.

As I look at the above list, I notice that many of the leaders named were also spiritual teachers. These people knew that the center of their being is Spirit. I believe that putting Spirit back at the center of our hearts, our lives, and the ways we lead, is crucial to our future as a species. Thus, all seven Vital Keys, which comprise the "Master Key," are really about the spirit of leadership. Humans have a spiritual dimension, and we cannot lead fully if we have left a major portion of ourselves behind, or have omitted it from our choices and decisions. Therefore, ***to grow as leaders, I believe we must also grow in spirit***. To this end, I include in this book practices designed to increase our communication with, and understanding of, that inner source.

When people more clearly understand their unique gifts, their place in the world and the wisdom within their own hearts, they lead with divine power and love, and they become the extraordinary leaders they were meant to be. Some of these leaders have been my clients, and I have had the privilege of witnessing their incredible journeys first-hand. This has been a source of great inspiration for me. I've also drawn inspiration from the courageous people I have encountered in my travels around the world.

To all current and aspiring leaders around the globe, I honor you, and hope that this book will serve as one little torch to help light your path.

"We're here for a reason. I believe a bit of the reason is to throw little torches out to lead people through the dark."

~WHOOPI GOLDBERG
(Actor)

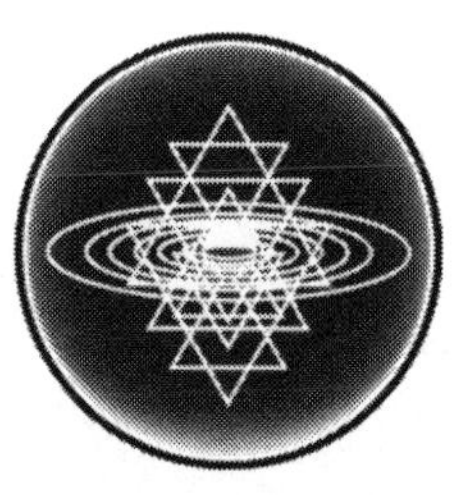

Vital Key #1: Consciously Choosing "Power With" versus "Power Over"

"Born within our human expression is the type of power that can harm or kill. Born within that same human expression is the type of power that can manifest without harm, and transform lives and the world for the benefit of all."

~WHISPERS FROM THE HEART OF THE WORLD
(Great Spirit's Messenger)

Power is all around us, within us, and affects most aspects of our lives, yet we may be completely unaware of where our ideas about power come from. Surprisingly, many of our concepts about power actually come from childhood. If we look back on our lives, some of us might easily recall traumatic events that significantly shaped our early beliefs about power. Others of us might have to search harder, for such events may be nearly forgotten, even though their impact was profound. These experiences told us what power was, how it was wielded, and whether or not we had any. I'd like to share with you one of my earliest memories, because it did just that. Although it was an experience that sadly reflects the type of power that can and did kill, it also stimulated my belief that power could also be used to transform lives to benefit all.

I sat on my mother's lap watching our black-and-white TV. I felt her stiffen as she leaned in to listen intently to an urgent news bulletin being read by a visibly shaken Walter Cronkite: "From Dallas Texas, the flash apparently official, President Kennedy died at 1 p.m. Central Standard Time, 2 o'clock Eastern Standard Time, some 38 minutes ago... Messages are beginning to come in from around the world and from the cities of the United States where a nation is in almost ... uncontrollable shock. They're weeping in the streets. Schools have to be dismissed. My own [neighborhood] school had to be dismissed because the children are weeping so much they couldn't stay..."[1]

Hours later, the television was flooded with images of the motorcade procession and the subsequent assassination. I was not yet four years old and for the first time in my life, I saw my mother cry. This was so disturbing to me that I reached out to comfort her, but really couldn't. I remember her saying, "We can't continue to live in a world where it's okay to kill our president." In my little being, I translated this to mean, "We can't continue to live in a world where we can kill anyone and anything."

This was my first experience of how damaging power could be. I remember that across the globe, people mourned our president's death and offered words of comfort and support. I believe it was during that day, remaining in my mother's arms while she cried, that I decided that one of the reasons I was here was to help create a world where harming others would not be tolerated, and where sadness could shift to global healing, friendship and support. It stimulated in me a dream to transform power to manifest the thriving world I believe is truly possible!

Power is one of the most profound tools of leadership, yet most of us are never formally trained in how to use it. Instead, we are "informally trained" by our culture to focus only on the harsh, authoritarian, and often destructive side of power. As a consequence, we tend to simply react to power situations in our lives. We "run on automatic," letting our conditioning choose our behavior, rather than consciously choosing what we really want to do. Here's a story that illustrates this:

For my father's 80th birthday, my younger brother gave him a special gift: a beautiful written tribute in which my brother described his fondest memories of growing up, and also the many ways our dad had contributed in the world. My brother emailed this to the whole family and asked each of his siblings to write something similar.

This email inspired me to ponder my own childhood memories of our father. A few days later, when the time felt right, I began to compose my contribution to this beautiful gift. As I wrote, I allowed the memories to flow freely onto the page. My intention was to express my deep love and gratitude, and to be completely authentic, writing from my heart.

What emerged were amazing stories of my dad's strength, courage and tenacity. He had been one of twelve children, and he'd faced many adversities including poverty, fragile health, and a mostly absent, abusive father. Yet, he emerged as a loving and philosophical man with a great generosity of spirit. I found myself writing about his curiosity, his MacGyver-like ingenuity, and his enduring belief that anything is possible. This strong faith helped him manifest powerfully, both in his own life and on behalf of others.

Then, suddenly, as I was in mid-sentence, a different memory came flooding in. I felt my heart racing as I recalled an incident where both of my brothers were "in deep trouble." They were getting "the strap," and I was hiding behind a piece of furniture, holding my breath so I wouldn't be discovered. I remembered desperately wanting to stop my dad from hitting my brothers, but I was afraid that I was too little to risk getting the strap myself. I was perhaps even more afraid that if I were big enough to do something, I might actually hurt my dad! I wanted to stop him so much it scared me.

The contrast between those memories and my reflections about the dad I knew to be a loving parent reminded me of how confusing such experiences had felt for me as a child. As I continued to write, tears blurred my words, finally giving way to clarity.

I saw how much of my life had been shaped by those moments of fear and powerlessness, as well as by gestures of love and strength. I saw how I had resonated with that love and so had consciously chosen to move ***toward*** *the "power" emanating from it; on the other hand, fear had repelled me, and so I, unconsciously at times, moved* ***away*** *from the "power" generated by anger. Since my dad was a source for both of these, it was no wonder I'd felt confused! As I reflected on this, my heart went out to the little girl I'd been, knowing that all I'd really wanted was for our dad to be happy with us, playing and laughing and teaching us naturally through his wise actions.*

I also saw how those fearful moments had made me conclude at a very early age that it was dangerous to be powerful. This came not only from the power my dad had demonstrated over my brothers, but also from my own feelings about his actions and how much I wanted to stop him. If I had been able to act on my feelings at the time, it felt like I could have done something I'd regret. Power felt dangerous, so for years I hid mine. Fortunately, this did not last forever, since I was blessed with such a vibrant heritage that I couldn't help but eventually express a sense of power in my life. From my dad's side of the family, I received the gifts of persistence, spiritedness, intuition and dedication, while from my mom's side of the family, I gained compassion, creativity and joviality.

In that moment of writing, I came to understand why I had dedicated my life to helping others to claim their power and use it more consciously, for the greater good.

I also saw how my dad's actions had been born out of the best of intentions: a desire to instill in us kids the value of discipline and to teach us "right" from "wrong" so we'd become responsible citizens. And I realized there was an even deeper level: I sensed that my dad had learned his retributive and violent behavior from his own dad, who no doubt did the same thing to him (but a thousand times more violently).

When this last insight came, I was flooded with overwhelming compassion, love and forgiveness for my dad. I knew I needed to share

these realizations with him, so I did. I completed my honest, heart-felt letter so that it spoke of both the light and the shadow that is our birthright as human beings. I thanked my dad for teaching me a great deal about power — both the kind I wanted to use and the kind I did not. For that, I was and will always be very grateful.

Throughout his life, and with unexpected mentoring along the way — especially from my gentle yet powerful mom — my dad slowly changed his relationship to power. Over time, he became more conscious of his choices with respect to power, learning to use it in ways that expressed his strength and integrity without violating others. My dad's transformation stands as a beacon, illuminating how we all have the power to change our conditioned responses.

Two Kinds of Power

What *is* power really? The word "power" originates from the Latin root "*posse*," which means "to be able to do something." This is a pretty neutral definition. As time went on, however, the word began to take on new connotations that were increasingly one-sided, such as "strength, vigor, might, especially in battle," "control, mastery, lordship, dominion" and "legal authority." These latter definitions moved the meaning of power in the direction of what I call "Power Over," as opposed to "Power With." Let me define these two terms:

- "Power Over" means using power in order to *dominate* others, generally through the use of force — physical, verbal, emotional, or otherwise. Power Over occurs whenever someone demands that an action be taken without the knowledge and/or consent of all those affected. In its most severe form, those affected are not even allowed to have a voice; they are provided no opportunity to comment or respond, either before or after decisions are made. Even more importantly, the people using Power Over gain most or all of the benefits of the decisions that are made, while those being "Powered Over" gain few or none.

- "Power With" means *sharing* power by treating others as equals, and effecting change through collaboration. Power With is far more balanced than Power Over, since it seeks equitable distribution of both power itself and of the benefits derived from whatever action is taken. Power With occurs when leaders seek consent in making decisions, and take into account the concerns of all those affected, regardless of their status. Power With invites everyone involved to participate in the decision-making, not just those "at the top" whose view may be far too rarified to know all the details of what Is, and of what is Possible.

I believe that power is a type of energy that comes from the Universe itself. For quite some time now, physicists and philosophers alike have told us that the entire universe is made of energy. I see that energy as a very potent creative force; after all, it brought the whole universe into being! A fraction of that immense energetic source is housed within every piece and particle of the universe — including each and every one of us. What we humans know as power, then, is our capacity to command a small portion of that universal creative force in order to direct it in our own unique ways. It's a fuel we harness to help us manifest our goals. That is really quite an extraordinary thing!

In fact, if we view power through that lens, it can only be seen as a divine gift and a blessing. If power weren't in play, nothing would happen. Like water, power itself is *neutral*; it can be used to sustain life or to destroy it, to bring harm or to bring beautiful work into expression. It is up to each of us to choose how we wish to use it and to learn how to use it wisely.

Now here's the key: when we use our personal power in a way that aligns with the larger flow of universal divine energy — and especially when we use our power to assist the evolution and development of all beings — then we have the ability to create positive transformation in the world. When we use our power this way, signals begin to resonate and echo, gathering support from the highest possible energy sources. This is the essence of using Power With. We align our personal will with divine will for the benefit of all. The conscious use of Power With helps create extraordinary actions and ways of leading.

"Divine will" may seem a strange term to use in our current culture. Some may find it challenging. I use this term to refer to a *transcendent flow of energy* that is recognized in spiritual traditions throughout the world and across millennia. This will be explored and discussed further throughout this book, but the key idea underlying Power With is that we try, as much as possible, to take the *entire* system into account when making decisions. *No one part of the system can persistently benefit at the expense of all the rest*, or the entire system gets out of alignment; this is ultimately inconsistent with divine energy. So, for example, making business decisions that financially benefit our own company at the expense of the wellbeing of other human beings or the natural world is typically out of alignment with the "good of all." It would therefore be out of alignment with "divine will."

To be truly powerful means to be in alignment with the whole. In other words, we seek to balance our own personal desires with the greater good. We don't go to one extreme, becoming victims or martyrs; nor do we go to the other extreme, becoming dictators addicted to forcing our will on others. Instead, we mindfully seek the path that honors a *balanced* use of power. This path may not always be readily apparent but if we hold our hearts steady and *allow* for divine flow, that path will unfold, and true manifestation can begin. Most of us know what it feels like to lose our sense of time and space, to be "in the flow." This is the divine power within us coming alive. It can be used for any creative endeavor, personal or professional — from hobbies and projects like gardening, art, music or sports, etc., to solving complex problems and creating solutions for the challenges in our lives.

Top-down leadership and management have dominated our world for centuries. This is Power Over. It is now time to recalibrate and reconnect to our divine power source with a conscious understanding of what power means in our lives, and how we use it on our own behalf and on behalf of others. Although there are times when Power Over is a necessary option, I advocate minimizing Power Over and maximizing Power With. And most importantly, I urge that the *choice* of which form of power to use in any given situation be made *consciously*, with care and deliberation, not because we're "running on automatic."

Ways We "Power Over"

Power Over takes many forms from the subtle to the blatant. It can be seen in any interaction in which one party tries to dominate the other. It may involve:

- Isolating others: ostracizing, shunning, ignoring needs and requests, "guilt-tripping," creating "camps."
- Demeaning others: mocking, ridiculing, name-calling, labeling, humiliating, making them feel inadequate, treating them as "less than."
- Blocking others: preventing or taking away access to money, jobs, rights, etc.
- Intimidating others: threatening to hurt them, their loved ones, or their culture.
- Attacking others: taking away home, land, resources, safety, life; violating others' bodies or beliefs; destroying their traditions; waging war.
- Denying or minimizing the importance of Power Over activities.

Power Over affects all levels of society, and includes (but is not limited to):

- On the national and global levels: war; pre-emptive strikes; genocide; colonization; co-option and destruction of sacred lands, traditions and natural resources; dictatorships; economic inequality and manipulation; sex trafficking and other human rights violations (including privacy invasion); "corporate-owned" governments and news media; force-based models (like "survival of the fittest" and "manifest destiny"); invasive medical practices; animal-testing; environmental destruction and pollution; violence as "entertainment."
- On the local and neighborhood levels: gangs; crime (murder, theft, rape, fraud, etc.); bullying; noise pollution; loss of safe environments due to toxic product use; loss of small businesses to global corporations; over-development and "sprawl"; tail-gating and "road rage."
- On the organizational level: sexual harassment; gender inequality (including "old-boy networks"); top-down management "steam-

rolling" and overworking employees; unfair hiring/firing practices; intimidation; gossip; non-transparent decision-making.

- On the interpersonal level: domestic violence (including child abuse and date-rape)[2]; bullying; gossip; labeling; "friendly" coercion ("Oh, come on, everybody's doing it"); codependent relationships; cliques; bigotry.
- On the personal level: neglecting, ignoring or violating our own needs and integrity, in favor of doing what is "socially expected" or because we are afraid of being perceived as "different." (Note that we are then using Power Over *on ourselves*, generally because it has already been "programmed" by the culture.)

Although incomplete, this list is rather disturbing, because it speaks to the enormity of business, economic, emotional and human loss. No one is immune to the repercussions of Power Over. How does it affect us and how did this type of power become so entrenched?

"Power Over" Hurts, Personally to Globally

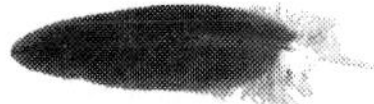

"When plunder becomes a way of life for a group of men living together in society, they create for themselves in the course of time a legal system that authorizes it and a moral code that glorifies it."[3]

~Frederic Bastiat
(Author, French Economist 1800's)

"Power Over others is weakness disguised as strength."

~Eckhart Tolle
(Spiritual Teacher, Author)

I have titled this section "Power Over Hurts," and this is usually true, but there are situations where Power Over is beneficial and necessary. These are generally in life-or-death circumstances where one person must make a split-second decision and use force to prevent disaster. For example, if a child is about to stick their fingers in an electrical socket or run in front of a rushing car, physically grabbing them and snatching them to safety ***is*** using Power Over, but I believe such use is justified. Firefighters, policemen, soldiers, etc., can run into similar situations where Power Over is needed. However, for most life events, Power Over is tremendously harmful and destructive, as illustrated by this story from a client, about corporate power run amok:

Joshua was a brilliant young inventor and engineer. He was hired by a midsized company to develop innovative healthcare products, including those used to reduce infant mortality in the United States and abroad. It was a noble goal, in keeping with Joshua's dreams of using his skills to "make this world a better place."

Joshua joined a small team consisting of two other engineers, Charles and Tina. Both were bright and energetic, and had worked for the company for three years. With a mixture of pride and humility, they shared with Joshua how their collaborative work had helped increase company profits by $10 million, while improving millions of lives. The jump in revenue had, in fact, helped provide the incentive to hire a third engineer — Joshua — onto the project.

Joshua discovered that working alongside his two new colleagues gave him an enormous amount of satisfaction. The three of them respected each other's talents, evoked each other's gifts, and gave each other support and encouragement as needed. They worked equally well both independently and synergistically. Plus, they really enjoyed each other's company. This made for a rich, stimulating work environment that produced consistent high quality results on time and on budget.

In only three and a half years from the time of Joshua's arrival, the company's profits shot from $40 million to $150 million. Joshua's team was thrilled, as they had been instrumental in conceptualizing and testing each new product. At the same time, the company accumulated credibility through other, non-financial measures of success: It was awarded a rare Tier One vendor rating by the largest retailer in the country, and their healthcare products received the highest customer

satisfaction ranking. These results would be considered outstanding for virtually any company, and they were directly due to the contributions of Joshua's team.

Then, with projections of even greater success on the horizon, the company's upper management made the decision to buy out another midsize company, believing that this would help them expand without having to "reinvent the wheel." The decision was made unilaterally and primarily on the basis of finances. With the buyout, they would acquire: a centralized U.S. distribution facility, which would reduce shipping costs; manufacturing facilities in China, which would reduce production costs; and new administrative offices in a different state, which would reduce maintenance costs. And, because the other company was experiencing serious financial challenges, it was acquired at a very low price.

On the surface, this decision seemed extremely positive, but it was made in Power Over mode — top-down authoritarian rule with little or no input from the employees who would be most directly affected. That choice sowed the seeds of calamity.

There were three significant problems: First, upper management never consulted any of their employees regarding the impact of this decision on their work. Second, management withheld the very important fact that they would be moving their administrative offices to new headquarters in another state, forcing employees to either move or no longer be part of the new division. Third, as part of the buyout agreement, the leadership team agreed to take on the other company's employees without a clear understanding of the financial impact or a plan for how those employees would be integrated.

The company immediately went into crisis. Faced with integrating the new engineers, upper management hastily created a new supervisory position and offered it to Joshua. The role, however, was poorly defined and Joshua didn't want to surrender the impact he was making with fellow engineers. He turned it down.

*In a crunch, upper management scrambled and hurriedly hired Max, someone from the outside, to manage both the new hires and Joshua's team. Max was well versed in design, but not functionality — crucial for quality control. He was also used to wielding power in a top-down management style. Within two weeks, Max made the following statement to Joshua's team: "If you don't make my plans work the way I tell you to, I'm going to f*** all of your careers!"*

The team was shocked. Joshua's first instinct was to go to the company president, with whom he had some rapport, but he feared it might backfire and that he'd be accused of lying, so he said nothing. Meanwhile, Max convinced the president that the engineers were all "prima donnas" who needed to be "put in their place." So, in the ensuing months, Joshua's team — whose work had made the company over $110 million in three-and-a-half years — was forced to dismantle their proven collaborative approach. Now working completely separately, they had to follow step-by-step procedures laid out in huge manuals, and be micromanaged on a daily basis. This proved disastrous.

In a very short time, the engineers lost their passion. They felt abused and under-appreciated. Yet, despite their deep frustration, they still retained their commitment to produce quality products on time and within budget. But trust was eroded. Meanwhile, Max's behavior went unchecked. The president was overwhelmed with the number of tasks he was juggling to complete the buyout. Like many at the top unintentionally do, he lost touch with the pulse of what was occurring in his company. He trusted Max, the new lead in charge of the engineers, and he didn't have time to oversee that work as well. So Max steamrolled his way along, wielding his personal power at the expense of the entire company.

Before long, the internal dysfunction began to show up in company performance. Deadlines were missed and major corporate customers, expecting products to be delivered by the promised delivery dates, began to charge over $1000 per day in late fees and penalties. Max, in a desperate attempt to retain control, reacted by creating a new organizational chart, once again without input from any of his

subordinates. He then called a dinner meeting with the three engineers.

Joshua, Charles and Tina felt a ray of hope, imagining Max was going to bring them back together as a team to help recoup the lost profits and company reputation. However, Max began the meeting by throwing the new org chart on the table. When the three engineers saw their names at the very bottom, their hearts sank. Tina fought back tears. Charles looked shell-shocked. Joshua, visibly angry, blurted out, "This sucks! If it weren't for us, there wouldn't have been any buyout. We delivered every project on time and under budget. There were no recalls in three years, which is unheard of. Is this how you reward great work?"

The meeting did not end well, and almost resulted in physical violence.

Within a month, Tina got another job. Charles, with a growing family and house payments, stayed. He didn't want to "rock the boat," but was extremely unhappy. He began describing himself deprecatingly as a "company drone"; it was clear he felt diminished, humiliated, and no longer enthusiastic about his work. Joshua, feeling utterly violated, became reactive, inadvertently damaging his connection with his wife, kids, and those to whom he reported. It wasn't long before he was fired.

Surprisingly, the company did survive — barely. Their profit margin shrank to almost nothing as productivity declined. With twice as many employees, they produced only half as many products. The buyout, intended to save money, effectively lost money instead. And the human cost? Immeasurable!

Although Max seems to be the "culprit" in this story, the destructive use of Power Over that broke up a "dream team" and brought a highly successful company to its knees originated with upper management. It was the top leadership who gave Max free rein, allowing him to do whatever he wanted without oversight, and who made the buyout decision in the first place without consulting those most affected. As with most organizations, the company did not have a governance structure in place that could check or deter Power Over behavior. As a result, Power Over descended from the highest levels and affected everyone in the company, *including* Max. Although Joshua and his team tried repeatedly to convince Max to

keep them together, they never felt safe taking their concerns to the president, a telling reveal in a Power Over situation. People who are being Powered Over generally feel this way — unheard, and in jeopardy if they try to speak out. Had upper management been more open from the beginning, much suffering might have been avoided.

There is a saying that "hurt people hurt people" — that is, people who have been wounded often respond by passing on their hurt to others. Our deepest hurts usually originate in childhood. In adulthood, those original injuries (or "core wounds," as we'll discuss later) can trigger knee-jerk reactions that can hurt both others and ourselves. In the above story, for example, it is significant that Max spoke offline to some of his fellow employees about having had an abused and troubled childhood. This likely contributed to his choices when put in a position of power.

Using Power Over either forces others' actions or ignores their needs. No one likes to be forced or ignored. People who are Powered Over feel anger, resentment, and a desire to retaliate, or else they withdraw. This, in turn, can create new wounds, along with anxiety, low confidence, loss of self-esteem, and loss of inspiration and enthusiasm. Such disempowerment is also a constant source of stress, leading to the feeling of not being safe in the world. Powered Over people cannot fully be themselves, and therefore cannot contribute their best work. Prolonged Power Over-ing can also cause depression and post- (or sometimes *ongoing*-) traumatic stress disorder (PTSD). It can also give rise to or intensify physical illnesses, as indicated in Louise Hay's book, *Heal Your Body*.[4] The exact illness varies depending on the trauma, but every system in the body can be affected, and the illnesses can range from mildly annoying to life-threatening.

People who use Power Over on others also experience negative health effects. These are presented in the same Louise Hay book, again with every system in the body potentially being affected. Over-control can lead to OCD (Obsessive Compulsive Disorder) and physical abuse. Leaders who consistently assume: "If I want it done right, I have to do it myself" are under the same spell of Power Over. They generally end up feeling both overwhelmed and unsupported, and may even feel betrayed by the

system in which they're caught. The use of Power Over also alters our psychological make-up. Recent research into violent video games that teach children to smash and destroy everything in their path indicates this kind of "play" wreaks havoc on the children's psyches, and gives rise to serious emotional and social problems.[5] Power Over damages relationships, destroying trust in both directions: those Powered Over don't trust because they're being oppressed, while those who Power Over don't trust because in their hearts they know people dislike and oppose them.

Whenever a leader uses Power Over, the negative effects are multiplied by the number of people that leader dominates. Whether in the home, workplace or the world at large, people who are Powered Over feel unheard, without leverage, and certainly not equal participants in the decisions or the events that define their lives. This diminishes both their input and their output. At the very least, it subdues joy and at the worst, it robs the world of their voice and problem-solving potential.

Power Over can lead to out-of-control behavior in all areas of life. On the home front, Power Over destroys marriages, scars children, and leads to millions of dollars in health costs and lost productivity due to stress, illness, domestic violence, child abuse, and psychological damage.[6] The negative effects of Power Over have been most recently spotlighted in both national and international sports, but particularly with five of the major leagues in the U.S. — the NBA, NFL, NHL, MLS and the NBL (National Basketball Association, National Football League, National Hockey League, Major League Soccer, and National Baseball League) where athletes were perpetrating violence against their families, partners or other players.[7] In addition, the use of Power Over in the home usually leads to Power Over being passed on to the next generation, creating an endless cycle of self-propagating violence.

In the workplace, Power Over creates an atmosphere of distrust and resentment, characterized by low morale and gossip, as well as breakdowns in communication and teamwork. This vastly reduces productivity and leads to low employee retention rates. Many organizations actually split apart as some members choose to support the leader, while others follow the more dangerous route of speaking their truth and risking job loss. In an article titled "Reward Workers, then Reap Rewards" in the *Albany (NY) Times Union*, November 20, 2012, Harvey Mackay revealed the very personal impact of Power Over leadership: "According to various surveys, seven out of ten people go home every night with the feeling that they work for an organization that doesn't care about them. That equates to one hundred thirty million people in the United States!"[8]

In the world at large, Power Over is destroying life, lands, and entire cultures and species. The old adage "power corrupts and absolute power corrupts absolutely" is the epitome of Power Over.

"In the councils of government, we must guard against the acquisition of unwarranted influence, whether sought or unsought, by the Military-Industrial Complex. The potential for the disastrous rise of misplaced power exists and will persist."

~**DWIGHT D. EISENHOWER**
(34th President of the United States)

From the U.S. to Afghanistan, from South Africa to the Middle East, stories of global Power Over abound. Even though each country is unique, all Power Over stories sound alike — no matter that they come from such disparate places as Jordan, Syria, Greece, Turkey, Libya, Iraq, Iran, Bosnia, Serbia, Croatia, Ukraine, and so many others. Some conflicts seem never-ending (like the Israelis and Palestinians). And one of the most tragic outcomes is the unintentional passing on of the destructive Power Over beliefs and behaviors to the children. Here is but one example from a newspaper in Zaatari, Jordan:

> "Like all the small children in the desert refugee camp here, Ibtisam, 11, is eager to go home to the toys, bicycles, books, cartoons and classmates she left behind in Syria. But not if that means living with Alawites, members of the same minority offshoot of Shiite Islam as

Syria's president. 'I *hate* the Alawites and the Shiites,' Ibtisam said as a crowd of children and adults nodded in agreement. 'We are going to kill them with our knives, just like they killed us.'"[9]

These children's refusal to share a playground or a classroom with their "enemy" dramatizes the challenges that confront any effort to find a political solution to the conflict. Meanwhile, the easy talk of blood and killing exhibited by such young children illustrates the psychic toll all of this is taking on the next generation in so many countries.

This pattern extends around the globe: Tibet continues to be persecuted by China; Africa suffers from decades of Power Over colonization and resource exploitation (e.g., the mining of "blood diamonds"); the United States staggers under the planet's most expensive healthcare system that delivers some of the worst health statistics in the developed world[10]; ecological disasters abound; global economic and monetary crises cripple employment in Greece, Spain, Italy, etc. In short, Power Over is causing harm in every area of our lives — physical, emotional, mental and spiritual — on every front and in all parts of the globe.

To make matters worse, the media, seeking the highest drama in order to increase ratings, Powers Over us with excessive focus on "the disease of the day" (e.g., Ebola), terrorist attacks, "false flag" operations (e.g., "weapons of mass destruction"), and any tragic recent new story. Our physiological response to fearful information is the same whether it is real and immediate or only speculation.

Because all of this feels *so* overwhelming, many of us simply give up even trying to find solutions. However, each and every human being, and especially those who seek extraordinary leadership, do have options. They can begin to rely on new types of power interactions — those that involve Power With, which take into account the more inclusive Wholeness of all of humanity, lovingly recognizing others as equals. If today, every human being suddenly began to honor Power With in his or her own lives, the system would rapidly transform! But even if that doesn't happen, every individual who even *tries* to apply Power With begins to turn our system towards new balance and healing.

Distorted View of Money = Power = Value

I cannot leave our discussion of the detrimental effects of Power Over without mentioning money, for its use and abuse in our current world is gargantuan. Presently, the more cash or assets someone has, the higher their "class," and the more influence or power they have in the world. I don't believe this idea was written into our Constitution or the Declaration, yet this is the way our society has developed. This is, in fact, a terrible distortion of the original intent of money. Originally, money was created for the fair and equitable exchange of goods and services; it played a *limited* role in a much larger story. Now, however, money equates directly to power, and most of us have "bought in" — as with all societal programming. Many people find themselves slaves to the idea that without money, they have no power and thus, in certain circles, *no value.*

In fact, we have so internalized the equation "Money = Power = Value" that we gauge everything in our world by what we can *sell* it for: land, trees, animals, natural resources, beautiful vistas, anything we make. We have lost the sense of the *intrinsic value of life* and of qualities that make life worthwhile, like peace, joy, beauty, contentment, love, and feeling connected to All That Is. This is epitomized by the following story broadcast on National Public Radio: In one African village, young girls hoping to go to their prom must make a big show of wealth, emulating what they see on TV and YouTube videos, or they will be deemed "not valuable enough" to go. Failure means being completely ignored by the entire community. In this village, it is so important to appear rich for the daughters' sakes that families will risk massive financial debt, including having no food on the table, in order to avoid being shamed and ostracized — *for a prom!*[11] Similar phenomena are as prevalent in the West, especially in the U.S., just not reported so publicly.

*"Anything that leads away from the 'time is money' belief is good.
As is any movement away from having money
as the gold standard of life."*

~Bodil Jönsson
(Physicist)

The Roots of "Power Over": Fear vs. Love

"Power is of two kinds. One is obtained by the fear of punishment and the other, acts of love. Power based on love is a thousand times more effective and permanent than one derived from fear of punishment."

~MAHATMA GANDHI
(Spiritual Leader)

The choice to use Power Over is fueled by a perceived need for *control* — at any cost. The core emotion behind this need is *fear*. Fear divides and separates us, while love unifies. Fear in and of itself is not bad; it's energy, just a tool, and sometimes a very useful one. In the early days of human evolution, when we had to flee from wild animals and protect ourselves from the immediate environment on a constant basis, fear helped to keep our species alive. It provided a warning mechanism in the face of danger, urging us to act quickly to save ourselves and others. Correspondingly, fear motivated our ancestors to anticipate possible dangers and to design methods to *control* their environment. Fear spurred them to develop their physical and mental skills, to create weapons, build better shelters and devise faster means of travel — all helping us to survive.

But our species is long-past the time when wild animals lurk at every turn and we need to rely on adrenaline rushes to run faster and jump higher in order to stay alive. Our historically useful fear-based behaviors and belief systems no longer serve us, but we have retained our attachment to them, "re-writing" the causes. Instead of tangible physical dangers, our fears today are almost exclusively ***social*** in nature. These fears include the fear of failure, of not being good enough, of being made fun of, of being perceived as selfish or inadequate, of not being loved or lovable, etc. We even fear success. To complicate matters, mainstream media exaggerates or even manufactures additional fears by sensationalizing what's really happening, and by hyping shallow consumerism that encourages conflict with anything that differs from societal "norms" — including other societies.

Underlying these fears is a fundamental belief that other people are probably going to hurt us, so we'd better protect ourselves. On the basis of "the best defense is a good offense," we "protect" ourselves by stepping into a Power Over mode: We try to prevent others from hurting us by forcing them to do things our way — i.e., by controlling them. Ironically, this yields yet another fear: the fear that others will control *us* if we don't control them first! All of this creates a general environment of dread in which domination and retaliation are the culturally-acceptable standards for dealing with every issue in our lives — as individuals and as nations.

Establishing a healthy understanding of natural fear, our ancient ancestors passed on their wisdom *consciously*, teaching their children which animals to respect and what environmental warning signs to pay attention to. But our culture today passes on its unhealthy fears largely *unconsciously* — through judgmental and punishing looks, words and other behaviors — via family, peers, the media, etc. Often before we are even able to speak, we have already been conditioned to accept these fears as both valid and natural, when in fact they have been unnaturally "programmed" by our culture. We accept the dangers these fears represent as being as real as a wild animal attacking us, when actually the dangers of social fears are entirely of *human choosing*. And because those "teaching" us were themselves unconsciously taught, we operate and pass these fears and beliefs on without even realizing it (like my dad did when he used violence because *his* dad had used violence and because it was supported by all the societal norms of the day — e.g., "Spare the rod, spoil the child" was actually publicly spoken by our then-President.)

Spirit teaches us to love ourselves and others. In contrast, our societal programming teaches us to fear and dislike ourselves and others. Because of this incongruence, such programming creates imbalances in our psyches called "Core Wounds." Basically, we are expected to harm ourselves to satisfy the culture's distorted "norms." Since it is unnatural to want to hurt ourselves, the culture has to force its programming into us. Therefore, our first experience of Power Over is when we "buy into" this coercive system and accept Power Over approaches as natural and viable.

This programming then forms an unconscious base from which we

operate in the world. Because it is unconscious, it can cause us to react in ways which contradict how we *consciously* want to act, and which may be completely out of proportion to actual circumstances. We're no longer operating in our truth, we're just *reacting* — generally in extreme ways, such as by lashing out or withdrawing. In this mode, we make poor choices which may seem good at the time, but really aren't in the long-term best interests of anyone, including ourselves.

An even more damaging consequence of fear-and-control-based Power Over programming is its suppression of our natural spiritual inclination to *connect.* Instead, we separate from each other and from the divine. Power Over is the ultimate ego-ic way of saying that we do not need divine support. We're choosing to "go it alone," using our personal power — which is *finite* — instead of aligning with divine power based on love — which is *infinite.*

In order to tap into that infinite power, and shift from fear-based Power Over, we must begin to invite love through our hearts. Love recognizes the larger Whole of which we are a part. It recognizes others as fellow travelers worthy of our respect, thereby encouraging Power With. Yes, power and love can coexist! True power, connected to the divine, contains the highest vibration of love — a piece of wisdom that is often missing in our dialogues about power. And this true and infinite power, demonstrated through Power With, can emerge only after we identify and begin to heal our core wounds.

Core Wounds

> *The Dalai Lama, after traveling in the West, was seen to have tears in his eyes when told that Americans do not love themselves.*

Core wounds are psychological-emotional beliefs or imbalances that are usually created when we are children, just learning about how the world works. For example, in most Western cultures, children are taught from an early age to judge and criticize themselves and others according to standards that are often hypercritical or unattainable. This creates fear because we know we cannot meet the standards. As children, we have limited power, and so we usually internalize our fear. This leads to invisible wounds in our psyches, which show up later as unconscious and unhealthy behavior patterns that wreak havoc over time.

We can also think of core wounds as deep hurts and beliefs we create about ourselves that result from painful early experiences in which *our sense of self was threatened.* These wounds, and the societal conditioning that created them, give us a distorted view of who we really are, and this creates inner conflict as long as they remain buried and unexamined. What may have temporarily served to protect us in our childhood becomes quite destructive and no longer serves our healthy development as adults.

Systematic patterns of core wounding often occur in families and cultures because of shared belief systems, and these can be energetically passed down through generations. Virtually all of us suffer core wounds of one kind or another; the issue is whether we become sufficiently aware of them so that we do not merely react out of them, but instead make conscious choices that reflect the kind of leaders we want to be — leaders who have a positive impact on our world.

"The cruelest aspect of this story is that those who are ... deeply traumatized ... somehow attach the meaning of existence around this victimization ... in such a way that they're defined by their victim status ... It's out of that victimization process that so often the wound is transmitted."[12]

~JAMES O'DEA
(International Peacemaker, Author)

Many of our core wounds revolve around issues of power; adults often end up addressing power in the same ways they were taught as children. In our culture, this is usually a Power Over way based on fear. If we do not sufficiently love *ourselves*, we can be "triggered" by whatever core wounds sit in our subconscious. For example, many people in the world today

carry a fear of power, particularly those who were abused or ill-treated in some way as children. Their traumatized psyches have organized themselves around a rejection of power, with self-talk that may sound like this: "This feels horrible! I'm never going to use power this way! In fact, I'm going to avoid power altogether." This may seem virtuous, but it is a denial of our divine inheritance. We have a divine right to our power, and it is important not to give it away.

Or, a child may go in the opposite direction and, after regularly witnessing power being used abusively, learn to equate power with anger. Anger then becomes their power tool; they learn to control others through anger. Anyone who was overly controlled as a child may have concluded that the only way to operate in the world was to control others in return, through anger or even violence. We may feel we have to manipulate and control because it's the only way we feel safe.

Here is a story about one of my own core wounds, and how I (eventually) recognized it for what it was:

> *Even as a child, I was an advocate of non-violence, and my hitting anyone was exceedingly rare and uncharacteristic. Outside of skirmishes with my older brother, the first time I ever hit someone occurred one day in fourth grade. I was tiny and the boy I hit was huge. The action of hitting him created complex cognitive dissonance inside of me. I felt simultaneously triumphant, sad, embarrassed — and overwhelmed by my own power. This is what happened:*
>
> *Every single day, for weeks on end, Billy harassed me. He taunted me, cut in front of me, and blocked my way, making me late for class. I felt angry and confused about what to do. Then, one day, something snapped. My power-packed punch was fueled by my anger. I knocked Billy off his feet, and people cheered me on. My teacher saw the entire event, ran in, grabbed me and whisked me away. Everyone was laughing because a little "squirt" like me had knocked down the "giant" Billy — like David and Goliath.*
>
> *My actions were neither conscious nor premeditated; I simply reacted. Afterward, I had to face the consequences of my unplanned response.*

On the positive side, Billy never harassed me again. I got to eat lunch and reach my classes on time. But on the negative side, each day in the halls, I feared his retaliation. On top of that, I felt a confusing mix of emotions inside. I felt triumphant because I had finally gotten Billy to leave me alone. But I also felt sad and ashamed because I had humiliated him, and, in a way, I had also humiliated myself because I didn't believe in violence.

To add to my confusion, I was "rewarded" by others who felt empowered by my "courage" in facing the bully head-on. I also sensed I might have been too bold, considering the risks: Billy was twice my size, and had he chosen to pummel me back, I would have been mincemeat! Also, in retrospect, if he had hit his head in just the right place when he fell, I could have killed him — a possibility that still twists my stomach in a knot today.

As a result of this event, I stuffed my power deep inside of me. It took years for me not to fear that ferociousness. Only much later, when I was studying "cognitive dissonance" in psychology, did I begin to recognize that this event was indicative of a core wound inside me related to power. At a very young age, that wound generated the unhealthy belief that: "My being powerful will lead to destroying others (and possibly myself)." I also realized that this incident reminded me of my earlier experience of power with my dad, and that his core wound reflected a different belief: "If I don't defend and protect myself, I'll be walked all over and destroyed."

When faced with the choice of how to handle the bullying, I was essentially torn between these two unconscious and conflicting beliefs: my dad's fear that "I have to defend myself or I'll be destroyed" and my own fear that "If I use my power, I'll destroy myself and others." Alternatives to punching Billy might have existed (e.g., I could have stood up to him without physically assaulting him, or I could have asked friends to walk with me, etc.), but I didn't even think of them; I just reacted out of those conflicting beliefs that derived from unconscious inner wounds.

Sometimes, the only way to take on someone who is Powering Over us *is* to do it head-on. But for me, the choice to hit Billy was not right. I knew that by the way it made me feel after I did it. By the same token, I am not implying that my anger or the emotion of anger itself is unhealthy. It is the reactive *misuse* of anger (i.e., causing harm), just like the misuse of power, that wreaks havoc when core wounds are running the show. This was especially true in my case, as my typical preference was to work through conflict in a loving way with no harm — but that was lost as these core wounds took over my child's mind.

It is important to understand that our emotions are natural forms of energy; they are meant to flow out and be released, with love and mindfulness. Many of our core wounds exist because we were conditioned by society to "stuff" our emotions — especially so-called "negative" ones, like frustration, anger, envy, etc. — imprisoning these energies in our bodies and psyches. Trapped emotions fester, and often lead to internal harm in the form of illness, or external harm in the form of violence and destructiveness. Considering that so many of us have core wounds around power, it feels important that we each ask ourselves: How has my early conditioning affected my use of power?

As leaders, it is necessary to address the healing of our core wounds. This begins with recognizing what core wounds are. It involves learning how to manage our emotions so we can direct our powerful energy in positive ways. Developing "emotional fluency" is an essential skill for moving into Power With leadership. Some of us, including myself, must first acknowledge that we *have* power. Even though I was (and still am) very small physically, I am very powerful, which used to scare me because I was afraid I'd hurt someone like Billy, just like I was afraid of hurting my dad. So, in the past, I would deny my power and stuff my emotions (and often be Powered Over), while my dad would make sure other people knew they couldn't hurt him (with the unconscious default of Powering Over them instead). As I grew to understand how essential my power was to the work I was called to do in the world, I began to explore how to evoke my own power more effectively, while addressing the emotions that needed to be expressed in the healthiest ways possible. And it is my

experience with the leaders I have worked with that, when their core issues and emotions are resolved, they are also much more likely to choose Power With.

"Power With" Heals

"I am not interested in power for power's sake but I am interested in power that is moral, that is right and that is good."

~DR. MARTIN LUTHER KING, JR.
(Civil Rights Activist, Spiritual Leader)

When a leader chooses Power With, when he or she chooses love over fear, they align their personal power with divine power, and *so* many things can change. First of all, the disempowerment that comes with Power Over can lift, and all the associated issues can begin to shift. Confidence, self-esteem, enthusiasm and mutual support can be restored. When the leader models deep listening, people begin to believe they have a say in what happens, and respect and trust increase exponentially. The leader begins to inspire others instead of forcing them, and people feel revitalized. Stress is reduced, and responsibilities become shared. The attitude of alignment begins to filter through all layers of the group, organization, family, or world. As more and more voices are heard, and their perspectives valued, they, too, can naturally begin to align their personal will with divine will. When people are excited to contribute their gifts, the doors to innovation open. It is a powerful transformation, within and without.

Power With does not incite a desire for violence because it isn't using force as its base. It is using our mutual connectedness and shared desires; it is using the power of infinite divine energy, and this means that it does not need to make anyone "less than" in order to proceed. With infinite underpinnings, there is room in Power With for everyone to shine without anyone losing anything.

Power used in alignment with the divine is such a joy to witness because it empowers everyone. The leaders also get to relinquish their anxiety-producing overwhelm, the feeling that they "have the world on their shoulders" and "have to do everything themselves." Leaders who make the shift from Power Over find, to their relief and delight, that the more collaborative choice of Power With engenders such trust that they can finally distribute power and responsibility without fear. Because Power With allows each individual to align their will with their highest expression, each can then serve with their own divine power and not hide, but shine brightly, illuminating and revealing all parts of themselves. With no need to hide, their qualities naturally reveal themselves without being contingent on ego-ic recognition.

To embrace Power With is one of the greatest stress relievers I know and sets the stage for healthier action in the home, in the office, and in the world. When people feel seen and heard by the leader, there is such energy generated that projects can be completed in far less time, with greater ease, increasing profits and morale. Wouldn't it be fantastic if everyone felt enthusiastic about going to work instead of dreading it? So instead of trudging through the week and pronouncing, "Thank God, it's Friday," we might begin the week singing, "Hooray, it's Monday!" I have actually seen this happen with several business clients I have worked with. What a gift when it does!

In the same article mentioned previously, Harvey Mackay described how some CEO's have consciously chosen to use Power With approaches on a daily basis in order to shift away from traditional top-down leadership. One such CEO is Robert Chapman of Barry-Wehmiller, a manufacturing company with seven thousand team members and $1.6 billion in sales. One of Mr. Chapman's visions is "to send people home every night feeling fulfilled."[13] Chapman solicits ideas from employees and encourages them to discover, share and be appreciated for their gifts. The results: high morale and employee retention, better employee and familial relations, shared responsibility and support for the entire company as well as each individual.

According to Chapman, "even when the recession hit, company orders dropped by 35%, and employees were worried about layoffs," the company continued to choose Power With approaches. Instead of arbitrarily dictating a solution with only profit in mind, Chapman gathered employee teams to come up with humane ways to meet the challenges of the economic crunch. The plan that emerged was for all employees to take four weeks off without pay, selecting the best time for their families. The 401(k) match also needed to be suspended, but employees supported the decision because they knew that it was done to save people's jobs.[14]

This is quite different from a well-known company's use of Power Over and non-transparency, which forced employees to work during Black Friday, resulting in anger, resentment, protests and extremely negative PR. That particular organization and other profitable companies have every opportunity to use more employee-supportive approaches during financially challenging times. In fact, they would be shocked at how loyal their employees would become!

Our most brilliant and effective leaders, mentors and guides are those who live by Power With. They impart wisdom without ownership. They demonstrate courage and strength. When needed, they take well-thought-out risks in order to help evolve our consciousness and create a better world for all. They exhibit a willingness to be vulnerable and admit weaknesses or areas needing improvement. They find ways to discover who their people *are* and evoke the best in them, nurturing their gifts and strengths. They avoid labels, don't box others in or engage in backroom gossip. They are in service to humanity, not self-aggrandizement. These extraordinary leaders leave a legacy that can be carried forward even in their absence.

I believe that Martin Luther King, Jr., a minister by training, came to understand, at a very deep level, what the source of true power really is and how it was meant to be used in the world. The last segment of his "I have a dream" speech[15] is the epitome of consciously choosing Power With — the alignment of personal will with divine will for the benefit of all. That connection with the Whole is what people loved, admired, and wanted to align with. King learned from Gandhi, another deeply spiritual man, and now we continue to learn from them both.

I would like to share a story about how Power With transformed many lives that had been harmed by Power Over. Portions of this story are reminiscent of the great challenges and transformation that occurred for several of my former clients and colleagues. (Note: in this story, by their request, I am using the actual names of the people involved.)

Several years ago, I met and worked with an extraordinary man named Sequoyah Trueblood — a man of great peace and wisdom who is filled with deep gratitude for life. Sequoyah came into this world as a Native American, enrolled in the Oklahoma Choctaw Nation. He spent his entire childhood in poverty, and was severely abused regularly by both his guardians and his teachers in order to "beat the savage out of him." He was also sexually abused, suffered from childhood incontinence as a result, and lived in a state of constant shame and guilt. Power Over was all he knew.

In high school, his athletic prowess (fast runner, football star) helped rebuild some of his self-esteem. He also developed a much-needed and very strong faith as a result of several miraculous experiences, the first of which was when a man suddenly appeared to him in the forest and said, "You're Sequoyah Trueblood; you're being taken care of," and then the mysterious stranger disappeared. This helped Sequoyah believe that he was protected and cared for, even if it was not always obvious in the visible realms.

At age 17, after a rushed marriage with a child on the way, Sequoyah joined the Army. Despite tremendous fear, he also felt very honored to be serving in the United States military. This was due, in part, to his being the nephew of Pushmataha, the "Indian General," considered by historians to be one of the greatest of all Choctaw chiefs. Pushmataha served in the War of 1812 for the U.S., was instrumental in leveraging further independence and influence for America, and is buried in D.C.'s National Cemetery. Sequoyah was often guided by visions of this man, and was moved by this heritage to serve our nation similarly.

Versatile, strong and very bright, Sequoyah quickly moved up the ranks, from private to squad leader to positions of increased security and secrecy, including intelligence and counter-intelligence activities. Due to his extraordinary capabilities, Sequoyah was recognized by military commanders and offered a post in the Army's corps of elite Special Forces: that is, he became a super-soldier.

Power Over continued when, as part of his new job, he was exposed to an array of drugs that enabled him to perform at extreme levels, but eventually changed the chemistry of his brain. The chemical change made it almost impossible for Sequoyah to control his behavior, except while performing his high-alert military duties. At times, the slightest provocation would send him into a violent rage in which he would beat up anyone around him. This was useful on the battlefield — he was awarded a purple heart and 17 decorations in all — but extremely damaging to the rest of his life.

As his family grew, Sequoyah found himself unable to cope when he was home. His army training, coupled with the excessive use of military-issued amphetamines, had made him so sensitive to sound that he could not handle any loud noises. This made it impossible for him to be around his children and wife in responsible ways. He would fly into uncontrollable fits of violence, until one day, he was so enraged that he beat both his wife and oldest son. After he calmed down, he concluded that he had to leave and possibly never return. He filed for divorce, and this triggered a series of bizarre and shrouded events that resulted in Sequoyah being coercively sentenced to jail, and his family being barred by the military from seeing him.

While in jail for up to 44 years, Sequoyah met three men who significantly and positively influenced his life. Serving as counselors, these men — a Zen master, a psychologist, and a hypnotherapist — worked with substance-related violent prisoners to help them change their behaviors through hypnosis and other mental and internal techniques. With their help, Sequoyah began to learn Power With ways of operating. He learned methods to calm his mind, body and being so that he wouldn't just react, but would be able to ***choose*** *his behaviors. This was not easy, but over time, Sequoyah became proficient. His intensive inner work also made him very aware of how much he had*

been programmed from a young age to Power Over or **be** *Powered Over. This awareness inspired in Sequoyah a strong empathy for others who were also struggling to find their way in the world.*

Sequoyah's changes so impressed his hypnotherapist that he invited Sequoyah to become his assistant in the prison. Sequoyah began to help other prisoners work through their violent behavior and ingrained responses. In time, he became a deep listener and healer for nearly everyone who came in contact with him. On the basis of his amazing metamorphosis, the penal system released Sequoyah early from his sentence, and he began to travel in the world, working with many people to help them heal core wounds and transform their relationship to power. He became a spokesperson and mentor for non-violence, bringing people closer to heart-centeredness and spirit — leading by wisdom and evoking that in others.

But in spite of his reformation, Sequoyah remained estranged from his family — a fact that troubled him greatly. He made repeated attempts at communication, but military interference and his earlier violence, coupled with the suicide and attempted suicide of two of his sons, had rendered his remaining family too frightened, angry and traumatized to respond. Finally, Sequoyah's partner, Suzanne, intervened on his behalf and, after sharing information from John Perkins' book, "The Confessions of an Economic Hit Man," was able to arrange a meeting between Sequoyah and his oldest daughter. This gave Sequoyah an opportunity to share his current work with part of his family — work that involved deep connection with spirit, alignment with divine power, and healing the soul regarding relationships with others and the planet.

Through his peace work, a situation later arose (generously supported by the Foundation for Global Humanity) in which Sequoyah could meet with his entire family on neutral ground. He was glad and grateful when many of them, however reluctantly, agreed to participate. When the family arrived, there was initially a tremendous amount of tension in the air, but this softened when Sequoyah's new spirit became apparent; as his daughter Stephanie, who was quite resistant, said, "The moment I looked into your eyes, that all changed." When everyone was

seated, and Sequoyah humbly stood up and offered prayers and ceremony for healing, his family was further surprised by his gentleness, forthrightness and obvious open-heartedness.

Sequoyah opened up the floor for his family to speak by saying: "I know that I have hurt you and done great harm. I want to apologize for what I have done, and if there is any way to repair the damage I have caused, I want to do it. I know that the first step is for all of you to speak your truth and let me hear it. Please tell me, how have I hurt you? How have I done you harm?"

Each family member then spoke in answer to this call. When they were done, Sequoyah spoke of how ***he*** *believed he had harmed them. There was a tremendous outpouring of truth, emotional cleansing, and courage. Sequoyah asked Spirit to guide him and help him to show his family that he was a changed man, that his life was different now, and that he really wanted to make a positive difference in the world.*

He came to call this his Redemption Story — a story built on Power With: owning our actions, acknowledging our responsibility for misdeeds, offering apology and reparation, creating "restorative justice circles" where everyone gets to speak, listening intently to even the harshest truths, expressing empathy, and offering prayers and ceremony are all Power With behaviors. They align us with spirit, with each other, and with our deepest core, and this creates a path toward healing. Sequoyah had transformed because he was connecting with spirit and connecting with his heart — which had now become his life's purpose.

Because of Sequoyah's commitment to Power With, he and his family were able to reconcile after years of pain (with the acknowledgement that it is an ongoing process). The family is now in touch frequently, and his daughter Stephanie has begun to help him with his peace work, including opening the doors for oil executives to be exposed to these wise and loving ways to lead. In the end, Power With gracefully and gently replaced Power Over. This process of healing and reconciliation is continuous, and all the energy released from it impacts all other transformations for healing — both within Sequoyah's family and out into the world.

Thankfully, we have other inspiring examples of Power With healing Power Over in the world: Nelson Mandela, the Anti-Apartheid revolutionary and politician who served as President of South Africa from 1994 to 1999, also understood the principle of aligning one's power with the divine. Despite the abuses he experienced while imprisoned without just cause, he treated the prison guards and all others with honor and respect, and befriended them. He wanted them to understand that the power they were used to, was based upon fear. Even when Power Over was in his face daily, he surrendered control, viewing both guards and fellow prisoners as equals. The guards were so taken by Mandela's humane and loving approach, even while he was experiencing their oppressive ways, that they often broke the rules to help him to continue his humanitarian efforts. They grew to respect and love him, as he did them. After Mandela was elected president in the first fully representative multiracial election, he and his administration continued this work by dismantling Apartheid's legacy of racism, poverty and inequality. This is the conscious use of Power With that allows extraordinary leaders to positively transform our planet.[16]

The Dalai Lama is the political and religious leader of Tibet, the very spiritually-oriented country that was seized and overrun by China more than 50 years ago. The Lama was forced out of his home and into exile, thousands of Tibetan monks and nuns were tortured and killed, Tibet's most sacred and fertile lands were ravaged and used for dumping toxic waste, and the Tibetan heritage was disclaimed with all Tibetan children being forced to be raised and educated as Chinese. In spite of this, the Dalai Lama's power is aligned in such a way that he has been able to surrender to these events while simultaneously not giving up. This is why he is such an inspirational world leader and teacher. He has learned to smile and joke in the face of great adversity, with deep compassion for others, even those whom many describe as his "enemies."[17]

I would be negligent if I didn't also speak about two remarkable women who were not political leaders, but "merely" citizens whose courage inspired the world. Most recently: the young Iranian woman, Malala, who was shot in the head by a Taliban executioner for speaking out about human rights, including the right of women to be educated. Her strength and miraculous recovery testify to how she has aligned her personal power in service to her people and all people in the world.[18] The second is the equally courageous Immaculeé Ilibagazia, a Rwandan woman who saw her entire family massacred during the genocide of 1994, and who was hunted but miraculously eluded the same fate by hiding for 3 months in a tiny room with 7 other women. When she eventually escaped, she refused to return death for death: instead of seeking vengeance, she made a point of seeking reconciliation and an end to violence, and has become an international spokesperson for peace.[19]

***"You can't forgive without loving.
And I don't mean sentimentality, I don't mean mush.
I mean having enough courage to stand up and say,
'I forgive. I'm finished with it.'"***

~MAYA ANGELOU
(American Author, Poet)

These stories also demonstrate an important element of Power With: breaking the cycle of violence. To get from Power Over to Power With, we each must make the fundamental choice that "The Buck Stops Here!" when it comes to Power Over. We each have this power: we can choose to *stop* retaliating against Power Over with more Power Over in order to "get even." We have the choice instead to forgive the ill treatments, abuses and injustices and say, "I will **not** respond to Power Over with *more* Power Over. I will respond with Forgiveness and Power With." This is how we heal.

It is true that after so much Power Over domination, most people cannot do this without first being given the opportunity to acknowledge the hurts they have suffered. This is the impetus behind "truth and reconciliation" and "restorative justice" movements: everyone involved in conflict comes together to talk — both those who used Power Over and those who were Powered Over. The damage done is *not* ignored or swept under the rug.

Like Sequoyah's family, everyone harmed is given the opportunity to express their suffering fully and in truth, and those who did the harming must listen and receive. Often, some type of apology or reparation is required. Without this, reconciliation is often impossible. Even with it, it is still often quite difficult. But the choice to Stop Powering Over is core.

"The best way not to give up power, is to notice that you have it in the first place."

~ALICE WALKER
(Author)

In the end, Power With is a gift to ourselves. It allows us to be who we are and give ourselves love and gratitude for that, without the need to "prove ourselves" or to be constantly striving to be "better than." We honor and value other people just as we honor and value ourselves.

This was expressed beautifully by international peacekeeper, James O'Dea, during the first session of my "Extraordinary Leadership Telesummit" in 2013. James is a former director of Amnesty International, a past president of the Institute of Noetic Sciences, and the current lead faculty member of the popular Peace Ambassador's training hosted by the Shift Network. James carries wisdom about power that speaks to his indelible experiences in war-torn regions like Rwanda, Israel, Palestine, Turkey and Northern Ireland. His words have inspired millions of people, including some of our more prominent leaders, to raise their consciousness around power. Here is what he said:

> "I had an extraordinarily powerful and enlightened mother, and she had a mantra that she repeated to me from time to time, for years ... She would say to me: *'Remember that you're as good a man as anyone who ever walked the face of this earth.'* That's a powerful and amazing thing to say to a young child! 'You're as good as any person who ever walked the face of this earth.' Very, very empowering. And then she would say, *'But you are no better than the person who takes away our trash.'* And it was that mantra, repeated again and again, of

> equalization of power, of saying 'don't you ever feel inferior, and don't you ever feel superior' that I think gave me the strength ... to speak with President Reagan and President Bush and President Clinton and presidents from around the world with [the sense that] ... I was no higher and no lower!"[20]

May we all walk with such dignity and strength!

"Power With" Is Not Necessarily a Panacea

Having said all this, I must also say that it would be inaccurate to imply that "once you lead with love, *everything* will fall into place." *Sometimes* it happens like that, but sometimes things are more complicated. I know — from my own experience and from the shared experiences of those extraordinary leaders that I have had the great good fortune to work with over the years — that love and Power With approaches are crucial keys to personal and global transformation, but I also know that transformation is not always easy or simple.

Our culture has been committed to Power Over for thousands of years. Like a heavy train running downhill, it can't stop or reverse instantaneously. People currently dominating through Power Over may not want to change. They fear loss of status and authority. They don't *want* to share their power; they *like* dominating. It's probable that such people will not only resist using Power With themselves, but will also actively try to prevent others from using it. Such Power Over "junkies" might be in positions of recognized power (like managers or high-level political and organizational chiefs — CEO's, etc.), but they could also be in subordinate positions. Regardless, they may not like the "touchy-feely" nature of Power With. They may dig their heels in, refuse to cooperate, and use Power Over approaches like ridicule, refusal to participate, and creation of oppositional "camps" — all tactics meant to sabotage attempts to transition to Power With. Others may interpret the lack of Power Over as a license to "goof off."

Apart from outright opposition, Power With is also subject to the fact that some people just like to complain! These people find fault no matter what a leader does, how egalitarian their approach, how respectful or empowering their manner, and no matter how many shared desires and goals are met. Such people just enjoy complaining, and their influence may sway others who are "on the fence" about the changes that Power With requires. Also, some people fear change, even when it's for the better, preferring the "devil they know" to the "saint they don't."

Sometimes, the change to Power With can only occur if championed by a leader already in a position of significant power. For example, Joshua and the other engineers in the story demonstrating how Power Over hurts, might have been as loving as possible, but that was not enough to change their company. *Sometimes* one individual's powerful heart-centered actions can change a large group of people, but sometimes they remain a solitary "voice crying in the wilderness." It is important in such situations not to give up on the whole approach. It might be necessary to leave that particular organization or relationship and seek out more fertile ground where Power With is more welcomed, and where a leader committed to Power With can find allies. I liken this to knowing where to tap a drum to get the best resonance. If we keep hitting the drum in the wrong spot, all the output will be flat and uninspired. But when we find the "sweet spot," the drum *sings*.

I also want to acknowledge that not every relationship or organization can function if they attempt to deal with issues that actually require more of a therapeutic context. Power With inspires deep sharing and commitment, but it also requires that everybody — leaders as well as "followers" — do daily inner work on their own wounds and programming to become and stay "clear" about their actions and motivations. This can be exciting and inspirational when insights are revealed and later integrated, but it can also be daunting, especially when the process is unfamiliar. We all need to do self-assessments and be honest in our responses. This is not always easy, and some people may become discouraged or "turned off" about doing it at all. These things just reflect the growing pains that are a normal part of personal and organizational evolution. We each must determine which path we want to follow and what is most important to us. As with all change, just because others fall by the wayside, it doesn't mean that we can't continue on *our* path. This book is about Extraordinary Leaders. These are the ones who are willing to do what it takes to initiate and support real change in the world.

It might also seem that Power With will only work when *everyone* commits to it. But we have to remember the "hundredth monkey" effect and the work of Gregg Braden, which proposes that when a very small fraction (actually the square root of 1%) of the population makes a definitive change, it can propel the entire population to change.[21] In a world of over 7 billion people, this means that it will only require about 8500 people making a change to have an impact on the whole planet.[22] This is similar to the "butterfly effect," in which tiny, individual changes can add up over time to produce great transformation in the world (as reflected in the Krishnamurti quote at the beginning of this book). We have to start somewhere, so let's each start with ourselves, and with those places in our lives where we *can* exercise our power. The more each of us chooses Power With approaches, the more we can slowly help the world to transform.

There are many new mechanisms that have been created to assist the process of changing from Power Over to Power With. I will be talking about these in more depth in Vital Key #7, "Manifesting Dreams and Transforming World Systems through the Heart," but they are also summarized within the section below that discusses "Power With Experiences and Structures." These include new forms of governance and formalized systems of communication that counterbalance the entrenched Power Over systems that we might feel we have to battle to overcome. Help is available! These new systems incorporate activities like empathy training, anger management, and non-violent communication techniques along with traditional organizational trainings like strategizing, project management, and so on. Our world *is* already changing; let's continue to help it along.

A Call To Action: Consciously Choosing "Power With"

"As we transform beliefs, we transform hearts, evoking the wisdom of power and the power of wisdom to effect change from the inside out."

~Whispers from the Heart of the World
(Great Spirit's Messenger)

As leaders, we hold the responsibility to understand the world of power around us. We must start by acknowledging the historical misuse of it and how our own socialization and position in society have affected our relationship to power. In my work with clients in leadership positions, I observe that these issues are often ignored or swept under the rug. We cannot afford to continue this! We are being called on to raise our consciousness about power and to work on freeing ourselves from any unconscious tendency to use Power Over.

Identify Your Motivation

Our critical first step is to acknowledge power and all its complexities. When making critical decisions, I ask leaders (and myself): What is the motivation behind your use of power relative to this decision? Are you motivated by ego, or are you seeking to align with divine will? The quickest way to get to the truth is to ask:

Am I acting out of fear or love?

If the answer is "fear," then we must attend to the source of that fear — see if we can calm it and transform it into love. The very asking of this question helps every one of us become more aware of our motivations. Sometimes, we stay in our positions because we're afraid to move. We may find, like Jerry MacGuire in the movie of the same name, that we "hate what we have become" and we "hate our place in the world." Asking the question, "Am I doing this out of fear or love?" and honestly listening to

our answer can propel us into becoming the person we really want to be. As with MacGuire, we will "lose the ability to bullshit."

Go Towards What You Fear

Another helpful practice is to move *towards* what we fear. This helps to negate fear's hold on us, and its corresponding habits of Power Over and control. As James O'Dea shared during the Extraordinary Leadership Telesummit:

> "When we think about power, [it brings up] the fear that someone has the power to hurt us ... That's when it gets dangerous, doesn't it? And that's precisely when I say, 'That's when you should move *towards* it.' It's like aikido ... The best protection is often moving towards the energy. And that's the beauty of aikido and its power teachings ..."[23]

Resolve Core Wounds

To begin to shift from Power Over, we must also address our core wounds around power. This step is one of the most significant in terms of creating long-term sustainable personal change. Like any exploration of personal issues, it's important to seek supportive mentoring, and in some cases professional counseling, to address these inner wounds. The process might include identifying beliefs that were established long ago to protect us from harm. For example, someone who believes they're "never good enough" and is disempowered as an adult, might have felt as a child that if they kept their mouth shut, their parents might someday believe that they would be "good enough." In that case, we might be asked to identify specifically how that belief helped us when we were young, and whether it serves us or harms us now. In those places of increased awareness, new, more life-affirming beliefs can be created (or may emerge spontaneously) that support our actual goals as leaders. Related and very beneficial inner work includes Vicki Abadesco's workshops for children to help create "a bully-free world"[24] and "inner child" work such as that popularized by John Bradshaw.[25]

Cultivate Empathy

Empathy is often described as the ability to "walk in another's shoes," to understand what someone else is feeling or thinking. In fact, empathy is also a deep knowing of our *own* innermost core; it is the ability to recognize ourselves in others. This is reflected in the Hindi greeting "Namaste," which means "the divine in me bows to the divine in you." In such reflection, no one is "less than" and no one is "greater than." There is only All That Is. We see our own value without becoming egotistical, and we see the value of others without diminishing ourselves. Empathy also allows us to experience each other's deepest pain and core wounds so that we may better understand one another, teaching us to respond with ever-increasing compassion.

Do a Self-Assessment About Power

Here are some questions for leaders to ask themselves:

- What does power mean to me?
- Where do I hold power in my body? (Knowing this helps us identify when we're abusing power.)
- Am I aware of my triggers, the things that cause me to default to Power Over tactics?
- Do I manipulate to get my way? Or do I use power in a healthy way to align with the divine so I can manifest in positive ways?
- Have I spent a good portion of my life fearful of my own power or other people's power over me?
- How have I disempowered others? Have I done this by undermining people's abilities to share their gifts?

Especially if we are leading groups or organizations, it's important to assess whether a tendency to use Power Over has undermined our effectiveness. Here are the top nine indicators that tell us we are using power in unhealthy ways:

1. Trust is eroded, an atmosphere of fear and/or gossip reigns.
2. We no longer inspire our team and they speak poorly of us, respect is lacking in both directions.
3. We do almost everything ourselves — no leverage or not delegating enough (affecting health and lifestyle, no time with family).
4. Conflict is increasing.
5. We are bludgeoning and/or overworking our employees.
6. We are losing employees to competitors, low retention/loyalty.
7. We are out of touch with people in the trenches; the right hand doesn't know what the left hand is doing, we're losing the forest for the trees.
8. We are over-managing or micromanaging unnecessarily.
9. We show poor quality of goods and services, decreased output, missed deadlines.

Take the time to ask colleagues and team members to give feedback about all of these questions and indicators as well (since, e.g., if we're out of touch, we might not *know* we're out of touch, etc.). Then aspire to demonstrate greater trust, respect, and fair distribution of power and responsibility within the organization. Be ever-aware of, and listen to, the voices of your people and teams. Create cultures to ensure fair representation, healthy conflict resolution and balanced feedback for workflow and processes.

Change Your Relationship with Money

As I mentioned before, our relationship to money has an impact on the way we view our place in the world, and the overall meaning of our existence. We are all valuable no matter what the surface shows, but the focus on money is still ingrained in our world systems. How might we change that? I believe we have an opportunity now to shift away from the obsession with money and wealth — which obviously causes much pain when attached to one's meaning in life — and to focus instead on people's gifts, talents, and *inherent value* — returning to the original intent to create a fair and equitable exchange of goods and services. We need leaders who will carry this message forth, particularly to young people.

Commit to "Power With" in Relationships

I invite us all to consciously commit to operating via Power With in our families and interpersonal relationships as much as we possibly can. This means that we consciously choose to infuse all our actions and behaviors with love, and attempt to navigate through our fears rather than letting them run the show. We do this by becoming aware of any knee-jerk desires to control out of fear: fear of chaos, fear of loss of financial stability, or fear of loss of perceived power (i.e. "I'm the boss"). Then we consciously shift to loving engagements centered on shared power and responsibility. This lets us tap into divine power and align our life path with that. The more we do this, the more we invite others to do the same, and this process can "domino," evoking the best from spouses, partners, children, neighbors, colleagues, and even bosses and higher-level leaders.

This extends to using Power With in our relationships with children. So many of us were shut down as children when the adults in our lives used Power Over out of their need to protect or control. When kids are over-controlled, they feel incompetent, like they can't do anything right. They begin to equate power with control and assume that power resides outside of them. As a consequence, they can become defiant, withdrawn, or fearful. Our children need to learn a more balanced engagement with power. They need to understand that it can be used for good, that the positive use of power can inspire change personally and globally. They also need to develop emotional literacy so they can make the choice to opt into love rather than fear. Young people, particularly those who feel that they have little to no influence, also need the opportunity to participate in something that allows the light of their power to shine. These are tomorrow's leaders. Do we want them to be hurt people who in turn hurt people, or do we want to stop the damage now?

One word of caution: in shifting from Power Over to Power With, we must watch out for any inclination to revert to Power Over *within* Power With scenarios. I have seen this particularly in couple's therapy, where a dominant partner will twist the therapeutic process to their own purposes, in order to regain control. For example, Imago Therapy is a practice used for relationship counseling that utilizes non-violent communication techniques. In Imago Therapy, couples are encouraged to listen respectfully to each other while taking turns sharing their concerns. These interactions can sometimes become quite emotional, and "timeouts" are used to cool down if things get too heated — with the intent that dialogue will be re-established when tempers have calmed. Timeouts are really important for the process, and very effective when used properly. However, in my work with clients, business leaders and relationship upheavals, I have personally witnessed dominant individuals use timeouts to *silence* their partners: if they don't like what they're hearing, they'll call for a timeout, thereby sweeping the contentious issue under the rug. This is not using Power With! We need to be attentive to control issues and manipulations that might be hiding in the shadows.

For spiritual couples and businesses, sometimes there are similar imbalances in the use of meditation practices: they might be used to "check out" rather than tune in to a connection with source. They also might be unconsciously used to ignore or avoid issues altogether, sweeping conflict and challenges under the rug. This can often include judgment around emotions, e.g., that expressing emotion is not "spiritual." This is not so! Emotions often reflect our deepest truths — truths that need to be spoken. In Power With, we do make the choice to express our emotions in the healthiest way possible, without "blasting" or "dumping," and with a No Harm policy in place as much as we can. Again, I highly recommend tools like meditation and timeouts, but they must be used mindfully, not manipulatively.

Commit to "Power With" in the World

I have a cousin who often wonders what would have happened after 9/11 in America if we had, as a nation, chosen to engage in a collective ceremony that focused on loving each other and those in the world whose hearts were then filled with sympathy and empathy for us. This is, after all, what those who *died* in 9/11 did: they phoned their loved ones to tell them they loved them as their airplanes were crashing or the fires were raging and they knew they were going to die. I don't know of anyone who phoned their loved ones to say, "You've got to kill the bastards who did

this!" Even if we couldn't at that moment love our *attackers*, we could have consciously chosen to focus on intensely loving our families and friends as a way of shifting our energetic from victimhood and revenge, and this might have made for a very different world today. We can still do it now, years later, with any news event that makes us angry or fearful. We can always choose to focus on the higher energetic; that is our spiritual birthright.

Also, we can look to extraordinary leaders who already model the behaviors we would like to emulate. We can all learn from the best positive examples of master teachers, like Martin Luther King, Jr., the Dalai Lama, Amma, James O'Dea, Albert Einstein, Abraham Lincoln, and others who have been inspired by the power of the divine moving through them in service to the world (knowing also that everyone is human, and can make mistakes).

Consider "Power With" Experiences and Structures

Individuals whose default behavior is to Power Over may not be equipped to react any other way. Their way has become the norm; they may feel trapped by habit, and need training and support in order to change. I'm speaking of trainings in things like "emotional fluency," anger management, non-violent communication (NVC), restorative justice, and other alternative forms of social healing. I also advocate participating in Rites of Passage, Vision Quests, Native American talking circles, other restorative justice and bully-free processes, archetypal training, expressive arts projects, dialogue groups, etc. For more resources, go to my website at www.leadbywisdom.com.

It's time to turn some of our outdated and unhealthy systems inside out. We need to create systems, structures and processes that promote Power With and inhibit habitual Power Over patterns. There are approaches to organizational design — more enlightened forms of governance such as Sociocracy, Holacracy, and others — that can help us build greater empowerment and collaboration into organizational decision-making. A

brief history and summary of these systems are presented in Vital Key #7, "Manifesting Dreams and Transforming World Systems Through the Heart."

I encourage exploration of these alternatives. Let's innovate to create healthier systems in all arenas of life. Let's be willing to look for what works in other countries, and conduct experiments. Let's reclaim our power and create a society that really works for all.

Practice Acceptance and Surrender

This is brave work. Our vision must be clear, not clouded by illusion. Our job is to do what we can in the best way that we can, and release the rest without unconsciously giving away our power. Surrender does not do this, although it *does* give up *control*. We can tell the difference by how we feel: When we give away our power or just give up, we feel an underlying sense of frustration, discouragement, worthlessness or meaninglessness. But when we surrender, we feel at peace — even if our final goal is not yet in sight.

For those who do not resonate with the word "surrender," I would like to offer the following simple steps derived from a process called "Allowing Alternatives," which I was given by my colleague and friend Mike Two Bears, a former major oil executive who currently leads and participates in spiritual ceremonies from many traditions:

1. Stop.
2. Be still (and know what is).
3. Let everything be (as it is).

The first step (Stop) is to make us aware of our own reactivity and give us the chance to become neutral. The next step (Be Still) is to create a "breathing space" to recognize what is true in the moment without pre-judging; I think of this step as putting us in the frame of mind of the old "Dragnet" TV show's "the facts ma'am, just the facts." The final step (Let Everything Be) deepens our non-judgment by inviting us to recognize that whatever is occurring is doing so for reasons that we may not fully

understand at present, but which will unfold as time goes on. This step also encourages us to become detached from assumptions of "good" or "bad" and from wanting to assume that what's happening is personal. These three steps help to frame the possibility that what is happening might be exactly what is needed, and to consequently "give us permission" to stop trying to force a behavior or an outcome.

One thing seems certain, if we continue to choose fear and Power Over, the disease of control will continue to be the norm — to the detriment of all. But if we open ourselves to love and Power With, a different path is possible. A more beautiful future can be created through collective commitment, much like the collective dream shared in the Introduction to this book. I am but one citizen of this world, yet I can't help but hope that we, as leaders, will choose to embark upon this daring, uncharted and transformative path together. This is the shift that must occur for us to survive and thrive in collaboration with our home, Mother Earth. That's why I believe so fervently that the conscious choice to use Power With is such an important key to extraordinary leadership.

Vital Key #2:
Seeking and Speaking Truth

"Truth seeking without being righteous, but looking for the heart of the truth of what's happening, is a powerful transformational agent." [1]

~JAMES O'DEA
(International Peacemaker, Author)

Extraordinary leaders share a collective dream of a better world, a *thriving* world. That world demands that we each, more consciously, step into truth. We cannot resolve the very real problems facing us today — poverty, a failing economy, poor healthcare, energy depletion and water crises, to name just a few — by continuing to operate within our current "house of cards." Yet our governance and social support systems have been co-opted by a complex web of lies, distortions and suppressions of the truth. These unhealthy mechanisms have been designed, not to serve, but to control and dominate. Acts of dishonesty and deceit are rampant throughout our culture, and are destroying the lives and health of individuals, nations and the Earth itself. In fact, lying creates many of the same problems as Power Over. This is because it's actually a *form* of Power Over: by corrupting the truth, liars can manipulate people and situations to their own advantage.

We may even have come to "expect" lies from people in positions of power. Yet, no matter how entrenched this practice is, nor how corrupt our systems, *our souls call us to reconnect to truth and speak it out loud.* This is no small task, as truth has been repressed for centuries — so much so that lying and lack of transparency have become tacitly accepted as "inherently human." In spite of this, I believe we not only *can* evolve to become more truthful beings, but that we *must.*

As leaders, we need to rededicate ourselves to truth, reversing the old embedded trends. The call to extraordinary leadership is a call to generate life-affirming and sustainable solutions for world problems. This requires us to create a solid foundation of truth-telling, with grace. We must also be willing to let go of the portions of our current systems that no longer serve. This will allow the space for us to construct a new "house" — one that is built on a foundation of truth.

Imagine Truth as Our Daily Experience

When I was very young, I used to have a recurring dream that I lived in a world where everyone could read each other's minds. It was a world where people would turn sharply and say, "Hey, I heard that!" to whatever we were thinking. This transparency eliminated the desire — or, indeed, the ability — to lie or withhold. Even though our thoughts were not always pleasant, this absolute honesty brought people closer together because there was no longer any feeling of separation or need to hide what we thought or felt: we all knew where we stood with each other.

This is not just a dream: I've had the privilege of experiencing cultures where mind-reading is actually the norm. I participated in a multicultural ceremony in Colombia in which the spiritual leaders of four different indigenous tribes were clearly able to read the minds and energy fields of all the participants. I have had similar experiences with other indigenous tribes including Peruvians, Native Americans and the aboriginals of Australia. Even in Western cultures, many people who do intuitive and energy work find that they can read other people's fields and communicate with other species, including animals and plants. I resonate

with and experience this myself — as "out there" as that may seem to some people. As in my dream, such communication is amazingly liberating: when others sense our unspoken truths, there is no need to hide any part of ourselves. This creates a solid foundation for truth consciousness. I sense that, in the distant past, all humans had this capability.

Today, I believe that we, as leaders, are being called to dedicate ourselves to a greater truth, to take on more responsibility for both speaking truth (carefully expressed) and operating with greater transparency. We are being called to encourage and inspire others to do the same. The goal is to unveil truth in such a way that we reduce fear and increase hope. I am committed to this in my own life. Imagine if millions of us across the globe committed to this, too. What a legacy we could leave for our children!

The Reality: Cultural Deceptions

"Deception may give us what we want for the present, but it will always take it away in the end."

~RACHEL HAWTHORNE
(Author)

Many nations and cultural groups have been held hostage to lies maintained by leaders who are supposed to represent the people. For example, the decisions of a few people in leadership roles in the financial industry alone have had drastic consequences for millions of others, placing our nation's economy in peril. Similarly, when our leaders initially disseminated information regarding hydro-fracking (high pressure liquid injections in the earth to extract oil or gas), it seemed like a safe alternative to oil drilling. People supported it because they believed they knew the truth. However, information was suppressed that would have revealed fracking's actual damaging effects on both aquifers and geological stability (increasing earthquakes). Truth was suppressed to support monetary gain for a chosen few, at the direct expense of those

who live in the affected regions, and the health of the Earth itself. Similar suppressions have occurred in many other industries. Let us ask our leaders to take on a new charge of greater transparency and to unveil truth to the people so that we are more informed about decisions made on our behalf. Let us demonstrate courage and faith by revealing our greatest secrets so that our lives and future are no longer held hostage.

Some lies run very deep. Millions of people in the industrialized West want to obtain "the American Dream": bigger and better homes, cars, conveniences, entertainment, etc. Some may still achieve this goal, but for many, that dream is shattered. This is heartbreaking for some, but it reveals a larger truth: if all seven billion of us followed the trajectory of the U.S. population elite, it would bring humanity to its end. The dream of the few is unsustainable for the many.

Similarly, many of us have been indoctrinated with the notion of "Continuous Growth" — in business, in finances, in everything! "If you're not growing, you're stagnating." This behavior does not exist in Nature. In Nature, continuous uncontrolled growth is known as "cancer." This is not a desirable model to build systems around. But who wants to give up the dream of a better life? Even spiritually-motivated people need money to create stronger businesses, to be more generous and to make a greater positive impact in the world. But this is exceedingly difficult when the economics of our systems have been based upon lies — large-scale lies that have unknowingly been accepted as true.

Even our beloved democratic ideals do not hold up under scrutiny. Wars, colonialism, the ravaging of cultures and lands, the buying off of other governmental leaders and the selling of drugs for arms have all been done in the name of "protecting democracy." I encourage us all to remember the words of progressive statesman Senator Hiram Johnson, articulating his sentiment in 1917 relative to WWI, "The first casualty when war comes is Truth." (With rather strange timing, Johnson died during WWII, the day the bomb was dropped on Hiroshima.)[2]

On the grandest scale, when corporations, governments and world leaders lie, the results can include social unrest, rebellion and wars, crises in all

world systems (financial, social, ecological, et.al.), suppression of innovative solutions that would *help* these problems, and vast waves of hate and hostility when cooperation and understanding are most needed — as the following story illustrates:

In late 2010, a movement began in Arab countries that later became known as "the Arab Spring." This seemed to be a grassroots movement to bring a new way of life to the people of those countries. On New Year's Day in 2011, I found myself deeply distressed by what I was reading in the mainstream media about this movement's effects in Egypt. Reports of massive violence and destruction abounded. I wanted to do something to help.

I tuned in to my inner wisdom and asked, "What can I do about this? Which way should I turn? Should I just give up and assume that one voice means nothing?" My inner wisdom responded, "No, no, no! I refuse to believe that." It seemed to reverberate in my chest cavity, as if I had spoken out loud. That evening when I went to bed, I continued to pray for guidance, and received a dream that contained an unexpected and very challenging request: I was told that I should go to Egypt myself. This is what I heard:

> *"During the intense struggle between the dictatorial rule of Mubarak and the wishes of the Egyptian people, we ask you to visit that land, to travel there with an open heart and an open mind. Although your current position is that of a transformational consultant and filmmaker, your role will be that of a peacemaker, for that is another of your gifts. We ask you to deeply listen, and as an anonymous representative from the U.S. with no agenda but to hold sacred space, to hear the heart calls from your fellow human beings."*

This request startled me for several reasons. First, there were obvious dangers in traveling to a place with so much reported violence. Secondly, there were potential dangers in being an American, carrying camera equipment and asking questions. Thirdly, I was, at the time, just recovering from a very serious car accident, which had immobilized me for several months. However, I have learned that when these beneficent intuitive messages come to me, it's best for me to listen and follow through.

So, the very next day, I began an intensive research project into the safety, security, and legal concerns associated with such a journey, including contacting the Egyptian news service and Consulate. I also studied the demographics and logistical issues so that I could plan effectively. My research continued for two months, and several times, things temporarily looked impossible. But in the end, all the twists and turns were successfully navigated, and on March 1st, shortly after Mubarak stepped down, I booked a flight to Cairo, Egypt.

When I told my family and friends of my plans, most of them expressed horror: they didn't want me to take such a risk, and begged me not to go. Partly to allay their fears, I sought out a travel partner who could also serve as a bodyguard and translator if necessary. Synchronicity led me to a six-foot-tall, 200+ pound military man with an affable personality, an open-minded attitude, and previous travel experience in the Middle East. His background was a wonderful complement to mine.

When my plane landed in late March 2011, it took me a few moments to register that the airport seemed to be deserted. The reports of violence and hostility had clearly been heard, and people were staying away from Egypt. As I walked through the unbelievably silent terminal, I began to feel really edgy. I seemed to be completely alone. Suddenly, I was startled by a brief, yet explosive noise that sounded like a gunshot.

Heart racing, I looked frantically around and discovered a maintenance employee who had just dropped his broom. I laughed and sighed in relief, and felt compelled to do a self-assessment. Breathing deeply, I realized how all the media hype had already gotten under my skin and made me petrified by a completely innocuous event. In that moment, I made the conscious decision that I needed to move through my fear if I wanted this spiritual journey to succeed. Otherwise, my fear would block my heart, and I would be unable to hear the voices of the people I would be interviewing. Quietly, I asked for protection, and for my fear to serve as a discerning alarm, but for my heart to lead the way as I

entered into these foreign lands.

The next day, my bodyguard/translator joined me, and we began to travel the land and speak with the people. I soon discovered that things were very different from what had been reported. I saw no violence and, to my great surprise, my colleague and I were welcomed and honored even though we were Americans, and I was a woman. We traveled from Cairo to the Great Pyramids to Alexandria to the farmlands and to deep pockets of poverty, listening to the voices of the people all along the way.

Consistently, they expressed a desire to love, be loved, live without so much struggle, to speak freely in support of human rights both at home and abroad, and to feel like their lives had meaning. Indelibly etched in my memory is the deeply-wrinkled face of a kind-eyed, 90-year-old man. With tears welling up as he spoke, he emphasized the non-violence he had witnessed, saying, "I am so proud of the Egyptian people, and I am more proud of all of humanity!"

This was emblematic of sentiments across the nation. Everyone I spoke with wanted a new type of leadership that would restore human rights, allow freedoms that had been curtailed, and represent the people's wishes in a truthful way. They expressed frustration at not knowing where to find such a leader, but every single person I encountered across the country wanted the change to be non-violent.

This was in direct opposition to what was being reported about Egypt in the mainstream world media! The clincher came for me on a night when I Skyped my parents back in America. I had just spent the day in Tahrir Square where millions of Egyptians were gathered. My parents were frantic because U.S. news reports showed rioting and bloodshed in that very square. I had just been there, and had seen ***no*** *rioting or bloodshed.*

I returned home profoundly moved by my experience. The Egyptian people wanted what American people wanted, what most people want, and they were trying to get it as peacefully as possible. Yet with all the mainstream media focused on "There's violence there," I am sad to say that violence eventually erupted — about three weeks after I returned home. I truly believe that erroneous news reports that focused world expectations on negative results helped to actually ***create*** *those negative results, including the rippling downward spiral of Egypt's economic foundation (heavily reliant on tourism). I further believe that the violence that occurred most likely originated with those who were vying for "Power Over" control in Egypt and not from the majority of the Egyptian people.*

This experience is representative of events I've observed all around the world. With the constant spread of distortions and propaganda in the news, both in the U.S. and abroad, I believe that we are currently in a crisis of truth throughout the globe. As always, this crisis also represents an opportunity for transformation. In spite of the fact that violence did erupt in Egypt, I remain heartened by the fact that millions of people were working together to try to effect positive non-violent change. This resonates with the collective dream expressed in my personal story in the Introduction to this book. The desire for greater truth is part of the shared dream for our world that I believe we can still manifest.

Remember: When two or more are gathered in the name of truth, there is a much greater chance that deeper, more inclusive truths will emerge. When more and more of us choose to align ourselves with this quest for deeper truth in service to all humanity, amazing transformation can occur. What would our world be like if we were able to do this? What if there was enough momentum to cause all those in leadership roles to step into a more truthful way of being?

Ways We Lie and Why We Do

The topic of truth is a tricky one. In the United States, when people are put on the stand in a court of law, they must swear or affirm "to tell the truth, the whole truth and nothing but the truth." But do we always know what the truth is? And can any human being be 100% objective (or even 1% objective about certain issues)? Keeping these concerns in mind, I'd

like to define some terms:

"Truth-telling" means doing our best to state facts as we know them in the most straightforward way possible, making an effort to avoid bias and self-interest. The conscious *intention* to be truthful is primary. As with any skill, the more we practice, the better we get.

"Transparency" means making information readily accessible, not trying to hide important facts. Truth-telling and transparency are subject to other considerations, including timing, safety and the impact on others.

"Lying" means purposely hiding or misrepresenting the facts. Lies come in several forms.

- **Lying Directly**: This is the most straightforward type of lie (although not necessarily the easiest to spot). Here the individual purposely misrepresents the truth, either by denying it or by manufacturing false "facts."

Our culture overtly disapproves of direct lies and advocates punishing those who are caught in them; however, this same culture supports *indirect lying* in many ways. Indirect lies include:

- **Lying By Omission**: The person lying intentionally leaves out important facts in order to mislead others. What is said is technically true, but it is incomplete, and thereby creates a false impression. Our culture indulges this kind of lie in advertising, political campaigns, and other arenas. This lie is the reason the U.S. courtroom oath includes "the whole truth."

- **Lying By Silence**: Here, a person knows something is untrue or disagrees with the status quo, but doesn't speak up for fear of the consequences. The silent lie is often in play around bullies, sexual abusers and others who use Power Over to generate fear: those who disagree keep their mouths shut, often allowing other people to be mistreated or harmed rather than draw potentially dangerous attention to themselves. (This has been seen especially with cult and religious abuses often unveiling more complex mechanisms protecting the lies.) Our culture encourages this type of lie by

placing strictures early on, encouraging young children not to be a "tattletale" or a "snitch." It also tacitly encourages it by supporting Power Over in nearly all areas of life.

- **Lying By Labeling**: By applying a label, the liar can twist the facts for or against a particular person or event. Human Rights violators have a long history of using this lie: applying derogatory names to people of certain races, cultures or religions reduces or removes their humanness, allowing them to be mistreated and abused. Similarly, the status quo is often maintained by labeling those who question it as "quacks," "weirdos," "non-team players," etc. Even when untrue, these labels often stick, deterring much needed change.

- **Lying Through Spin**: Applying "spin" is technically not lying, but certain facts are purposely exaggerated or distorted in order to make a person, product or event appear better or worse than they actually are. Spin has become extremely popular in our culture where it is used routinely in advertising, political campaigns and throughout the media.

All these forms of lying also interact with each other. Lying by labeling is often teamed with lying by silence (e.g., human rights violations perpetrated by one group are allowed to continue by others who keep silent); direct lies frequently need to be followed up by lies of omission or silence (to cover up the original lie); spin often leads to direct lying (as spin increases, this becomes only a small step), and so on.

Why do we do these things? According to Dr. David Smith, Ph.D., "The tendency to tell tales is a very natural human trait ... it lets you manipulate the way that you want to be seen by others."[3] In other words, we lie mostly to help ourselves. Usually, the intent is not to be hurtful to others — but others can be collateral damage. Smith has identified the six most common reasons people lie.[4] These are presented below with real-life examples from my clients during consults and strategy sessions:

1. **Lying to Be Nice:** "That suit looks great on you" (when we don't think it does at all). The underlying impulse may be altruistic, but it makes us

inauthentic. Ironically, this lie can also be very hurtful if the other person discovers what we really think.

2. Lying to Make Oneself Feel Better: "I can afford this; I'm bound to get a bonus soon" (when no bonus is expected). Instant gratification may feel good, but such lying can lead to run-away debt and/or addictive behavior.

3. Lying to Save Face: "So sorry, I never got the email" (when we did, but didn't want to answer it). Although this can save us embarrassment, Dr. Smith cautions that it can lead to the unhealthy pattern of giving ourselves "permission to be irresponsible."

4. Lying to Avoid Confrontation: "You're a terrific employee, but we no longer need your position, so we're letting you go" (when we really want to fire this employee and hire someone else in that position). Avoiding confrontation can feel good in the short term, but over time, it stunts our growth and deadens our connections because we never really learn to stand up for others or ourselves.

5. Lying to Shift Blame: "My boss made that decision, not me" (when they didn't). As with confrontation, it may be a relief to avoid blame, but we have to be responsible for the consequences of *all* our choices. This kind of lie can put us forever on the defensive, and render us unable to handle bigger issues. In addition, others will resent us for not taking responsibility that's rightfully ours.

6. Lying to Get One's Way: "I have a doctor's appointment; you'll have to deal with the auditor" (when we're really going out to play golf). Although we may get what we want, we violate our integrity. We also feed an erroneous belief system that we don't deserve what we want (since we "had" to lie to get it). In addition, the other person is being manipulated, and if they find out, they're most likely going to be angry or upset.

Oddly enough, when we lie we are actually *giving away our power*. It may not seem that way in the moment, but we are compromising ourselves on many levels, and that diminishes us. Even if nobody else knows we're lying, *we* know. This has consequences for our health and self-worth. In addition, people who are being lied to can often sense the lie, even if they can't "prove" it, and their attitude and behavior towards us will shift in negative ways. Finally, any behavior that creates distrust, anger or hurt interferes intrinsically with our ability to use the vital Power With approaches to issues and projects.

To the above list, I would add two more reasons we lie:

7. Lying to Gain or Maintain Power Over: This is like lying to get one's way, but on a much larger scale. An example is a corporation that continues to sell a product that is known to be faulty or dangerous, and/or withholds negative product test data from the public (e.g., the tobacco industry, the cell phone industry, certain automobile manufacturers, certain pharmaceutical companies, etc.) Other examples include political groups and other organizations that conceal wrong-doing and even criminal activity in order to maintain their positions of authority. This tendency is pervasive, affecting all areas of our lives — financial, social, environmental, and more.

8. Lying to Protect Someone: This lie is very complex, and is discussed separately in the Endnotes.[5]

If any of us think we are exempt from lying, research shows that each of us lies, on average, between 2 and 11 times every day depending on the situation, and according to some studies, 60% of us have a hard time getting through a ten-minute conversation without lying at least twice![6] These statistics are shocking because most of us feel we want to tell the truth — including me. Having grown up Roman Catholic, I was taught that "lying is a sin." I've never consciously wanted to lie; yet, there have been times when I didn't speak the whole truth because I didn't want to "hurt someone else's feelings," or because I had unconsciously hidden truth from myself.

Not only does the research seem to indicate that more than 90% of Americans lie on a regular basis, but we also have a most difficult time admitting that we do.[7] We'll invent all sorts of excuses and

rationalizations to assure ourselves and others that we haven't lied. In short, we lie about lying!

Is this an inevitable part of being human, or is it something programmed into us by our culture? In her book, *Liespotting*, Pamela Meyer seems to think it's intrinsic. She mirrored this message during her TED (Technology, Entertainment, and Design) Talk saying that, "Lying's complex ... It's woven into the fabric of our daily and our business lives. We're deeply ambivalent about the truth. We parse it out on an as-needed basis, sometimes for very good reasons, other times just because we don't understand the gaps in our lives ... We're against lying, but we're covertly for it, in ways that our society has sanctioned for centuries and centuries and centuries. It's as old as breathing. It's part of our culture; it's part of our history. Think Dante, Shakespeare, the Bible, News of the World."[8]

On the other hand, my experiences with indigenous tribes and others who are able to engage telepathically, indicate that lying is *not* intrinsic to our species. Telepathic communication naturally engenders truth-telling and dissolves the separation that makes lying desirable. Therefore, I believe that lying is *learned* (i.e., culturally programmed[9]), and that this behavior develops in cultures that have lost the understanding of what I call "Spirit at the Center." This (sadly) includes many Western cultures. Note that "Spirit," here, does not have to equate with religion. When we have spirit at our center, we live by a set of beliefs and behaviors that honor our connection to others and All That Is, respecting each other's voices and the truth that we uniquely represent, minimizing harm to one another.

Lying Hurts

"The truth may hurt for a little while, but a lie hurts forever."

~EILEEN PARRA
(Human Resources Manager)

What happens to us internally when we lie? Does lying feel good? For most people, the answer is "No, not at all." When I lie, I feel it viscerally;

my solar plexus constricts involuntarily. Lying creates anxiety and stress due to "cognitive dissonance" — that is, most of us feel that "a liar is not who I want to be."

Research studies have looked at what happens to the health and well-being of people when they persistently conceal the truth over a long period of time. During the American Psychological Association's annual conference, Anita Kelly described a study she conducted at the University of Notre Dame in which she spent ten weeks tracking the health of 110 adults.[10] Half were asked to stop lying during the study period, specifically to "make no false statements" (although they could keep secrets, dodge questions or omit the truth). The other half of the participants weren't given any instructions about lying, except to report the number of times each week that they "fibbed." In addition to taking a weekly lie-detector test, participants filled out questionnaires about their physical and mental health, and about the quality of their relationships.

The results of this "science of honesty" study revealed that both groups lied less, and those explicitly instructed to stop lying experienced significantly greater improvements in their health. In fact, reducing the number of lies told (even minor ones) by just one translated to four fewer mental health complaints, and three fewer physical complaints per person per week.[11] That's a dramatic impact. Imagine *this* extended across our planet!

Although research on how lying affects health is rather scarce, most of the studies indicate that lying triggers the release of stress hormones, leading to increased heart rate, blood pressure and a more suppressed immune system. Barbara Brennan, author of the book *Hands of Light*, spent years researching the connection between energy and chakras, ailments, and the thought patterns that lie behind them.[12] Her work showed that holding beliefs that no longer serve us contributes to "dis-ease." Louise Hay's work, *Heal Your Body*, also demonstrates this. There seems to be a powerful, mutually reinforcing relationship between lies, unhealthy beliefs and disease.[13]

Lying not only hurts us physically, it also affects our relationships. First, it affects our relationship with ourselves by compromising our integrity, reducing our self-esteem, and corrupting our use of power. Most people feel guilt and shame about lying, even if their lies are never detected by anyone else.[14]

Persistent lying can also skew our view of the rest of the world: we can project our own behavior onto others, and assume they are lying too. This erodes our trust in others, even as our own lies erode their trust in us. Since trust is the foundation of healthy relationships, this can destroy intimacy and friendship.[15] This is seen in couples who end up in affairs and are unable to reveal the truth — it is emotionally painful and usually takes a long time to rebuild trust, if ever. As with "the boy who cried wolf," lying can make others unwilling to believe or assist us even when we are telling the truth. It can also make them less forgiving of any other offenses or mistakes we might make.

Within businesses and organizations, a reputation for being untrustworthy can make a person unpromotable or get them demoted, fired or expelled.

When leaders lie, people's respect for both them and their organizations dwindles, and trust diminishes in ways very similar to those just discussed. A great deal of energy is wasted as other people try to get at the truth. Gossip and discontent become commonplace between people and within teams. The atmosphere grows increasingly toxic. Productivity and morale plummet.

In addition, when corporate leaders lie to "protect" their own interests, it destroys creativity and innovation — both within their company and without. History is filled with inventors of new techniques and technologies who had their inventions quashed by the "powers that be" who didn't want to lose their control of the market, and the dollars that went with it. These inventors were labeled "quacks" and their inventions were demeaned and dismissed. How many people know of Nikola Tesla's concept of free energy, demonstrated nearly 100 years ago? How many people know of the alternative methods of agriculture or healthcare that are available today? How many people know about alternatives to combustion-based vehicles? Even in the burgeoning computer industry, some innovations were suppressed for years because they would have shrunk profits for the then-leaders of the field.

Truth-Telling Heals

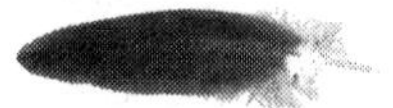

"Honesty is the first chapter in the book of wisdom."

~THOMAS JEFFERSON
(3rd President of the United States)

Truth-seeking and truth-telling generate benefits on many different levels. Individually, we experience a boost to our physical, emotional and mental health. We also save all the time and energy we used to spend generating and covering up our lies. This will translate into heightened confidence and courage, enabling us to take more calculated and meaningful risks.

Organizations mold themselves around their leaders. When a leader is personally committed to truth, it has a transforming effect on everyone around them. It increases confidence in the leader's ability to lead, it elevates trust levels throughout the organization, and it increases productivity and morale as people spend less time speculating and gossiping. In a trusting climate, people are also more willing to bring forth issues previously hidden or unmentionable. Suppression undermines organizations, but bringing things to light frees energy. Truth-telling at the highest levels of power enables the greatest degree of innovation and creativity to spring forth from the people. In sum, a truthful, trustworthy leader is a source of inspiration, and when people are inspired they become empowered to take on the things that matter, such as the preservation of cultures, species, Nature and the Earth itself.

I would like to share two relevant stories about truth-telling:

> *In the early 2000's, I was teaching at a university that specialized in training military personnel. My subject was about leadership in Human*

Resources management. Among my students was a young man named Saul. Saul was handsome and personable, and was apparently being groomed to become an officer. However, in my course, he was under-performing in the extreme. He frequently skipped class; whenever he did show up, his participation in the discussions and activities was minimal; and his assignments were either incomplete or not handed in at all. I knew my students had duties as soldiers, so I was willing to be very flexible if they had schedule conflicts, but Saul never came to me to discuss any problems. When the midterm grades went out, I gave him the grade he had earned — an F.

A few days later, a Major showed up in my office. He explained to me that Saul needed to get a B in my course in order to qualify for a particular officer position which the Major and others wanted him to get. I said that I would love for Saul to get a B in my course, in fact I would love for Saul to get an A in my course, but up to that point, the quality of his work was getting him an F.

*The Major became more emphatic. "No. He **has** to get a B. You are going to give him a B. Are we clear?"*

I replied that, no, with all due respect, we were not clear because I was not willing to lie about any student's work. He persisted. Cautiously, so did I.

*I said, "I really believe in the material I am teaching. This course is about leadership. What kind of leaders are we creating if I do what you ask? What kind of leadership are you and I modeling for these students if we give high grades to someone who hasn't done the work? This course is about managing human resources! Is **this** how we want to manage them: lying about them and rewarding nonperformance?"*

*The Major was respectful, but unyielding. He repeated that Saul **had** to get a B. We went back and forth on this for some time. I said that I understood if Saul had a military assignment that was taking him away from my class, then he might have problems getting the work done, and that if that were the case, I would be more than happy to give him an "Incomplete" or let him drop the course without any grade. But this*

was unacceptable to the Major. Saul would not be eligible for the desired position unless he completed my course and got at least a B.

Finally, after more reiterations of our respective positions, the Major said, "Are you willing to lose your job over this?" I told him I would not want to lose my job, but if I was being forced to give this student a B he hadn't earned, I would quit before I would sign my name to that, particularly because of the impact it would have on the rest of the class.

Shaking his head, the Major left my office.

The next day, my supervisor came to me. The Major had been to see him. My supervisor was part of the school's administration, but was also a military man who understood the promotion system. Although he was unhappy about the situation, he also tried to cajole me into giving Saul the required B. He implied this was a special case, and I should just "look the other way"; I wouldn't be asked to do this for every student, but just this once ... couldn't I???

I told him what I had told the Major: "What kind of human resources leaders am I training when I have to diminish myself and the other students by giving free grades instead of having students earn them? I can't do it."

I spent the next several days very concerned about the entire scenario, and agitated and unhappy that I might lose my job. In addition, although I had said nothing about the situation to any of the students, it became clear to me that they all knew something was going on. They knew that Saul had not been performing, and they also seemed to expect that he was going to get away with it. They were irritated and upset at this prospect. I knew that if I was fired, it was possible I would be replaced with someone who would be willing to sign off on a fraudulent report card for Saul, and that would be harmful and undermining to everyone else in the class.

After about a week, the Major again appeared in my office. The first words out of his mouth were, "You're a hard-ass, aren't you?" He said that my supervisor had told him that I wasn't going to change my

position, so he had come back himself to try one last time. When it became absolutely clear to him that I really would rather quit than lie, he was still dubious, but reluctantly said he would go and talk to Saul.

What happened next was nothing short of miraculous! Saul suddenly became a new person. He came to my office and we discussed his situation. It turned out that he did have a lot on his plate, including a very heavy course load. He was doing really well in all his other subjects, and he had been led to believe that he could "blow off" my class because his grade was "taken care of." Now that he knew otherwise, he began to show up in class every day and really do the work. He not only turned in every assignment on time, he also caught up on all the assignments he had missed — and he got an A or a B on everything he did. He also became an active participant in the classroom. The final project involved role-playing a human resources scenario. Saul edited his team's video of the process, and did a fantastic job.

At the end of the semester, I was delighted to give Saul the B he required because by that time he had completely earned it. In fact, if he had worked the same way for the entire semester, he would have gotten an A. Had he not stepped up to the plate, I would have given him the F he'd had at midterm, and taken the consequences. As it turned out, I didn't lose my job, since the Major got what he wanted too — but he got it honestly.

It was also very clear that the other students knew what had been going on, and they were demonstrably pleased at the way things unfolded. They would have been very angry if Saul had gotten away with getting a reward he didn't deserve. Instead, they all felt the satisfaction of truth being honored and the integrity of the course material being mirrored in real life. This was the best possible outcome for all.

Everyone involved in this situation emerged energized and empowered. Saul went on to a military assignment the next semester, and I truly believe he was better at his job for having had to earn his required B. The other students were spared the resentment and cynicism that was brewing when they thought Saul was going to get the

grade without earning it. And I didn't sacrifice my truth or principles out of fear.

In the above story, everything "worked out." It is not always this easy, as this next story shows:

In the 1980's, I was introduced to Matthew, a potential client who had been a local politician in his town. Matthew had experienced an extremely successful first term in office. He loved being a public servant and felt that he was good at it. From everything I'd heard, the people in his constituency felt the same way. Infused with that spirit, Matthew began to campaign for a second term.

Halfway through his campaign, he was approached by Jack, the town's supervisor. Jack had a request that related to yet another politician whose name was Dave. Many years earlier, Dave had been a big help in getting Jack elected, and Jack felt a sense of loyalty. Now, Dave had been accused of taking bribes, and Jack asked Matthew to make statements to the press to the effect that Dave was innocent. Matthew was shocked by this request because he and Jack both knew that the charges were ***true****. Matthew had heard Dave talking about taking bribes: Dave had referred to it as his "little indiscretion"; he had definitely done it. Matthew knew that Jack, too, was aware of this. Although Jack was Matthew's boss, the two men were also good friends, and Matthew had always believed Jack to be an honest man. He was stunned that Jack was asking him to lie. He could not believe Jack was serious.*

"I am very serious," Jack assured him. "And if you don't do this, I guarantee you will not be re-elected."

Matthew was horrified. He felt blind-sided. It was bad enough to be asked to lie — but now he was also being threatened, and by a friend! He didn't know what to do. He loved his work and wanted to continue in public service, but he felt sick about sacrificing his honesty and reputation to do it.

Matthew sat with the dilemma for several days. Then, finally, he made a

decision. He told Jack that he just couldn't lie. As soon as he refused, all sorts of rumors started to spread about him. None were true, but they destroyed his reputation. He did not get re-elected.

Matthew spent a year in a bleak depression. He ***missed*** *his job. He missed being able to bring positive change to his community. He was discouraged by the lies that had been told about him — when he had refused to lie himself — and he knew that people who had believed the lies still bad-mouthed him.*

What finally pulled him out of his despair was his fourteen-year-old daughter saying, "I am so proud of you, Dad, for not compromising your voice, your truth." Although others who knew him well were also proud of him, having his daughter say this to him was the most significant.

As he related this story to me years later, he said, "That had such an impact on me!" Every parent wants to set a good example for their kids, to be a mentor for their development. Matthew's choice cost him his career, but it confirmed him as a truth-teller, a man of honesty and honor — and it demonstrated that for his children. He believed that if his daughter was ever in a similar situation, she would probably choose truth-telling over lying because of her father's example.

Matthew never served in public office again, but he found other ways to serve the public. He became an educator. I find that choice such a perfect ending to his story. I will never forget how he summed up this experience:

"I might have lost the election, but I saved my soul."

This is an important part of this vital key: the profound changes that come into our lives as a result of embracing the spirit of truth. Gandhi created a word to express our use of these deeper truths in our lives. He called it "Satyagraha," which literally means "Truth Force." It equates to the Tibetan Buddhists' description of the divine force of wisdom, exemplified by the god "Manjushri." This is a figure that holds in his right hand a sword of pristine awareness to cut through to the essence of what is, while in his left hand he carries a book representing wisdom.[16]

Truth-Telling Can Be Dangerous

"In a time of universal deceit,
telling the truth is a revolutionary act."

~GEORGE ORWELL
(Author and Futurist)

The above stories illustrate the value of truth-telling, but they also demonstrate the risks. In both cases, the truth-teller was threatened in an effort to get them to keep silent. It would be irresponsible to advocate truth-telling without acknowledging the potential consequences and dangers. In a culture still committed to Power Over, truth-tellers can find their paths suddenly very difficult. Individuals who speak their truth have (in order of increasing danger) been ignored, mocked, ridiculed, labeled as quacks and liars, vilified and defamed, lost their jobs, had their reputations destroyed, had their entire careers derailed, had their lives and families threatened, and some have even died or disappeared under mysterious circumstances.

There is a long list of people who have experienced these things for speaking their truth in a non-truth-seeking climate. These include, but are by no means limited to: Nikola Tesla, Paramahansa Yogananda, J.I. Rodale, Jim Garrison, Daniel Ellsberg, Lois Gibbs, Karen Silkwood, Erin Brockovitch, Jeffrey Wigand, Kathryn Bolkovac, Joe Wilson and Valerie Plame, John Perkins, Catherine Austin Fitts, and Edward Snowden (see Endnote[17] for details of these people's lives). These names span nearly a century of American history, and that is just the tip of the iceberg.

Each of these people was attacked and/or threatened in one or more ways, and told not to reveal their information — but they persevered. These are acts of courage. In fact, every vital key in this book demands that people shatter the normal paradigms of their lives because those paradigms are mired in Power Over. That's why I call this book "*Extraordinary* Leadership." Extraordinary Leadership demands more of leaders than our current paradigm. The courage to become true to

oneself is one of the most challenging decisions we can face as human beings.

Sometimes, we don't even have to *reveal* truths to be threatened; we only have to be in a position to do so. Several of my former clients, who worked for security organizations, have had their health and lives threatened just for trying to *leave* their job. Some became mysteriously ill, and some have had to live in semi-seclusion after exiting (this has also been the case for people who attempt to reveal truth within organizations later identified as "cults" or "secret societies" — see Endnote[18] on "Institutionalized Lying").

Events like these are very real and very sobering. I do believe that our willingness to stand tall in our truth, with flexibility, is vital if our world is to evolve as it must in order to overcome our current multitude of global crises. However, I also believe that we can take steps to minimize the risks as much as possible.

Minimizing Risk

As indicated above, truth-telling can be perceived as a subversive act, especially when there are other people, often in powerful positions, who are *invested* in the lie, deception or cover-up. To better ensure our success and safety when unveiling hidden truths, we must be careful how we go about shedding light on them. It's important to do so in a way that leads to the most beneficial outcome. Before proceeding to reveal a significant but hidden truth, it is important to weigh all the factors and find a way to proceed that isn't reckless, and that protects, as much as possible, the integrity and viability of the source.

It is also important to carefully strategize so that we minimize as much as possible the risk of being labeled "quacks," "nuts," "traitors," etc., although this risk can never be completely eliminated. That's why the notion of unveiling truth in what I call "divine timing" might make a huge difference in how that truth is perceived. Divine timing involves "tuning in" to our divine inner core for guidance and asking: "Is what I am about to say or do going to move the situation forward to clarify it and create resolution — without any additional harm?" If the answer is "no," then the timing may not be right. It is also important to honor our logical side by conferring with wise mentors and advisors. These are people whom we trust who also know the "lay of the land" and can advise us as to whether or not this is the right time to act. In the case of my trip to Egypt, not only did I listen to my divine guidance, but I also spoke with knowledgeable people *in Egypt* before departing. In sum, the practice of divine timing involves a combination of logic and intuition, and takes all things into account before making a decision. When divine timing is right, the positive benefits outweigh the negatives.

Truth-revealers must also pay close attention to details when beginning the disclosure process. Edward Snowden, mentioned in the above list, was an American computer professional who leaked classified information from the National Security Agency (NSA) that raised public awareness about the extent to which the U.S. government appears to be spying on its own citizens. As revealed in the film "Citizen Four," before releasing his information, Snowden made sure that trustworthy and publicly respected news reporters and other people had witnessed the undeniable evidence of abuses. Only then did he make his announcement to the public.[19]

For the sake of our integrity, it is also crucial that our motivations are clear and clean. It is imperative that we act on the basis of a commitment to the greater good, and not out of personal anger, vengeance, showmanship or distorted attention-seeking "heroism." Snowden's truth-telling has cost him a great deal, and necessitated much sacrifice. He can no longer live in the country he loves; he is away from his family, and he has been accused of being a "traitor creating harm." In spite of this, he has continued to express his position carefully and with determination, maintaining a stance consistent with the basic ideals of the American Constitution:

> "I take the threat of terrorism seriously, and I think we all do, and I think it's really disingenuous for the government to ... exploit the national trauma [of 9/11] that we all suffered together ... to justify programs that have never been shown to keep us safe, but cost us

> liberties and freedoms that we don't need to give up, and our Constitution says we should not give up ...[20]
>
> "Being a patriot means knowing when to protect your country ... knowing when to protect your Constitution ... from the violations of, and encroachments of, adversaries. And those adversaries don't have to be foreign countries. They can be bad policies. They can be officials who ... need a little bit more accountability. They can be mistakes of government ...[21]
>
> "I've been asking the United States [government] — the press has been asking the United States government — for a year now if, after a year, they can show a single individual who's been harmed in any way by this reporting ... Is it really so serious and can we really trust those claims without scrutinizing?"[22]

In cases where a decision might lead to great harm, I recommend distributed decision-making be employed, as encouraged by new enlightened governance practices[23] (unless there is consent that the leader makes a unilateral decision). Such decisions also need to be informed by the next Vital Key of Integrity. This helps us cleave to our "true north" and stay on course.

Sometimes truth-telling goes down more easily if we include creative alternatives for how to transform untenable situations. It is also a way to shift out of our Power Over paradigm. Whereas Power Over wants punishment for exposed evil-doers, Power With allows those caught in a misdeed to retain their dignity while also giving them a chance for atonement (including addressing potentially buried shame). For example, when we truthfully unveil the harm that certain industries are perpetrating, we could simultaneously suggest creative forms of reform and reparation. A case in point is cigarette companies diverting a portion of their (vast) profits into educational programs that discourage children from smoking. There are also many cases of companies retooling old, harmful products to make new, healthier ones. As a more graceful means of supporting change, polluting industries could voluntarily begin to retool *before* they are forced to, rather than hanging onto the old paradigm with bleeding fists. For example, oil companies could divert

some of their (even vaster) profits into supporting renewable and non-polluting energy sources. Such shifting by the current mega-power brokers would need to be carefully scrutinized to avoid corruption seeping in that would undermine the transformation.

Finally, truth-telling is sometimes supported by using humor to soften the blow. Our current world crises are satirized daily by radio and TV personalities who perform the role of "activist storytellers" by turning world news into comedic — but highly informative — routines. These include Stephen Colbert, John Oliver, Ellen DeGeneres, Caroline Casey, and others. Some of these celebrities even lampoon the media industry itself, which has compounded the problems of truth-telling by catering to sensationalism and steering away from topics too "controversial" for their corporate and advertising "overlords." I so admire the brilliant John Stewart from *The Daily Show,* who persistently parodies the tragic absence of truth with the greatest degree of humor and undeniable insight.[24]

Given the risks and dangers, are there times when leaders should refrain from telling the whole truth? I have to say "yes," especially when telling the whole truth would create more harm than good and/or endanger lives. That, in fact, is the guidepost. For example, I still have not released the video footage I shot in Egypt. It might be powerfully supportive to do so, but it could also put the courageous individuals that wanted to be videoed, at risk. This caution, however, is not a license for leaders to withhold truth for their own *personal* gain or for the benefit of retaining and protecting a status quo that is creating harm. As mentioned previously, this issue is a complex one. (For more detailed information, see Footnote[25] on "Lying to Protect Someone".)

"The truth does not change
according to our ability to stomach it."

~FLANNERY O'CONNER
(Author)

Sometimes, in spite of our best efforts, truth-telling destroys existing structures. In some cases this is because the structure was built on a weak foundation, and needed to come down, harsh as this outcome may be to the lives invested in it. Enron and the entire dot-com bubble-burst, Bernie Madoff and banking scandals, all of these truths needed to come out, but it cost many people their life savings and brought our economy to its knees.

Sometimes, truth-telling shatters the lives of those telling it because our culture is not ready to hear the truth, no matter how well-timed or well-intentioned. There is no simple or sweet solution to this. In part, we live in dangerous as well as extraordinary times, and life itself inherently contains risk. Each of us must look into our own hearts and souls and decide what is most important — retaining the status quo that may be crushing us inside, or speaking out with our voice of truth and putting our lives on the line. It is a question of choosing our "core allegiance."

Re-Discovering Your Core Allegiance

In the Leadership Telesummit Series I hosted in 2013, I interviewed Foster Gamble, the co-creator of the film "Thrive," focusing specifically on this vital key of Truth. When asked a question about Edward Snowden, Foster had this to say:

> "I was deeply inspired by what he did. I had some sense of what it takes to risk your life to tell the truth for the benefit of your loved ones and your species and your planet. What he did was so courageous and so impactful, and it continues to be ... But the question that this really, I think, brings up for people is: to what is your core allegiance? Is it to the rule of law, no matter who makes up the laws? Is it to your nation-state? Is it to the flag? Or is it to your own core morality?"[26]

In a rather risky interview by Brian Williams, the long-time anchor for NBC, Edward Snowden clarified his core allegiance. Listen to his carefully chosen words:

> "[T]here have been times throughout American history where what is right is not the same as what is legal. Sometimes to do the right thing,

you have to break a law[27]...

And the key there is in terms of civil disobedience, you have to make sure that what you're risking ... doesn't serve as a detriment to anyone else ... I don't believe the United States is, or ever should be, a security state. If we want to be free we can't become subject to surveillance, we can't give away our privacy, we can't give away our rights ... And we have to say there are some things worth dying for... and I think the country is one of them."[28]

I'd like to share a story, on a much smaller scale, about a situation that placed me face-to-face with this same question of core allegiance:

For several years, I worked for a well-respected organization that provided healthcare management systems. Having just been promoted to a consulting position, I was assigned to a project where, I was told, workflow was thwarted and personnel issues were interfering with the critical delivery of systems for the West Coast. The project was "bleeding finances" and yielding "incomplete products with mediocre quality." My assignment was to report directly to the project's lead manager, Jayne. I was to work with Jayne to assess the issues, and to turn the project around so that it would be both profitable and effective.

During initial meetings where I was being briefed on the situation by upper management, I was stunned by the unhealthy degree of gossip versus objective, verifiable data being put forth about Jayne. I was also concerned that very few creative solutions were being brought to the table. My own initial observations of Jayne's work and competency didn't fit with what I was being told.

I thought my role was very clear until I discovered the underlying truth about why I had been promoted and assigned to that project. Jayne had for some time been raising concerns about health and ethics in the workplace. Management, not wanting to hear or deal with these issues, had labeled her a "complainer," "not a team player," and, finally, "crazy" in order to undermine her credibility.

Unbeknownst to me, upper management was actively meeting behind

closed doors to devise ways to get rid of Jayne. Due to my extensive background in psychotherapeutic practices, I was essentially being asked to substantiate that "she was not mentally fit for her position" and needed to be removed.

Unfortunately, at the beginning of the project, I fell into the trap of lying by silence, fearful that speaking my truth would cost me my new job. It took me a whole week to realize, to my grave discomfort, that I was guilty of this "slander by silence."

Meanwhile, upper management continued the negative comments and distortions about Jayne to convince me that she deserved to be removed and that, in order to do that, they only needed my "supporting data." Thankfully, I was complicit for only a very short time. Then I was brought back to my senses by a very significant dream.

> *In the dream, I saw a woman in a straitjacket. She was "the woman to be taken down." At first, I could not see her face clearly, but as the dream went on, she morphed into Jayne's. She looked me directly in the eyes and said, "If you truly want to change the climate of companies like this, you must be willing to uncover the deeper truth and risk your own livelihood so that other people can see that greater truth too."*

Waking from that dream, I made three significant decisions:

1. *The next time the bosses started bad-mouthing Jayne, I would respectfully stop them and ask a series of specific questions designed to get at the truth. I would also share what I had observed of her to date — which was, for the most part, quite positive. Not privy to the whole picture regarding their reasons for her impending dismissal, I knew I had to stay true to my clear observations and create alternative solutions that honored* ***both*** *her and the company.*

2. *If I had an opportunity, I would request a lengthy meeting with Jayne to learn about her perspective on the situation, her personal and project goals, and how she wanted to proceed. Then we would dialogue about how I might support that, if it seemed like it was*

beneficial for the whole organization.

3. *I would request, repeatedly if necessary, that a larger meeting be called that would include all parties — including Jayne.*

Jayne took me up on my request for a meeting with her, and I began to understand what was really happening. I discovered that she was even more competent than I had observed and that the problems went even deeper than I had thought. I tried repeatedly to arrange a meeting with all parties but was told "There's no time for that." Management didn't want to hear anything positive about Jayne and refused to engage in constructive dialogue about the problem.

It was critical for me to take the path of standing up for Jayne's humanity and gifts. Uncovering the greater truth was absolutely what my soul was calling me to do. I am a truth-seeker, and want to promote authenticity, not encourage lies and manipulations. My dream was a gift; it awakened me from the somnolence of complicity that I'd fallen into, the place that any of us might fall into when we feel coerced or pressured.

Although I had been described as an "excellent diagnostician," I was determined not to let labels define people, but to use terms only as guidelines for healing the human spirit. Not only did I decide not to diagnose this woman the way management wanted, but I decided to observe the entire group to better understand why they wanted me to do this in the first place. The more curious I became, the more my discernment grew.

What I discovered was that the upper management team was itself embroiled in some extremely unhealthy group dynamics that verged on sociopathic behavior or, at the very least, plays for power and control that undermined trust. However, when I tried to bring this perspective to their attention, they balked and implied that if I didn't report Jayne's incompetence then ***I*** *would be demoted or fired.*

After making numerous attempts to shift this dynamic — while also reflecting on what I wanted to contribute in the world — I made the

> *decision to leave the organization. My experience with Jayne was not the only factor impacting my decision, but it was a significant one. The bottom line was that I wanted to work for a company that valued truth-seeking and was committed to finding constructive, positive ways to address problems. For example, rather than getting rid of someone based on gossip and lying by silence, why not try to see where their gifts and talents, in balance with their weaknesses, could fit more effectively?*
>
> *Leaving this organization wasn't easy, but I'm very grateful for what I learned about my own core allegiance. Shortly thereafter, Jayne, while appreciating my efforts to retain her, felt so devalued by the others that she also left.*

Making such choices enabled both Jayne and me to stop "collaborating in a lie," as Pamela Meyer says, and instead declaring: "Hey, my world, our world, it's going to be an honest one ... where truth is strengthened and falsehood is recognized and marginalized."[29] Foster Gamble adds that the question of "What is your core allegiance?" is:

> "...more and more important, because life as we know it on planet Earth hangs in the balance of each of us answering that question. And if the law happens to fit with your core morality, that's great. Then you can stay within the hassle-free zone. But if a Jew running from the Nazis in the '40s in Germany approaches you, and they ask you to hide them, then to what is your ... core allegiance? Is it immoral because it's against the law to hide a Jew during the Holocaust? Is it immoral to hide a slave who's running away from imprisonment? ... What whistleblowers like Manning and Snowden and Drake and Hudes — and the list is growing, fortunately, Catherine Austin Fitts and Adam Trombly and so many more — ask us to do, is face that question and answer it for ourselves."[30]

No matter how entrenched the systems we work in, our souls call us to reconnect to truth and speak it out loud.

A Call to Action: Re-Dedicating Ourselves to Truth

"We can't make informed decisions without knowing the greater truth."

~WHISPERS FROM THE HEART OF THE WORLD
(Great Spirit's Messenger)

There is a path forward, but it does not look like business as usual. To begin to chart the course to a sustainable future we must sort truth from lies and from the deceptions that so often successfully masquerade as truth because we refuse to question them. So where do we begin to look for these new truths?

A recent and inspiring example, one that I resonate with deeply, is the film "Thrive." This film is the result of Herculean efforts put forth for over a decade by its creators, Foster and Kimberly Gamble and their team. The film describes how unveiling previously hidden truths might be exactly what our world needs at this time. It is so clear that our systems are failing, but what is not publicly known is how hard some people are working to create positive change. The film attempts to get at the root of *why* these systems are failing, and to present alternatives. It also reveals how people who challenge the status quo have been threatened and their innovative work discredited, confiscated or destroyed because it competed with the powerful interests who are profiting from our ignorance. "Thrive" unveils the hidden mechanisms that spread fear and lies to keep us ignorant, and asks why it is that some of these heroic innovators have met mysterious deaths.[31]

I found this film riveting. I was also astonished at how closely it reflected the hidden picture that had begun to reveal itself to me through years of work with various clients — from corporate and military people to foreign and domestic students from multiple cultures. Like the Gambles, I've had the good fortune to engage with people who had the courage to speak their truths to the world, even when some in power tried to silence them.

In making the choice of where to put their allegiance, many of these people learned that their silence might be the kiss of death for humanity, so they decided to speak out. They came to realize that if we are to survive and flourish, we must build our foundations on love — the kind of love that is intended to be unconditional, non-judgmental and ever-present.

This is a call to action for all leaders. The individuals who are working diligently to reveal the truth and to bring innovations into the world need our support. The more we can pay witness to them, the more we may be able to tip the scales toward protecting their work, lives and families. Ceremonies and prayers can also help create a sacred container to protect them energetically. Through our encouragement, these innovators can continue their work to help our world.

Commit to Becoming a Steward of Truth Yourself

Here is my list of the top seven commitments for leaders regarding Truth:

1. Commit to becoming a champion of truth — a truth-seeker and a truth-teller.
2. With regard to decision-making, commit to seeking the truth about the impact of upcoming decisions on the future wellbeing of all those who will be affected, from family and company, to community, to other species and our planet. Ask questions such as the following and track the effects of the decision:
    a. What impact will this decision have on morale? Have the decisions for the group been made by consent? Check trends in employee retention, feedback and job satisfaction; are they improving?
    b. How will this decision impact our income, new client accounts, and the outcomes that new clients were seeking?
    c. What is the effect on public opinion and trust in the community?
    d. How will this decision affect communication and relationships, both at work and at home?
    e. What about the environmental impact?
    f. Equally as important, how will this decision affect my relationship to, and love for, myself?

3. If there have been lies, deceptions or cover-ups in the past, explore possible ways of revealing the truth now.
4. If you perceive that your "hands are tied" or you feel that you or others are under threat, be strategic. Create alternative ways to develop support so that truth can be revealed in such a way that if anyone is intending to harm you, it will be much more difficult for them. You may decide the timing isn't right and it would incur too much harm.
5. Become informed as much as possible about where deceit has occurred, without villainizing. (See the section below on "Paradigm-Shattering Information" for a place to start.)
6. Support the enactment of laws to maintain our First Amendment rights, as well as seeking truth and transparency with as little harm as possible now and for future generations.
7. Explore trainings that might be applicable to you and your organization that are specifically focused on improving communications, decision-making, and understanding how truth can impact organizational climate (like Stephen R. Covey's "The Speed of Trust" workshop, new forms of governance and related workshops, and trainings associated with this book through my company, Lead By Wisdom).

Support Truth-Telling Within Your Entire Organization

Here is my list of the top seven ways to rebuild trust and encourage truth-telling:

1. Connect with others in such a way that they feel seen. Be fully present (e.g., not multi-tasking by being on your cell phone at the same time).
2. Listen without an agenda, then mirror back what you think you heard, and listen to ensure that you were accurate.
3. Be genuine and authentic in speaking your own truth. Allow yourself to be vulnerable.

4. Don't make other people "wrong" just because they don't share your perception or point of view.
5. Be clear in your communications. Double check what you think you committed to and make sure it matches what others expect.
6. Follow through on your commitments (i.e., be truthful in your promises). If you have to break a commitment, manage back respectfully and create new, more doable outcomes and deadlines.
7. Create circle meetings with guidelines that ensure that each voice is represented.

Support a More Truthful Society and World

"If you would be a real seeker after truth, it is necessary that at least once in your life you doubt, as far as possible, all things."

~RENÉ DESCARTES
(1600's French Philosopher)

Carl Sagan once said, "One of the saddest lessons of history is this: If we've been bamboozled long enough, we tend to reject any evidence of the bamboozle. We're no longer interested in finding out the truth. The bamboozle has captured us. It's simply too painful to acknowledge, even to ourselves, that we've been taken. Once you give a charlatan power over you, you almost never get it back."[32]

In her TED Talk, Pamela Meyer said something that struck a chord in me:

> "Lying is a cooperative act. Think about it; a lie has no power whatsoever by its mere utterance: Its power emerges when someone else agrees to believe the lie. ... I know it may sound like tough love, but look: If at some point you got lied to, it's because you *agreed* to get lied to. Truth Number One about lying: Lying's a cooperative act. Now not all lies are harmful. Sometimes we're willing participants in deception for the sake of social dignity, maybe to keep a secret that

> *should* be kept secret ... But there are times when we are unwilling participants in deception. And that can have dramatic costs for us. Last year saw 997 billion dollars in corporate fraud alone in the United States. That's an eyelash under a trillion dollars. That's seven percent of revenues. Deception can cost billions. Think Enron, Madoff, the mortgage crisis. Or in the case of double agents and traitors, like Robert Hanssen or Aldrich Ames, lies can betray our country, they can compromise our security, they can undermine democracy, they can cause the deaths of those that defend us."[33]

It is up to each of us to seek out the truth of events in the world and their effect on our lives and future. We have been taught not to trust each other and to perpetuate war both within our souls and with each other. But these paradigms are coming to an end. As Foster Gamble says, "So many people are waking up to what's really going on that that old scheme of duping us is no longer working."[34] Assisted by world-connecting technologies such as the Internet, more and more people are sharing information formerly hidden, and exploring new ideas, structures, tools and inventions. Here are some ways we can all participate in this:

- If interested, fund projects that support paradigm-shifting work.
- Support independent news media whose primary aim it is to unveil the greater truth without sensationalizing (like *Democracy Now, Coast to Coast,* National Public Radio, etc.).
- Research on your own where the truth lies (no pun intended).
- Create dialogue groups, councils or think-tanks/heart-tanks (mine was called Divine Leadership) that include in all their decisions the impact for seven (or more) generations into the future. These can serve to inform decision-making with collective wisdom.
- Investigate gaining access to the Bilderberg's annual meeting or to other secret meetings that determine global affairs.[35]
- Share paradigm-shattering Information.

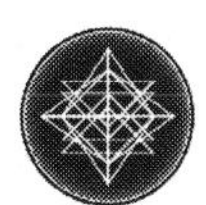

Paradigm-Shattering Information — What *Is* the Truth?

"All truth passes through three stages. First, it is ridiculed. Second, it is violently opposed. Third, it is accepted as being self-evident."

~ARTHUR SCHOPENHAUER
(1800's German Philosopher)

Not every leader wants or needs to address our global "untruths," but it is incumbent on us all to be aware of them, and how they might impact our work and the direction of our nation and our world. Gathered from decades of first-hand accounts from clients, current research from colleagues, and the well-articulated "Solutions Hub" of the Thrive Movement, here are some of the topics that seem most critical at this time:

#1. "Made-up Money" — We are immersed in an economic and monetary system that creates false debt, demanding it to be paid by our citizenry. In the recent mortgage collapse, the entire system was "made up" — from deceptive housing and land mortgages with loans that could not possibly be paid back, to banks that covered the loans with no more than 10% collateral. In this system, banks were making a double profit, first from the created-out-of-nothing interest and then from the properties themselves, which the banks ended up owning when the inevitable foreclosures occurred. I know people who experienced this first-hand. Who was responsible for this made-up money and who paid for the bailouts?[36]

#2. Healthcare through pharmaceuticals has turned the Hippocratic oath inside out. Today, prescription drug dependency in the U.S. is at an all-time high (affecting many of my top-impact clients), effective healthcare alternatives are suppressed (because they threaten profit margins), and pharmaceutical profits are skyrocketing. Invasive tests and procedures are the norm when alternatives exist and are being successfully practiced in other parts of the world. As an example, a friend's mom, suffering from

a cancer that was ravaging her body, wanted to try the Rife machine. But this protocol has been deemed "illegal" in the U.S., so my friend had to seek it out secretly, driving to Canada, only to be told that pressure from the pharmaceutical companies forced a shift in the protocol, now rendering the original "illegal" even in Canada; the alternative protocol did not work. My friend's mom died several months after this ordeal. Let's invite and support great solutions like Lynne McTaggart's "What Doctors Don't Tell You" (a publication recently banned, then reinstated after protests, in the UK) to inform the public about cutting-edge research on healing practices.[37]

#3. Mainstream news is far from "the whole truth," except for some independent media programming. Propaganda promotes and distorts the separation of "left" from "right," encouraging hatred and violence.[38]

#4. Various untruths in the legal and penal systems reduce our rights. This includes such things as censorship, surveillance and the fact that corporate voices dominate our human ones. Frequently, laws are pushed through without the public's knowledge or comment, as media distractions serve to keep them hidden. Our penal system is now a privatized moneymaker rather then a platform for restorative justice.

#5. Human rights violations abound in the world. These deceits are still alive and well, as evidenced by the continuance of slavery, human trafficking, racism and gender inequality, including unequal pay. According to various sources, including a U.N. report by independent researchers and organizations like the Australian-based Walk Free Foundation, as many as 30 million people have been forced into slave labor as prostitutes, child soldiers or child brides — "in all ways that matter, as pieces of property, chattel in the servitude of absolute ownership."[39]

#6. At seven billion people and counting, we live in peril of overpopulation if we continue to abuse our resources. There is evidence this challenge is being "handled" in secret via projects that promote eugenics, the questionable High Frequency Active Auroral Research Program (HAARP), chemtrails, rampant pesticide use, and nuclear testing. Is it right to have a few people decide how to manage overpopulation? There

are many saner, more humane ways to address the issue.[40]

#7. Campaigns are used to distort the truth in order to convince the public to support warring activities against our so-called "enemies." For example, Vietnam's Gulf of Tonkin incident, later deemed a "false flag" operation, involved a distortion of the truth, as verified by former Defense Secretary Robert McNamara.[41] Similarly, 9/11 became a pivotal point for the enactment of "anti-terrorist" laws that frequently supersede our democratic processes and violate our rights under the Constitution. We publicly demean countries we've actually become dependent upon, using them to sell drugs for arms (client-verified) or ousting their leaders if they won't serve U.S. interests. Only later are secret truths revealed.

#8. Innovations and inventions, especially those related to "free energy" (as advanced by Nikola Tesla and others) that threaten "Big Oil," have been, and continue to be, suppressed or discredited as "quackery."[42] These threaten profit margins and the international dependency on oil, which is related to the arms trade and the balance of global power. This all continues at the expense of the future of humanity and our planet. What if, instead, oil magnates considered the possibility of funneling monies into the very things that threaten their extinction? What if they supported the use of free energy and the redistribution of resources with equanimity to help reduce hunger, poverty, etc. How transformative that would be!

#9. Our public education curricula seem to have been designed with hidden agendas. For example, most history books do not accurately convey the treatment of the Native American people by the U.S. government. (My recollection is that Manifest Destiny was presented as the greatest national goal "no matter what it took."[43]) Nor do the texts cover the speeches made by Eisenhower or Kennedy regarding the dangers of the "military-industrial complex."[44] And they certainly contain little about high-level secret societies. Science books tend to exclude evidence for alternative and reverse-engineered technologies such as ormes (orbitally rearranged monoatomic elements), atomic and molecular microclusters, light-based cellular and DNA effects, and the plethora of experimental evidence for ESP, remote viewing, and human abilities to interact with matter using only thought and/or energy. Science textbooks also fail to discuss the concepts traditionally associated with alchemy, as well as the metaphysical implications of quantum mechanics. Books on nutrition fail to present the negative effects of pesticides, GMOs (genetically modified organisms) and the activities by companies like Monsanto to control the use of all original seeds, and monopolize profits around food production. Archeological books do not include evidence of artifacts potentially attributable to species from other planets, or data that contradicts mainstream evolutionary theory. In short, few textbooks present more sides of the truth, nor attempt to help students understand why some inventions "succeed" and others "fail." Educational textbooks rarely expose the complex, behind-the-scenes interactions that actually shaped the energy industry. These power plays, threats and suppressions have transpired for well over a century and they continue to determine which discoveries and inventions will see the light of day. The suppression of "inconvenient" truths continues.

#10. Efforts are being made to control the weather. Ostensibly, this is being done to save lives and protect property. However, such power is being wielded with unpublicized agendas. We need to uncover the truth about projects like HAARP and global experiments with chemical testing. There are plenty of real-life examples of substances known to cause cancer still being sprayed in residential areas, and secret nuclear tests that contaminate the water systems of whole regions. Additionally, there are people who are now tracking a potential correlation between certain government-sponsored projects and bizarre weather anomalies such as rain in areas that are typically arid, earthquakes, volcanoes and other violent conditions. What type of impact is this having on our own biological systems and our Earth long-term?

#11. There appear to be larger, hidden agendas at work throughout all our systems, as many researchers, documentaries (such as the "Thrive" movie), and my own long-term observations and investigations suggest. What has happened with UFO research and encounters with alien beings from other planets and star systems (those whom indigenous people refer to as "the Star Nations")? What about the secret societies like the

Bilderbergs, the Illuminati, Skull and Bones (Yale-based), Rosicrucians, Freemasons, etc? Many of our Presidents and leaders belong to these secret organizations, so what impact are they having on us?[45]

Humanity is at a critical juncture. The time is *now* to pierce through to a deeper level of truth. Let's begin sharing and being transparent with the truth of what exists in our world. Some of the information we uncover can be potentially shattering, but let's not shy away merely because of fear. There are ways to introduce disquieting information so that it can be embraced; we can learn to do this lovingly and skillfully.

It is my belief that this nation, the ultimate melting pot, can free itself from lies and distortions about who we are and who the "other" is. In fact, we must do this if we want to see our collective dream become a reality. On an individual level, we can become more aware of personal shadows that cloud our ability to seek and speak truth. I invite us all to stand with people like my dear friend and honored colleague "Woman Stands Shining." She is Diné (Navajo), and dreams of creating a movement she calls a "global wiping of the tears," wherein the truth about all the persecutions and genocidal actions of the past would be spoken, and all generations would be healed. I urge leaders to delve deeply and not be afraid to ask questions. When faced with decisions, let us lead by wisdom and reveal the truth of who we are, and who we aspire to be, for our species and for our world.

Vital Key #3: Honoring Integrity by Walking Our Deeper Talk

"Watch your Thoughts, they become words. Watch your Words, they become actions. Watch your Actions, they become habits. Watch your Habits, they become character. Watch your Character, for it becomes your Destiny."

~UPANISHADS
(Sacred Vedic Sanskrit texts)

I'd like to invite everyone on a journey, a journey I took with fellow team members from the Foundation for Global Humanity (FGH), a deeply committed, heart-based organization.[1] The mission of this visionary foundation is to document and preserve remarkable and little known ways of healing and being, both indigenous and contemporary. In the Autumn of 2011, we were called to participate in a special event convened by the four primary indigenous tribes of the Republic of Colombia in northwestern South America. This journey included a call to foundational integrity at the center of our being — in our minds and especially in our hearts.

These indigenous peoples, who live in and around Colombia's Sierra Nevada de Santa Marta mountain range, believe it is their sacred task to help sustain the balance and integrity of the spiritual and physical world. In their role as guardians of the earth, the elders of these four nations —

the Kogi, Wiwa, Arhuaco and Kankuamo — regard their lands as the beating heart of the world. These sacred lands serve as the spiritual father and mother of the four living Elements sustaining life on this planet: water, wind, fire and earth. Here resides sustenance for all of our spirits.

The highly trained spiritual ritual priests of these nations, referred to as the "Mamos," were guided to the understanding that it was now time to teach and share their spiritual knowledge with the world in order to help lead others into the new consciousness that wants to emerge. With the intention of contributing to the transformation of the human race by reminding us how to live in harmony, they invited all who were interested to come to South America to witness and experience their ancient ways of being. They issued a call to all of humanity, and about 250 of us came together to participate. This gathering was identified as "The Dawn of a New Time."[2] I was blessed to be included.

What I experienced there, in the heart of Colombia with these sacred human beings, was one of the most profound events of my life:

> *Upon our arrival after a very lengthy journey, we were called to a meeting with the Mamos. We gathered at the entrance of their village and stood, waiting, in the pulsing heat. FGH had been asked to film their spiritually-rich lives on their powerful land, but before we could begin, the Mamos would need to "read" us to determine whether we could proceed further with the project. We knew this initiatory process was essential, yet we had no idea what it would entail.*
>
> *No one spoke as each of the Mamos, the wisdom keepers, clothed in exquisitely woven white robes, leggings and headdresses, approached and silently greeted each of us. More than ten of them were present. They formed a semi-circle in front of us. As they stood regally, I felt a very strong energy emanating from the core of their beings, a combination of vibration and light that I've since come to believe is emblematic of their alignment with All That Is. It was as if their mere presence spoke these words: "We are sacred vehicles through which spirit can emerge on this planet."*

Then, they began what I can only describe as "scanning our souls." No words were spoken as the Mamos gazed deeply into our eyes as if to "register" what was in our hearts and minds. They did this for what seemed a very long time. We stood, as patiently as possible, in this unfamiliar land while heat vapors rose around us and hungry bugs burrowed their way into our skin through our fully clothed bodies that we thought were protected. We did not know the full impact of what we were experiencing.

As the process took place, I felt a range of emotions. There was a tinge of fear — the fear of being exposed as a fraud, or of being deemed "not good enough." But that passed within seconds as I began to feel my heart surge. Never before had I been "seen" in this way. I felt that the Mamos were seeing me for who I truly am. I savored the extraordinary feeling and, as their soul gazes touched mine, I could "hear" them say, "Yes, they are pure of heart and they are willing to have a life review here and now. This is good, very good." And the word "good" seemed to translate to "You are open-hearted, willing to expose the truth of who you are, with humility and love. You are welcomed here."

This process went on for many hours — how long exactly, I don't know. As the process concluded, I knew I had participated in a profound practice in which the state of our integrity had been witnessed and mirrored back to each one of us, without judgment.

Toward the end of our time with the Mamos, we were informed that some of those gathered with us had been graciously asked to leave. Although those who departed might have felt a bit disrupted or perhaps even intimidated, they also seemed to intuitively understand why they could not be "registered." (Note that the Mamos themselves had to be in deep integrity for the "scanning" process to work; otherwise, those scanned could feel resentful.)

What if each and every leader courageously submitted to a life review, as we did? What if they each had the state of their own integrity mirrored back to them, without judgment? I believe it would change the world.

Losing Our Integrity Hurts

"Conscience warns us as a friend before it punishes us as a judge."

~LESZCZYNSKI STANISLAUS
(King of Poland in the 1700's)

What is the state of integrity in our world? One way to gauge is to ask: Do we, as a society, trust our leaders? Do we trust our leaders in government, in the banking sector? Do we have faith in those entrusted with our financial, educational and healthcare institutions?

Global Integrity Loss

A recent ABC/Washington Post poll demonstrated that ratings regarding the empathy of elected leaders (as measured by questions such as: "Do our leaders understand the problems of people like you?") have plummeted, dropping from 72% in 2009 to 50% in 2014.[3] The same poll found that 52% of Americans believe that the U.S. should "mind its own business internationally" in terms of getting involved in foreign wars, and 66% thought that "greater involvement in the global economy is good."[4] In several research studies and surveys conducted by Roper, news agencies, and, in particular, the Pew Research Center, only 37% of Americans expressed confidence in our current president to make the right decisions for our country's future — a significant decrease from the 61% who trusted him when he first took office.[5] Sadly, this kind of drop in confidence is not unusual.

Why are most of our public leaders *not* trusted to act with integrity? In announcing her candidacy for a congressional seat, Marianne Williamson, the inspirational spiritual teacher, author and lecturer who popularized a greater understanding of *A Course in Miracles*, put it this way:

> "What we're talking about here is the fact that we have developed a legalized system of corruption in the United States ... If only short-term economic gain for the corporate sector is allowed to be our economic bottom line, then there is no room for anyone to get to say, 'But what about the children? What about the health of the Earth? What about the health of the society? What about the health of the air? What about the health of the water?' There's no room for conscience. Anytime you have any person, or any system, which does not operate with remorse [or] with conscience ... that's called a sociopath!"[6]

As uncomfortable and inconvenient as it might be, we must acknowledge that most of our systems have become corrupted in such a way that they certainly don't foster integrity. Even more problematic is the fact that corruption tends to feed upon itself. Systems led by leaders out of touch with their moral compass tend to create mechanisms to hide that lack of integrity. We saw this with the mortgage crisis and subsequent international financial crisis. We see it in campaign financing, and in the U.S. Supreme Court ruling that redefined corporations as people. We can see it on an even larger scale in the unregulated strong-arm tactics employed by pharmaceutical companies, in the penal system being re-created as a for-profit enterprise, and in countless other systems that have gone haywire.

We can't help but see it in the environmental crisis as well. When disasters happen, they are in the news only briefly (if at all), and then go off our collective radar. Can we really begin to estimate the long-term impacts of environmental abuses like oil spills, nuclear disasters, genetic manipulation, toxic chemical overload — and so many more? What happened to the updated reporting on the nuclear materials released by the Japanese tsunami? What is really being sprayed in our skies by the pluming chemical trails that now criss-cross our airways? What happened to the massive oil spill in the Gulf of Mexico? What is really going on with HAARP?

We are out of integrity with our home, Mother Earth. It's time to take responsibility for all these acts of recklessness, and make different choices.

There is increasing evidence that governments that were once thought to be "of, by and for the people," are now for some other agenda. This forces the Crisis of Integrity to spread across the globe. For example, when is it ever beneficial for a culture — an entire civilization like Greece with its rich and diverse heritage — to sell its most precious monuments to private investors? This behavior is an act of violence against our world. It symbolizes how the very few with the most resources and power have become morally bankrupt to dangerous extremes. Similarly, are Americans aware how much of their country is owned by other countries: by the Dutch, the Chinese, etc? How is this beneficial to Americans? What marks the fall of an empire? A lack of appreciation for the arts, and the misuse of every resource become the seeds of self-destruction. A once-thriving nation crumbles because of the cancerous behaviors of a greedy, power-hungry, and seemingly heartless, few.

The impact of this assault against integrity is far-reaching; the following is a summary, highlighting what happens when we lose our moral compass:

- Forms of governance lack "checks and balances," and "shadow organizations" arise.
- The elite hoard resources and create a climate of fear that encourages integrity breaches.
- Entrenched laws and policies lead to corruption, engendering civil unrest.
- Unjust practices and inhumane acts like war and human rights violations increase.
- Our planet and its resources are exploited and abused, leading to the potential destruction of many species, including our own.
- Contradictions between what our systems are ostensibly designed to create and the conditions they actually foster are exacerbated; there is a pervading sense that the "game is rigged" to favor the privileged few. And when the rules are broken, the consequences differ greatly,

depending upon who does the breaking: the punishment is greatest for those at the margins of the playing field.
- Efforts to convince the public that the "game" is fair are intensified; those who criticize the game are shamed, ostracized, threatened or removed (Power Over).

Speaking of games, these persistent integrity breaches remind me of the game of *Monopoly*, a game that I wanted to revise to include rewards for ethical behavior and penalties (similar to restorative justice) for moves that demonstrate "moral bankruptcy." The game would include forgiveness, and rewards for those who dramatically change the way they do business, especially whether they take into account the long-term impact of their profit-seeking behaviors. Let's play *that* game instead, where everyone has an opportunity to win, and competition is based on competing against an internal ideal, rather than trying to destroy each other![7]

Integrity crisis indicators also include:

- General attitudes of separation/otherness and non-inclusive world-views.
- A sense of superiority, often fostered by certain religious groups or traditions that (ironically) tend to justify injustice towards those they deem as "less than."
- The perpetuation of gender, race and class identification in ways that privilege the few over the many, and limit social mobility.

As with Power Over, the underlying dynamic of this mass crisis of integrity is one of *fear*. When we bear witness to the inherent wholeness of the Universe where everything that exists is a part of One, we can't help but experience love in its highest form — just as many of us did when we gathered with the Mamos in Colombia. But fear contradicts this wholeness, telling us that our survival may be threatened by the existence of the "other"— the other person, nation, species, belief, etc. Unchecked fear is inherently divisive; it splits us off from the whole and, in turn, severs the roots of integrity because love and unhealthy fear cannot inhabit the same space — a scenario we also witnessed in our

relationships to Power and to Truth. In the political realm, fear is often tactically and strategically used (i.e., misused) to create divisions between us, to splinter us, and to distract us from recognizing our innate interdependence — the acknowledgement of which would make us focus on the greater wellbeing of all. Fear is often manipulated by those who want to control us; they fill the airwaves and the media with it, often pointing towards a targeted segment of society as being to blame for some present (or imagined future) scarcity.

When the mass collective focuses on destructive fears, a split is created in our world, encouraging separation within the population. The Occupy Movement, for example, referred to "The 99%" versus "The 1%" (i.e., 1% of the world population has more wealth than the other 99% combined), or the 47% identified as "takers" in the 2012 presidential campaign. There are so many examples, but the one that is most striking to me relates to how we react in times of economic instability: in such a climate, caring about the greater good seems overwhelming, so we let our concerns narrow down to protecting just our nation or just our family, rather than attending to the world-at-large.

Identifying differences is not divisive in and of itself. It is when differences are used to "prove" that the "other" is the "enemy" or "inferior" that they create havoc. Wouldn't it be better to use the energy of all that emotional charge to come up with creative solutions for the truly pressing issues of our world?

"No snowflake in an avalanche ever feels responsible."

~STANISLAW JERZY LEC
(Polish poet-satirist, post-WWII)

Each of us, as leaders, must take responsibility for the integrity crisis. It is up to each of us to make a strong, collective commitment to be guided by integrity, by our moral compass. If each of us begins to work on ourselves, our inner transformation can slowly transform the external world — that, I believe, is also part of our collective dream.

What is Integrity?

"Integrity is choosing your thoughts and actions based on values rather than personal gain."

~**SHERI STAAK**
(Business Blogger)

In seeking to delineate integrity as one of the vital keys necessary to evoke wiser and more extraordinary leadership, I discovered that the word "integrity," like the word "love," is hard to define. Yet, we all seem to instinctively recognize when love and integrity are present.

Integrity comes from French and Middle English roots, and is usually defined as "the quality of being honest and having strong moral principles," or as "the state of being whole and undivided, the condition of being unified or unimpaired."[8] In modern language, we refer to this as "walking our talk," a congruence between the words we speak and the actions we take.

Words are very potent; they are the bridge between our innermost beliefs, ideals and principles, and the external world. Words have power. When we speak things aloud, we direct energy. Energy begins to flow in accordance with our words. But when we act in ways that contradict our words, this energetic force is disrupted, and it feels chaotic — to others and to ourselves. When leaders do this, it's especially alarming. This is why it is so important for leaders to recognize their responsibility with regard to maintaining integrity in word and deed. It is also why integrity and truth-telling, the previous chapter's vital key, are so tightly intertwined.

We can think of integrity as being practiced at the intersection between the internal and external. In fact, I suggest that we take this even further. In our Western culture, we usually think of "integrity" as "walking our talk." That's important because, for us to be in integrity, there *does* need to be an alignment between our words and our actions. Yet, I also believe that there is a much deeper level of meaning to integrity, one that the

Mamos exemplify so beautifully — that integrity ultimately reflects our *wholeness*. This means integrating more of the Whole into our thinking, into our actions and our being, bringing forth the highest possible degree of moral congruency. It's not just relying on one part of ourselves — like our rational minds — especially when we need to make important decisions, but taking the time to create congruence with all of our parts. And, most importantly, integrity means acting in ways that acknowledge our relationship with all beings and the Earth, as One.

This is what I mean by our "deeper talk."

It is this standard I'm referring to when I ask: Are we being morally responsible to the Whole and consciously considering the impact of our actions on all beings, future generations and the future of our planet? To truly comprehend what it means to be "integrated," to be "whole and undivided" or "unified" is to recognize the degree to which we have a tendency to split apart. Human beings are complex; we are made up of many aspects: body, mind, heart and spirit. To be in integrity, all of those parts of us must be in harmony. Bioneers' co-founder and president Nina Simons uses the word "congruent" to describe the feeling: she says, "It's when all of myself is heading in the same direction."[9]

Think how often we feel a split between our head and our heart. Similarly, our body and its appetites may send us in one direction, while our spirit pulls us in another, and our intellect perhaps yet another. True integrity requires that our different aspects cohere. When they do, we can be immensely powerful. In fact, integrity is one of the healthiest and most important sources of personal power. Many indigenous cultures understand this and have developed practices and rituals to help foster this deep internal congruity. By contrast, contemporary Western society often fails to attend to this real, human need, fostering distraction instead. That's why we often feel fragmented.

The practice of integrity begins within. Here, we strive to bring all the different aspects of ourselves into alignment with our "moral compass," a concept first introduced years ago in the wonderfully insightful essays that make up *The Responsible Person*, edited by Howard and Tracz[10].

This "moral compass" is a foundational worldview that embraces the principle of No Harm toward others and ourselves. It's the practice of asking questions like these:

- Am I in touch with my core essence, the greatest expression of who I am? How coherent am I at my core? Is my head at war with my heart? Am I ruled more by my thoughts or my passions or my sensations? Does intellect override body? Am I in balance?
- Are my actions toward others guided by a moral compass? Do I use that moral compass in my workplace, in my community, and beyond?
- Am I aware of my connection to the greater whole? Do I take responsibility for how my individual actions impact my culture and that of others, the land, all sentient beings, our entire planet and ultimately our universe?

When we consider these questions, we realize that Integrity is not a single act, but a *continuous process* of realigning from the inside out. When all aspects of ourselves are aligned, we become coherent and authentically powerful. Integrity that arises in this way is an energetic force whose effects ripple outward infinitely. Coherent integrity reverberates throughout all of our relationships, and ultimately spirals outward as our personal contribution to the evolution of the human presence on the planet. And in our hearts, we also know that when that coherence is broken, it is up to us to recognize it and reverse the trend. Only then can we actually lead with greater wisdom and make the positive impact we wish to create. This is the "new" integrity we, as leaders, are being called now to stand for and embrace; this is also what I mean by "walking our deeper talk."

The Cost of Misaligned Integrity

"In looking for people to hire, you look for three qualities: integrity, intelligence, and energy. And if they don't have the first, the other two will kill you."

~**Warren Buffet**
(CEO, Berkshire-Hathaway)

When we are faced with challenging decisions, do we stop to ask ourselves what actions would be most in alignment with our own integrity and moral guideposts? As leaders, do we ask ourselves questions like, "Is what I am about to do or say in alignment with my highest self? What impact will the decision I'm about to make have on all those affected, both now, and seven generations or more into the future? Who will *I* become if I take this action?"

In forgetting (or avoiding) these questions, leaders run the risk of making decisions that cause harm. Unless we bring integrity considerations into the very heart of our decision-making process, we can find ourselves damaging trust and potentially destroying people, organizations, communities and nations, even if this was never the intention.

Most leaders I know do not want to leave legacies of destruction, but rather legacies of positive, beneficial results. However, unless leaders consciously attend to their own moral compasses and hold themselves to a certain standard, they may find themselves making decisions that are way off their core values. I've seen it hundreds of times in my work with businesses and corporate leaders. In that space of power, it is far too easy to justify tiny "innocent" slips. But because everything is connected, our "micro" choices do not stay "micro." They spiral out, leading inexorably to ever-expanding corruption. Finally, they spill out into the public eye as money laundering, illicit affairs, drugs for arms, or "false flag" operations intended to incite unnecessary wars, etc.

Without *actively attending* to integrity and inner congruency, leaders set themselves up for crisis. The more our actions and ways of being are out of alignment with our central healthy beliefs, the more we begin to experience dissonance within ourselves. The effects can show up in many ways, ranging from physical, emotional and/or mental health issues to problems in the relational and/or spiritual aspects of our lives.

When people ask me for help with leadership challenges, they may express any number of symptoms. Leaders might describe feeling anxious, overwhelmed, unable to sleep, or ineffectual in their work and/or personal lives. They may also express feelings of shame or humiliation.

Shame often leads to impaired decision-making and self-sabotage as well as dysfunction and disease. Leaders may also experience a sense of guilt and, depending on the degree of disconnection, that guilt can escalate. It can show up as insomnia, hypersensitivity, uncharacteristic aggression or even paranoia. In a desperate attempt to cope, these leaders might act in ways that are out of character, including secluding themselves. As one of my greatest mentors once said, "When this happens to most leaders, they feel like shit, and then they suppress it. That suppression sometimes lasts their entire lifetime!"

The presence of unacknowledged guilt and shame leads to unhealthy psychological dynamics such as reactive emotions and destructive behaviors. These, in turn, tend to erode trust and loyalty within organizations. Symptoms include bad-mouthing, lost productivity and damaged reputations in our workplaces and communities. Knowing that we can all jump track with integrity, I recognize the incredible value of approaching these topics without judgment but with active compassion.

Furthermore, small breaches in truth or integrity, seemingly minor in themselves, can take their toll over time. In the previous vital key on Truth, I reviewed statistics indicating that people have a tendency to lie, on average, 2 to 11 times per day. When I first heard that statistic, I didn't want to believe it — especially of myself. But I set about monitoring myself carefully, and I was able to verify that it was sometimes true. I had to "own up." And, even though the lies I told were innocuous, usually for ease in navigating social situations, I began to notice something else: living with all those untruths actually consumed a great deal of my vital energy.

Any aspect of ourselves that we disown or bury away never really leaves us, but becomes a part of our "shadow." We tell lies — or show up as less than our real, authentic selves — because we feel the truth is unacceptable. At the moment of the initial hiding, this may be expedient; but over time, we can surrender so much of ourselves to the shadow that we are no longer in touch with our true, essential selves. When this happens, integrity disappears.

Most of us want to see our leaders taking "right actions," choosing wisely and making decisions that create the most benefit and the least harm. Yet we have seen many examples of political and corporate leaders, as well as sports "heroes" and other public figures, who have broken our trust. I believe these brilliant, amazing people fell because long-standing, unhealthy and unconscious fears and beliefs began to influence their actions and critical decisions. Since many of our deepest, most intractable fears and beliefs are buried in our unconscious, they operate outside of our awareness. Unless we consciously strive for mindfulness, and work to bring integrity to our forefront on a regular basis, our hidden fears and beliefs can slowly erode our integrity without our conscious knowledge. This is why we can fail to notice that we are out of integrity, even when it is obvious to others.

Some leaders do make a *conscious* decision to sidestep integrity, but for others the loss of integrity is more like a slow and infiltrating disease, ravaging the soul one piece at a time. Many public figures, considered great leaders and mentors, one day find themselves caught in a downward spiral, mystified as to how they ever got there. Sometimes the corrosion is so unconscious or so hidden in the shadows that it takes getting *caught* — being publicly humiliated or even imprisoned — to get us to realize the extent of our harmful behaviors. Sometimes this is the best thing that can happen because a crisis wakes us up to what is really important.

What is it like to be publicly caught in acts that are out of integrity? Many of us have memories of former President Nixon adamantly insisting, over and over, with nervous agitation, "I am not a crook!" Most humans prefer to deny their guilt and shame. But as painful as it is, being "called on our shit" or asked to "eat humble pie," whether as an individual or as a nation, can be a gift. The public exposure of moral bankruptcy is stressful and humiliating, yet it can also serve as an opportunity for redemption and renewal. We can emerge from our trials wiser people, capable of teaching, mentoring and exemplifying how walking the path of integrity creates a healthier life. It is my hope that people like Lance Armstrong, Tiger Woods, innumerable politicians and all other public icons who have made decisions that caused harm, will have the courage to take steps toward

greater integrity and restorative justice that will inspire all of us to "walk our deeper talk."

In order to make sure that I continuously internalize these concepts, I ask myself, "When have you been out of integrity, Joyce?" Just the very recognition that I *have* been at times, evokes feelings of shame because I value integrity so much, and consider myself a person of high integrity. But I haven't always met that standard. Now I'll take this revelation one step further and share a personal story. Although this incident happened almost 20 years ago, it still feels sensitive, so it's challenging to share it. But I do so because it represents such an important turning point in my life. This experience helped me to reprioritize integrity, which led me to a much more congruent way of being. But before I could do that, I first needed to encounter my shadows. That was not easy. Fortunately, I was blessed with some wonderful mentors and a deep faith. Both helped me to come to terms with the ways I had been out of integrity.

> *I remember the first time I became really conscious of a shadow in myself, one that was so buried I couldn't look at it. I had come to think of myself as a conscious person who cared about the welfare of all beings (including myself). I was a deep listener, someone with a great deal of integrity, and someone who was willing to fight for the truth. How gut wrenching, humiliating, and unnerving it was for me, then, to come up against a truth I had unconsciously hidden from myself, a truth that brought me to my knees and forced upon me a profound and uncomfortable recognition of this piece of my shadow.*
>
> *Because of my deep faith and my connection to Spirit, I never thought I would find myself in an abusive relationship. I had vowed, in my teens, that if a man ever raised a hand to me, I would leave immediately and never return. And so I had — for all of my life. Furthermore, during the first decade of my career, I had assisted many women (as well as children, families, and prisoners) to climb out of the recurring cycle of abuse. So imagine my horror and surprise when I found myself in that very same position!*
>
> *I won't go into all of the details, but I was nearly strangled to death. As my partner's large hands pressed ever harder against my throat, I*

heard him say, "I can bury you anywhere, and no one will ever find you!" I knew that I was very close to death when, suddenly, I felt the presence of angels, the very team of angels that had first appeared to me when I was young. Suddenly, I knew that I was not meant to die in this way and, with a surge of intense energy — like that of a mother gifted with the strength of Hercules to save her child — I pried his hands off my neck and ran as fast as I could to safety.

For a very long time, I considered what had happened. I was advised "off the record" by a top-notch lawyer specializing in this type of abuse, that pressing charges would consume a large portion of my life and would probably not gain any positive results in the end. I am the type of person who doesn't like to assign blame; yet there was no denying the reality of what had been done to me, and I needed some kind of closure. Without excusing my partner's violent act, nor denying that he was directly responsible for his actions and behaviors, I knew I wanted to dig more deeply to understand this disturbing event in my life. I was guided to consider how my own behaviors might have contributed to creating that situation, including the potential influences of past lives.

One day, while I was working with colleagues on a project that involved peacemaking and restorative justice, a realization hit me like a ton of bricks. I suddenly saw how many of my actions regarding this man had been contradictory or incongruent at a deep level, and how that inner incongruence could have contributed to creating volatility in our relationship, culminating in my almost losing my life. What I saw was this:

Years previously, I had experienced a painful divorce after a fifteen-year marriage. Shortly thereafter, health crises with my parents compelled me to leave my teaching position in Florida and move to New York to support my loved ones. When I was able to regroup, I applied for teaching positions nationwide, and ended up taking a job that was not only far away from my family, but also paid only a fraction of what my experience deemed fair and reasonable. But the sequence of challenging events in my life had so undermined my sense of self-worth and inner peace, that I was unconsciously operating out of fear — out

of a "poverty mentality" — rather than out of faith, trust and love. And, because I was operating out of fear, I felt humiliated about not being able to be "in the flow" with great abundance, powerful strength of character, and deep faith — elements that had always been my most familiar ways of being. I was blind to my own motivations.

And during this period of spiritual blindness, I made another choice that I had never made before, and which was also triggered by fear: I agreed to date a man who was one of my "superiors" at work. Although I cared for him as a fellow human being, I did not want to "be" with him as an intimate partner. But I agreed because I was fearful of losing my job; I felt that if I didn't do as he wished, I would be fired. In making such a choice, I was operating directly out of fear and lack of faith. I was also operating from a place of non-truth — deceiving even myself. As a consequence, my relationship with this man was founded on a lie, and that colored my own energetic. In other words, I created a vibration far different from what I truly wanted for myself. I'm sure that was confusing and frustrating to him, and that it played a part in triggering some of his violent behavior.

I am in no way excusing what he did, but I am acknowledging that the consequences of my own choices included drawing such a partner to myself. And, in a very strange, convoluted way, it was as if the frightening event that helped to remove me from that relationship was also what was needed to shake me into a deeper awareness of my own truth, and help me re-discover my own moral compass. It was a powerful lesson (one that I would never want to manifest again!) in how much I needed to change. It forced me to evolve — in the ways that I had always intended for my sacred walk on this Earth, but which I had not previously accomplished. It made me take complete responsibility for my life.

When I became aware of that truth, it was as if every particle of my being changed, and I was set on a new path, a new trajectory of evolution. I shifted from a potential victim to a consciously creative, deeply loving and responsible human being. Once realigned with my

own integrity, I found I could mentor and lead much more fully — with divine guidance, of course.

As painful and challenging as this experience was, I am eternally grateful for the gifts I received in its wake. An oft-quoted Martin Luther King, Jr. expression that resonates is "... and the truth shall set us free ... free at last, free at last, I thank God Almighty I am free at last." In a state of semi-despair, King knew he had to come to terms with his own shadow and own up to violations of integrity in his personal life: his affairs and the unexpected violence he unleashed after walking a path of non-violence for the majority of his marches. When King came to the recognition that he had violated his own integrity, he, too, experienced shame and humiliation. Coming into this awareness was one of the most transformative events of his life, inspiring him to speak that last portion of his famous "I Have a Dream" oration.

Reclaiming Our Integrity Heals

***"I am at peace with myself. I have a good name ...
My name stands for integrity."***

~**JEFFREY WIGAND**
(Cigarette company whistle-blower)

Regaining our integrity after losing it feels like being given a new lease on life. We feel renewed and restored, even if the process has involved shame and embarrassment. In my personal story above, I reclaimed lost "shadow" parts of my being and came to see how I had given my power away. These insights served as tremendous healers and teachers for my soul. I have had additional experiences where reclaiming my moral compass restored me, even though the process was unpleasant. The first of these happened at a very early age:

As a young child, I so wanted to honor my mother for Mother's Day. Usually, I made art projects, which she liked. But the year I turned seven, I wanted to do something different. I had seen this really beautiful gemstone pin with hearts in it at a local store that I visited a lot, and I got it into my head that this pin was the perfect gift for my mom. My challenge was that I received no allowance, and so had very little money. All I had was a penny jar. On Mother's Day, I meticulously counted all my pennies, and was thrilled that I had just enough for the gift I had selected. I hoisted the jar into a satchel, slung it on my back and rode my bike to the store.

Excitedly, I flew through the doors and made a beeline for the jewelry department. Out of breath and with my heart racing, I found the pin that I had spotted weeks before. To my dismay, it was now packaged as two pins in one box, and the price was now beyond what I could afford. I was shy by $3.50, which was a huge amount for me at that time. Since it was already Mother's Day, I believed I had to get the pin then or never. My mind and heart began an internal dialogue:

My heart cried, "If you don't buy it now, you'll have nothing for your mother on Mother's Day!" Simultaneously, my seven-year-old mind chattered, "It's too late to earn more money. Maybe you can just take the pin and leave what you do have. No one will ever know, and besides, it's for a great cause." My heart responded, "But that wouldn't be right, would it?" My mind argued, "Why did they change the packaging? If they hadn't done that, you could afford it. You're only shy $3.50. You can take it. It's okay. You're making the best decision under the circumstances!"

I really wasn't sure how to resolve this dilemma, but I nervously made the decision to leave my jar of pennies in the jewelry department and take the boxed gift without telling anyone. I walked slowly out of the store, jumped on my bike and rode home as fast as I could. During the ride, I rationalized that the pin was such a beautiful and perfect gift that what I had done was okay.

I got home, wrapped the pin and handed it to my mom. Then, I burst into tears, feeling overwhelmed with guilt, but unable to share why. My mom, perplexed, opened the gift and loved it, just as I had envisioned her doing. ***That*** *felt perfect, but nothing else about the experience did. My guilt took over for hours that evening. I couldn't concentrate. I wasn't myself. I was agitated with everyone. I couldn't even take in my mother's huge smile and kiss of thanks "for such a beautiful, thoughtful and loving gift."*

What was happening to me was that I was recognizing that being out of integrity totally negated the joy I might have felt at my mom's reaction. All night long, I was plagued with the thought that I had actually stolen something. I knew in my heart that stealing was Not Right — and I didn't need to get caught to know it. I prayed to God to help me repair the damage I'd done.

When I woke the next morning after my guilt-drenched sleep, I knew exactly what I had to do. I asked my older brother if I could borrow money to pay the difference for the gift (with a promise to pay him back as soon as possible). He reluctantly agreed. Then I rode back to the store, asked for the manager, and told him what had happened. He chuckled, saying he had wondered where that jar of pennies had come from. He thanked me for my honesty, and for "really being the person he knew me to be." This exchange had a profound effect on me and, in that moment, I knew that I would not steal, in whatever form, again.

I learned so much from that tiny moment in my life, and I chose to use it to fuel my desire to be the best person I could possibly be (while still being lovingly generous to my mom and anyone else).

Years later, my resolve was challenged. As a teenager, I was solicited by a number of classmates to shoplift clothing, but I declined, expressing concern and curiosity about their motivations. I asked them why they felt compelled to steal, even though they had money. Their response was, "We're bored, it's exciting, and we can get away with it." After sharing with them what had happened to me as a kid, I explained that the choice to steal would have prevented me from being trusted by others and

myself. I would have been living a lie and would have to hide, as these classmates were doing. Even more important to me was the fact that stealing was harmful to other people. If enough people did it without getting caught, the store might go out of business, costing diligent workers their jobs, and forcing shoppers to have to go elsewhere for goods. I gently explained how the negative consequences could be far-reaching. I also asked them to envision someone stealing something from *them*. How would that feel? I encouraged them to stop and I believe that many of them did.

That early commitment to continuously strive to be in integrity brought, and continues to bring, extraordinary results into my life. The more I practice this sacred inner alignment, the more centered I become, and the more I feel able to connect with the wisdom within and around me. I have found that this naturally inspires others, and I am so grateful that I can make that contribution to their lives.

That's one of the reasons why I love the transformational leadership work I do; I have the opportunity, when my clients trust me, to help "watch their back doors." Anyone can become unintentionally derailed. We each can become blind to our own shadows and to the impact of our rash or unhealthy decisions. As leaders, we need objective and supportive mentors who can shine light on our blind spots and help us to see the best pathways, the choices that maximize positive impact, while minimizing harm. Just as I have had amazing mentors who watched my back, I too am deeply committed to assisting others to reconnect with their core integrity so they can realign their life walk with their deeper talk.

The reclaiming of our moral compass can have positive impact on health, both personal and organizational. It can reduce the stress and anxiety that being out of alignment causes. It can also help pull teams back together if they have become disjointed. As leaders, our alignment is infectious. We can inspire everyone around us, galvanizing entire organizations, even nations, into positive change.

We each have the choice, in every moment, to change the trajectory of our lives. Even if we have become selfish or power-hungry, we can choose to become men and women of deep integrity, honor and heart. I believe in our inherent ability to make such changes, however monumental they may seem. I believe in our ability to realign with the integrity that lies at the inner core of all of us. If that happens, global healing *will occur.*

In fact, the transformation of our global integrity crisis is already underway. It can be witnessed, for example, in the humanitarian work of powerful leaders. For example, former President Jimmy Carter works through Habitat for Humanity and other significant collaborations relative to restorative justice. He also participates in the Council of Elders initiated in 2007 by Nelson Mandela.[11] The Council's notable members include Kofi Annan (former Secretary-General of the United Nations), Mary Robinson (former President of Ireland and former U.N. High Commissioner for Human Rights), Desmond Tutu (Nobel Peace laureate and former Chair of South Africa's Truth and Reconciliation Commission) and many others; "The Elders" serve as an independent, international, non-governmental organization working toward peace and human rights. As witnessed in organizations like "The Elders," transformative acts include attempts by global leaders to engage in diplomatic negotiations and dialogue, and to put formerly hidden agendas on the table, rather than initiating senseless wars. The efforts of the Mamos (Colombia's spiritual leaders) are similar, calling upon the global community to support them in protecting the sacredness of their land and all the beings that live there.

Another great example of transformation can be found in the Occupy Movement, especially when the focus is on collaborating to find creative solutions.[12] It's also evidenced in the work of global leaders like Oprah Winfrey, Deepak Chopra, John Milton, Joanna Macy, Jean Houston, practitioners of George Leonard (the Integrative Transformative Practice) and many others who teach people about forgiveness and meditation, and compassionate engagement with others and with the Earth. Worldwide Intentionality projects, Creativity for Peace, James O'Dea's Peace Ambassador training, and other such convocations jump-start integrity by encouraging us to leap beyond paralyzing victim/perpetrator paradigms.

In short, reclaiming integrity begins with each of us. And to anyone experiencing great resistance to this idea, I say that they have the

potential to become the most inspiring of all — because they not only *can* do it, but others are not expecting it!

Reclaiming Integrity Can Be Dangerous

As with truth-telling and Power With, not *everyone* will be overjoyed if they see us making a conscious shift toward greater integrity. Entrenched systems that rely on Power Over and the subjugation of populations for the benefit of an elite few do not encourage individuals to step into their integrity. Those who attempt it may even find themselves facing attacks and threats — especially if they hold highly visible positions. Many of us of a certain age have witnessed the assassination of leaders who tried to act with integrity.

It is not always easy for leaders to maintain their moral compass because of all the forces in place that are intended to prevent it! Looking back at each of our presidents over the past 200 years, how beholden were they to hidden agendas on numerous fronts? Were they subject to power brokers who pulled strings to get them elected? Were their hands tied and, more importantly, were their hearts held hostage?

I openly acknowledge the very real pressures that leaders face, pressures that can wreak havoc with integrity. And it is especially difficult when leaders are gifted with vision; there is such a large gap between what we see as possible and the reality "on the ground." There are so many powerful interests invested in the status quo. Anyone who has had their livelihood or their life or the lives of their loved ones threatened may feel obliged to forfeit their integrity. We might feel compelled to rationalize breaches of integrity because the ingrained systems are "too hard to change," even if the consequences are harming humanity and our planet.

As with truth-telling, integrity requires us to *examine our core allegiance.* Extraordinary leadership may not be for everyone. But for those who feel its needs tugging at their souls, integrity is the only choice.

A Call to Action: Integrity Matters

"The ends you serve that are selfish will take you no further than yourself, but the ends you serve that are for all, in common, will take you into eternity."

~MARCUS GARVEY
(Journalist-Activist)

For several years now, I have had a recurring dream that all the leaders who have gotten caught up in the pursuit of money and power — instead of the pursuit of liberty and happiness for all — experienced a series of visions. These visions were designed to awaken them to the urgency of reconnecting with integrity and with the original, divine purpose of their lives. Much like Charles Dickens' famous character Scrooge, whose visionary journey had such a profound effect, the leaders in my dream were transformed into men and women of deep integrity. They were redeemed, and thereafter recognized for their kind-hearted and selfless acts.

My intention in focusing on integrity as one of the vital keys is to encourage each and every leader to highlight integrity and move it into the forefront of his or her conscious awareness.

As I've said, we are in the midst of a global integrity crisis. Yet, even though the threat of violence, including the tragic deaths of presidents and spiritual and cultural leaders, may have engendered fear and suppressed the public expression of integrity, it has not destroyed it. We have merely experienced a collective "winter" in which our connections to our higher selves have been temporarily forgotten. Now we are being called to rise up. We each have the opportunity to become our best selves: leaders who demonstrate courage, determination and heart-centered integrity, guided by a strong moral compass. It is not necessary to fight for positions of leadership only to become puppets to them. Remember, there is strength in numbers, and if we want support for our commitment to integrity, we can *ask* for it. Humanity and the Earth are crying for this. Are we

listening? Isn't this who we truly want to be?

We are being called to utilize our energy and time for larger things. We are being asked to move beyond fear, shame and guilt, and to share all of our gifts and speak with honesty and courage. By doing so, we will free up resources we never knew we had, and crack open our hearts to receive both guidance and support from our communities, our world, our higher selves, and All That Is.

As we each bring our own energetic fields into greater alignment, we will be assisting others to do the same. This is the science of transformation: the force of our integrity spirals outward from within each of us, intersecting with the integrity fields of others, giving rise to fields of ever increasing coherence.

My hope is that leaders can serve as angelic forces on Earth, shepherding in a new era, in which we all radiate more integrity. Over my years of working with issues of integrity within myself and with my clients, I have created some practices to help foster that potential; these are listed below.

Conduct a Life Review

What will it take to move our hearts more fully into divine alignment? Remember the Mamos and the tribes that gathered for "The Dawn of a New Time"? We might begin by considering a life review.

> *One day during our journey in Colombia, our team learned why this gathering, which required great effort, had been called. Spirit had spoken through the Mamos, and asked the tribes to seek help from the Western world. Why? Because both the Colombian government and the drug cartels were surveying the tribes' sacred lands, seeking to multiply their profits by exploiting its resources, including redirecting its sacred waterways — the source of the purest water I have ever tasted. The "Dawn" gathering was intended to open people's hearts. The Mamos believed that the release of all this heart energy would raise the vibration, rendering it impossible to damage that sacred place.*[13] *When I heard this, I knew deep inside that we were there because we,*

too, had heard the call of Great Spirit. (It is unknown at this time whether the tribal land will be preserved or not.)

Just as the Mamos from the heart of Colombia saw the potential crisis in their lands as reason to invite those present to participate in a life review, our global crisis of integrity invites each of us to conduct our own life review. As leaders, we are being asked to step forward and examine the impact of our choices.

I encourage all leaders — both emergent and incumbent — to embark upon this deep examination of their lives. Imagine the impact this could have on others and the world!

I am reminded of a little known, yet highly-recommended book, called *Integrity*, by Dr. Henry Cloud. There were many gems of wisdom in that book, and one of the most thought-provoking for me was Cloud's question (paraphrased): What is the wake, like the wake of a wave, that we leave in our lives? Dr. Cloud specifically stated, "The wake is the results we leave behind. And the wake doesn't lie, and it doesn't care about excuses. It is what it is. No matter what we try to do to explain why, or to justify what the wake is, it still remains. It is what we leave behind and it is our record."[14]

Cloud was asking each of us to consider this question not merely at times of trauma, or on our deathbeds, as many do, but each and every day as we walk in this world. Are we leaving a wake of destruction and sadness, of hurt and anger? Or are we leaving in our wake a world made better, a world that is more humane or just or kind?

I ask all of us to consider what Cloud's question means, in all its depth. I ask us to consider what it might be like for others to witness our life review. And if we have left harmful wakes, large or small, I ask that we release the shame. I encourage us to ask for forgiveness from others, and to forgive ourselves. Let us allow the love that is so greatly needed to take the place of shame, supporting us as we begin the restitution process.

Accept Your Whole Self, and Practice Forgiveness

After working with many people to help them acknowledge their tendency to slip out of integrity by lying, I noticed that when they were encouraged to share their deepest secrets in a safe space where they would not be criticized or condemned, great healing occurred. We need to create such spaces for each other. This, I believe is one of the ways to support the emergence of extraordinary leadership.

We must learn to *accept our whole selves.* Working through a process of self-acceptance will help us to see how our fears — about our imperfections or unacceptability — have kept us from being fully alive.

As we begin to embrace all parts of ourselves, including the fact that we may have intentionally or unintentionally harmed others, we begin to see more of the truth of who we are. We begin to understand that we are the creators of our lives, and that if we are unhappy with those lives, we have the power to change them. With courage to look deeply within ourselves, we can acknowledge how we'd like to grow. If we take the time to reflect, we can also see the myriad ways in which we have *already* contributed to the world and how others have supported us to do so. Just think of all the beings — people, animals, plants — who make our lives possible and give it meaning in even the smallest ways: those who might have just held out their hand (or paw), or smiled at us. We all have allies, seen and unseen, even those of us who have experienced many challenges in life.

Can we come to a place of forgiveness for ourselves so that we no longer hold on to the notion of needing to "prove ourselves?" This is almost a subversive act in our current system, since nearly every element in it — from the media to business to schools etc. — *demands* that we prove ourselves every day. Can we have the courage to Just Say No to playing this destructive game?

Sometimes pride prevents us from admitting the harmful things we've done. Out of pride (or shame) we also cover up our hidden beliefs, such as the fear that we are "not worthy" or "not good enough," or that we'll be persecuted unto death if we strive to live in integrity. Learning to accept more and more of ourselves — not only our human flaws and vulnerabilities, but also our divine and sacred aspects — is powerful medicine.

Peace is generated from the inside out; it comes from being in alignment with our inner truth. This inner peace fosters the transmission of vibrations that encourage coherency in all. Through energetic exchanges that are not necessarily seen, but are felt within our bodies and our pineal glands, we can help soften our experience of how we view the world, evolving from defensiveness and judgment to discerning consideration. Because we are in such a state of alignment, our actions and ways of being will appear to have the quality of ease. When this is so, we will become beacons to others.

Realign Your Moral Compass to Include Others

"If there is any one secret to success, it lies in the ability to 'get' the other person's point of view and see things from that person's angle as well as from your own."

~HENRY FORD
(American Auto Industrialist)

"If you judge people, you have no time to love them."

~MOTHER TERESA
(Spiritual Peace Leader)

One of the most poignant stories in the Bible is the account of Mary Magdalene, a woman condemned by the public. She was on the verge of being stoned when Christ intervened and said, "Whichever one of you is without sin, let that person throw the first stone." Of all the vast multitude of people, not one could throw a stone. By his simple statement, Christ, like other master teachers, brought people's consciousness back to center. He reminded us that we all have done things we wished we hadn't. Each of us has had missteps. When we can admit to that and reconcile ourselves to our own humanness, we help everyone to heal, and we create the opportunity to more deeply connect with people, inspiring them in

ways we may never know. Let's take another look at the sacred ceremony with the wisdom keepers in Colombia.

> *During the gathering, the tribal council members requested that all attendees participate in a cleansing ritual. Each person was given two hand-woven threads and instructed to hold one in each hand between their thumb and index finger. Then we were asked to review all the ways in which each of us had harmed or offended others, going as far back as we could remember. The two threads represented and spiritually "absorbed" our two sides — our "shadow" and our "light." These threads were later purified in a ceremony using the water of the sacred rivers with the intention of helping us to reintegrate.*
>
> *This practice encouraged each of us to take responsibility for any acts, large or small, conscious or not, that may have harmed anyone or anything, including our Mother Earth. This was very humbling.*
>
> *Although this practice was intended as a private confession, the Mamos were trained to sense what an individual might be avoiding. If the Mamos noticed any unwillingness on an individual's part to be responsible for their life review, they would identify those who were not ready and ask them to leave. Those who were asked to leave seemed to understand, somewhere deep inside, why they had to go. Although some were resistant at first, they all ultimately respected the Mamos' request and departed.*
>
> *This ceremony also revealed an essential aspect of the Mamos' way of being: no one is superior to any other. All of us have shadow sides and things we wish we could forget. The Mamos themselves engage in this same practice continually, and they carry bags around their necks that act as constant reminders to stay true to their life's mission.*

This cleansing ritual had a profound effect on us: our hearts felt liberated and clear, like fresh springs. Wordlessly, it encouraged us to strive to retain that purity of heart, not just for the duration of our stay in Colombia, but for the rest of our lives. Imagine if every human being engaged in this practice. What shifts would occur! And what if leaders led the way? As I reflect on this possibility, I get goosebumps. We could change the trajectory of our entire planet.

Embrace the Power of Apology and Atonement

When I think back on times when I have slipped out of integrity, I remember feeling confused, frustrated and humiliated. Once I quieted my agitation, I was able to reflect and ask myself if I was walking my deeper talk. When I recognized that I wasn't, and that my actions had potentially harmed others and myself, my desire was to do everything possible to realign with my divine integrity.

Sometimes, an apology is required. In our personal and professional relationships, when a spouse, partner or colleague genuinely apologizes, we admire them because we recognize the courage required. And how do we react when we witness a fellow leader or a public figure, someone who was elected to represent our citizenry, genuinely apologize? It is so powerful and healing because it releases bound-up energy, energy that then ripples from one being to the next, creating a vital matrix of renewal. An example that comes to mind is Prime Minister Kevin Rudd's heart-felt public apology to Australia's indigenous peoples. More of this would certainly be great for our planet!

Not only does a sincere apology heal hearts, it also helps to renew trust — but only if it is truly coming from our authentic center. An apology cannot be used manipulatively to increase a leader's "marketability." Improving public opinion may be a by-product, but if that is the original *intent*, the apology is not pure, and people will sense that.

Many times, an apology alone is not sufficient. The situation may call for a more complex process in which people who have been hurt are given a forum to speak about their experiences, like the dialogue ceremonies that took place in Rwanda after the 1994 genocide, and the "Truth and Reconciliation" processes conducted after Apartheid in South Africa. With skillful facilitation, the meeting area becomes sacred space, and the words that carry the pain of past hurts transmute, creating an energetic vibration filled with courage and connection. Through the alchemy of this process, both victims and perpetrators begin to see themselves in the other, and are able to hold the other with greater understanding and less judgment. When we have hurt others and walk in their moccasins in this way, we are able to release our own pain, for there is also pain in holding unacknowledged guilt and responsibility.

In my experience with many organizations over the years, leaders who are willing to begin a dialogue with others about integrity are opening themselves up to a great opportunity — an opportunity for the healing and transformation of all involved. The shifts that I have witnessed within such leaders and their teams have been quite expansive and with long-term effects.

Of course, these ideas are likely to meet with some resistance. Some may argue that "what's done is done," that "it's time to move on," and that revealing hidden truths is like "airing dirty laundry." I contend that, if the process is done with as little judgment as possible, it can serve as an opportunity to work through conflicts, and the "laundry" eventually gets cleaned up in a healthy way.

I also want to mention that sometimes the process of coming into integrity also requires atonement of some kind. In this vein, I am reminded of David M. Kennedy's book *The Modern American Military*. In an interview regarding themes from this book, Kennedy tells one of the most heart-wrenching stories I've ever heard. A U.S. soldier was faced with the decision of whether or not to shoot an "enemy." His soldier's training had taught him "do not hesitate or that hesitation and breath might be your last." But in the seconds just prior to pulling the trigger, this soldier noticed that the enemy had an infant strapped to his chest. The soldier had to make a decision, and make it fast. After another excruciating second passed, the soldier decided to pull the trigger. He now lives with devastating pain and guilt resulting from that choice.[15] It is understood that being a soldier necessarily demands the willingness to kill others; it's part of the job. But this job sometimes requires a soldier to go against his or her own innate integrity.

This soldier is not alone. Many times we find ourselves in situations where we face conflicting demands, and we can only do the best we can. But when a soldier — or anyone else — finds themselves agonizing over a past action, some form of atonement may help them forgive themselves and move toward healing.

In the powerfully moving film, "The Five People You Meet in Heaven," based on the book by Mitch Albom[16], a veteran named Eddie, who works at an amusement park, dies in order to save a little girl. In death, he discovers that he has embarked on a journey through five levels of heaven. At each level, he meets a person who had a significant impact on his life, or he on theirs. The movie introduces the possibility that atonement is one of the ways to heal from morally challenging choices that caused unnecessary harm or death, like the choice made by the soldier in David Kennedy's book. These atonements can be done even after death has occurred, as is formally done in a number of spiritual traditions, such as the Kabbalah. Our willingness to atone contributes to the raising of the global vibration. Atonement is life-affirming, unveiling the purity at the core of the human Heart.

Daily Practices to Help Stay in Sacred Alignment

When I reflect on our human walk with integrity, my mind often turns to my friends, Sequoyah Trueblood and his partner, Suzanne Eugster. They both mentor others and hold space for healing, especially for youth and veterans. As previously mentioned, Sequoyah served honorably in the U.S. military for many years and has witnessed many of the horrors of our world. Yet, he always walks with spirit, uttering a simple yet profound mantra: "Great Thanks, Great Peace, Great Love."

Sequoyah has journeyed many times to Colombia. Blessed with the privilege of interviewing him in a three-part video series for the Foundation for Global Humanity, I was able to capture just a small fraction of Sequoyah's incredible experiences there.[17] In addition to being "registered" by the Mamos, Sequoyah was specifically called by one of their sacred leaders, Mamo Munevos. This was a call in preparation for taking on the full extent of his life work: helping to reopen and heal the hearts of human kind. (The Mamos consider Colombia to be the "heart of the world," and the mountains of that land to represent the four chambers of the heart.)

Sequoyah and Suzanne's deeper walk includes the willingness to critically examine all aspects of their lives, to seek redemption with open hearts, and to encourage healing through their wisdom teachings. We are blessed to have them on the planet at this time. I was invited to share many days of ceremony with these special souls. I offer the details as a template for us all to integrate, if we can, into our lives:

> *The day begins with songs for healing. Prayerful melodies are lovingly stirred into the brewing coffee. My heart fills with gratitude and ever-present peace as Sequoyah's eyes and smile silently beam, then are voiced out loud — "thank you" to everyone and everything in the room and beyond. This practice is so simple; we could all choose to do it.*
>
> *And the day proceeds: shared meals, shared laughter and deep, appreciative listening. Later, a group gathering in preparation for a sweat lodge provides another opportunity for cleansing, prayers, songs and healing — opening even our most tenacious "blind spots" or "shadows," and bringing them to light. Through these practices, Sequoyah and Suzanne tend the fire of integrity in their hearts, taking actions that support the truth of who they know themselves to be. In this way, they inspire themselves, each other, and the rest of us to attend to our integrity.*

I encourage everyone I know — clients, family, friends, and now, all who read this book — to try this, or to create their own ways to express their integrity every day. In this way, we can work together as individuals to bring our collective dream into reality.

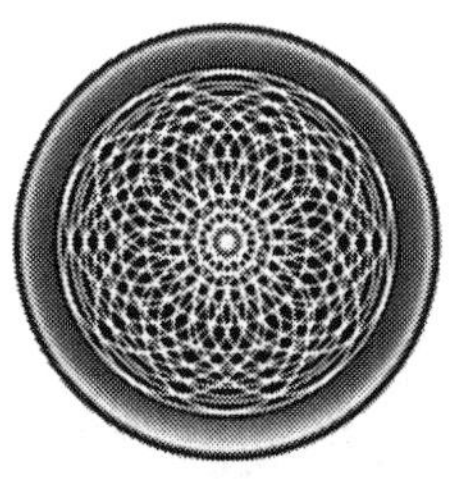

Vital Key #4:

Dissolving Unhealthy Separation, Honoring Uniqueness Within the Whole

"We are tied together in the single garment of destiny, caught in an inescapable network of mutuality. And whatever affects one directly affects all indirectly. For some strange reason I can never be what I ought to be until you are what you ought to be. And you can never be what you ought to be until I am what I ought to be."

~DR. MARTIN LUTHER KING, JR.
(Civil Rights Activist, Spiritual Leader)

This vital key marks a sort of turning point within this book. The first three keys — which deal with Power, Truth and Integrity — have immediate and obvious repercussions in the external world. When we change how we use Power, people notice it immediately; when we change our attitudes towards Truth and Integrity, again, it is recognizable in both our actions and our words. The next three keys that follow, however, are more subtle, and increasingly so; they involve deeper levels of our inner being, and our model of the universe. These keys relate to Wholeness, Balance, and our attitude towards the Miraculous. We may make important internal changes relative to these later keys without other people necessarily being aware of it, but this does not mean these keys are

less important. Our inner lives motivate and inform our outer ones. Developing our inner selves expands our capacity to be extraordinary leaders.

Separation, Uniqueness and Wholeness

There's a paradox at the center of our existence: we are simultaneously *One and Many.* We are distinct individuals, yet we are all inter-related. The Universe is one Whole, yet it has endless facets and faces.

The way that cultures deal with this paradox has profound implications.

For several centuries now, Western societies have emphasized Separation at the expense of Wholeness and connection; we have a long history of valuing "rugged individualism" and the heroic journey of "going it alone." By comparison, Eastern philosophy and indigenous traditions tend to see everything as part of a greater whole; these traditions value relationship and interconnectedness.

The West's "Journey of Separation" has deep roots; it arose out of esoteric and metaphysical causes that are outside the scope of this book. Our pursuit of separation has brought us certain benefits: It has allowed us to focus our attention on the study of specific aspects of the material world, resulting in many scientific and technological discoveries. As individuals, the emphasis on separation has enabled each of us to more fully explore and express our unique gifts and paths — something that would be difficult or impossible if we were all merged together.

However, this Journey has also created problems. Believing in Separation as the basis of reality has caused many in the West to conclude that we live in a purely mechanical universe devoid of loving interconnection, indifferent and cold. This makes us feel terribly alone. This, in turn, makes us afraid — in a deep-rooted and largely unconscious way. Our fear then makes us separate even more, leading to a vicious cycle.

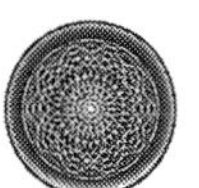

This has now extended into our societal programming. Our world has become entrenched in Separation, over-valuing it to the point of forgetting Wholeness altogether. It has become "every man for himself"[1] which, coupled with the Power Over philosophy of "might makes right," is tearing our planet apart. We have forgotten that we are not just individuals, but also a single humanity, and indeed, a single world. We have forgotten our inherent interconnectedness.

This is painfully tangible as we observe world events. The news is filled with stories of our fear, distrust, hatred and divisiveness. One example is the recent (Autumn, 2014) race-related riots that spread like wildfire nationwide. Laws that trample human rights and promote racial profiling exacerbate the damaging effects of our unhealthy extreme of separation. Our collective beliefs serve to shape these and other experiences in our lives. As with any "ism," violence erupting from racism magnifies the split of those who wish to further separate and those who wish to come together to attend to the deeper causes — i.e., our core wounds, experienced both personally and collectively.

We have an enormous need for healing these wounds, created from our long-term, historical and ancestral fears. But in order to heal, we must first understand how deeply our false sense of separation is embedded in our subconscious.

We are *both* separated and connected; we are both individuals *and* parts of All That Is. I believe it is our purpose, in developing extraordinary leadership on Earth at this time, to marry these two views together and incorporate a more balanced, unified view into our lives and into the ways we operate. As leaders, we are being asked to undertake the sacred task of re-weaving our world together, to honor uniqueness within the whole. To accomplish this, we must first come to terms with the dynamic of separation in both its healthy and unhealthy manifestations. Only then can we make more conscious choices and become exemplars for others.

Ways We Separate and Why We Do; Unhealthy Separation Hurts

"Relationships are assignments.
They are part of a vast plan for our enlightenment."

~MARIANNE WILLIAMSON
(Spiritual Author, Speaker)

In general, we want to separate from something when it hurts us or makes us feel uncomfortable. We may try to separate from other people, from the world and its issues, or even from ourselves. We can do this physically (e.g., we move out, move away, quit a job, stop interacting with someone, etc.), emotionally (we stop feeling friendly towards the other, begin to fear or distrust them, no longer share our thoughts or feelings, etc.), or mentally/spiritually (we change our belief system, attitudes, or way of being in the world). Sometimes these separations are healthy for us; more often they are not.

Separation is healthy when it is done in order to honor ourselves — our identity, integrity, self-worth, personal path, physical safety, etc. For example, it is healthy to separate from an unhealthy relationship. When we leave abusive people or harmful situations, we demonstrate that we value ourselves enough to care for our physical or emotional wellbeing. This enables us to more fully contribute our gifts to the world. We also distance ourselves from those engaged in perpetrating the harmful behavior, thereby "taking a stand" for integrity. This helps us reclaim our moral compass and inner truth. Such separations are healthy and beneficial. Leaving an abusive person or organization can also give us perspective on the socially unhealthy aspects of their harmful choices, empowering us to make different choices that have more life-affirming impact. Our separation can inspire others in similar situations to have the courage to separate as well, thus improving the energetic base of the whole community and world.

Separation is unhealthy when it involves devaluing ourselves or others. For example, if we engage in vengeful or abusive behaviors towards someone who has harmed us (e.g., plotting, bad-mouthing, gossiping, back-stabbing, physical violence, etc.) we are violating our own integrity by succumbing to Power Over, and undermining both parties. Even if we separate for healthy *reasons*, it can be an unhealthy act if we *do it* in an unhealthy way. Let's say we have a friend who routinely mistreats us and they won't modify their behavior. It is healthy to distance ourselves from this person either by leaving the friendship entirely, or by doing inner work to retain our center in spite of the other's behavior (e.g., so we stop getting "sucked into arguments" or becoming disempowered by mockery, etc.). We honor ourselves by avoiding emotional manipulation, and we create a grounded space in which to speak our truth with integrity when necessary, thus honoring both parties. On the other hand, if we separate from this person by focusing on our own hurt and the other's "wrongness," becoming non-communicative, seething, belittling, hating, etc., it is unhealthy. We diminish our own emotional truth and balance, and degrade the other's ultimate humanity. We might do this with organizations, cultures, and nations as well.

"To let each second be a new birth experience is to look without condemnation on the present. It results in totally releasing others and ourselves from all errors of the past..."

~DR. GERALD G. JAMPOLSKY
(Psychiatrist, Author)

Unhealthy separation creates harm to both others and ourselves. Ultimately, it becomes a trap — because we remain interconnected anyway, but now in a dysfunctional way. The next few pages present various kinds of separation, both healthy and unhealthy, and how they can affect us.

Healthy Separation from Others

To reiterate, we desire to separate from others when they make us feel uncomfortable; this is healthy when it is done out of regard for ourselves or a process; it is unhealthy when it undermines or demeans any of the parties.

Many times, the choice to separate arises from how we or others use power. For example, if someone is engaging in harmful Power Over, we may separate to escape their treatment of us, or to avoid being an unwilling participant in their treatment of others. This can happen with any relationship, personal or professional, and may involve behaviors such as disrespect, cruelty, manipulation and control, or physical attacks up to and including assault and sexual abuse. Getting away from such activities is a healthy choice.

This is similar to separating from people and organizations when their behavior conflicts with our values. Reasons can include prejudice, unfair practices, illegal activities, or being socially or environmentally irresponsible, harming other species or the planet. As with Power Over-based reasons, we separate to stay in our integrity and to distance ourselves from that which is not our truth.

We may also need to part from others when there is a misalignment in goals or desires. No one has done anything "wrong," but we are simply not a good "fit" for each other, and we must separate in order to get our needs met. An example might be moving out of a neighborhood because it is too far from our work, or there aren't enough children or elderly, or the population is not creative enough for our interests, or desired services are not available, and so on. Such separation is healthy, as long as it is done without villainizing others.

We can also outgrow a situation, and find our values and interests no longer aligning with people or organizations with whom we used to resonate. This can happen especially with couples: they may find the need to separate, temporarily or permanently, in order to fulfill their sacred and unique paths. If this is done via methods such as "conscious uncoupling," which honors both partners as well as the relationship itself,

it can be very beneficial.[2] It is certainly better to separate than to remain together in a toxic and unloving atmosphere. It's also important to remember that separation doesn't mean the complete removal of love.

"At some point, you have to realize that some people can stay in your heart but not in your life."

~**SANDI LYNN**
(Author)

Very often, we *must* break away from others in order to develop in a way that honors our highest and best selves. For example, we are called to separate from our family of origin in order to individuate as adults. In some cultures, this transition is acknowledged with a formal "Rite of Passage" ceremony, which gives "permission" and support to the process. Healthy separation for teenagers reduces confusion and self-destructive behaviors, and helps set the stage for becoming balanced adults.

Separation from others can also help us develop greater discernment, especially about what constitutes healthy friendship in the first place. When a friendship has *not* been healthy, a little distance can provide great clarity. For example:

> *When I was in my teens, I had a very close friend named Tammy. We had a great deal in common, and enjoyed each other's company. But as time went on, Tammy wanted us to spend almost every waking moment with me. I began to feel smothered. I felt that I was giving too much and becoming drained. Eventually, I realized that I had to step away for a while just to regain my inner balance. This was a difficult decision because I loved Tammy, and did not want to end our friendship. So I explained to her how I felt and asked for a "timeout" to regroup, assuring her that I fully intended to reconnect again afterward. Sadly, Tammy was angered by my request, and refused to be friends any more.*
>
> *I took the time I needed for my own wellbeing, and then tried repeatedly to reconnect with Tammy, but she refused. Although I accepted her decision, I felt sad that she didn't want to be together in a way that*

would be healthy for both of us. I could see that our relationship had been out of balance for me, and while I wanted to transform it, Tammy did not. Although difficult at the time, this experience helped me to become more conscious about relationship equality.

This story also highlights that a temporary separation can create space for us to understand the *intention* for our connections. Many of us just "fall" into relationships because it's convenient, because we feel a void within ourselves, or because it was "expected" of us. Some people can even take jobs, marry or have children for these reasons! Separating can help us to gain perspective, determine what we really want, and then make *conscious* choices. I am a strong advocate of using discernment in each of our relationships. We can respect and appreciate people and still not want them in our intimate lives.

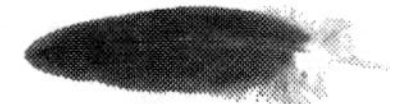

"There can be a tendency in all kinds of relationships to cling to the status quo until something better comes along.."

~**GREGG BRADEN**
(Author, Spirituality and Technology Researcher)

Separation can also help us to break old patterns and give us the space to create new ones. This is especially true when boundaries have been violated or interactions have become heated or corrupted. Removing ourselves can give time for emotions to cool down, and for new energies to arise. All of this is healthy.

Sometimes a separation may be beneficial to one party, but it is not the *optimal* action: instead, all parties (and the world at large) would benefit from finding a harmonious *resolution* to the conflict. This usually involves valuing each other's unique qualities and setting functional boundaries. Seeking professional mentoring can also help to address concerns objectively, and create new pathways for alternate solutions to emerge.

All of these separations from others can be healthy provided we accomplish them in a healthy way — that is, not demonizing or dishonoring ourselves or others. For this, I believe we must meet three

criteria: (1) we need to speak our truth (with minimal harm, consciously sharing, not blasting) about the situation with the parties involved; (2) we need to attempt to engage methods to resolve problems in an up-front way, if possible; and (3) we need to make a "clean break" if critical issues escalate abusively without resolve, or if other harmful threats are present.

Unhealthy Separation from Others

"It feels as though we're hurt by what someone else did. But what really has occurred is that someone else's closed heart has tempted us to close our own."

~MARIANNE WILLIAMSON
(Spiritual Author, Speaker)

Unhealthy separation occurs if (1) we separate for healthy reasons but do it in an unhealthy way, or if (2) the reason for separating is, itself, unhealthy. The former was addressed above; the latter is addressed below:

The most common unhealthy reason to separate is due to unresolved internal issues, usually related to core wounds and some type of fear. For example, we might want to insulate or isolate ourselves because we are afraid we can't perform to other people's level of expectations. This can happen in schools, as well as within athletic and other teams. Or we may have a fear of intimacy, and flee when someone gets too close. Or we may fear the loss of our independence because we don't know how to set healthy boundaries. These are unhealthy separations because we are devaluing ourselves: diminishing our own power, squelching our truth, or reducing our self-worth by believing that others are better or more important than we are.

Fear and self-worth issues can also cause us to force *others* to separate. For example, many companies lose excellent employees because their talents threaten the *boss's* self-esteem. I've heard many a client speak of having to deal with a superior's verbal abuse and unfair treatment due to such conflicts, which eventually caused them to exit from their organization. For the employee, leaving such a situation is healthy if it cannot be resolved. However, the boss in such cases is engaging in very unhealthy separation behavior: they devalue their employee's gifts because they have already devalued their own.

We can also force separation onto others when we are frightened by their differences from what we consider "normal." Many disabled people and those with unusual personal characteristics have experienced this forced separation, and it can be devastating — because they have not *done* anything "wrong," but are getting rejected simply for *being who they are*. Children are especially susceptible to this, but adults are not immune. I experienced this unhealthy separation repeatedly in my own childhood, and as it had a profound effect on my character and my desire to support heart-centered relationships, I would like to share part of my story:

My personal journey with separation started when I was born: I arrived covered with black fuzz on my forehead and all over my back. My mom actually handed me back to the hospital nurse because she thought I couldn't be her child, and that a Native American mom somewhere else in the hospital was equally worried about receiving the wrong bundle!

Thankfully, my parents quickly learned to accept me, though my appearance at birth remained a mystery. Perhaps, I was intended to enter this world intrinsically honoring my indigenous relatives and All My Relations, not just my blood heritage of Eastern and Central European.

In grammar school, I experienced dyslexia, and I also had a lisp. These made it almost impossible for me to learn how to read effectively, separating me from those who could. I was subject to labels, derogatory statements and judgments made by other kids, and even some adults.

My "second sight" was another matter. Sometimes it was amusing, like when I knew who'd win the World Series before it happened (a fact that was verified when we all watched the game in a large assembly at school). But sometimes it frightened others when I could sense that someone would be hurt, become sick or even die — like the little boy who passed away suddenly on the playground. Some of the teachers seemed to want to punish me for "knowing" of that child's impending

death, and they told the other kids to stay away from me.

I felt like I couldn't possibly fit in. For most of my early childhood, I felt extremely isolated. Yet, for some reason, I was determined not to let people's rejection get to me. Even as a young child, I had a strong faith that enabled me to believe that I'd be okay no matter what, even though I often felt very alone. This faith, and my parent's determination to instill a positive attitude that "I could get through anything," allowed me to seek out support from people I knew could help.

My cousin, four years older, was brilliant with language. I tentatively asked if she could help with my reading difficulties. To my relief, she said, "Yes." Every week, my parents drove me to her house where she worked with me on my reading. I recognized her unique gifts and she responded by eliciting mine. Under her loving guidance and determination, my unexplored qualities emerged, and I began to read with eager delight.

To experience that mutual valuing of each other at seven or eight years old was foundational for me: The generosity extended by my cousin propelled me to want to do the same for others, and helped forge my character. Along with earning very good grades, I became The Empath, The Diplomat, and The Caring One. So, when a new student from Egypt came into our fourth grade class, I was asked to be her "diplomatic guide," especially when conflicts arose. My intuitive abilities and my genuine curiosity about her culture helped me to understand her better, and enabled me to act as a bridge for other students.

For several months, this Egyptian student and I seemed to be great friends. So I was shocked and devastated when she suddenly began to treat me badly. I knew that I didn't want to acquiesce in being "walked all over," so I tried to talk with her about it. She didn't like that, and asked to have me removed as her "guide." I sadly stepped away from that assignment, choosing to continue to honor her while not retracting my concerns. This was an unwanted, but necessary separation that was transformational for me. My teacher called it "a hard and courageous act." The experience of connection was rich and joyful; the separation was painful and sad — but I knew that standing up for myself was the right thing to do.

To truly understand separation though, I guess I needed to experience something even more intense. No matter our race, creed, color or socio-economic status, we all face challenges. It's a natural part of being human. Depending on how we respond to difficult circumstances, they can help us build character and become the people we are intended to become. So it was with me:

At the age of 12, I was diagnosed with scoliosis (curvature of the spine) and directed by my doctors to wear a brace in order to minimize the progression of the curve. The brace protruded to my neck, visible for all to see. Even though I was the same person I'd always been, wearing that piece of equipment changed how people saw me (maturity clothing was all that would fit): I was now perceived as being weird and scary. The mere sight of the brace evoked the worst name-calling and mockery I'd ever experienced. To make matters worse, these verbal assaults were not just generated by strangers, but by my closest companions.

I was ostracized, and lost every person I had considered a friend. This was the most painful forced separation I'd ever experienced. I really wanted to connect with fellow human beings in a heart-centered way, and I felt I was being denied that simply because of the way I looked. Years later at a high school reunion, I discovered that people had seen me as "ugly, scary, and unapproachable," despite the fact that I continued to be warm and loving, reaching out whenever possible. They avoided me because "they didn't want to get what I had." To my great surprise, some confessed to carrying guilt about how they'd treated me for over 20 years.

Most people who are physically challenged have experienced similar rejection in one form or another. People who chose to connect with me after I began to wear the brace were those who were also challenged (physically, emotionally, or socially). One who became my best friend had something similar to elephantiasis. It distorted her entire appearance; her head was enlarged and severely out of proportion with the rest of her body. If I thought I had it bad, I wasn't even close to experiencing the prejudice and cruelty she had to endure. So many of

her classmates made fun of her that, after a while, I found myself constantly defending her — which sometimes upset her as much as the ridicule.

My new circle of companions did share incredible heart-felt connections, fueled in part by their separation from everyone else. However, I observed with sadness that they ***also*** *exhibited prejudice against others different from themselves: specifically, they said bad things about the people who said bad things about them! It became clear to me that misunderstanding differences and fear of the unknown was causing all of it, not how anyone actually looked. My connection to spirit helped prevent me from becoming bitter: I could see, even as a kid, that it wasn't personal; it was based on fear and something deep in our psyches that I learned, years later, to understand as "core wounds." Because of these many experiences, separation and the deep desire to connect are both very real for me.*

These experiences had a tremendous impact on my life, ultimately molding my character by inspiring me to connect more deeply with everyone I encountered. However, for many, such early experiences create or enhance core wounds and lead in the opposite direction, giving rise to additional separations (including from their own bodies and feelings, as discussed in sections below). Extraordinary leaders are those who pay attention, through good times and bad, to each and every heart-felt, authentic connection. They cultivate, through their ways of being, the notion of relating as the indigenous do: for All Our Relations.

"How far you go in life depends on your being tender with the young, compassionate with the aged, sympathetic with the striving, and tolerant of the weak and the strong; because someday in life you will have been all of these."

~GEORGE WASHINGTON CARVER
(Botanist, Inventor, Agricultural Chemist)

The emotional stress of unhealthy separation from others can lead to physical and emotional illness. In families, it can lead to abuse, divorce, and children becoming estranged from parents. This can ripple outward to affect those not directly involved in the conflict: e.g., children may be forced to "take sides" when spouses are at odds with each other; parents separated from children might never be allowed to see their grandchildren; friends may be forced to choose between one friend and another. This is exhausting to everyone, and can magnify the separation by creating new conflicts.

The toxic effects of unhealthy separation in our personal lives can spill over into other areas, including work (and vice versa). We can lose patience and empathy, snapping at people who haven't done anything "wrong," and we can find ourselves chronically agitated, less able to deal with other events. Or we can become withdrawn, depressed, and even suicidal — and we may not seek help because we feel so isolated already: "I don't belong, and nobody cares." Children who are being bullied at school or in their neighborhoods are especially susceptible.

Separation in businesses, just as in intimate personal relationships, can take the form of toxic atmospheres rife with shaming and blaming. The effects of this unhealthy separation can vastly reduce individual performance and productivity as well as the synergy and effectiveness of teams; it can increase employee turnover, and corrode loyalty, potentially disrupting entire organizations. This can be seen, for example, when employees quit on the spot due to an explosive argument, without taking the time to process why. Another example is when there is such built-up resentment that key players in projects leave just prior to a deadline in retaliation for poor treatment, leaving everyone in the lurch. As the blaming and shaming continues, contracts are lost, client relationships are degraded, and profits are compromised. Stockholders can lose faith, pull out, and publicly criticize, causing more separation.

In addition, business leaders who have separation issues at home can fear that if they reveal their family matters, it could threaten their standing in the business world. For example, I have witnessed repeatedly how heartbreaking and life-altering it is for presidents, VPs, CEOs, and others in leadership positions to lose connection with a child. Clients (mostly men) have admitted in the privacy of my consulting office that such loss feels significantly more painful and damaging to them than anything that occurred in their business. And yet, they fear talking about it to anyone in their circle because they believe they will appear weak.

Often when unhealthy separation is in play, we feel a "push/pull." Being together is difficult, but being apart is lonely or dismantling — of a family or a partnership. It seems like, whether we stay or whether we go, we hurt! The longer the separation behaviors continue without resolution, the more difficult it may become for reconciliation to ever occur. People can turn to drugs or alcohol for relief from the stress, compounding the problem for themselves and others.

Separation from Local, Cultural and World Communities

"Although the connections are not always obvious, personal change is inseparable from social and political change."

~DR. HARRIET LERNER
(Clinical Psychologist, Author)

Separation from others may extend to the larger community, culture, or even the world. We may find ourselves wanting to separate from these groups and systems because of a misalignment between our needs or belief systems. This may be healthy or not. If we separate to honor our own needs, without diminishing others, it's healthy. If we instead try to do harm (e.g., vandalize or destroy property, start riots or kill people) in punishment or protest, it is unhealthy because we are violating our own integrity and creating even more separation. Attempting to shift Power Over situations by applying more Power Over usually doesn't work (although it is sometimes used as a "stop-gap" measure).

As leaders in a time when sweeping cultural change is needed, we may feel an urgency to disengage from the current systems and culture. *How* we do this becomes very important because we are role models for others:

it's crucial that we demonstrate healthy ways of separating.

For example, we may find that our culture's prevailing "norms" do not resonate with the kind and quality of life we want to lead, and so we may physically separate by moving to another community or country. This is healthy if the new location better meets our needs. Or we may separate from our society, culture or world *emotionally or behaviorally* by taking a stand for what we believe in, even when it isn't "popular." This might be as simple as changing our buying habits — e.g., to support healthier food or more ethically produced products. Or we might create organizations to educate others or rally support for chosen causes. Or we might enter the political arena and try to change the system from within. We might get involved with new forms of money, governance, healthcare, food production, etc. Or, on an even deeper level, we might focus on trying to "change the ground of being" by doing spiritual and energetic work within ourselves to shift underlying issues. This is the subtlest of all methods of change, but it may be the most powerful in the end: as we change our inner state, it creates ripples of change that flow out into the world. We become the heart of the butterfly in the "butterfly effect."[3] These methods of separation are all innately healthy because they honor our own needs and our best understanding of the world's needs without villainizing others, demeaning the collective left behind, or using force or violence.

We may also separate ourselves from society and the world by joining a closed community, such as a monastery, ashram or convent. This can be a beneficial response to systemic issues, but I do offer a cautionary note: it is important to be clear about our motives. Are we truly drawn to dedicating our lives to spirit, or are we trying to hide from the discomforts of being human? It is usually better to run *towards* something than to run *away* from something.

Separating from the larger systems becomes unhealthy when our reasons are based on unresolved core wounds. For instance, we may want to disconnect from our society or culture when we have fears about "belonging" or "fitting in," or when we fear that a different way of life is going to overpower our own. In these cases, we may separate ourselves to feel safe and/or avoid change. Conversely, if we have been victims of a

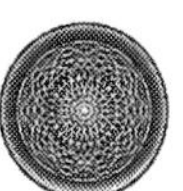

systemic form of Power Over (such as genocide or racial or other prejudice), we may feel justified in now "punishing" the dominant culture for its past treatment of us or our ancestors — i.e., "You owe me, so I can get away with it..." This ends up increasing our sense of isolation rather than healing it, and we perpetuate the lack of understanding — which diminishes everyone involved.

In the extreme, we separate from our communities or the world because we fear for our very survival. The ubiquity of conflicts and wars, the threat of systems collapse, and the apparent limitation on supplies of food, water, money, etc., can make us want to disengage from the larger society in order to focus on the survival of ourselves and our immediate loved ones. A healthy way to deal with such concerns is by lending our support to new, potentially transformative initiatives — so we can *all* get out of the danger together. But we may instead choose to become insular, turning our efforts entirely towards self-protective behaviors, minimizing our outreach to strangers, neighbors, communities, etc. In this survivalist mindset, other people are seen as threats rather than fellow travelers. Although we certainly have a right to try to get our needs met, such separation is usually unhealthy: if we trample over others to insure our own survival, we deny that we are all connected and ultimately, deny our Wholeness. Becoming anarchists who want to kill anyone from "outside" only perpetuates Power Over. Unfortunately, this fear-based fervor can take whole societies hostage. On the national level, we may close our borders, invoke police states, and ban books, broadcasts, and internet. This increases our isolation even more, becoming a relentless downward spiral.

Unhealthy separation from the world community proliferates prejudice and hate:

> *One evening not long ago, I was driving home from a meeting, and turned on my radio. I heard chanting in a foreign language. I didn't understand it until the reporter translated into English, and then it was all too clear: "We hate America, we hate America, we hate America." Regardless of how this chant originated, the sentiment pierced me like a knife, speaking volumes about our separation from nation to nation, and people to people.*

Separating from others in this way dehumanizes them and paves the way for violence and war to become acceptable "solutions" to be used against those whom we consider "less than" (or those whom we believe treat *us* as "less than"). Rioting and civil wars, plus crime and violence by gangs, mobs and secret organizations, then become the "norm." Gender, race, class, and religious inequalities, and even genocide become justified because anything different is "less than." In direct response to being devalued by others, we can also develop a sense of entitlement, feeling that we "deserve" to take whatever we want from those who are degrading us. This is a vicious cycle leading to global terrorism and war after war after war.

This "disease of separation" is seen on a global scale in the pervasiveness of human rights violations, sex trafficking, selling drugs for arms or oil, increased socio-economic tension between the "haves" and the "have-nots," the compromising of governmental oversight and protective agencies (like the CIA, FBI, and their international equivalents), and the degree of top-down control accompanied by increased surveillance and the persecution of those who dissent.

As leaders, we all need to ask ourselves how we contribute to the forces of separation, and what hidden wounds we carry that may be influencing our thoughts and actions. Becoming more conscious and aware can help us make better choices to relate in healthier ways to our fellow travelers on this journey. This includes fellow travelers of other species in the world around us.

Separation from Nature

"There was a time when humanity recognized itself as part of Nature, and Nature as part of itself."

~TED ANDREWS
(Metaphysical Author, Teacher)

There are no healthy separations from Nature except to find shelter from inclement weather or natural disasters. Yet, separation from Nature is today's norm. We spend more and more time in artificial environments, we look upon Nature as a source of raw materials to be exploited rather than a connected part of our being, and we mostly engage in efforts to Power Over the natural environment. Why?

The primary reason we disassociated from Nature was because it scared us: even now, we fear its raw power in the form of tsunamis, volcanoes, hurricanes, drought, firestorms, etc. Out of this fear, we distance ourselves and apply Power Over, but this is unhealthy because we *depend* on Nature for every aspect of our survival; ironically, even the technology we use to Power Over the natural environment is built out of raw materials *supplied* by that natural environment.

We may also disconnect from Nature in order to thwart our conscience so we can continue exploiting Nature's resources indiscriminately. To stop would mean the loss of our financial edge and sense of supremacy, so we separate ourselves instead. This allows us to retain our ego-ic mythology that we are "in control." This behavior may be fueled by the ingrained belief, held by many in the West, that "mankind has dominion over Nature." These words, found in certain translations of the Bible and other sacred texts, have been misguidedly interpreted to mean "humans are *superior* to Nature, and have a right to exploit and destroy it." This unfortunate belief has justified horrific abuses, and needs a major overhaul. I believe a more accurate interpretation is that "humankind has *stewardship* of Nature." Stewardship is a very different relationship than domination. Exploitation and superiority are intrinsically separation-based, while stewardship reminds us of our inherent connectedness, wholeness and responsibility. If we acknowledged this connection, we'd see that the destruction of Nature is really hurting us too.

What are the effects of our false separation from Nature? We have subverted our own future in favor of short-term Power Over domination. We disregard the sanctity of other species, destroying them, their habitats and their food chains (i.e., the genocide of non-humans). We disregard the land and its systems, interfering and exploiting at will for greed, personal convenience, or weapons to use against other people and nations; drilling, fracking, mining, damming, nuclear testing, HAARP, CO_2 and chemical overload, toxin-based agriculture, and now biological tampering like GMO's, have endangered the stability of the plant, animal and sea kingdoms — the entire ecosystem upon which human life depends. We disregard our own health and vitality, as well as that of our children and future generations, in the name of "control" (i.e., fear). Our disrespect for Nature bleeds over into disrespect of everyone and everything. We forget to teach our children to love and cherish Nature, or even to know how to become stewards for it (many don't know where their food comes from). We create laws to give Nature-destroying corporations rights in opposition to Nature. We value and applaud excess and continuous growth, in opposition to Nature's model of balance and cycles.

These behaviors have produced a planet in crisis, or what Polly Higgins, a lawyer turned legal activist, calls "Ecocide."[4] If we succeed in disrupting the natural systems far enough, our technology, strong though it seems, will not save us. Even now, our world is so out of balance that only a few are actually *thriving*. We see this in widespread health crises related to toxins in everything we eat, drink and breathe. We see it in dying and infertile land from decades of unconscious farming methods that over-employ artificial fertilizers and ignore the need to rotate crops or tend the land in more sustainable ways. We see it in weird weather anomalies resulting from tampering with natural systems to the breaking point: I recently heard a story on National Public Radio that spoke of the direct correlation between human actions, climate change and the dramatic rise in earthquakes in Oklahoma. *Yes, Oklahoma* (as opposed to California). Here is the startling statistic: The U.S. and Oklahoma Geological Survey stated that in 2013, Oklahoma suffered *183* earthquakes of magnitude 3.0 or greater — a shocking increase from the *2* per year it experienced over the preceding 30 years! The report stated that the most likely contributor to this dramatic increase was "geologic waste water disposal by injection into deep formations" — i.e., hydro-fracking and standard oil-drilling by-product disposal work.[5] (This is *on top of* the damage such work causes through contamination of dwindling aquifer and ground-water supplies.)

"Humankind has not woven the web of life. We are but one thread within it. Whatever we do to the web, we do to ourselves. All things are bound together. All things connect."

~CHIEF SEATTLE
(Native American Mystic, 1780-1866)

I also want to highlight one other very consequential aspect of our separation from Nature: the abuse and mistreatment of animals. Evidence, accumulated over decades of research, paints a disturbing picture. We are seeing a migration of behavior patterns: animal species formerly observed as being supportive and loving are now exhibiting "unnatural" behaviors that foster separation. This trend directly relates to their mistreatment by humans (i.e., abuse and long-term confinement). Dr. G.A. Bradshaw of the Kerulos Center (www.kerulos.org), whose motto is "to create a world where animals live in dignity and freedom," provides one of the more poignant depictions of this destructive development. She tells the story of a group of elephants who were observed killing rhinos. This was a huge anomaly in elephant behavior; they do not naturally act violently against others. After years of study, researchers discovered that when elephants are taken into captivity (particularly at a young age when they are still bonding), often to be overworked (sometimes to death) or abused in circuses or other entertainment venues, they become aggressive and violent. Neuro-biologists and biological psychologists who studied them now believe these elephants actually developed PTSD (post-traumatic stress disorder) because of their unnatural severing from their parents, which then caused them to act out. These researchers believe that elephants are meant to bond with others in their herd, learning, growing and playing with each other. In this way, they are not dissimilar from humans; we, too, need healthy bonding (what attachment theorists call "secure attachment") in order to be Whole — and suffer when it is absent.[6]

In addition to our physical survival, separation from Nature also threatens us in other ways: our spirits are bound up with Nature, and when we lose our sense of connection, we lose one of our greatest wisdom teachers. Dishonoring Nature dishonors our deepest core. We can change this! As leaders, re-establishing our sense of the sacred natural world is a crucial part of healing ourselves and our planet. Reintegrating respect for everything around us will also increase our ability to be respectful of ourselves and other people, infusing our leadership in the world with a new dynamic of heart-centered wisdom and fearless integrity.

"Nothing is inconsequential. Each grain of sand holds amazing secrets. Each event contains mysterious messages. Every encounter with another being is a point of contact on which the universe pivots. When we enter into this frame of mind, reality as we see it becomes a vast opportunity to experience the interconnectedness of all creation."

~RABBI DAVID A. COOPER
(Jewish Mystic, Teacher, Author)

Separation from Self

In the Introduction to this book, I said that all the vital keys inform one "Master Key," which is: to re-create the world outside of us, we must re-create the world within. All of the separations discussed so far have been with externals — people, organizations and systems outside of ourselves. But separations are born first *inside* of us. This is why it is so important that we, as leaders, become aware of the many ways in which we can disengage on the inside — that is, from some part of ourselves. As before, this can be healthy or unhealthy. All healthy separations from Self are *temporary only*; if we permanently separate from any part of ourselves, that's a core wound — and it is out of our core wounds that the unhealthy separations in the world have been born. Therefore, healing our unhealthy separations from ourselves is vital for positive global transformation.

Separation from Body

We separate from our Body whenever we ignore it or lose track of it. This happens when we are in meditation or having an "ecstatic experience" where the boundaries of our body dissolve and we feel oneness with All. This is a healthy separation (as long as we come back!): the body is actually invigorated by the energies flowing through it, and we can experience miraculous healings of illness and injuries through such an experience. Similarly, we separate from our bodies when we sleep, a process both beneficial and necessary for health. People with chronic health conditions may develop conscious separation techniques involving meditation, visualization, biofeedback, etc., to help them manage and cope with pain. In all cases, these separations from the body are temporary, and they are healthy because they honor the body's natural processes.

We can, however, separate from our body in unhealthy ways, such as when we ignore its needs for food, sleep, exercise, and healthy environments. We tend to do this because we believe something else (usually work) is more important. (It isn't.) These separations can cause a variety of health problems ranging from exhaustion to acute or chronic illness. Tired and undernourished bodies don't support clear decision-making or communication, and can make us clumsy and accident-prone. We also don't have the physical support needed to retain mental or emotional clarity, making us short-sighted and short-tempered, seriously impairing leadership.

Separation from the body can also show up as a denial of our sexual power. We can feel overwhelmed by the potency of our body's urges, and we may try to detach in order to feel "safe" and in control. This is unhealthy: it's important to embrace our sexual vitality as it helps to generate our life force energy.

We also separate unhealthily when we make negative judgments about our bodies — usually because we feel our body is "unacceptable" in some way. Such negative judgments can come from a material cause. For example, we may actually have trouble functioning due to a congenital disability, a chronic illness, or an injury. This may make our body feel like a burden from which we want to escape. This is not a nurturing attitude, and shifting such judgments can often help the body to heal and function better.

Usually, though, our negative body judgments come from the *culture*: e.g., we are labeled, mocked or ridiculed for being "ugly," "fat," "skinny," or simply for looking different from the "norm" — a norm which is typically *media-generated* and either unattainable or unnatural. Unhealthy separation from our body due to such judgments can escalate from disliking ourselves to active self-abuse such as cutting, attempting suicide, or gaining excitement only from dangerous or reckless activities like extreme sports. We can also become addicted to alcohol, drugs or sex as a means of escape. (In my personal story, I was exposed to other people who made judgments about my body, but was fortunate enough not to "buy in" to what they said, and was able to avert this kind of separation from Self.)

Separation from Emotions

We separate from our emotions whenever we ignore or compartmentalize them. This can be healthy when it is done *consciously* and temporarily. In crisis situations, for example, where a cool head is needed, we can create healthy separation from our emotions to think more clearly rather than become submerged in fear, vengeance or other charged reactions. In non-emergency situations, temporarily separating from emotional reactivity can give us time to integrate our head and our heart. Also, in deep meditation, we often find ourselves in a state of great peace and emptiness, totally free of emotional charge. This is healthy, and can help us gain perspective when we come back from our meditative practice.

More typically, though, when we separate from our emotions it is because we judge them as "wrong" or "bad," an unhealthy attitude that usually comes from cultural conditioning. For example, we learn to devalue our natural emotional responses if we have been ridiculed for them ("cry-baby," "wuss"), or if we have been punished by authority figures for straying from the "acceptable norm." This happens especially with boys

and men relative to the softer emotions: our culture allows and even applauds anger, but if boys show tenderness, grief or compassion, they are often labeled "sissies" or "wimps" and assumed to be weak. As with the body, the media reinforces these judgments.

We may also disassociate from our emotions because we find their intensity frightening, and feel they are too powerful for us. This is not healthy because we are denying both our truth and our power.

Unhealthy separation from our emotions usually shows up as suppression: we lose passion, joy and enthusiasm, becoming dis-interested in everything — work, sex, entertainment, and connection. We can become clinically depressed, or addicted to substances that can suppress us further. For example: the lungs store grief; cigarettes anaesthetize the lungs; many people become addicted to cigarettes while trying to suppress or cope with grief. Undervaluing emotions can also make us over-reliant on logic and reason or it can cause us to support false masks that cover up our authentic selves and denigrate heart-centered connections. Our culture has reinforced this imbalance for centuries.

At the other end of the spectrum, unhealthy separation from emotions can also show up as oversaturation, where we swing out-of-control, often without awareness: we may lash out at others without even realizing what we're doing, and without owning our behavior afterwards.

In addition, both emotional suppression and emotional excess can make us overly concerned about "what others think" and reliant on others for our moral compass because our connection to our own hearts is so impaired. When we separate from our emotions in unhealthy ways, we also lose much of our access to intuition.

All of these unhealthy emotional separations create problems that are especially critical if we are in leadership roles. Whether we are out-of-control or "walking zombies," we certainly cannot make clear decisions, and our disconnected behaviors can damage others' trust in us. When we lose touch with our emotions, we cannot feel empathy or make authentic connection with others. Disconnection from our feelings can precipitate addictive behaviors and substance abuse. It also increases our intolerance of those who *do* express emotion, and this can lead to friction and misunderstandings, especially with people from other cultures that are more demonstrative. Both extremes of emotional separation can also give rise to numerous physical illnesses. In addition, separation makes us deny our "shadow" aspects, which can increase inner conflict, leading to self-destructiveness and loss of identity, as well as a tendency to over-react to others who express the aspects of self that we've denied.

Separation from Mind

We separate from our Mind when we ignore or lose track of it. As with Body and Emotions, this can happen when we engage in healthy relaxation and self-enrichment techniques such as meditation, yoga, etc., and such separation is healthy. Our minds get a chance to rest, free of "chatter." This is especially beneficial if we typically engage in self-sabotaging mental activity such as perfectionism, negative self-talk, or OCD (Obsessive Compulsive Disorder). In the West, we typically over-identify with our minds, and so we may find it beneficial to disengage from thinking in order to learn how to open our hearts, or to increase spontaneity and connection with others.

Unhealthy separation from our mind comes when we feel some of our thoughts are "unacceptable." This is usually due to the judgments of others, as was the case with my precognitive abilities. If we have been labeled "brainiac," "nerd," or "geek," we may "dumb ourselves down" in an effort to fit in (many underachieving kids fall into this profile). At the other end of the spectrum, we can accept judgments of "moron" or "lame-brain" and give up altogether since "What's the point of trying? If I'm stupid, I'm stupid." Sometimes, separation from mind contributes to emotional separation, as in the case of gifted children who refuse to dumb themselves down, but instead develop a sense of superiority over others, often in retaliation for having been mocked for their gifts. This often carries over into adulthood, showing up in how we lead. Sometimes our minds are judged "unacceptable" by the culture simply because we think differently or have belief systems that are outside the cultural "norm." As

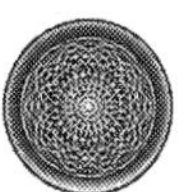

with other separations, the media tends to reinforce this "norm," frequently with hidden agendas around power and control.

Devaluing our mind can make us overly dependent on other people's opinions and ideas because we're out of touch with our own. It can also induce reliance on mindless distractions (like violent movies and most TV) so we don't have to think. This further increases our separation from Self. When we undervalue our mind, it can become difficult to complete projects on time, to coordinate our activities, or to engage in collaborative efforts; we "can't keep things straight" because we've disabled one of our important parts. As leaders, this makes us lose touch and become unreliable. We can become "spacey" and ungrounded, getting into accidents, tripping, losing things, and forgetting. If carried to the extreme, this can lead to *actual* memory loss and conditions like Alzheimer's disease.[7] Separation from our mind can also prevent us from having a balanced perspective on issues. For example, we may become hyper-focused on future plans to the exclusion of practical necessities. Belittling either our emotions or our mind lessens our ability to integrate our head and our heart, our logic and our intuition, and this greatly reduces our problem-solving ability and our access to innovative solutions. As with other separations from self, we can become dependent on addictive practices.

Separation from Spirit

"When we understand us, our consciousness,
we also understand the universe, and the separation disappears."

~**AMIT GOSWAMI** [8]
(Theoretical Quantum Physicist)

We separate from our Spirit when we deny its existence, or ignore it and its urgings. There are no healthy reasons to separate from spirit. Most unhealthy reasons are culturally generated, and so this is perhaps the most insidious of all separations from Self. We are spirit beings inhabiting physical forms! When we disassociate from spirit, we deny our innermost core. This can create wounds in still other parts of ourselves, increasing the likelihood of additional pain and unhealthy separations.

In spite of our inherent spiritual nature, our culture often mocks or dismisses many spiritual activities — calling them "woo-woo," "superstitious" and "unscientific." When we allow ourselves to be "bullied" in this way into separating from our spirit, we perpetuate this behavior, and then we, too, can end up mocking, ridiculing, demeaning and dismissing anything that smacks of the miraculous or magical unless it can be explained by current science (which is often spiritually void). We distrust and disbelieve in intuition and spiritual principles and practices. This stance greatly limits the field of possibility for addressing problems, especially when we are faced with critical decisions as leaders.

When we detach from Spirit, we may avoid sharing our gifts if they have been relegated to "taboo" zones. This includes everything from psychic gifts such as precognition, distance viewing, and multidimensional communication (being able to talk with animals, plants, angels, ascended beings, etc.), to working with energy and other alternative methods of healing and consciousness-raising. Even though millions of people are benefiting from practices such as meditation, yoga, aikido, biofeedback, etc., the societal base is still one of deep suspicion and dismissal of these things. We may choose to "side" with the culture to avoid being labeled, embarrassed, ostracized or even threatened. For example, when I was a kid, and many adults were "weirded out" by my precognitive abilities, I learned to pretend I didn't have such abilities when I was around those adults.

When we undervalue our spiritual core, we also lose sensitivity to other beings and the Earth itself. These then become "other," which we can treat with cruelty and abuse because we have lost touch with the spiritual thread connecting us all together. Empathy disappears along with heart-centered responsibility. This can give rise to the externally-directed unhealthy separations discussed in other sections.

We may also separate from spirit if we equate it — as our culture often does — with *religion*. Although the basis of most religions *is* something spiritual, the actual practice of religion today is more often political and social in orientation, and frequently involves an elitist viewpoint that is

inherently divisive. This is particularly true with cults and radical sects. The "we/they" viewpoint that such religions hold is inimical to our inherent connectedness and spiritual core, and this has caused many people to want to separate from religion in order to distance themselves from its hypocrisy, control, judgments, demands, manipulation and even physical and sexual abuse. Leaving such religions and cults *is* healthy. But it is important not to "throw the baby out with the bathwater" by interpreting these *human-based* violations as a reason to separate ourselves from Spirit itself. We can instead use our separation from the abusive organizations to give us the space to regain our perspective and reclaim our true spiritual connections.

Many Westerners have been brought up to believe in a God that is judgmental and bent on punishing us for our "sins." In dread or disillusionment, they can turn their back on Spirit altogether rather than live in continuous fear, guilt, or shame. Others become discouraged by personal trauma or global conditions: "When bad things happen, where is God? It's better not to believe at all." These separations involve deep core wounds that can be healed if the person is willing.

Separation from Spirit is perhaps the most damaging way we can separate from ourselves because it motivates so many other separations. Without a spiritual base, we are easily thrown off center by external events or the actions of others, and we will often gravitate to using Power Over "solutions" to problems. We lose our sense of belonging to the whole, as well as the value of our own unique self. This can lead to feelings of unworthiness, meaninglessness and despair. This, in turn, can lead to self-abusive behavior or reliance on drugs, alcohol and other addictions to "fill the void" left in our lives by our lack of connection. We also lose part of our moral compass, and we can begin to depend on external authority to define our center, since we have no access to inner guidance that we trust. Without connection to our own spirit, we lose spiritual connection with our fellow travelers, including Nature and other species. We lose perspective and can become tyrannical or demeaning, create conflicts, shatter trust, destroy connection, reduce the possibility for collaboration, and generally create an atmosphere of friction and disrespect. For someone in a leadership role, the rippling negative effects of all this can be disastrous.

Technology: Agent of Connection or Separation?

Our modern technologically-oriented culture has given us one additional cause for unhealthy separation: the technology itself! This technology has been designed and built from a model in which there is no "Spirit at the Center" and we are alone in the universe. When we immerse ourselves in this technology, it "entrains" us to itself. For example, fifty years ago, children mostly played outdoors — in Nature and usually with other kids; today, computer games have usurped both Nature and proximate human playmates. Similarly, the Internet is a great international connector, but simultaneously it tends to be a physical and emotional separator. This is reflected in the following poem snippet from the spoken-word video "Look Up" by Gary Turk[9] :

> " ... All this technology we have ... it's just an illusion.
> Community, companionship, a sense of inclusion, yet
> When you step away from this device of delusion,
> you waken to see a world of confusion; ...
> a world of self-interest, self-image, self-promotion,
> where we all share our best bits, but leave out the emotion ... "

"Smileys" do not substitute for heart-felt interactions, and multi-tasking with electronics while we're talking with our friends, family or colleagues interferes with deep listening and reduces the quality of our connection. As much as I respect and value the gifts of technology, I also believe that the overuse and blind misuse of it leads to a type of unhealthy separation that denies the depths of our humanity.

"It is especially difficult for modern people to conceive that our modern scientific age might not be an improvement over the pre-scientific period."

~MICHAEL CRICHTON
(Author)

Reconnecting Heals: Moving toward Wholeness

"A person with Ubuntu is open and available to others, affirming of others, does not feel threatened that others are able and good, [is] based from a proper self-assurance that comes from knowing that he or she belongs in a greater whole and is diminished when others are humiliated or diminished, when others are tortured or oppressed."

~DESMOND TUTU
(Archbishop, Spiritual Leader)

In the light of all the crises of Separation we seem to be facing, we can often feel powerless. But the solution lies in our remembering the true nature of our power: *being in alignment with the Whole.* Wholeness is, in fact, the true nature of the Universe. On the energetic level, every part of All That Is is already interwoven and interacting with every other part across all time. Native American traditions use the phrase "All My Relations" to mean the relatedness of *everything* in the Universe, and modern physics is validating this ancient view. Materially, everything that exists can be traced back to the same star stuff. Energetically, we each stretch out infinitely into All That Is. We live in an interconnected Universe, and it's important to keep this in mind as we lead. It will help to prevent unhealthy separation and will re-establish unity where there has been division.

During one of my Extraordinary Leadership Telesummit interviews, JoAnne O'Brien-Levin, a wisdom keeper, powerful thought-partner and editor, described the journey she took to navigate from unhealthy separation toward wholeness, especially regarding healing the suppression of the divine feminine:

> "I think, at some point, I began a quest almost like a spider woman to try to weave together all these things that I felt in my body, ... feeling in my body the separations and the way in which parts of me were being marginalized, even by myself, and where could I find tools to

> weave that back together so that I could be a whole person ... [T]hat journey has taken me to look for wisdom ... ultimately to indigenous people to find what I thought to be the most holistic way of thinking about what a human being is, what life is all about, what Nature is, what the cosmos is."[10]

Ancient spiritual wisdom has long taught that we can access this wholeness and interconnectivity through our *hearts*. Scientific research is now providing evidence that supports this ancient wisdom.[11] When human consciousness becomes coherent and synchronized, it can affect the behavior of physical objects. Random number generators (RNGs) are small electronic devices that ordinarily produce completely unpredictable sequences of zeroes and ones. But when a great world event synchronizes the *feelings* of millions of people, networks of RNGs become subtly structured such that the ones and zeroes are no longer random. The probability that this is due to chance is less than one in a billion! This research suggests evidence of an "*emerging noosphere*," or the rising of a unifying field of consciousness described by spiritual teachers from all cultures. And what else might it tell us? "*Coherent consciousness creates order in the World.*"[12]

Let's follow this train of thought. It implies that the more coherent our *individual* consciousness, the more we contribute to creating greater coherence in our collective consciousness. And the more coherent our collective consciousness, the more order and coherence we can create in our external reality. This makes it possible for the many crises of separation we currently see in our world to dissolve into a unity of connectedness — if we all stay true to such a vision.

"The sun shines down, and its image reflects in a thousand different pots filled with water. The reflections are many, but they are each reflecting the same sun. Similarly, when we come to know who we truly are, we will see ourselves in all people."

~**AMMA**
(Spiritual Teacher, The "Hugging Saint")

Because our body, emotions, mind and spirit are interconnected, separation in one area can lead to problems in one or more of the others: we can become ill, imbalanced, and dysfunctional. As leaders, we need to be as Whole as possible in order to tackle the issues in our lives and the world. To begin to heal separation from Self, leaders must reclaim their rejected parts and weave them back into their consciousness. Learning to appreciate and express all our aspects is a crucial part of becoming extraordinary leaders. When we reconnect with all parts of ourselves, we grow into balance and inner harmony, often healing illnesses and chronic conditions, and gaining access to guidance, wisdom and insight. Such healing also increases our ability to connect deeply with others and our world.

When we reconnect with families, we can heal issues between partners as well as generational rifts. When there is an opportunity for dialogue, we can create reconciliations, perhaps even after a lengthy estrangement. Healing requires patience and the commitment to maintain a quality connection over time. And even if we find we cannot actually live together in the same house, we can at least honor each other from a distance, i.e., by creating a *healthier* separation.

When leaders make the effort to create more connection within their organizations, they can transform teams, projects and productivity. The effects can be startling when more of people's talents and skills come forth, and new and exciting possibilities arise. I'd like to illustrate this with the following multidimensional story:

> *I was working as a business analyst and manager for a major corporation. The company, which had over 90,000 employees, served the government and health sectors. My team was under a tremendous amount of pressure to complete a very complex project in which we were expected to deliver excellent quality on deadline and "not one minute later." (This was literal: every minute late amounted to thousands of dollars lost!) This necessitated long hours as well as a willingness to collaborate, keeping conflict to a minimum. Each segment of the project was required to be completed before the next segment could begin. So when Tom, my managing programmer, said he*

was having trouble with a programmer in another department, things came to a screeching halt.

Concerned about delays, I asked Tom what was causing the conflict. It was as if merely posing the question uncorked months of suppressed anger. Tom had nothing but negative things to say about this other programmer, and he expressed them in a completely out-of-control manner. Venomous words spewed out until I finally found myself shouting, "Please stop!" After calming him down, I asked Tom to explain in a reasonable way why he despised this man so much. As I listened, it became clear that his reaction was triggered by his views regarding the company's policy of outsourcing certain work to less expensive labor from other countries. In Tom's view, these jobs were being "stolen from Americans."

In fact, more than a dozen new programmers with cultural roots in India had recently been hired. A number of them happened to have the same name: Raj. Unfortunately, upper management had begun referring to these individuals by number, as in "Raj 1," "Raj 2," "Raj 3," etc. Although we tended to joke about these name choices, this action, in fact, bothered me because it made the men seem interchangeable, like they had no real identity or inherent value.

I saw now that Tom's anger about the company policy had found a target: one of the many "Raj's" — a man that, in fact, he had never met in person, only talked to on the phone. These outsourced programmers, who worked on the other end of our immense building, had been hired because of their excellent programming skills. Outsourcing this work had enabled the company to save a considerable amount of money while maintaining quality. All of the other Raj's were performing brilliantly, and in fact our Raj had performed that way for the first few months as well. I questioned Tom more deeply to try to understand what caused the shift.

Our project was massive. Each segment was supposed to have written specifications detailing what had to be done. Tom hated writing specs, but because he was one of the best programmers in the company, he was given some leeway in this regard, and usually just gave ***verbal***

instructions to his team. This worked okay with all the Americans, whom Tom respected, but when it came to Raj, whom he instinctively disliked because of "stealing an American's job," Tom would give "instructions" that were incomplete and vague. He would call and say things like, "We're working on section X. You know what I need. Get it here by 2:00pm." Then, when Raj would produce the wrong code or fail to meet the deadline, Tom would label him an "idiot" (again) and fly into a rage. He labeled all the Indians "idiots" in spite of the fact that others in the company had found these programmers to be fast, accurate and gifted.

Up until recently, Tom had been working with a second programmer who had always provided Raj with the requisite written specifications, and Raj had always performed excellently. Tom insisted that this other programmer had been "holding Raj's hand," and now that the other programmer had moved to a different position, Tom refused to do such "babying," especially not for a "lousy outsourcer." Tom had no idea that he was treating his American team members vastly differently from Raj. He felt Raj was stupid for failing to "get" the logic of what needed to be done, and he was unconscious of the fact that he was actually expecting Raj to read his mind.

Now that I had the bigger picture, I stepped back to assess the situation. Our team only had 18 hours to complete our part of the project, and we needed Raj to complete his work before we could finish ours. It was imperative that we resolve this issue, so I made a series of requests. I asked Tom to agree to my intervening to help expedite the process. When he did so, I asked him if he had written out exactly what Raj needed to do. Tom answered, "No. I shouldn't have to do that." I asked, "Do you trust me? Do you value my opinion?" Fortunately, he did, on both counts. Tom and I had shared a cubicle for months, and he respected me (as I also respected him), so he answered, "Yes."

I said, "Okay. I am really concerned about what's happening here. You've never met this guy in person. You have no real idea what he can do. You have massive prejudice because he's outsourced. You have no idea of the circumstances under which he was hired. He works here;

that's the reality. And we have a project that we have to complete in 18 hours. Can you put your prejudices aside so we can get this project done?" Tom laughed, because he thought I was a little crazy sometimes, but he trusted me here, so he agreed: "Okay, I'll do it this ***one*** *time."*

I responded, "Please write up a detailed list of the things you want this man to do and a timeframe. If he doesn't get it done, or he does a terrible job, I will document it and bring it to our supervisor. But! If he ***does*** *get it done, I am asking you if you would please go and meet him and thank him." Tom agreed, probably assuming he would never have to do this because "Raj was an idiot."*

With Tom's list in hand, I made my way across our huge "campus" to Raj's office. As I stepped into his cubicle, my attention was drawn to an image on his monitor. Instead of the company logo, which was the default screensaver, Raj had a gorgeous picture of an Indian god. It was absolutely beautiful, and seemed to radiate a positive and benevolent energy. Raj seemed startled that I'd noticed his screen, and he rapidly switched to the company logo. Still feeling the energetic vibration of the image, I couldn't help exclaiming: "Wow, what was that on your screen?" Raj became visibly upset and said, "Nothing, it was nothing! What do you want?"

I told him how our team was under deadline and that our managing programmer was frustrated with his (Raj's) work, and concerned that we wouldn't finish on time. Raj told me about his failure to get proper specifications for several weeks. I could tell that he was upset by his untenable position. I intuitively sensed that Raj was non-confrontational, and therefore never challenged Tom's inadequate instructions. Instead, he had just "plugged away" trying to produce what was wanted by sheer magic. He declared that Tom had "never given him a chance." It was clear that he was ***not*** *an "idiot," and that he had not been enjoying being treated like one.*

When I gave Raj the written specification, he assured me he could do an excellent job and complete the task within the allotted time. I was grateful and told him that I'd follow up as soon as I heard he was done. Since we'd finished our essential conversation, I decided to go back to the image I had seen on his screen. I tried to describe to him how beautiful it was and how it had moved me. As I did so, his eyes moistened. He pulled the image up on his screen again and explained that it represented the power of the creator in his spiritual tradition. "When I was hired to work here," he said, "I prayed to be the greatest creator I could be, to contribute to this company to help make it the best company it could be. This image reminds me daily of that hope." He then asked if I would please not tell upper management that he used it because he didn't want to be fired.

Moved by what Raj had just shared, I assured him that I'd do all I could to support his efforts to keep his job, and asked him to please get back to me as soon as he completed the tasks for our project.

Raj agreed, and I hurried back to my cubicle. I decided to tell Tom the whole story, and asked if he would please open up his mind and heart to allow Raj to contribute to our team. He said that he would, provided Raj "got the work done, and done well." Without hesitation, I said, "He will!" My faith was rewarded. Tom had predicted it would take Raj four to six hours to complete the assignment. Within two hours, Raj had completed his work and emailed it to Tom who was stunned by this rapid response, and even more surprised by the outstanding quality of the programming. Feeling very grateful, I requested that he acknowledge Raj in person, as we had agreed.

I was buried in the work I needed to complete to meet **my** *deadline when I heard someone call my name. I looked up and saw Raj and Tom approaching my cubicle, arms around each other's shoulders like buddies after a battle. Grinning, they said, "Thank you for helping us to get to know each other." With the most joyful shock, I said simply, "You're welcome. After all, that's my job!"*

Tom and Raj actually became friends. They both shared a deep love of computers and programming, and talked shop endlessly (now, in person) both on-site and off. Tom, who had known nothing about the Indian culture, found that he also resonated with Raj's image of god, and was both intrigued and attracted by it because he, too, wanted to create in the best way possible, sharing Raj's desire to impact the world in a positive way.

Shortly afterward, the vice president of our division called me into his office. In the company's atmosphere of tension and pressure, I felt quite nervous. He looked at me and said, "What the hell did you do to those two guys?" My heart leapt to my throat, but he continued, "Whatever it was, keep doing it!" I broke into a huge smile and, as I hurried out the door to make my deadline, I said, "I would be happy to!" We completed our enormous project on time and with laser accuracy.

Miracles like this happen when each person on a team sincerely wants to contribute, when they're encouraged to do what they love, and when everyone values and trusts each other. But to get to this place, each person on a team must be *seen and heard* by the team's leader and all its members. In this example, Raj was initially not seen, quite literally. Not only that, he was fearful that if he were to be truly seen, he might be rejected, even fired. Yet, when he was seen for who he was, he exceeded all expectations. Tom also felt unheard, in that his frustrations and his views about outsourcing were festering beneath the surface. Once I listened to him and helped him consider another perspective, things began to shift. He too felt valued, both by Raj and by me. This enabled him to open up his mind and heart. He began to see Raj as the unique soul he was, and to appreciate his contribution. Tom's lifelong prejudice against "foreigners" — fostered by his having grown up in an insular community — dissolved when he gave Raj a chance, allowing him to find a kindred spirit in a man from the other side of the world. His anger about outsourcing vanished as well. Lastly, I too felt seen and valued for the unique gifts and talents I brought to the organization.

This story also illustrates the second aspect of this chapter's Vital Key: valuing uniqueness. Because he came from a different culture, Raj could bring gifts and interests that none of Tom's American friends had. Rather than decrying and resenting these differences, Tom was able to become curious about them, and to eventually honor them. This is a route for us all: to transmute the hatred generated by millennia of separation and turn it into curiosity and appreciation.

When our individual uniqueness resonates with that of others, magic often occurs. It can generate more energy than we could ever imagine,

leading to extremely synergistic collaborations. This phenomenon isn't confined to organizations; it can extend to whole societies if they are willing to change how they interact with other cultures. For example, in my travels, I was dismayed to discover the degree of prejudice many indigenous people feel towards Americans and Europeans. In my visit to Colombia (in Vital Key #3 on Integrity), the Mamos wisdom keepers had assumed that people outside their tribes would not understand or respect their ceremonies and ancient teachings. To their credit, when they realized this was not so, they made a public apology. This showed great integrity and helped to unify everyone in the gathering. It filled us with unconditional love, and enabled any prejudices and negative filters we Westerners had to also dissolve away. Imagine if the Palestinians and Israelis could do this. Imagine if America and terrorists could do this! The Berlin Wall came down. Anything is possible.

Animals, too, are healed by reconnection. Linda Kohanov[13], in her books and work with equine-assisted therapy, reveals many stories of abused horses who, when treated with love and dignity, not only recovered their true natures, but went on to help humans recover from their own emotional and physical traumas. J. Allen Boone, in his book, *Kinship With All Life*[14], recounts many experiences of animals that behaved aggressively or fearfully towards humans because of mistreatment, but became docile, contented and helpful when humans treated them with respect and affection. In the case of the anomalous aggression shown by elephants in the previous section, the elephants, too, returned to their center when offered love and care. In Dr. G.A. Bradshaw's video, "Elephants, Us and Other Kin," she says:

> "Gradually, in the peace and security of the [rescue-]sanctuary milieu, Mini [one of the rescued elephants] was able to shed the identity of her abusers. She was able to access the seedbed of 'elephant consciousness' once again and revitalize. She spends her remaining years tending to her ailing sister elephants. In a culture of transient living and disposable relationships, where the individualized self reigns supreme, it may be difficult to grasp the depth of Mini's psychological transformation. But attachment theory, and the interdisciplinary annealing that it has helped catalyze, teach that the

> wellspring of life does not lie in one person or the other, but *in the spaces between*. Neither is it privileged by one species or another ... In the words of neuro-philosopher, Alva Noë, 'The life is not inside the animal ... The life is the way the animal *is* in the world.'
>
> "... So yes, my answer is yes. Elephants can recover. *We* can recover, but only if we are willing to relinquish the mandate of human survival in favor of life of other animals ... 'Renewal will come,' as Dr. Pim Van Lommel writes, 'only when we acquire another consciousness, *when our power of love becomes stronger than our love of power*.'
>
> "Mini ... and so many others [rescued animals] forced to relate to life through experiencing near-death, dare to live for someone *outside* of themselves. The wild ones emerge radiant, teaching the need for emulating, not pitying, those who have suffered so mightily. Their testimonies issue monuments commemorating survival in the bloody past. Instead, they urge those of us who remain, to *live*, not just survive. Activist John Seed offers this antidote to what can become overwhelming and paralytic despair: 'I try to remember that it's not me trying to protect the rain forest; rather I am part of the rain forest protecting itself. I am that part of the rain forest recently emerged into human thinking. We are not alone if we live for and through love.'"[15]

I saw this in Colombia. I have seen it in other places. I have seen it in my own life. When people connect through the heart — in love and without seeking ego gratification — their vibrational frequency rises and expands exponentially. This can create unimaginably miraculous events and extraordinary leadership. Uniqueness in collaboration with Oneness is a Whole New Human Story. As leaders, we are being called to help write that new story.

Reconnecting Takes Strength

This may not be easy. The world has a great deal of inertia in the direction of Separation. Sometimes we may not feel our connectedness, and so we'll have to trust our process. Or we may need to *healthily* separate from

portions of the world to maintain our inner reliance on the underlying truth of Wholeness. This is especially the case with separating from media-generated fear and sensationalism. Extraordinary leaders know the value of listening to their inner wisdom, and those who have brought about radical change for good have always had to hold their course in the face of tremendous odds and opposition — like Desmond Tutu, Mother Teresa, Amma, and many of the truth-tellers in Vital Key #2, etc.

A Call to Action: Cultivating Connection, Honoring Uniqueness

"Once upon a time, the tribe of humanity embarked upon a long journey called Separation. It was not a blunder as some – seeing its ravages upon the planet – might think. Nor was it a fall, nor an expression of some innate evil peculiar to the human species. It was a journey with a purpose: to experience the extremes of Separation, to develop the gifts that come in response to it, and to integrate all of that in a new age of Reunion."[16]

~CHARLES EISENSTEIN
(Author, Speaker)

As leaders, I believe this Key calls us to perform three urgent tasks:

1. Foster Reconnection with, and heal unhealthy Separations from, Self, Others, our Communities, Organizations and the World.
2. Create more Wholeness.
3. Honor Uniqueness — our own and that of others.

Foster Reconnection, Heal Unhealthy Separation

Our task is not to dissolve all separation — that would be neither possible, nor healthy — but we must work our way back from the extreme

separation that characterizes our world today, and which is leading to so much destruction. This task is much larger than any one individual leader can accomplish; it is a collective task. But what each of us can do as leaders is take a discerning look at all the many forms of separation that impinge upon our lives, and begin to heal them.

Starting with ourselves and with our intimate connections — partners, family, friends — we can each take steps to prevent unhealthy separation from occurring, and to heal rifts that already exist. If we tend to respond to conflicts with unhealthy separation behaviors, we can choose to consciously change our habits by engaging in practices that foster reconnection rather than polarization, such as constructive dialogue, truth-telling, anger management and non-violent communication. If others in our circle are behaving in divisive ways, we can each choose to attempt to change such interactions or, if the other(s) will not change, to healthily remove ourselves from such interactions. We, as leaders, can send the message that we don't want to behave that way anymore, and encourage others to cease and desist through our own modeling of positive change. We can also help those who are "stuck" in separation to move beyond it by filling ourselves with compassion for them. We are all in this together, and nearly every person who engages in cruelty, abuse or Power Over does so because *they* were treated with cruelty, abuse or Power Over. This includes everyone from the school bully to international terrorists. We need to do what is necessary to keep ourselves safe, but we can also create space for the possibility that others will transform if nourished with connection. No one is beyond the reach of unconditional love and divine intervention.

We can each take note of any biases and prejudices we may have against other genders, races, religions, classes, creeds and traditions. When we find ourselves tending to demean or having a knee-jerk reaction to others, we need to work on consciously balancing our concerns with connection and understanding. One way to do this is to actively engage the other:

travel, read books about other cultures, religions, traditions, etc., purposely talk with those who are different. Pay attention to relationships that encourage separation and choose to follow a different path. Change begins with each of us.

Within families, we can try to reconcile differences and create environments that respect and validate each person and allow for healthy development of both children and adults. There are fantastic programs across the globe for children and families regarding healthy group interactions as well as counseling for individuals, couples and families. Many indigenous tribes are encouraging the use of ceremonies specifically intended for developmental rites of passage, already with great impact.

Our personal journey of reconnection must start with reconnecting with the deepest center of who we are — that is, with our spirit. Spend time each day in conscious communion with this invisible part of being. This may mean taking time to meditate, do energy work, read inspirational words, or be in Nature. I encourage all who wish to become extraordinary leaders in our global transformation from Separation to Reconnection to consider the following in their daily lives:

Cherish each physical body, they are sacred vehicles for our expression in the world. Honor each emotion; they speak our inner truths. Do get help in managing out-of-control emotions if necessary, but do not "stuff" them down or judge them; they are gifts to help us grow. Value thoughts within the greater framework of Wholeness. We will not pass this way again. Go out into Nature with an open heart. Treasure the senses: look, listen, smell, touch, taste when appropriate; all that we are and all that we create as humans comes from Nature, and when we leave this world, our bodies will return to it, to nourish generations to come. We are a part of eternal cycles of life and death. We do not dominate that on which we are utterly dependent. Instead, we can aim to work in *concert* with Nature for the benefit of all.

Create More Wholeness

"Indigenous cultures across the globe have recognized for millennia the spirit in all life and the interconnectedness of people with the natural world ... There is an understanding that our bones and the stones of the earth are made of the same minerals, that our breath comes from the trees and plants, and that our blood is of the ocean."

~PAM MONTGOMERY
(Herbalist, Plant Communicator)

As today's leaders, we must be *champions of increasing Wholeness in all we do.* Our task is to include more of the whole in our decision-making. The well-respected organizational leader, Peter Senge refers to this wholeness practice as "getting the whole system in the room" so that the voices of all concerned (human and non-human) can be expressed and heard.[17] This means re-including Nature in all of our decisions. The problems of our world are multifaceted. Only when our listening is equally deep and multifaceted, can real solutions emerge. This is the healing energy of Wholeness. The more we connect with heart energy, and passionately integrate it within our minds and bodies, the more we will free ourselves from the chains of spiritual debt carried over for millennia. We relinquish these debts through forgiveness and unconditional love.

Honor Uniqueness

"Individuality is only possible if it unfolds from wholeness."

~DAVID BOHM
(Theoretical Quantum Physicist)

The third aspect of our task is to find ways to honor the uniqueness found in all individuated forms (human and non-human). This new focus will help us to heal all of the harm that unhealthy separation has caused. We do this by recognizing how that uniqueness contributes to the Whole and by finding ways to support each being to blossom and contribute their unique gifts. A puzzle missing only a single piece is nevertheless *not* Whole. If any one of us fails to express our uniqueness, we die unfulfilled, and the world is impoverished.

And when we give the gift of Honoring Uniqueness to others, it multiplies a thousand-fold. Valuing uniqueness in our partners, children, and all others in our lives enriches them, us, and the world. I've had the privilege of witnessing sons finally being truly "seen" by their fathers, for example. The importance of this kind of thing cannot be overestimated.

Just as we cannot love another if we do not love ourselves, so too, we cannot honor others fully if we do not honor ourselves. We can value our own uniqueness without needing to be "better than" others. What is it like when people truly see our unique gifts and value? Anyone who has ever experienced it knows that it creates an extraordinary feeling of expansiveness, joy, and gratitude. It makes us want to contribute even more.

Honor Nature and All Life

"Our task must be to free ourselves by widening our circle of compassion to embrace all living creatures and the whole of Nature and its beauty!"

~**ALBERT EINSTEIN**
(Theoretical Physicist, Philosopher)

As leaders, we can support and spearhead movements aimed at shifting cultural mindsets that treat animals, plants and the Earth as unfeeling "raw materials" that can be used without respect or compassion, and that are here strictly for the benefit of humans and corporate interests. Each of us can make choices to eat foods and use products and services that arise from methodologies that respect and cherish Nature, such as sustainable, humane and organic farming methods, healthier forestry, life-affirming power-generation (non-fossil fuel and minimal or non-polluting), ethical research, and so on. We can make choices that support "green" products, processes and philosophies. We can further support organizations that research, develop and manufacture such items, like The Rodale Institute, Bioneers, The Biomimicry Institute, permaculture and organic gardening organizations, etc. We can also support organizations that are doing research into our interconnectedness and the miraculous possibilities that arise out of honoring these connections, such as: the Institute of Noetic Sciences (IONS), the Foundation for Global Humanity (FGH), Institutes for the Achievement of Human Potential, Continuum Movement, the Alliance for Wild Ethics, the Center for the Advancement of Human Potential, the Monroe Institute, wiser.org, etc.

Honor Your Connection with Others and the World Community

"It's time for parents to teach young people early on that in diversity there is beauty and strength."

~MAYA ANGELOU
(American Author, Poet)

Within schools, leaders can encourage transformation by teaching children respect for Nature, respect for other cultures, and respect for each other. There are many schools introducing programs to educate students about bullying behavior and what to do about it. Through this powerful, anti-bullying training (e.g. organizations like Soulshoppe.com), children learn to develop empathy and trust.[18]

Within organizations, leaders can look for signs of unhealthy separation between employees, and between employees and management, and put in place structures and techniques that foster greater connection. These include processes of shared governance, as well as dialogue circles and diversity training.

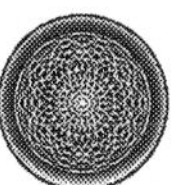

Expanding from that, there are now a plethora of spiritual and evolutionary practices available to us, including meditation, yoga, Reiki, creative expression, mindfulness, intentionality experiments, global healing and so on. It has been my observation over the past 25 years that if just one of these practices is introduced into a group or organization, even in political arenas, people are happier, more creative and more productive. They also seem to want to collaborate more, and have more trusting attitudes. This can radically alter the landscape of how we work with others throughout the world. These and other innovative practices, including the implementation of new more inclusive governance models, are also being used effectively to bring peace and healing to areas hit by catastrophes and conflict. As leaders, we can support and educate others about such practices.

As described earlier, human rights abuses and trafficking, cultural obliteration, genocide and ecocide are all acts of separation on a mass scale. Leaders can speak out about these issues and work to change public policies to address and heal separation. A beautiful example of this was seen during the recent "Wisdom of the Origins" Conference, sponsored by the former SEED Graduate Institute. Extraordinary leaders from around the world — including the 13 Indigenous Grandmothers, global peace ambassadors like James O'Dea, representatives from the United Nations, The Shift Network and many others — convened in New Mexico to create a "Declaration of Commitment to the Indigenous Peoples."[19] This written document, created through heart-felt collaboration, offered apology and atonement for atrocities against indigenous tribes worldwide, and formally acknowledged their innumerable contributions to humanity and the planet. This was a singular example of leaders consciously and publicly initiating cultural restoration and healing, and I felt blessed and honored to witness, participate in and film this moving event.

In closing, a Native American legend foretells the coming of the "Warriors of the Rainbow." These are leaders who would be "free of petty jealousies, and [who would] love all mankind as their brothers, regardless of color, race, or religion."[20] Their role is to "teach the people of the ancient practices of Unity, Love and Understanding." In *The Seer and the Sayer* by

Victoria Hanchin, Indigenous Grandmother Dona added her understanding of the Warriors of the Rainbow as those who would remember what they are here for — to create a legacy of greater good for a world that works for all in alignment with indigenous wisdom.[21] This sounds remarkably like the vision of the world expressed in our collective dream. *This* is what we are here for: to reconnect and heal unhealthy separation, to foster more wholeness, and to set an example by honoring the unique gifts of all beings. And it is the wisdom of extraordinary leadership to manifest that dream by forging these practices into our lives, organizations, and world — for All Our Relations.

Vital Key #5:
Dancing with Dynamic Balance

"The major work of the world is not done by geniuses. It is done by ordinary people, with balance in their lives, who have learned to work in an extraordinary manner."

~GORDON B. HINCKLEY
(Mormon preacher, teacher)

Life is full of dualities and extremes: light and dark, soft and hard, head and heart, body and soul, logic and intuition, masculine and feminine, action and reflection. As humans, we're sometimes drawn to extremes, but as leaders our task is to navigate these polarities with grace and skill, so that we can model and demonstrate for others how to proceed. To accomplish this, we need to develop a special knowing, an ability to recognize when things are starting to go out of balance, and how and when to steer them back into equilibrium. In the words of the Kenny Rogers song, we need to "know when to hold'em, and know when to fold'em."

What is Dynamic Balance?

"Your hand opens and closes, opens and closes. If it were always a fist or always stretched open, you would be paralyzed. Your deepest presence is in every small contracting and expanding, the two as beautifully balanced and coordinated as birds' wings."

~RUMI
(Sufi Mystic and Poet)

Dynamic balance is the process of purposefully tuning in to what is needed, and then behaving in accordance with that tuning-in. This may be done daily or moment-by-moment, depending on circumstances. Dynamic balance is a refined and never-ending dance. It is alive. We must be in integrity to dance this dance well, and we must be willing to do what is *necessary* according to our dynamic perception.

Some people carry a belief, or even a worry, that balance is boring, that being in balance implies being "static," "on the fence," never having an opinion or a passion. But this is not the case. Balance is only static or neutral if a particular situation *calls* for that, according to our discernment. If a situation calls for us to do nothing, then we do nothing, but not out of boredom or indifference, but rather out of a deep knowing that *non-action* is what is *needed.* Dynamic balance is a highly mobile and incisive way of being that is actually quite challenging — just like complex dancing. It requires us to be responsive, responsible and willing to make mistakes — with humor and grace — in service to the dance.

For a wonderful demonstration of dynamic balance, we only need to look to our bodies. Bodies naturally want to remain in what is called homeostasis, a state of equilibrium. Our environments forever challenge that homeostasis, and so our bodies are constantly dancing between motion and pause, activity and rest, taking in and eliminating, inhaling and exhaling; our bodies constantly adjust to changes in temperature, cell chemistry, inner electromagnetics and a myriad of other functions in

order to remain alive and healthy.

Sadly, our culture often creates situations in which we are encouraged to either ignore our bodies or overload them with stimuli, and this absolutely knocks us out of balance. Sometimes the knock happens so slowly that, like the proverbial frog that doesn't notice the water getting hotter, we just go along until we suddenly receive a major "wake-up call." This call can feel like getting whacked in the head with a 2x4, and it can happen to any of us. Here's a story of how it happened to me:

> *When I was married, my then-husband and I went through a period of about seven years when we moved repeatedly in support of his work. Finally, seeking more financial stability, we decided that it was my turn to look for a full-time position. What happened next seemed quite magical.*
>
> *We were living in upstate New York, and we both wanted to return to the warmth of Florida. We picked a town on the Florida map and scraped up enough cash to purchase a 13-week subscription to the local paper. I also wrote down in my journal exactly the type of job I wanted. I was a professional psychotherapist, and I was looking for a unique position. I was interested in the transformational aspects of education, and I wanted to work with children to help identify their core gifts and proficiencies and foster their creativity. In describing my dream job, I named the population and kind of work environment I hoped for, including the flexibility to work in Nature, outside the 9-to-5 "box."*
>
> *I spent the next 13 weeks scrutinizing the classifieds, diligently identifying every potential position, and applying for many of them. Meanwhile, I kept dreaming about the job that I had meticulously outlined, even describing the personalities of my future colleagues. Twelve weeks went by without a real hit, and I began to feel a bit of frustration and discouragement. As if in answer to my silent request, every night of that final week, I was gifted with dreams that insisted I not lose faith. On the 13th Sunday, I saw it, printed in black and white: my Dream Job!*
>
> *The job description was almost verbatim what I had written in my*

journal, and my husband nearly fell off his chair when I read it to him. Overwhelmed with gratitude, and mindful that hundreds of people would be applying for this job, I wrote the most heart-felt and passionate cover letter I'd ever written. In order to improve my chances, my husband and I went out on a limb and drove to Florida, so that I'd be available if I received a call for an interview. To put this into perspective, this was a 1400-mile road-trip! But I was determined, fueled by my intuition and logic, plus my love for my husband and our mutual wellbeing.

I did indeed receive a call within a few days, after which began a series of events that tested both my faith and my determination. First was the job interview, which involved being grilled by 22 people rotating in and out and seated around the biggest table I had ever seen. I sat on one side and the president of the grants organization sat on the other; we were separated by what seemed like miles. The interview lasted five grueling hours, but it ***did*** *result in a job offer — which I immediately accepted. In doing so, I ignored the insight that cautioned, "Be careful, this feels excessive," because the job appeared so ideal.*

My work involved an innovative program, funded by a grant from the state. During my first year, I served as both a therapist for 35 emotionally handicapped children and as their liaison with their teachers, healthcare practitioners and families. Because of this holistic approach, the children improved exponentially. They were feeling valued, they excelled in school, and they began to heal in every aspect of their lives. Their families were healing as well. For that first year, everything felt beautifully balanced; this truly was my dream job. Everyone else seemed to agree, as I kept getting excellent reviews from the children, the families, the teachers, the school principal, and my immediate supervisor — information that all went back to the grant administrators. Everyone was happy.

Then, at the end of the year, everything changed. I learned to my dismay that the grant had been written with a stipulation: after the first year, state law required the lead counselor (me) to serve ***all*** *newly diagnosed "emotionally handicapped" students in a multi-city area.*

Suddenly, my caseload expanded ***tenfold****.*

Thirty-five students had been just doable; now I was required by law to serve three hundred. By the end of the first month, I was exhausted and I could barely keep track of my students' names. Having witnessed many times the negative consequences of burnout on clients, colleagues and personal relationships, I had promised myself that I would quit if I ever felt that happening to me. I spoke to my boss, requesting that she hire another therapist to help with the work, and I offered to train this person. My boss replied that the grant did not allow for the funding of additional personnel.

Against my better judgment, I chose to remain in the job, even though I knew I was no longer effecting the positive change that was so important to me. But being a very vibrant woman in my 20's, I thought, "Never mind, I'll just work harder." I spent hours reviewing each child's records and family history while also practicing mnemonics to help me remember everyone's name and life story. I kept this up for months, until one day, in the ladies' room, I noticed I was passing clumps of blood, and I knew that something was dreadfully wrong. Each day, it got worse, and I got weaker. I continued to petition for the grant to be re-written to either limit the number of children I served or to fund additional therapists. And all the while, in spite of everything, I kept getting excellent evaluations.

Then, two pivotal events occurred. First, I requested that my boss set up a meeting with the grants administration president to discuss the untenable situation. My boss did so, and the president and four others from the grants board came to hear me present my assessment. At the end, I stated that if something didn't change, I would have to leave the program because I was burning out. I'll never forget what happened next: the president stood up and, grinning from ear to ear, said, "You don't look like you're burning out to me, honey. You always look good. Carry on!" He then sauntered out the room. Infuriated, I wanted to quit on the spot, but knew I needed to calm down before making such an important decision.

The second pivotal event occurred two days later. I went to see a physician who immediately prescribed a colonoscopy. Afterwards, the doctor called me into his office, looked me straight in the eyes, pointed his finger at my face, and said, "Young lady, if you do not change your lifestyle, you'll be dead by the time you're 40!"

This admonition struck me like a blow to my heart. I was in my 20's. I felt I was deeply committed to living a rich, impactful and also balanced life — and I was failing! When I got home, I burst into tears. It was a lot to take in, and I felt like a caged animal. I knew I had to bring my health back into balance, but that decision would throw the rest of my life into chaos. Yet, the decision was very clear to me. I had to choose my physical wellbeing over my job and the economic security it provided.

It took both insight and courage for that doctor to call me on my poor choices — choices that had propelled me way out of balance — and to tell me as forcefully as he did. I'm forever indebted to his extraordinary leadership on my behalf. His words, which still haunt me, changed forever the way I approached self-care. I vowed that I would do everything possible to keep my body and being in balance for the rest of my (hopefully very long) life.

And so I left my "dream job." Afterwards, I learned that the grants administrators were forced to eventually hire ***three*** *full-time people to replace me, and those three still couldn't handle the demand of the newly increased emotionally handicapped population. After another year of high employee turnover and mediocre results due to overwhelm, that promising, innovative program's funding was cut. A wonderful and effective idea had turned sour because, without dynamic balance, success was not sustainable.*

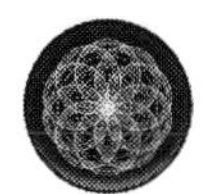

Out-of-Balance Hurts, While Dynamic Balance Heals

"I feel exhausted if I teach too long."

~DALAI LAMA
(Tibetan Spiritual Leader, Global Peace Advocate)

Dynamic balance is crucial for leaders. If we are destabilized, our normal life processes and natural healing are compromised, and we become vulnerable in many other ways. We're distractible, and we often can't think straight. If we're not able to make clear-minded decisions, manifestation is far less likely to occur. Arguments become more prevalent; we lose our emotional fluency. We may act rashly, diminishing trust at home and at work. This becomes more devastating the more influential the leader.[1]

Because we humans are so complex, we can get out-of-balance in many ways. To help raise our awareness I'd like to explore several of these ways in some detail.

Self: Dancing with Dynamic Balance

Let's start with ourselves — our bodies, minds, emotions and relationship to spirit can get out of balance. We can also get out of balance with others in our lives.

Bodies: Finding Balance with Our Sleep

One of the most critical things we tend to ignore is our need for good, sound sleep. We seem to think it's not really all that important, and that we can skimp on it. But neglecting this need is incredibly damaging. Studies show that after only 7 nights of too little sleep, more than 700 *genetic* changes are possible. These changes harm our immune, digestive, skeletal, cardiovascular and nervous systems, and impair vital body processes including those related to aging, handling stress, repairing tissues and removing toxins. Insufficient sleep negatively impacts our memory, mental clarity, and our ability to feel joy and pleasure (serotonin levels). Sleep deprivation can also cause psychological disorders ranging from anxiety all the way up to psychosis — including experiencing paranoia and hallucinations.[2] (Remember that depriving "the enemy" of sleep is one of the military's most effective torture techniques!)

Remember, too, that Dreamtime can be a source of great insights. Many important discoveries and inventions "came" to people via their dreams. These nightly visions inform many of our more personal experiences, too, often providing us with clues and counsel about what is going on in our lives and how we might handle issues. This can enhance our waking lives and impact our ultimate human potential.

I would venture to say that most leaders today are sleep-deprived. It's one of the casualties of our fixation on an unachievable ideal: the "heroic leader" who can do it all. When there doesn't seem to be enough time in the day, these leaders forfeit their sleep to catch up, forgetting the repercussions. They are often talented innovators, but when they're sleep-deprived, all hell breaks loose. Like walking zombies, they're not fully present, and so they can make decisions that compromise their organizations, or they become reactive in ways that exacerbate conflicts. They can be unfocused, overly emotional or physically clumsy. They might lose a contract because they weren't able to effectively convey their thoughts in a presentation. No leader is immune to this, including those in highly influential positions, such as presidents and prime ministers. Imagine the consequences.

To make matters even worse, many people take drugs to prevent sleep in the hopes of enhancing performance. Sometimes this is even mandated: This has happened for many in the military (like Sequoyah in the story in Vital Key #1), where leaders advocated the use of mega-amphetamines to ensure superhuman degrees of alertness and responsiveness from soldiers. When the urgency of the danger passes, these men and women can't slow their bodies back down to sleep. To counterbalance, they are then given depressants or powerful sleep aids to reverse the process. The

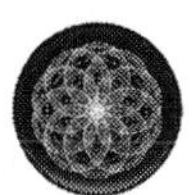

ultimate long-term consequences of these radical practices create near-irreversible changes in the brain chemistry of those enlisted to serve and protect. They are unable to balance their emotional expression and often unintentionally harm others. Veterans Affairs is just beginning to address the lifetime damage associated with these practices.

I believe that sleep time is intended to be restorative for all sentient beings. If we have challenges with sleep, our body *is* trying to tell us something. We need to pay attention to find the right balance.

Bodies: Finding Balance with Our Nutrition

Another critical need for balance within our bodies is sound nutrition. When we are not adequately supported with fuel, or when we eat foods that are contaminated with synthetic additives, GMO's, or imbalanced amounts of certain ingredients (like salt, sugar or fat), etc., we cannot function well, and we open ourselves up to a myriad of illnesses and diseases. Although I cannot summarize them all here, there are thousands of books and studies on the topic of wise nutrition and the problems resulting from eating unconsciously. Suffice it to say, we cannot be vibrant leaders if we are destroying our bodies with toxins and unhealthy food. The expression "you are what you eat" is actually an important phrase to help us, as leaders, become conscious of what we are putting in our bodies.

It is also important to listen to our own unique body's needs, because what is an elixir for one person might be poison for another: for example, wheat is the "staff of life" unless you're allergic to gluten.[3] Our bodies inform us every second if we take a moment to listen. As with all issues of balance, we need to *pay attention* to how our body responds to what we eat: Do we feel energized after meals, or drained and unable to focus? Do we get a stomach ache whenever we eat a certain food? Do we feel "out-of-sorts" every time we dine at a certain restaurant? Failure to listen to *our* body's personal wisdom can lead to illness and decreased functioning even if the food itself is intrinsically "healthy" and nutritious.

We also need to be aware of our habits around food. If we wolf down our meals (which I am sometimes guilty of) or if we skip meals because we're in a hurry, this takes a serious toll on our body's ability to process the nutrients we do take in. If we get into mealtime arguments with family or colleagues, or if we simultaneously ingest unsettling news reports while eating, this also affects our body's ability to process. In short, we can eat really high-quality food and still develop digestive disorders, ulcers, and/or have nutritional imbalances because our body can't metabolize properly due to the stressors we introduce each time we eat.

Finally, we also need to be aware of our cultural programming around food. An alarming number of people today, including leaders across the globe, suffer from life-threatening disorders related to food. These include obesity, diabetes, allergies, anorexia, and bulimia. These issues have to do with the Power Over environments we live in, our unexamined core wounds, and our culturally-ingrained beliefs about how we look and what's important. In addition, we need to become aware of systemic problems within the food industry and the questionable motivations and tactics surrounding food's promotion. These issues also have to do with Power Over and separation from Nature.

When our bodies are nutritionally out-of-balance, it affects our performance in many areas of our lives. Sometimes we may not realize how we're "slipping" until we get a wake-up call in the form of a serious illness, or we can just continually feel "run down" — as if we already had a chronic illness. Such behaviors are all too common in our world. Remember: Dynamic Balance requires us to *pay attention and do what's necessary*. We need to treat both our food and our eating habits as if they are vital to our survival — because they are!

Bodies: Finding Balance with Stress

Stress is one of the major factors affecting our overall balance. We can be energized by the challenges of our lives, as James O'Dea points out in his book *Creative Stress*, but then we must also take time to "unwind."[4] This is a call to dance with dynamic balance by integrating exercise, meditation, or simply being in Nature, into our daily routine. Ignoring this need can

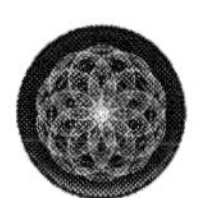

lead to a variety of physical, mental, and emotional problems: physical illnesses range from getting the flu to developing a chronic condition such as ulcers, heart disease, high blood pressure, etc.; mental problems include diminished perception such as suddenly becoming clumsy, uncoordinated or having poor judgment — on the road, in the boardroom, or at home; emotional issues include becoming over-reactive and less tolerant of ourselves and others.

In our current world, we can't avoid stress altogether, but many of us actually increase the stress in our lives by the choices we make. Millions of people work in jobs they hate, are in relationships that have become toxic, or live in environments that are making them sick. Jobs, relationships and environments can all be changed! Dynamic balance demands that we tune in and listen to our own truth. Maintaining the status quo when our bodies desperately want "out" not only creates physical health problems, but it can also lead to rage, domestic violence, depression, apathy and poor performance in all activities.

Emotions: Finding Balance

"There can be no transforming of darkness into light, and of apathy into movement, without emotion."

~DR. CARL JUNG
(Swiss Psychiatrist, 'Collective Unconscious' Explorer)

"Red is such an interesting color to correlate with emotion, because it's on both ends of the spectrum. On one end you have happiness, falling in love, infatuation ... passion ... On the other end, you've got obsession, jealousy, danger, fear, anger and frustration."

~TAYLOR SWIFT
(American Singer-Songwriter, Actor)

Emotions are strong energies, and they are meant to *flow*. They can invigorate and inspire us, notify us when something is wrong, and help us express the fullness of who we are. They are an integral part of being human. However, in our culture we are encouraged from childhood to lie about our emotions, to suppress them or to use them in unhealthy ways. This causes emotional imbalance across the landscape. Signs of such imbalance can include unresponsiveness, uncontrollable crying, explosive outbursts and arguments, or a constant fear of consequences that prevents us from standing up for ourselves, or for what we want or believe in. When our emotions are out-of-balance, we either allow them to take over our lives, or we suppress them and shut them down. Because our culture's current philosophy tends to foster Power Over, which represses truth, integrity and wholeness, we see these imbalances regularly.

People who Power Over others have frequently allowed their out-of-control emotions — like rage, vengeance, or a distorted joy in seeing others suffer — to take over. This can lead to physical health issues like high blood pressure, ulcers and heart disease. When our emotions are running the show, we frequently act before we've thought something through, leading to regret, harm, and even loss of life. It also wreaks havoc with relationships: explosive people create fear and a general sense of unease, causing others to withdraw because they have lost trust and confidence. Being explosive also reduces our ability to have or express empathy, and it can "program" our children to have an unhealthy attitude towards their own emotions — thus creating a vicious cycle. It may even lead to child abuse and post-traumatic stress disorder (PTSD) in others. We cannot effectively lead if our imbalanced emotions call the shots, because we will say and do things that are not in anyone's long-term best interests. It is critical to note that in our culture women are often labeled "overly emotional" for vehemently expressing their truth, while men who run on the emotions of anger and rage are very rarely so labeled; in fact, male anger is often seen as "normal" in leadership circles. This gives rise to two issues of balance: women struggle to know how much is "enough," while men fall into the trap of too much being "necessary."

At the opposite end of the spectrum are those who "shut down" their emotions. We see this frequently in people who have been repeatedly

Powered Over by others: they become unresponsive no matter what's done to them, and have a "what's-the-use" attitude towards life. Ironically, when we shut down, we are actually Powering Over ourselves by suppressing our own emotions. This decreases both our productivity and our availability to others. As with over-emotion, repressing emotions also creates many problems, the biggest of which is that we can never fully be ourselves. Our gifts and our lives are co-opted, diminishing our contribution to the world. In time, long-pent-up emotions can unexpectedly burst forth, causing the shut-down person to suddenly become emotionally *over*-reactive, often without filters, potentially leading to violence and destructiveness directed at others or themselves. If we are parents, our behaviors set an example for our children. Are we training them to "buy in" to the Power Over model? Are we taking away their voice as well, and helping to perpetuate the cycle of imbalance? We can certainly shift this with our choices.

Relationships: Balancing Self-Care with Other-Care

"Problems arise in that one has to find a balance between what people need from you and what you need for yourself."

~JESSYE NORMAN
(American Opera Singer)

Leaders, especially entrepreneurs, are typically at one end of the self-care spectrum, not asking for help or support, and wanting to do it all themselves. This creates instability and may lead to burnout. It can also cause us to miss the opportunity of co-creating and cross-pollinating with others' ideas and ways of operating. We can develop tunnel vision and narrow minds, and lose touch with the rest of the world. On the opposite end of the spectrum are those who don't want to take any responsibility for their own growth. This is unhealthy too. Both ways represent a lack of self-care.

Another way this dichotomy can show up is as a struggle between passion and compassion. If passion is overemphasized, as it can be in love affairs or when a leader is highly visionary and expending a lot of energy on their work, there can be difficulty remaining grounded. We may feel scattered or overextended energetically. This can lead to many types of disease, and it can also impair our ability to follow through on commitments or to get results. (This kind of imbalance can also happen when teenagers experience raging hormones or during menstrual cycles.) Too much passion can also lead to self-absorption and a lack of empathy. If taken to extremes it can lead to the chronic use of Power Over to get one's way.

On the other hand, too much compassion can become distorted, dropping us into codependent relationships or compromising our own self-care because we're spending so much of our life taking care of others. Physiologically, this can show up as exhaustion, anxiety, sleeplessness, and digestive disorders. Many healthcare professionals suffer from health problems themselves and don't feel they have the time to stop because their patients *need* them so much. This is out of balance. We become poorer leaders when we neglect ourselves for the same reason that "you can't love another if you don't love yourself." A commitment to Balance calls for leaders to do just that — love themselves. When I work with leaders, I always encourage them to commit fiercely to their own self-care and personal development, but balancing that with compassion for others.

Relationships: Balancing Work with Family and Friends

"You can't truly be considered successful in your business life, if your home life is in shambles."

~ZIG ZIGLAR
(Author, Motivational Speaker)

This aspect of dynamic balance is often easy for leaders to ignore. But if they do, the effects are the most devastating. I cannot tell you the number

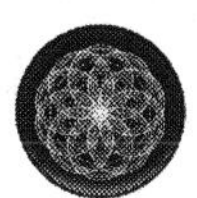

of leaders I've worked with who recount the same story: coming home very late one evening (as usual), and being shocked to discover their intimate partner of many years has walked out — in some cases, for good. If leaders give so much at work that they have little left for their families or friends, their personal lives fall apart: their spouses/ significant-others may unexpectedly leave them, or their children might end up ill (because unconsciously it may be the only way they can receive the attention they need). If the imbalance is extreme enough, children or spouses/partners may even become harmfully reactive or suicidal.

Our relationships are vital to our wellbeing. The more attuned we are to their importance, the more likely we are to recognize when they are getting out of balance. This recognition can help us repair the situation before it's too late, and we actually lose someone we love.

> *One day, June, a client in her eighties, shared with me this story about her dad, Albert. Albert was an extremely successful businessman with such a demanding schedule that he spent very little time with his family, even though he loved them very much. One afternoon, June and her mother arrived for lunch at the same restaurant where Albert was having a business meal. Naturally, they noticed each other, and waved. When Albert's business colleagues saw this, they asked him, "Who is that charming little girl?" Shocked to realize that his associates had never met his family, Albert replied, 'That's my lovely daughter and my wife!" This was a wake-up call for Albert that his "charming little girl" was every bit as important as his work. From that day onward, he reprioritized, insisting on spending time each week with June, doing a variety of creative and fun activities. Although she had not been resentful of her father's absence (since that was all she had ever known), June was elated when he chose to transform.*

Many leaders, and particularly men, give priority to their desire to provide for their families while sacrificing their family life. It is crucial for such leaders to realize that their family's needs extend beyond financial support. This is part of the Power Over imbalance discussed in Vital Key #1 in which Money = Power = Value. We can think that our most important value to our family lies in the money we provide, but this is not so. Our loved ones need personal connection just as much as they need food, and so do we. Acknowledging this truth will help us be wiser and more empathetic leaders in all aspects of our lives. This is reflected in the fact that Albert later told June that he'd had no idea he was neglecting her until that event occurred. I have seen this with many leaders: their seeming indifference is often due to unawareness, a blindness to the obvious, and when they discover what is actually happening, they can and will transform — and actually welcome it.

Organizations: Dancing With Dynamic Balance

Like individuals, organizations can go in and out of balance dealing with such concerns as vision versus current reality, profits versus public good, consent versus top-down decision-making, etc. They must also toggle between action and reflection. When an organization is balanced, synergistic expression surges and, as with bodies, there is a feeling of "flow."

When dynamic balance is present in an organization, every team member feels heard and seen, inspiring them to work with enthusiasm, motivation, enjoyment and care. Projects are likely to be completed with high quality and on time. Complaining and counterproductive behaviors are minimized because problems are addressed when they arise, rather than being pushed under the carpet (e.g., employees are not told to "keep quiet and live with it"). Also, when there is balance, managers feel less weight on their own shoulders because respect and trust flow in both directions.

I've been a part of many teams and organizations where the importance of balance was not recognized, either by the employees or by the management, and before long, everyone began to experience the repercussions. However, each time, when the key of Dynamic Balance was effectively addressed, the positive potential and synergistic spirit began to re-emerge.

It is especially important for leaders in organizations to pay attention to imbalances arising from where team members fall on the continuum of introversion to extraversion. Introverts primarily derive energy from internal engagement, while extraverts primarily derive energy from

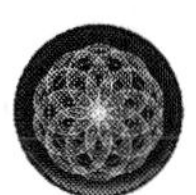

external activities. Our societal tendency is to reward more extraverted behavior. Extraverts are the ones who are more likely to speak up in a crowd and take quick action over any situation. Introverts are more likely to mull information thoroughly and speak with judicious economy only when they feel the time is right. Both extraverts and introverts can have deep knowledge, wisdom, heart-centeredness, and an equal desire to express, but because of our societal bias, introverts may be marginalized and not heard. In a dynamically balanced organization, all team members need to feel valued. Leaders need to be aware of their own style and any biases they might have toward others who have different styles.

When the expression from extraverts and introverts is out of balance, it can result in a natural build-up of frustration, in both personal and professional arenas. One approach to greater balance is to mindfully honor the gifts and contributions that exist along the *entire* continuum. The extravert doesn't feel a need to hold back and can therefore contribute immediate ideas that solve a problem or help advance a situation proactively, but their desire for action may not take into account the whole picture or the full impact of their decisions — on others, the land, or future generations. The introvert applies their talent for supreme observation and deep introspection, taking in information and distilling it down to its essence, but this takes time and they may need encouragement to speak up. Both contribute in positive ways. When either is ignored, everyone involved loses out on the tremendous potential of their combined holographic perceptions.

Imbalances within organizations can take many other forms, including power imbalances, relationship imbalances, or imbalances between the organization's internal model and the outer reality in which it is operating (i.e., a belief system that is no longer viable because the world has moved on). When organizations become out-of-balance relative to their power structure or their attitude toward "the bottom line," they can act in nightmarish and inhumane ways, as shown by the following story:

> *Robert was a brilliant computer expert who had been working as the lead programmer for a top-notch East Coast graphics design firm for over ten years. He referred to himself as a "hard-core introvert," and*

although he viewed that as internally healthy, he felt that he had difficulty expressing himself publicly, both at home and at work. At one point, he had also been diagnosed with Asperger's Syndrome, a high-functioning form of autism. He said, "I wasn't very good with people, but I did my best, and I was involved in treatment to help with my socialization and communication skills. This was critical for my job, as I was in charge of all the other graphic designers in my particular unit."

Robert performed impeccably for his company, and received numerous awards for his creative innovations that brought the company millions of dollars in profits. But he often had difficulty adjusting to change or any type of crisis that required his direct attention. So he left those issues to others "more equipped to handle chaos." However, one day something happened that could not be left in someone else's hands.

Robert's mother, thousands of miles away, became very ill. Fearing that she might be dying, she begged Robert to come and spend time with her. He explained the situation to his superiors. Their response was an unequivocal No. They told him, "Under no circumstances can you leave in the middle of these urgent deadlines."

As the days swiftly passed and his mother's pleas became more desperate, Robert asked repeatedly for some leave. Dismantling emotionally, he finally asked to speak with the company president. However, even the president refused to let him take time off. As Robert later expressed it, "It was as if the organization drew a line in concrete and there were no jackhammers to dislodge what was seemingly set in stone." Robert became angry, and began to shout at the president. He was nearly fired on the spot, when he received an emergency phone call that his mother had died.

Robert later told me, "With the gravity of the situation in plain view, you'd think that the atmosphere might have balanced out toward compassion — but no. No chance of that. I was told that if I went to handle my mother's affairs, I would not have a job when I came back. This may sound completely ludicrous, but due to my illness and inability to handle such conflicting imbalances, I was terrified that I would lose my medical insurance and my livelihood. And so, I did not go to my own mother's funeral! Now I have to live with that for the rest of my life."

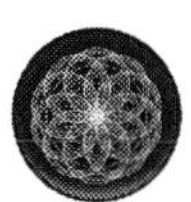

This company had lost all sense of proportion. In the name of money, they bludgeoned and diminished a hard-working and extremely productive employee who had a history of generating great benefits for the entire organization. After the above experience, this employee may have stayed on, but he never felt the same way about that company or his job again.

National leaders can also lose balance and clarity. The 2013 United States government shutdown mimicked our nation's economic illness, and the legislators chose to address the problem in a very out-of-balance way. The people of the United States paid for a bailout of banks and banking cartels. Private businesses cannot do this. When a business can't make payroll, most people cannot make the choice of staying on board without pay, because they have families to support, so they take the cut or leave. This is a perfect example of imbalance cascading throughout a system.

When organizations, governments, or large systems (e.g., economic, healthcare, education, etc.) get out-of-balance, synergy stops; there is no more "flow"; people become discontent. When employees are treated inhumanely, they can lose their loyalty, their motivation, their enthusiasm. They can either retreat inside themselves, no longer offering their gifts (some of which may be vitally needed for the organization's survival), or they may become verbally or even physically aggressive and defiant, sabotaging projects consciously or otherwise. Productivity suffers, with time and money overruns and lackluster results, because people's hearts are no longer in it. Just as with Power Over, corporate imbalance ultimately loses both money and personnel, not to mention innovation and strength. All imbalance is ultimately unsustainable; in the end, the structure crumbles.

A special case of organizational imbalance is called "The Founder's Syndrome." This is a common dynamic that affects many non-profits, although it can happen within for-profit companies as well. Founders birth organizations out of their passion for a particular issue or cause. Things proceed smoothly until the organization reaches a point where it must evolve beyond the control of the founder (much like any developmental stage of evolution — e.g., youth taking initiatory steps to becoming adults). The board and other members want to take the enterprise in a different direction, but the founder resists, wishing to remain in control. It becomes a struggle between a *singular* vision and a *shared* one. This can lead to a variety of Power Over ploys, including manipulation, back stabbing, gossip, secrets, and other undermining behavior.

These are natural growth pains, but if they are ignored, the entire organization can get seriously out-of-balance, with power struggles consuming everyone's energy. Over the years, I have witnessed at least seven very powerful organizations unwittingly fall prey to "The Founder's Syndrome." Of these, three completely imploded and dissolved without ever having addressed the roots of their demise, while two others lost several devoted employees and remained unaware of the negative internal dynamics which continued to fester, undermining future success. Only two of the organizations emerged from the experience with a new balance that was actually healthier and more effective than the way they had started.

We each need to tune in to our inner wisdom to determine what constitutes "balance" and its expression for us. Then we need to honor that — in our personal lives and in our organizations.

Personal to Global: Balancing Doing with Being

There are a number of imbalances that spring from *cultural assumptions.* These assumptions are so ingrained they are virtually invisible, like the air that surrounds us. Yet they have a profound — and destabilizing — effect. The first of these is the imbalance between Doing and Being.

"Doo-Be-Doo-Be-Doo..."

~FRANK SINATRA (SONG LYRICS)

(Singer, Actor)

"Besides the noble art of getting things done, there is the noble art of leaving things undone. The wisdom of life consists in the elimination of nonessentials."

~LIN YUTANG

(Writer, Inventor)

Our culture places a great deal of value on Doing — that is, accomplishing things in the external world. This view says that *action* is what's important, physical interactions and their results. But many cultures, past and present, hold that *Being* is as important as Doing, or perhaps even more important. Being involves our inner life, attending to our own health and wellness, communing with our spirit and our inner core — all things that are invisible to the outer world. Cultures that value Being as much as Doing value our connection to All That Is and our wholeness. They acknowledge the crucial importance of one's inner life, how essential it is for maintaining balance in all of our outer-world activities.

As a spiritually-oriented person, I thought I had the balance between Doing and Being "down pat." I thought I knew how to temper my strong desire to contribute in the world by paying equal attention to my inner wellbeing. I was blithely unaware that this lesson is not one that you "master" and put on a shelf. In fact, like all aspects of dynamic balance, it's really not intended to be master-able. Balance is like a living organism, pulsing in and out, inhaling and exhaling, forever. How did I come to this understanding? Well, unfortunately, Spirit had to use the 2x4 method on me — again:

> *Several years ago, I was working as a creative production director for the Foundation for Global Humanity, the organization that I mentioned in Vital Key #3 on Integrity. I loved my work, which involved interviewing and filming indigenous peoples and leaders all over the world. My outer life was extremely active, but I also felt I was devoting plenty of time to my inner life too — at least in part, because the nature of my work was so nourishing to my soul. One day, as I was driving a few miles from my home, I stopped my car at a very busy crosswalk. Suddenly, I was slammed from behind by a car whose driver was talking on a cell phone.*
>
> *The jolt impacted my brainstem, spinal column, nervous system and motor coordination. The trauma not only affected me physically, but also mentally, impairing my cognitive skills and my ability to interact with people. I was unable to solve problems, complete tasks, or perform the multitude of activities I was so used to taking on with ease. I could neither interview people nor operate a video camera. In short, I was*

unable to function "normally" in any way, shape or form, and I was definitely unable to work. This lasted for over four months, in which I spent the majority of my time resting in bed.

I had to completely regroup. On one level, it felt devastating. I wondered what in the world had happened to me. I didn't ask "Why me?" but I did ask "Why? What was this situation trying to tell me?" Some people might say, "Things like this just happen" — and sometimes they do. But this incident felt like a 2x4 being used to get my attention — not just part of me, but all of me. So what was it about? Two answers eventually emerged.

First, I had to ask for help just to be able to eat and sustain my bodily functions. This was not easy for me because I usually played the role of giver rather than receiver. Still, I did it. Many extended a hand of support, and I grew to love and appreciate that! But I also felt there must be a deeper lesson.

Second, during those four months, I was only semi-mobile, so most of my time was spent horizontal, staring at my bedroom ceiling. My brain was so scrambled, much like the stories you hear about athletes with severe concussions, that I could neither work nor read. Slowly, it came to me: I couldn't DO anything! I could only BE.

I already knew that in order to live most fully and expansively, we must be able to balance Doing and Being. I knew this intellectually, and I was already meditating and engaging in other daily practices to support balance, but apparently it was not about doing more — but doing less. In those four months I learned that the wisdom of Being is endless, and I had barely scratched the surface.

During that time, I could have vanished into an endless out-of-body journey, traveling between worlds and dimensions or meditating without end. Those things were rather easy for me, yet I also knew that this was not what I was being called to learn. I was being taught "to simply Be" so that I might learn to ***dance*** *with balance.*

Without too much thinking or over-mentalizing about my state of Being, I began to experiment. When I was first injured, a dear friend

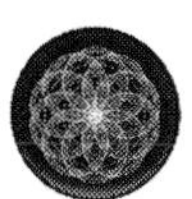

from across the country had sent me a dozen roses to wish me a speedy recovery. With assistance, I placed the roses on my dresser so I could see them from my bed. Every day, when I looked at those flowers, I felt my body expanding with gratitude. Love cascaded effortlessly between us, from me to the flowers and back again. This was such a genuine, heart-felt expression, that just recalling it now, I can feel myself welling up with tears.

Eight weeks into my challenging period of immobility, I was finally able to lift myself out of bed. I was heading to the kitchen to pour myself some orange juice when something wondrous happened. When I reached my bedroom threshold, I stopped abruptly, stunned by an insight that filled my awareness: Those lovely roses had been in semi-bloom for eight solid weeks! How could that possibly be?!

In that split second of awareness, I understood what it meant for me to just Be. In that state, I didn't have to Do anything. I only experienced love for those flowers and felt their love back to me. What an incredible gift! Knowing that love is always there, that it requires nothing but Being, I finally "knew" — that is, I gained wisdom through direct experience — how to Be the dance. And I understood that Being is the state of infinite loving presence in which all human and non-human life co-exists.

This experience with several months of non-doing gave me a multitude of gifts. Afterward, I made a point of always asking: "Is this a beneficial time to act?" I had not considered this question so intensely before. Just Being makes us intimately aware of time and no-time, of our bodies and nature as both physical and spiritual. The question, "Am I in alignment with a higher (global, cosmic) order?" begins to pulse inside us as we make decisions. It is like finding oneself in a totally dark room and cracking open a doorway to the light on the other side. The light comes in and everything changes.

Through my car accident, I also received deeper understanding of the power of thoughts, especially those fueled by love: I know that my loving thoughts kept those roses alive well beyond their normal term, and they also helped me to heal.

I emphasize that Being is not "better" than Doing. It is that we want to treat both as *equals*, and as equally necessary to our health and evolution. Most of our current technology is based on Doing. What would happen if we devoted as much time and attention to the "inner technology" represented by Being? What profound transformations could we bring into our world?

Personal to Global: Balancing Head with Heart, Logic with Intuition

"The very act of thinking has become relegated to only one type of mental rational aspect ... But really it's not like that ... [The word 'intuition'] now means 'Insight apart from reasoning.' It used to mean a sacred contemplation, a meditation ... [This] has obviously caused tremendous damage and we have to embrace the return arc ... because we need both in balance."[5]

~GLENN APARICIO PARRY
(Author, Founder of Circle for Original Thinking)

Head versus Heart and Logic versus Intuition are also imbalances that spring from cultural assumptions. There is an ancient Amazon prophecy about the Eagle and the Condor. This prophecy speaks of how human societies split to follow two different paths. One was the path of the mind, of logic and the masculine; this was the path of the Eagle. The other was the path of the heart, of intuition and the feminine; this was the path of the Condor. According to the prophecy, it is now time for these two to "fly together in the same skies" as equals and complements to each other.[6]

This prophecy also effectively describes the separation that has occurred *within* us — and the great need to bring the two together. The Eagle represents our left-brain, our logical, analytical, action-oriented side; the Condor is our right-brain, our intuitive, contemplative, insight-oriented side. Both sides are necessary to make us whole, but we in the West have valued the left brain over the right, and thus are out of balance with our own nature.

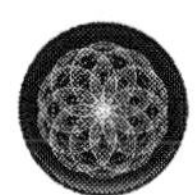

This inner imbalance is reflected in outer imbalance. The West has been dominated for thousands of years by the path of the Eagle, over-emphasizing activities based on logic and mind (giving rise to many of the problems discussed in previous vital keys). Balancing our analytical and results-driven behavior with heart-centered connectedness and spirit-based intuition (the path of the Condor) can move us back toward center.

In her amazing book and TED Talk, "My Stroke of Insight," Dr. Jill Bolte Taylor recounted her experiences during and after a stroke, which caused the left and right sides of her brain to be unable to communicate normally. This brilliant neuroscientist described the gift she was given by this shattering event, which was that she came to appreciate *equally* these two very different, but complementary, ways of experiencing and interacting with the world.

Jill found that her left hemisphere was the one that made her feel like a "solid individual, separate from the energy flow" around her, while her right hemisphere's view dissolved that separation. When she was in right-brain mode, the left brain went "totally silent" which meant that she experienced no "mind chatter." She said, "All of the relationships in the external world, and any stressor related to any of those, they were gone ... Imagine what it would feel like to lose 37 years of emotional baggage! ... It was beautiful."[7] As she continued her experience to near-death, Jill realized that she was still alive, and the following is what motivated her to recover:

> "And I pictured a world filled with beautiful, peaceful, compassionate, loving people who knew that they could come to this space at any time ... they could purposely choose to step to the right of their left hemispheres and find this peace ... What a stroke of insight this could be to how we live our lives!"[8]

Dr. Taylor's experience is an echo of the Eagle and Condor prophecy, reminding us that the seemingly opposing forces of mind and heart, logic and intuition, are each important *parts* of the Whole. We need to recognize the value in *all* of our parts, and integrate that understanding into our world systems, all the sectors of life including governance, technology, economics, health, etc. Here's a story demonstrating how this

was brought into business:

For several years, I worked for a medical firm that was creating a very large web-based system for dealing with medical insurance payments. The system was going to be used by doctors and patients over a wide geographic region. The website's designers were almost entirely young men who were inclined toward left-brain processing. Their focus was technical: getting an enormous amount of highly complex medical and bureaucratic procedural information into the system, and then streamlining that system so that the information would be distributed as quickly as possible to doctors, nurses and patients. This was not a simple task and required great ingenuity.

My main responsibility was to manage the writing of complex user manuals. To do this, I had to actually test the system myself. A prototype version of the system was up and running and being used — or it was ***supposed*** *to be — by several hundred doctors and patients. However, the company was discovering that the patients, most of whom were elderly, were refusing to use it. The company couldn't figure out why. When I began to test the system, I found* ***myself*** *getting lost and unable to follow the flow. I couldn't pinpoint why either, but I thought, "Geez! If I'm having trouble with this, how is an 80-year-old without computer experience going to manage it?"*

After several attempts at corrections, including content management and easier step-by-step instructions, the target population was still resistant. The company was in danger of being unable to complete their contract on time if they didn't find out what was wrong, and I was determined to assist in whatever way I could. The web designers believed the problem was due entirely to stubbornness, that "old people were computer-illiterate and unwilling to learn." This broad-brush prejudice disturbed me, and I felt it was an unfair assessment. I was convinced there must be more to it, but I couldn't identify the problem with my logical mind. So one night I sat and meditated on the question just before going to sleep. I was gifted with a very insightful dream:

In my dream, I saw an old man who looked just like George Burns in

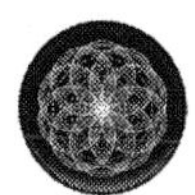

the movie "Oh, God!" He was covered with wrinkles and wore glasses that were about three inches thick. He stared through those thick lenses into my eyes and said (and I quote): "How the hell am I supposed to read the print on this goddamned website?? It's too small!" I could see that he was either clicking the wrong buttons or misunderstanding questions because he couldn't see them, and so he eventually just refused to participate in the entire process. It was brilliant!

The next day, I went and told the website designers what my insightful dream had indicated. They did not believe me. They all said, "There's no problem with the font size. It's plenty big enough." But they weren't looking with 80-year-old eyes. I said, "Okay, let's do a simple test. In the next release of the prototype system, add a one-page survey with the following question: 'Is this font size big enough?'"

Skeptically, they agreed to do this. The response was astounding. Approximately 80% of the patients said "NO!" This response was so overwhelming that the programmers immediately increased the font size, and wrote the final version of the system so users would have a choice of several (increasingly-larger) fonts. Usage transformed: nearly all patients began using the system.

A right-brained intuitive approach answered a crucial question that was not being answered by logic, and prevented the entire project from being scrapped. My colleagues thought it was unconventional and "out there" to get information from a dream, but they definitely appreciated the positive result obtained.

We might labor under the illusion that bringing more heart into our lives, and particularly into business, will make us sloppy, sentimental, and less productive. It's time to challenge that notion. The heart helps us to access our ethical and moral behaviors. It helps to bridge the gap between our spiritual selves and our human bodily selves. Both are sacred. For decades, I have been sharing the wisdom of the need to balance intuition and logic, head and heart, and I have seen corporations, non-profits, for-profits, and governmental agencies consistently manifest better results by bringing dynamic balance to this equation. They build effective collaborative teams, make discerning decisions and take adroit creative risks.

When human beings are free to dance on the continuum of head and heart, logic and intuition, being and doing — they won't be less productive, but more so, because they will be bringing *all of themselves* to the table — with greater health and passion too. Valuing all of our humanness is part of the paradigm shift towards dynamic balance.

Personal to Global: Balancing Masculine with Feminine

"The human race has exhausted the productive potential of the male-dominant model of civilization, and even before that, of the female-dominant model. We have seen the excesses and failures of both. The modern world desperately needs a new paradigm from which to explore its expanding universe if civilization is to survive ..."

~ARIEL TOMIOKA (QUOTING HER TEACHER "KYARI")
(Author, Spiritual Teacher)

Possibly the biggest imbalance that springs from cultural assumptions is the one between Masculine and Feminine. These terms refer to much more than just men and women; they refer to a constellation of capacities and perspectives that are built into the fabric of the Universe itself. In Asia, these universal energies are called "yin" (feminine) and "yang" (masculine). The yang or masculine principle is about power moving outward, i.e., external action. The yin or feminine principle is about power moving inward, i.e., internal action (like contemplating, imagining, and communing with spirit). Both of these energies are vital for us to thrive. To create balance in the world, both must be equally valued, and neither should predominate. Unfortunately, our culture has over-valued the masculine principle, and this has led to the devaluing of much of the feminine aspect, including heart-centeredness, connectedness, and intuition.

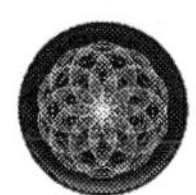

In my many professional roles — as a manager in both corporate and academic settings, and as an advisor or member on numerous boards, both for-profit and non-profit — I have seen things spiral out of control when the feminine principle is marginalized: the masculine principle is continually trying to take action (whether beneficial or not), while the feminine principle keeps calling for deep listening, intuition, and greater attention to wholeness. Many times when women attempt to speak up in these settings, or present an idea or insight, male colleagues interrupt. Women frequently either shut down, or they persevere only to get labeled a "pushy bitch." I've even been in positions where women were in the majority, and the feminine principles were still marginalized! That's how strong the paradigm is.

Devaluing the feminine is at the root of many of the problems already discussed in this vital key and others. Not caring for our body (our personal "Mother Earth") is one form of it. Allowing organizations to steamroll over individuals and their emotional needs is another form of it. Exploiting and destroying natural resources is yet another form of it. Dominant power behavior (Power Over) is, in general, an overly masculine approach. This is affecting almost everything in our lives and world. Bringing feminine and masculine back into balance is extremely important to our very survival.

As mentioned, masculine and feminine principles are actually universal. Physical males have feminine principles within them, and physical females have masculine principles within them. Therefore, devaluing the feminine actually hurts men as well as women.[9] In addition, women comprise about half of the global population and continue to increase in the overall workforce; their voices need to be heard, not silenced or diminished.

Bringing masculine and feminine into balance yields the same or similar benefits as other healing Keys — using Power With instead of Power Over, dissolving unhealthy Separation, honoring Truth, choosing Integrity, and balancing other elements in this chapter such as Doing and Being, Head and Heart — and for the same reasons. When we deny the existence of any part of ourselves, we are not in our Integrity and we have unhealthy Separation eating away at our sense of self. When we are out of balance with any part of ourselves, coming into balance heals and strengthens us. That balance can improve communication, increase collaboration, empower individuals and organizations, and heal physical, emotional and relational issues that spring from a lack of wholeness.

> *In the previous story about website usability issues, I was one of only a handful of women in a very male-dominated organization. In meetings, I noticed that most of the men tended to be somewhat dismissive of the women, even the female "techies." Luckily, about 10% of the males present were different: they were naturally very honoring of everyone in the group, regardless of gender or position. These men also happened to be in powerful positions. Because they acknowledged the value of my voice and presence, this eventually helped to convert the rest of the men to the idea, "Hey, maybe we should pay attention to the contributions of women and what they have to say." I am very grateful for their supportive leadership.*

I have also observed alpha males doing the same kind of overpowering and dismissing of input *from other men* if the other men were presenting in a more intuitive and/or gentle way — that is, the same issue of the feminine principle being overpowered, regardless of whether it came from a male body or a female one.

Just as with Doing vs. Being, and Heart vs. Head, the idea here is *not* for a masculine-dominated culture to now be "balanced" by having women take over! The only way out of imbalance is for *all* of our parts to be *equally* honored. Things are likely to get a little messy as we go through the process of rebalancing, and over-correction may show up for a while. In the long-run however, domination by *either* principle is out-of-balance! In fact, the whole *idea* of domination, with both "sides" fighting for supremacy is, in itself, a symptom of the masculine principle being out-of-balance. Women *do* want and need to be heard and seen, and this does need to be openly addressed because of the perpetuation of Power Over for the last several centuries. But no one will heal by over-valuing only half of the system.

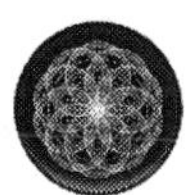

Men, too, need to heal from centuries of imbalance. In learning to *share* power, they will discover that nothing is lost, and much is gained. Pat McCabe, also known as "Woman Stands Shining," is a wonderful Native Diné (Navajo) Wisdom Keeper. During my Extraordinary Leadership Telesummit, she expressed this beautifully when she had this to say to men:

> "I want you to be as powerful as you possibly can be. I really want this for you. I will do everything I can to help you be that powerful man. The reason why I want to do that is that I'm asking you to use all that incredible power that you have, the power that you're designed to have, in service to thriving life ... That, to me, is the hope of the future."[10]

There are encouraging signs. In the past several years, the *feathers* of eagles and condors have been *physically found together* — actually on top of each other — in many places around the globe. Indigenous wisdom keepers believe this to be a sign that the prophecy of the Eagle and the Condor is coming true, and that humanity ***is*** reuniting its two halves. This gives me great hope that we can all learn to create that beautiful wisdom dance with Dynamic Balance, and lead with it going forward.

Balance Can Be Tricky in an Out-of-Balance World

In a world still dominated by Power Over, where out-of-balance is considered "normal," it may feel very weird to move towards balance. We may feel like alien interlopers in our own lives. Friends and family may be critical or frightened by our changes. We might get asked (angrily): "Don't you *care* anymore?" or "Are you crazy?" It is important to recognize that fear is almost always generated whenever someone challenges the status quo. This is true even when the status quo is painful! We can offer patience and compassion both to ourselves and to those who feel upset by our new behaviors and choices.

Sometimes, our move towards balance will actually cause long-time friendships or other relationships to dissolve. People who have come to rely on us being out-of-balance may feel frustrated, threatened or bereft when we don't want to dance that way any more. Again, compassion for everyone involved — including ourselves — is the key. For example, it's important not to let the resistance of others who are fearful of change prevent us from moving in the direction we want or need to go. This resistance might show up as aggression, angry arguments, "logical" reasons why what we're doing "will never work," and so on. We also need to remain aware of how much the culture supports out-of-balance in all areas of our lives, including entertainment, news, food, physical environments, leisure activities, etc. We may find ourselves needing to change the kind of reading material, radio programs, sports and other activities we allow into our lives to stay in balance.

Sometimes the resistance may show up inside *ourselves*. As with many of the other vital keys, when we start to change, it can cause "all our crap to come up." This is usually because of core wounds. All of the ways in which we are out-of-balance may become painfully obvious, whereas before, in our more *totally* out-of-balance lives, it was all a nice blur. This is when we need to have faith in ourselves, our spirit, and the process of transformation. We can feel overwhelmed and want to go back to the way it was, even though that way was imbalanced and didn't really work. We need to be forgiving and patient, and trust in our process. The spiritual teacher Ram Dass expressed this beautifully:

> "The universe is made up of experiences that are designed to burn out our reactivity, which is our attachment, our clinging — to pain, pleasure, fear, all of it. And as long as there are places where we are vulnerable, the universe will find ways to confront us with it. That's the way the dance is designed."[11]

We also need to recognize that there are particular situations and stages in our evolution and growth where imbalance is *likely* to occur. At those times, it's critical to identify this as a *systemic* issue, rather than finding fault with an individual. For example, adolescence is a time of great change, which often produces confusion, rebellion and a great deal of "out-of-balance-ness." It is important for both those experiencing the

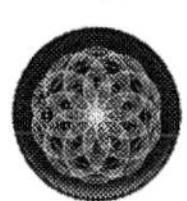

imbalances and those who have to live with them to recognize that these things are "normal." Our role, then, is to *guide* the other toward balance rather than trying to Power Over the imbalance. Similarly, in organizations, there are times when transformation occurs as part of normal evolution, and trying to hang on to "the way things were" can create a brutally out-of-balance environment. "The Founder's Syndrome" that I mentioned earlier is one such example. It is crucial in such times to discern the larger pattern, rather than blaming one person or a group for the balance problems.

This is particularly true when it comes to gauging *our own* growth and evolution. Many of us have been taught to be perfectionists, especially with ourselves. This can severely interfere with our dance with Dynamic Balance. In addition to causing us to beat ourselves up, it also short-circuits our connection with spirit. We have to lovingly retrain ourselves to know when something is "good enough."

What would you do in balance to help change the dynamic or systems that no longer serve? Sometimes, rather than relying on our default reactions (like gossip, bad-mouthing or withdrawing, etc.), we must "break down to breakthrough," regroup (and gather support to encourage healthy expressions of Power, Truth, Integrity and Wholeness) and attain a new balance at a higher level. For example, Robert, the computer programmer who was *not allowed to go to his own mother's funeral*, decided, after months of recovering from the experience, that for his own balance as a leader, he would 'fight' for himself and confront those responsible for his inhumane treatment. Hesitantly, but out of necessity, he solicited support from other colleagues. With their combined voices for balance, they were able to initiate and set important change into motion. As a result of these courageous efforts, new company policies were created that implemented structures to more fairly address handling both family and work crises.

And other times, we just have to leave! Several times in my career, I found myself in situations where the dynamic balance between masculine and feminine was so consistently dishonored that I chose to resign. Sometimes I held out far too long, hoping that the circumstances would shift into balance, but such changes usually don't happen unless the leaders set the foundation for that to occur. In other words, they must lead by example — and if they had been doing that, the imbalance wouldn't have been there in the first place. Decisions to leave are never easy, and may cause sleepless nights, but we have to determine within ourselves how torn we are about trying to encourage a change of heart versus how abusive it feels to stay.

A Call to Action: Bringing Greater Balance into Our Lives and World

"To achieve such a state of dynamic balance, a radically different social and economic structure will be needed: a cultural revolution in the true sense of the word. The survival of our whole civilization may depend on whether we can bring about such change." [12]

~FRITJOF CAPRA
(Physicist, Author)

Extraordinary leaders are greatly needed to ignite the evolutionary changes the world so desperately needs. These leaders must be heart-centered and open-minded — people willing to question, take risks and realign with the "Spirit at the Center" that our indigenous relations kept sacred. Their motivation must be to heal humanity rather than to satisfy an ego-ic desire for recognition. These leaders must be committed to the principle of Dynamic Balance in all its many forms. When that commitment is coupled with a worldview that affirms the value of all beings and our planet, then the ultimate balance will begin to form — the balance between human will and divine will.

What might this look like? Here are a few ideas of whole-scale changes our planet can use:

- Wouldn't it be amazing if teams of heart-centered, dynamically balanced leaders could collaborate with oil companies and nations to direct their efforts toward clean "free energy," energy that allows *all*

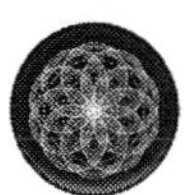

people to thrive, not just the privileged few? Simultaneously, this could save our earth from the devastation of Nature-destroying activities (previously-mentioned, e.g., oil spills, drilling, fracking, etc.)

- What if we committed to the health and wellbeing of all? What if we committed to complete veracity regarding the efficacy of pharmaceuticals and to remaining open-minded about exploring alternatives, both ancient and new?
- What if we ensured greater equality in the jobs given to domestic workers and those outsourced? There are unique ways to balance both, while providing training for those who need it the most.
- Wouldn't it be great if the whole world moved toward governance that is not corrupted by special interests, but instead is truly "of, by and for the people"?

The challenge is nothing short of monumental! It is urgent that we examine and retool *virtually everything*, from our core beliefs and assumptions to our socio-economic and political systems and structures. This change must be evolutionary rather than revolutionary. We don't need a radical shift to yet another extreme. We need persistent attention to dancing the dance of Dynamic Balance. Such an approach will be more effective because it addresses the notion that everything is connected: it is all one big system, and that system is designed for dynamic balance.

Begin with Yourself

As leaders, we must first do whatever is necessary to bring *ourselves* into balance. We must do this because the current systems, "legitimized" by Power Over, certainly won't do it for us. Chronic imbalance of power pushes our limits. Impossible schedules, outrageous demands, the model of continuous growth — these must be countered with our own inner truth: "Do I really feel good about this? Does this feel right, even, sustainable?" If the answer is "no," then we may have to make hard decisions that defy the prevailing cultural patterns — like saying "No" to top-down management styles, "No" to projects that would make a profit but damage the environment or harm other beings, "No" to eating fast-food that our bodies reject — "No" to a lot of things we've come to accept as "normal." The culture might not approve, and may even label us as "crazy" but by saying "No" to these things, we open up space to say "Yes" to those decisions that support Power With, Truth, Integrity, Wholeness and Balance.

When we *are* operating in Dynamic Balance, we feel it; our energetic field naturally wants to expand. We can see the bigger picture, and we're better able to "go with the flow" rather than forcing something that really doesn't want to happen. We're also better able to serve as impartial witnesses to our own actions and those of others, because we're not tethered to emotional roller coasters. The more we experience this, the more we will experience centeredness, focus and even peace within ourselves.

To help my clients attune to Dynamic Balance, I advise them to ask themselves a number of questions, such as:

- Am I out of balance in my life? If so, where?
- What might I do to bring myself back into balance?
- When I am out of balance, where in my body do I experience it and how? Do I feel energized or deflated? Is my heart open or closed?
- What emotions come up as I reflect on balance in my life and work?

First and foremost, each of us must attend to ourselves — our bodies, our minds, our emotional and spiritual wellbeing. This includes attending to our belief systems and our model of the world. There is no substitute for our own inner work. Below are some practices to help guide this journey.

Balance Your Body

First, we need to pay attention to the amount and quality of our sleep: ensure enough time to sleep; provide a restful environment (dark, quiet, turn off the phone ringer); "wind down" prior to sleep by engaging in activities to center and quiet the mind rather then "revving up" (e.g.,

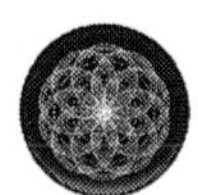

reading a thriller or watching the news prior to sleep may not be the best choice).

Other recommended practices are to not go to bed angry or with other emotional intensity, and to implement techniques for minimizing the negative impact of renegade emotions. Seek tools to calm down, including daily meditation practices to help create that inner space needed for a restful sleep on a regular basis.

If interested, the dreamtime space can also provide gifts, clues and solutions to challenges and problems faced or hidden during the day. We can explore on our own or join dream circles and community groups versed in evoking personal dream interpretation.

If sleep simply will not come (and it is not a chronic experience), try not to become anxious about it; the body may simply be re-adjusting. If insomnia is chronic, seeking professional assistance may help to determine the root causes and the most effective solutions for each person, their body type and their personality.

We also need to pay attention to our nutrition. What works or doesn't for our particular body? Analytical types may want to get a baseline of vital medical statistics — blood work, heart functionality, etc. — what is healthy for each of us statistically speaking, and are we willing to live up to our optimal self? If not already doing so, *read labels.* Buy food *consciously.* Along with that, we need to find the right balance for our particular body between exercise, recreational activities, rest, and work, as well as activities that nourish our minds and creativity.

Balance Your Emotions

Balanced emotional engagement improves effective communication, allows for calmer interactions, better relationships, and collaborations that work and create greater impact in the world. If we feel that our voice is being "shot down" or that what's important to us is being ignored, we still need to keep trying to express ourselves — but in a healthy way. If we're in a position to create forums where people can express their views and be heard, let's do so. We also need to practice discernment and constructive criticism rather than judgment for judgment's sake of self or others. We need to identify any areas where we are trying to overly control our emotions or other people versus expressing our emotional truth in a balanced way.

Emotional balance also includes identifying any extreme personal beliefs or expressions that could cause harm to others or ourselves, and bringing ourselves into a place of moderation. For example, we may show up with too much perfectionism because we really fear we're not "good enough." Ironically, this false identity might be preventing us from bringing forth our best work. How can we bring that into greater balance? Katherine Woodward Thomas and Clair Zammit have done some amazing work in this arena, and created "The Transformation of Identity MATRIX" to begin the process of personally exploring this subject.[13]

We also need to watch how we as leaders react in a crisis. Wise leaders and wisdom keepers balance emotional reactions very well — with calm, strong, decisive action, after contemplation and expressing emotions (including anger, upset and fear) in the healthiest ways possible. So, we need to pick our battles judiciously, and if our emotions are ignited, take the time to get centered. If we want to share our perspective on the primary reason for our upset and/or we want our message to be heard, we need to balance our verbal and non-verbal communication so that the other person can take it in.

A Balanced Approach to Money in Your Life

Creating a balanced approach to manage all our resources, including money, is foundational for extraordinary leadership. At times, this can be challenging because we've been indoctrinated with the idea that "more is always better," and the objective of a business is always growth, as quickly as possible. But that is not necessarily the best approach. We are meant to live in balance around giving and receiving — like breathing in and breathing out. If we tend to receive more than our share, we can create strategies and structures that facilitate giving — and vice versa. This

might be easier than we imagine. To bring more balance into our relationship with money, consider asking the following:

- Am I in dynamic balance around giving and receiving?
- How balanced am I toward money in both my personal and professional lives? Do I have enough? How much is enough? What do I consider greedy?
- What do I do, or want to do, with my money now, and in the future?
- Consider having a *dialogue with money* and be open to hearing the responses.
- Also consider exploring Lynne Twist's re-visioning of the nature of money in terms of "sufficiency" in her book *The Soul of Money*, and then asking: How does this new information affect my relationship to money and how can I balance that with the work I hope to do in the world? Another book that can help change our attitudes toward money is Charles Eisenstein's *Sacred Economics.*

Balance in Your Relationships

Leaders often feel that they can't be 100% committed to *both* their family and their professional life; they believe one or the other has to take a hit. This does not need to be the case — in fact, balance is crucial! Having gone through this journey with several clients, I can testify that it is possible to create a healthy balance between the two, so long as fierce self-care is in the mix. For example, leaders can make a commitment to limit the number of hours they devote to their work, delegate responsibility to others, and follow-through on their commitments to family as zealously as they do to commitments at work. This can involve creating date nights with spouses/partners, taking the time to play with children when they're young, and listening deeply when they're older. Leaders need to let their loved ones know they love them by giving them *quality time*, not necessarily objects and things. Those material objects might be appreciated, but they will eventually be discarded, while memories of a parent or partner who truly cares will last forever.

Balance Head with Heart, Logic with Intuition

A more integrated dance between the head and the heart is critical to move forward in our evolution. Inviting more of the heart if we tend to be in our head will allow for connections to be made and the relational parts of leadership[14] to flourish. Conversely, inviting in more of our head will improve our reasoning, and our ability to make decisions with full consideration of past errors and the learning that comes from them. It is very important not to suppress intuition, nor to villainize logic. Both are necessary to function within our world. Indigenous cultures, having danced this dance for many millennia, have much to teach us about ways to wisely integrate both head and heart.

Over the years, I have developed a method that incorporates Power With approaches alongside Truth, Integrity, Wholeness and Dynamic Balance into a "think-tank" framework. I call it "Divine Leadership: A Think-Tank/Heart-Tank Experience," which is part of my Extraordinary Leadership Certification Program. It emerged through my work with new forms of governance and has been extremely powerful and successful for participating leaders.[15] Many of those involved have graciously shared their insights from doing these practices, describing them as "significantly and positively impacting their lives, both personally and professionally." I invite all leaders to consider participating in a think-tank/heart-tank of this nature as part of their dynamic balance practice, like those offered through my business, Lead By Wisdom, incorporating each of the Vital Keys from this book.

Balance Masculine with Feminine

Leaders might consider using the following practices to evoke their divine feminine and masculine:

1. With curiosity, list all the feminine qualities you have. Note which ones you believe are life-affirming. Then list all the masculine qualities you have. Again, note which ones you believe are life-affirming.

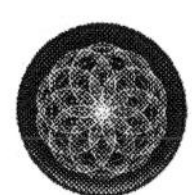

2. Which masculine and feminine qualities do you appreciate in those you work with or in your intimate partner or friends?
3. Try an exercise from "Woman Stands Shining":
   What do you inherently love and trust about the feminine?
   What do you inherently love and trust about the masculine?

Consider sharing your answers with others in creative dialogue in an effort to develop pathways toward greater balance.

Balance Doing with Being

We each need to determine for ourselves where our dynamic balance lies with Doing versus Being. Like everything else, it will probably change from moment to moment. I encourage us all to pay attention to the warning signs of burnout and *stop* before it happens. Take time to refresh and recharge: We do it with batteries and power tools; let's do it with ourselves! We don't have to be slammed from behind or whacked with a 2x4 to choose to honor our spiritual centers.

Whenever we find ourselves clinging to any sort of dualistic extremes — head over heart, masculine over feminine, Power Over instead of Power With — we need to stop, and then ask ourselves if this is really for the highest good. If it isn't, release it and seek dynamic balance. Dynamic balance doesn't mean that head/heart, logic/intuition, doing/being, masculine/feminine need to be in equal portions *every instant*. It is the *overall* balance that needs to be equal, with the ebb and flow depending on what is called for in each moment. If viewed from far above, it might indeed look like a dance: *Oops, too much head, not enough heart; Okay, now we need to include some logical steps for people to complete their projects; Ahh, now it's time to sleep,* etc. We respond to the changing rhythms of circumstances as a dancer might when the music shifts from the tango to a waltz or to jazz.

Commit to Balance in your Organizations

As leaders, we are the stewards of our organizations. We can assess how dynamically balanced our organization is by asking questions like the following:

- During meetings, do people feel interrupted or unheard?
- Are there frequent misalignments between and amongst the team members on issues, ideas, or solutions?
- Is there a constant push to make decisions without taking the time to reflect, troubleshoot or dialogue about the best solutions?
- Do meetings feel like they contain too much emotional processing?
- Are we frequently missing deadlines?

If the answer to any one of these (and other related) questions is yes, it's likely there are some imbalances within the organization that need attention.

Organizations also need to consider their balance between masculine and feminine principles. As leaders, it is important to assess what is happening overall in our organization regarding minimizing the feminine gifts of deep listening, receptivity, wholeness, silence, intuitive pieces or hidden influences.

- Ask: How balanced have we been in making our most important decisions?
- If decisions are routinely pushed through without adequate reflection, the masculine might need to be minimized and the feminine brought to the fore. Conversely, if there is too much processing without making crucial decisions, the masculine might need to be more accentuated.
- Create a space in which the masculine can be supported by the feminine and vice versa. Watch the results. (They will usually be amazing: forward-thinking and effective decisions will be made carefully yet in a timely fashion.)

A Balanced Approach to Money in Your Organization

There is no ignoring the reality of the economic crunch and the devastating impact it has had on a huge percentage of the population.

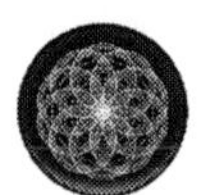

Stephen Dinan, creator of the Shift Network, cautioned that, when it comes to economic challenges, we should not "focus too much on a collective climate ... [because] that puts things outside of [our] control ... [and makes us] into the victim ..."[16] I support these sentiments, however, I also believe that people in leadership positions would help their teams tremendously by addressing their economic concerns in a straightforward and transparent manner. This includes work in circle structures (like dialogue groups and distributed-power governance meetings) to create consent around the balance of fair compensation and the exchange of goods and services, and other intrinsic motivations. Although addressing the fiscal issues of an organization can often feel like a juggling act with the leader as the "bad guy or gal," most people do appreciate this more direct and open approach.

To move your organization toward balance (and transparency) with regard to money, here are some questions leaders need to ask:

- How balanced is my organization with respect to money?
- How will I distribute funds when my business or organization grows? Do I apply the majority of funds to salaries or to programs?
- Do I put vendors in impossible positions by demanding "good, fast *and* cheap"?
- How much do I allocate for myself? Many entrepreneurs don't think of themselves when allocating monies for projects and salaries; they forget that they, too, need a buffer (like a passive income stream) to pay their bills in case they become ill or otherwise unable to work.

Reach Out for Support

We are all, at times, oblivious to our own imbalances. In our world of "do-do-do" and ever-increasing demands, we can become inadvertently blind to what is most important to us, including the people we love and care about. This is why it is so helpful to have a mentor, a dear friend or a support group — someone we trust — to "call us on our shit before it's too late," as some of my clients would say. It's important that we don't allow the ego-ic, prideful belief that "I don't need anybody's help" to bury us in a life that eats away at our core, robs us of joy and destroys our ability to lead with greater wisdom.

We can also reach out to the divine assistance that is always there to help us. When we do this, and reconnect with our highest selves and spirit on a regular basis, we are usually reminded to "stop and smell the roses." That is, we are asked to consider our feelings and relationships as being just as important as our actions. We are asked to truly care about our friends, families and colleagues as much as we do about our work and our desire for money and possessions. Spirit also reminds us to treat our beloved Earth as if it, too, were a dear friend — because it is. Seeking dynamic balance is well worth the effort; it seeds our extraordinary leadership so we can grow our extraordinary work. Our collective dream calls us forward in this endeavor, urging us to value and give voice to all our parts, all cultures, all peoples, all beings.

Vital Key #6:

Remembering Our Miraculous Nature

"There are two ways to live. One is as though nothing is a miracle. The other is as though everything is a miracle."

~ALBERT EINSTEIN
(Theoretical Physicist, Philosopher)

As we develop our capacities as extraordinary leaders, we will be called to connect more directly to our higher selves, our wholeness and All That Is. This call is especially significant for this Vital Key — to help us remember our miraculous nature. We live in very stressful times, as the daily news continuously reinforces, and it is easy to become discouraged. In private, many leaders have confessed to a deep and troubling concern that they are losing faith in themselves and in the future of our planet. Whenever we're tempted to give up on everything, that's a sign that we're forgetting the real truth, which is that we, each of us, are miracles living in a miraculous world.

I'm convinced that one of the reasons why I'm here on this planet at this time is to keep reminding us of that essential truth! I am also convinced that if we redirect our attention *away* from external chaos, and instead focus on remembering who we really are, we can positively impact the world in ways beyond what logic and intellect alone can conceive as possible. If we can learn to acknowledge and work with our own transcendence, we will begin to see possibilities, even under seemingly impossible circumstances, and it will give us the courage we need to lead during these chaotic times.

I will take this one step further: if we really understood how miraculous we are, virtually *anything* would be possible.

We Are Miraculous

"Miraculous: ... Occurring through divine or supernatural intervention, or manifesting such power; Highly improbable and extraordinary, and bringing very welcome consequences."

~OXFORD DICTIONARY

The human being is an amazing creature. We are capable, through training, practice and determination, of achieving astonishing things. Who hasn't been awed by athletic prowess, consummate artistic performances, or brilliant inventions? But I believe that no matter how accomplished we are, it's likely that we're realizing only a *small portion* of our true potential.

Everyone comes into this world with gifts and capabilities. Some we recognize and make use of, but many we never explore. I believe that each of us has untapped capacities, individual gifts and talents that we have never fully expressed, perhaps for want of encouragement or opportunity. On the global level, the boundaries of our collective power are unknown, our potential for synergy virtually untested. This is due, at least in part, to the overwhelming presence of Power Over, which keeps us separated. Remembering our miraculous nature invites us to change this dynamic.

What is Human Nature?

Throughout the centuries, many individuals have demonstrated "unusual" powers, such as precognition, distance viewing, seeing energy fields, and being able to communicate with animals and plants.[1] Giving credence to

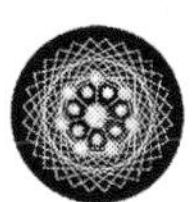

such capabilities may strain our current understanding of our human nature, but do we really know what our human nature is? Is it as fixed as we might think, or are there even more extraordinary gifts hiding, unexpressed, in the strands of our DNA? Even though our science has unlocked many details of our genetic code, a great deal of our DNA has no currently known function. Many esoteric researchers believe our "extraneous" DNA is responsible for mystical capabilities and interactions, and for collective possibilities that have not yet been explored.[2] Who and what would we be if we found the key to unlocking those hidden gifts?

As a species, we are still evolving. So, in truth, we don't really know what our limits are. Michael Murphy, in his groundbreaking book, *The Future of the Body*, makes that very case with respect to the human body. There is evidence, he writes, of enormous, yet-to-be-fully-developed potential. For example, there are extraordinary experiences of perception being extended in all kinds of ways. Some wine tasters can make ten thousand discriminations; some perfume testers can make 30,000 distinctions. People can train their eyesight to far greater acuity than was ever thought possible. Many people can hear beyond the "normal" decibel and frequency limits.[3]

And what about extrasensory perception (ESP)? Although anecdotal evidence of ESP has been around for centuries, scientific research is only now beginning to verify it. For example, people can be trained to perform what is called "remote viewing"[4], which is using the mind, usually with a specifically structured protocol, to seek impressions of an unseen or distant target (beyond our normal five senses). This is being explored at the Stanford Research Institute (SRI), the Institute of Noetic Sciences (IONS), the Monroe Institute and other reputable training and educational facilities throughout the world. Although our culture often "pooh-poohs" these activities, serious military- and government-sponsored research into these phenomena has been conducted, in secret, for decades.

Indigenous healers and shamans have, for thousands of years, divined the healing properties of plants through direct communication with those plants, or through dreams and visions.[5] Many Western doctors and pharmaceutical companies have begun collaborating with these healers to develop new medicines from the plants identified in this way.

There is also a growing body of evidence supporting the existence of phenomena such as psychic healing, channeling and past lives. Edgar Cayce, the "Sleeping Prophet," during his lifetime and beyond, helped to heal people from ailments of the body, mind and spirit using information he had obtained via channeling.[6] Thousands to millions of people in the world today do "energy work" on their own bodies, on others, on plants, animals and the world at large with positive results. Jane Roberts, an American author, poet and spiritual medium, channeled an energy personality named "Seth" to help to bring forward information relevant to topics like *The Nature of Personal Reality, The Eternal Validity of the Soul,* lessons in ESP and volumes more. She followed in the footsteps of previous pioneers in this field, and many have followed after her.[7] Dr. Ian Stevenson, the Canadian-born psychiatrist, was fascinated with the study of human perception, and spent most of his life researching the paranormal. Traveling extensively for over forty years to investigate three thousand cases of children who claimed to remember past lives, he became known internationally for his meticulous research into reincarnation.[8] Others, such as hypnotherapist Dr. Michael Newton, have followed similar paths.[9] These are but a few examples.

Such reports may strain the bounds of believability for many Westerners, but I bring them up to make a point: We need to drop any conviction that we know our limits — either personally or as a species —because we don't. The upper limit of our capacities is undetermined. In fact, it appears that the primary source of limitation is our cultural programming. How willing are we to explore beyond our current boundaries, beyond what our belief system says is possible?

"Our Miraculous Nature" refers to both the gifts we are already aware of and using, plus those not yet in our awareness. If up until now, we have related to the world with just a small fragment of our total being, it's because of our limited view of who we are. But if we begin to expand the boundaries of what we believe defines us, then the world all around us will expand as well, and more will become possible.

Our Miraculous Nature

When we are in that space of expanded possibility, the most unusual yet meaningful "coincidences" begin to occur. Sometimes these are small things, like two friends unknowingly buying the same uniquely patterned shirt on the same day. Sometimes the events are larger, and deeply emotional, like former colleagues who have not been in contact for ten years suddenly and simultaneously calling each other. We see this expansion of creative, curative power frequently with identical twins, especially if one has been injured. My mother is an identical twin, and whenever her sister has been ill, my family has witnessed their miraculous connection: the more strongly my mom believes that her sister will heal, the more quickly she does, and visa versa. Doctors often wonder how this happens, but if we remember our miraculous nature, it is not that mysterious. Identical twins usually know how real their connection is because they already have an expanded sense of themselves and each other.

The famous psychologist Dr. Carl Jung used the word "synchronicity" to describe such events. Jung coined this term to refer to the "occasionally observed phenomena of *meaningful interactions* of events, objects and internal states of mind."[10] He had been observing such incidents for decades and discussing them with the leading thinkers of his day, including physicists Albert Einstein and Wolfgang Pauli. Through these discussions, Jung clarified a description of synchronicity's operation. This was described in the "Synchronicity: Matter and Psyche Symposium" on www.matterpsyche.net as follows:

> "Where Einstein had found time and space to be relative to one another, Jung saw in synchronicity the relativity of matter to psyche. Just as the mystery of the effects of the observer on matter in quantum physics were demonstrating the relation of inner state to outer matter, so, too, were the local, material occurrences of events [outer world] related to inner states. In both ways, we were consciously observing the interaction of matter and psyche."[11]

Jung believed that synchronistic events are evidence of a unified reality —

the "unus mundus," or "One World." If All is One, then is there really any separate "self" distinct from the Universe? If the boundaries between the self and the Universe dissolve, then are there really any limits? Such a reality includes all the possibilities of using synergy between individuals, groups and entire populations, as well as between people and all other life on the planet. Some of these synergies are currently being explored as presented in later sections.

There is one additional dimension of our miraculous nature that I would like to address: I believe we have the potential to tap into the *divine power* that makes what we now call "miracles" possible. The more we recognize that we truly are one with All That Is, the more we will be able to exercise those divine capacities. The more open we are to this idea, the more likely it is that miracles will show up, in our lives and in our world.

I believe this understanding changes our "job description" as leaders. In sum, I believe our job is to *increase the probability of the miraculous occurring* in the world, including in our teams and organizations. And I believe we are already moving in that direction. Miracles do indeed surround us, and many of us have witnessed miraculous events in our personal lives, if not on the global stage. We simply need to shake off our temporary amnesia.

Why We Separate from, and Forget, Our Miraculous Nature

The world is itself miraculous, and all it takes to remind us of that is to witness time-lapse images of the development of a fetus, or the intricate interdependence of hummingbirds, bees, flowers and trees (as seen in the magnificent work of Louie Schwartzberg[12]), or the fascinating images sent back to Earth from the Hubble space telescope.

But this truth seems to fade into oblivion as our daily tasks, both at work and at home, demand our constant attention, and the various societal crises and distractions lower our energy and tunnel our vision. As leaders, we often get caught up in the demands associated with being

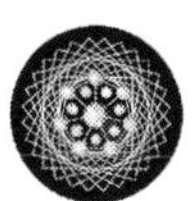

responsible for our companies and their deliverables, budgets and forecasts, as well as all the people we "take on." Then, we allow stress to creep in and overwhelm us. Listening becomes burdensome, and the idea of asking for help from anyone, much less the divine, gets buried. This is when we forget that we are interconnected and already One with All That Is. Instead, we think we are all alone, which blinds us to the unseen support that surrounds us. In this state, we can even find that a reminder to "keep believing" becomes an *annoyance.* Have you ever found yourself snapping at someone who says "keep the faith" when your business or home life (or both) feel like they're falling apart?

There's something perversely seductive about being in the "alone" place. We feel like the world is on our shoulders and only ***we*** are capable of delivering the goods. It's part of the myth of heroic individualism that American culture celebrates. But the moment we begin thinking we're heroic for going it alone is the very moment we forget our miraculous nature. Ironically, it's that very thinking that disconnects us from All That Is, and makes us much *less* likely to produce the "miracles" we (or our bosses) would like!

Even as children, we are not encouraged to acknowledge our miraculous nature. Instead, we are bombarded by external stimuli from every direction, and expected to act on all of it; in short, we're encouraged to Do rather than Be. We get rewarded for "concrete results" and admonished for "daydreaming" or being "irrational." In his book, *The Power of Limits,* György Doczi points out that "irrational" doesn't mean "without reason," but rather "*beyond* reason."[13] Our miraculous nature is indeed beyond our current, limited reasoning.

In addition, many of us experienced early conditioning that it was dangerous or inappropriate to explore some of our gifts. For example, if our parents were very pragmatic, we might have been discouraged from expressing our creativity or voicing a desire to pursue the arts. Others of us may have been ostracized or even punished if we spoke of dreams or visions considered precognitive, or if we seemed able to sense what people were about to say before they spoke, or if we happened to be able to communicate with animals or plants. *Most* children have these abilities,

but our culture programs them out. In this way, forgetting our miraculous nature is one of our earliest core wounds.

When such programming takes us over, we *appear* to lose our miraculous abilities. We begin to just take ourselves for granted, no longer feeling awe and wonder over ourselves or the world. Simultaneously, we stop acknowledging our special gifts. By the time we have become "responsible" adults, any memory of these gifts is so deeply buried, it may take a crowbar to retrieve it. This chapter's vital key *is* that crowbar! Those abilities are not really lost, but only submerged.

When I was a child, a reminder of our miraculous nature came to me in the form of a divine intervention. This was one of my most significant early learning experiences. It demonstrated the presence of universal support, and taught me that we never have to face problems alone:

> *One evening when I was eight years old and being watched by a babysitter, I saw a movie that encouraged an open attitude toward interracial relationships. Moved by the film, I concluded that I might some day want to marry a man outside my race. Excited, I shared this news with my parents.*
>
> *My dad responded, with great vehemence, "I would disown you!"*
>
> *I was astonished and stopped in my tracks. My sensitive little mind couldn't believe what my dad had just said, and he wasn't backing down. I was so upset that I ran to my room, grabbed my tiny suitcase, threw in a couple of outfits and ran out of the house — an action I had not ever taken previously or since.*
>
> *The only place that I could think to go was to my best friend's house about a half-mile down the road. My friend immediately asked me what was wrong. Through tears, I babbled my story. At first there was deafening silence and then, in a very defiant voice, my friend said, "I would disown you, too!"*
>
> *I was stunned. Was the whole world like this? I felt mortified that everyone seemed to think my idea was so radical that they wouldn't even want to know me! I felt boxed into a corner. I had to get away to*

try to make sense of what was happening. I ran out of my friend's house too, and toward the forest behind my grandparents' farm. By this time, it was dusk, but I ran and ran, tears streaming down my face, until I couldn't run any more. Finally, in total exhaustion, I dropped down onto a rock that was covered in moss. I cried uncontrollably until I could barely breathe.

Then, suddenly, a wave of peace came over me. I'd never experienced anything like it before. It felt like the arms of the Eternal Mother were embracing me with love, letting me know that it was all okay. As wave after wave of this vibration passed through me, I began to smile and felt compelled to lift my head. I peered into the night and saw the light of the moon illuminating an enormous tree in front of me. I looked up above the tree and saw what I can only describe as a very large angel. It was a figure of incredible luminosity that looked like what I imagined the Virgin Mother to look like, except this Being seemed both masculine and feminine. The angel gazed down at me and spoke in the most beautiful voice directly into my mind:

> *"Beloved child, we are with you. You are loved and will always be loved. What you experienced is something very harsh for your tender age, but we are here to remind you of what you already know. As you live your life, there will be times when you will need to turn away from those you love, because they do things that are against Great Spirit's loving nature. And even with that, we ask you to still honor your parents. Love them deeply, but know that there will be times when you must turn away. When this occurs, know that we are always here, and you can turn to us in times of need and in times of joy. Thank you for your courage. Thank you for your love. Blessings to you always, dearest one! We will meet again."*

And with that, the angel disappeared.

This experience was profound. I realized, in that moment, that my parents, although older and more knowledgeable, were human and fallible, and that, as much as I loved them, I'd sometimes need to rely on other sources for support. I believe this was an example of the miraculous "God source" or universal energy assisting me on my path.

From that point forward, I was determined to live my life serving humanity with the same loving energy I had experienced from that angelic being.

With that thought, I asked for assistance in returning home, as it was now very dark. I was guided to follow the sounds of a stream until I made my way back to the road that led home.

Although I spoke to my parents briefly about my experience, I didn't tell them all the details because my gut told me it was not the right time. But I did begin asking my father why he felt as he did and, as time went on, I developed a much greater understanding of his point of view and he of mine. Over time, we have "walked a mile in each others shoes," learning how to have deep compassion for each other as well as how to honor each other's unique perspectives. My parents have both changed significantly, stimulated in part by this event, and if I chose to be in an interracial relationship, I believe that my parents would accept that person with open arms. More importantly, I know I would be guided by a loving, divine source, no matter what.

My experience is by no means unique. Over the years, I've witnessed numerous examples of miraculous interventions where people have received guidance from an unseen source that shifted their way of being and leading in the world. This guidance could take the form of angels, spirit guides, Master teachers, loved ones who are passed, and others. From family and friends, to colleagues and clients, both in the U.S. and abroad, many people have told me that when they listen to their intuition or open themselves up to the great mysteries, they experience deep shifts in their lives.

I especially remember a time, years ago, when my father was terrified that one of my teenage brothers would be forever controlled by a cult he had joined. My dad was worried in a way I had never seen before; his many sleepless nights were negatively affecting his attitude toward our whole family as well as his performance at work. Then, one day, something happened that helped him come to resolution. He described his experience this way:

"All of a sudden, I heard this voice whispering in my left ear:

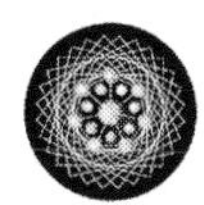

'Everything is going to be okay. Just let go, it's okay!' I quickly looked in both directions to see who was talking to me, but there was no one in the room. Over the years, I have received messages from God; they were sent to my heart or my mind. But that day, it must have been important enough that God wanted me to hear it in my ears, loud and clear." (And everything did eventually turn out okay.)

For decades, I have been facilitating workshops on "Balancing Logic and Intuition in the Workplace," "Harnessing Intuition in the Business World," "Creating Optimal Performance by Balancing Logic and Intuition" and "Leadership Beyond the Norm" (which included training in psychic development). Yet, even now, certain words will deter leaders because they fear these ideas are still "unacceptable." Why do we deny ourselves these gifts when, deep down, we know how beneficial they can be?

Change takes time. In the Vital Key on Truth, Arthur Schopenhauer was quoted as saying that all truth passes through three stages: first it is ridiculed, then it is violently opposed, and then it is accepted as self-evident. Our Power Over culture currently still ridicules and opposes mystical explorations that return sovereignty and power to the individual, even when these processes are firmly grounded in scientific experimentation.

The Scientific Bases for Miracles: The Power of Thought

"Miracles are a retelling, in small letters, of the very same story which is written across the whole world in letters too large for some of us to see."

~C.S. LEWIS
(Christian Theologian and Author)

Just to be clear, when I speak of the miraculous, I am not talking about self-delusion, made-up possibilities or drug-induced escapes. I am referring to events that somatically resonate and are experienced as *real* — you feel it in your bones, or in your solar plexus or in your heart; you may even experience goosebumps, regardless of the temperature,

tingling in your hands, surging energy flows inside your body, and so on.

Some of these events and experiences cannot be empirically tested. However, many of them can and have been. Although I don't necessarily believe that we *need* scientific validation to appreciate the positive impact of miraculous experiences, I applaud efforts to do so: they are pushing the boundaries of our current paradigms and, in so doing, creating new understandings of how the world works. This is especially true with regard to the relationship between consciousness and matter. Many of these boundary-expanding experiences have been excellently documented in books and papers from the Institute of Noetic Sciences (IONS), especially the works of Dean Radin[14]. Many others come from numerous sources worldwide.[15] Dr. William A. Tiller, a physicist and one of the original founders of IONS, has conducted scientific studies into radionics, acupuncture, homeopathy, Kirlian photography, auras, and a host of other psychoenergetic and subtle energy phenomena, and he has actually begun defining the mathematical equations for how consciousness affects matter and energy.[16] Dr. Peter Gariaev, the father of "wave genetics" or "fractal genetics," has demonstrated the ability to reprogram DNA using words and frequencies[17]; similar results have been observed within the international Human Genome Project[18] and elsewhere.[19] There are many quantum physicists who have found the imprint of the divine within the very fabric of space, time and matter.[20] Rupert Sheldrake, author and biologist, has deeply explored the interconnectedness of all living beings, and how our energetic resonances can affect each other.[21] There are many other scientists pursuing similar studies.

For years, Lynne McTaggart has conducted live scientific experiments exploring the power of thought. In my "Extraordinary Leadership Telesummit" interview with her in 2013, she spoke of several aspects of her fascinating work, including *The Field*, a vast sea of energy that connects us all; *The Bond*, identifying our relational bonding (cooperation and collaboration instead of competition); and her ongoing healing work through *The Intention Experiment*. She said:

> "What I've been wondering about a lot [is]: when you ... have lots of people thinking the same thought at the same time, does that magnify

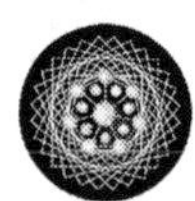

the effect? ... I wanted to test [if we could] use this for philanthropic things, to improve the world — instead of just trying to use intention to manifest more stuff, which is what we do a lot."[22]

Shortly after our interview, Lynne conducted a first-time (global online) philanthropic exercise in conjunction with Quantum University and their accompanying QuantumWorld TV station. The event was created to observe "the power of intention to heal an individual with a diagnosed illness under scientifically controlled laboratory conditions." I had the privilege of participating. The outcomes ranged from feeling the loving support of a global community to the miraculous healing of chronic illnesses.[23] The experiment also found that the *senders* of healing thoughts experienced as much benefit as the intended receiver, an effect also observed by well-known scientific healing practitioner, author and visionary, Barbara Brennan.[24]

Over the past decade, inspired by the groundbreaking research of Karl Pribram on alternative healing methods, Lynne has created several of these Intention Experiments, attracting thousands of participants from over 90 countries around the globe. These experiments have demonstrated the power of group intention. Not only does intention have the power to purify water and help crops to grow faster, but it also appears to help lower violence in war-torn areas.

In 2010, as a Monroe Institute trainer, teaching people about the nature of human consciousness, I conducted an experiment as part of Dr. Joe Gallenberger's research in an offshoot program called "Sync Creation."[25] The experiment involved sending loving thoughts to samples of unsprouted winter wheat seeds. We observed a *huge* difference, more significant than I ever imagined, between the growth of the seeds to which love was sent, and those that were ignored (controlling for other variables): the loved seeds grew about 80% faster than the ignored ones, and were significantly larger and healthier — that is, they truly thrived. This result was both miraculous and very moving. If sending loving thoughts to "just" wheat seeds (or water, as in Dr. Emoto's work[26]) can have such positive effects, imagine the potential effect of sending loving thoughts to *people*!

Remembering Makes Us Whole Again

Why is it so important that we, as leaders, remember and *embrace* our own miraculous nature?

First, as we've discussed in previous chapters, when we cut ourselves off from any part of ourselves, it diminishes us, and that, in turn, diminishes the whole world. But when we begin to remember our miraculous nature, we retrieve a portion of what has been lost. When we begin to sense our own higher selves and connection with spirit in our lives, we can help to heal many other issues and imbalances. As we ourselves become healthier, more vital and vibrant, that radiates out to others.

Second, our assumptions about human nature impact how we lead. If we have an impoverished sense of human possibility, our leadership will reflect this — with potentially tragic results. However, if we have an expansive view of human possibility, we will evoke the remarkable. This is particularly important now, as old paradigms are breaking down, giving way to new understandings. During my "Extraordinary Leadership Telesummit" interview with Lynne McTaggart, for example, I asked her about the most surprising observations of her work. She discussed how her experiments have challenged centuries-old scientific mindsets about competition, individualism and "survival of the fittest." She said:

> "It's really clear to me that we need to move forward with a very, very different paradigm if we are going to survive. ... [S]cience is just a *story*, like any other kind of story. It *approximates* what the human experience [is] and what the world is. Every time we make a new discovery, we re-write a new chapter. And the chapter that's being re-written now suggests that we are far different from what we've been told. ... [We] have to understand ourselves more as this interconnected entity ... an 'intergalactic super-organism,' as I like to call it. ... [We] also have to understand that we're a lot 'leakier' than we thought we were. We think of ourselves as these absolutely self-contained entities, but we now realize ... our minds traverse other people and things, and seem to affect them ... [In short, we're] much more connected than we thought.

> "[M]any of the problems that we face now have to do with that old and outdated model of competitive individualism. Because that's why we're in the mess we're in right now: *This is what selfish looks like.* It's the breakdown of every kind of societal structure ... in our healthcare model, in our financial model, in our educational model, in our ecological model — everything is kind of falling apart. This is not a sustainable model. We have to come up with a new one."[27]

And so, we come to the third reason why we, as leaders, must learn to remember our miraculous nature: because we are being called to lead the world through a vast paradigmatic shift, a shift from Separation to Connection. We are being asked to let go of the idea that we are just ego-ic personalities, making the world turn through our singular Herculean efforts (and exhausting ourselves in the process). We are being asked to embrace a *completely new sense of what it means to be human*, and to lead others accordingly. This will require us to stretch, to test the waters at the edges of our understanding. For if we truly accept the idea that humanity is one interconnected entity, how then do we lead? What needs to change?

Fourthly, our thoughts also affect others. What we think can impact other people (and other beings) in substantial ways. This has been extensively researched and discussed in books such as *The Secret Life of Plants* by Peter Tompkins and Christopher Bird, and *The Secret Life of Inanimate Objects* by Lyall Watson. Our thoughts are energies, and the energies we carry can affect entire systems, as revealed in additional works such as *Power Versus Force* by Dr. David Hawkins.[28] Therefore, as leaders, we need to consider the effect our thoughts have on those we lead. Our *negative* thoughts can have adverse effects, disrupting our teams, for example; we might, then, want to concentrate on positive, life-affirming thoughts, and on visionary expectations.

Finally, leaders who tap into their miraculous nature have faith in something larger than themselves: a benevolent guiding force that supports us as we live our lives and seek the greater good. Such leaders listen deeply to discern what this guidance is telling them, balancing keen observation of concrete facts with an ever-present trust. Then, when the unusual or unexpected occurs, leaders who accept their miraculous nature are able to respond with a minimum of reactivity or aggression. Instead, they retain a sense of strength and awareness. This enables them to handle conflict and crises much more effectively. They are unafraid to take risks or to step into the unknown, because they know that they will be supported no matter what the outcome. I have had the privilege of experiencing this myself, as the following story illustrates:

Several years ago, in one of my management positions, I was also asked to oversee the creation of a brand-new, health-oriented call center. My responsibilities included the training and oversight of the center's Customer Service Reps (CSRs) who were charged with fielding calls and delivering critical medical information in an accurate and timely fashion.

At first, things flowed smoothly. But after a few months, we began to experience personnel conflicts involving several of the CSR's. Heated emails full of verbal attacks were flying between several workstations, and the situation was threatening to escalate into physical violence. Most of these attacks involved one particular CSR whose name was Kim. She was one of our most articulate and knowledgeable service reps. The managers I supervised held several meetings aimed at resolving the issue, but nothing seemed to be working. If we couldn't come up with a solution, Kim was going to lose her job, and the call center was going to lose one of its best reps. I decided to step in to see if, with fresh eyes, I might observe something that was not yet obvious. I set up a time to meet with Kim directly.

The night before this meeting, I sat quietly and asked for wisdom to assist me in understanding the situation, which was negatively affecting our whole team. This request was my way of tapping into our miraculous nature. Whenever I do this, I find the responses usually come quickly, sometimes so quickly they surprise me. And the suggestions I receive are usually very effective so long as I'm paying attention and willing to listen. As often happens for me, the feedback came in the form of a dream:

I was in a very calm and peaceful room. There were clouds painted

on the walls and the sun was streaming through the windows. Suddenly, I heard the sound of frantic giggling. Moving toward the sound, I looked down and noticed a tiny person swimming in what looked like a martini glass. It was Kim. She looked beautiful, yet in disarray. She said, "Come swim with me!"

Puzzled, I responded, "Why are you inside of that glass? Why not come out here with me?" She replied, "I can't get out." Then the liquid in the glass started to spin. Within a few moments, Kim was drowning.

With a sense of urgency, I called, "How can I help?" Kim responded, "I don't know." Concerned that she was going to be sucked into the whirlpool, I stuck my finger (as enormous as a giant's compared to Kim) into the drink, and she grabbed hold of it. But she kept slipping back in. Each time she grabbed on, I noticed something new about her: she had a frightened look on her face; then she had bruises on her body; then she seemed ever so slightly pregnant.

In a flash of insight, I shouted, "Don't you want to see your baby being born?" Kim started crying, finally grabbed on tightly, and I pulled her out of the glass. Desperately, she sobbed, "Please help me. I keep drowning."

The dream ended abruptly. My eyes popped open and I sprang out of bed, urgently knowing I had to share this dream with Kim. When she stepped into my office later that day, I felt a hint of defiance in her. I greeted her gently, and asked if I could share a dream I'd had. She said "yes" with a most curious look on her face.

Midway through my recounting, Kim began to weep uncontrollably. She was stunned by my dream and confessed, through her tears, that she was a closet alcoholic, that her boyfriend abused her both physically and emotionally, and that she'd just found out she was pregnant. She was desperate to keep both her baby and her job, but she wasn't able to quit drinking on her own and didn't know what to do. Her violent outbreaks at work reflected the pressure she was holding inside.

My intuitive dream had opened the way. Now I had to shift rapidly into action. I knew that if Kim didn't get help immediately, my managers would have to fire her, and rightly so. I asked if she was ready to go into rehab. I promised to help her to get admitted and also to find a way for her to return to her job after treatment. She agreed. I called our human resources department; they located an appropriate local facility, and within three hours she was being scheduled for her program (which, in itself, is miraculous!).

Kim remained in rehab for nine months. She emerged a strong, healthy woman with a newborn daughter to care for. The president of our company gave permission for her to be re-hired, and within 30 days, Kim received our Employee of the Month award. Grateful for being so supported during this very challenging time in her life, she gifted the company back with her extraordinary service.

Although the decision-makers of this company were not necessarily used to respecting input from intuitive practices (in this case, dreams and visions), during my tenure, they were open-minded and honored my balanced expression of logic and intuition as well as my unique ways to lead. This experience reminded me that when we trust in our miraculous nature and are supported to do so, we can inspire others to face great challenges and invoke change for the better. Sometimes, these changes go beyond what we thought was possible, influencing shifts in ingrained policies and systems. When we listen to our miraculous inner voice and trust its messages, spontaneous miracles start to appear in our lives.

I believe that leaders in touch with the miraculous within themselves have the power to create whatever they can imagine, so long as those visions are in alignment with the greater good. This may seem improbable, but I know it is possible because I have seen it so many times in my own life. Such visions carry both enormous opportunity and great responsibility.

This is one of the reasons why the previous vital keys are so essential; together, they provide the foundation for this key.

Remembering who we really are generates more energy, more clarity, and the capacity to think outside the box. This unleashes *creativity extraordinaire*. As we continue to recall all the ways in which we are miraculous and can be more so, we will increase our ability to generate powerful solutions, to communicate more clearly and with ease, and to navigate through conflict in ways that heal instead of harm.

Miracles Are Not Necessarily By-Demand

It is true that the density of our earthly plane means some miracles are more challenging to manifest than others. Sometimes, in spite of our best efforts, we do not get the results we crave in the timeframe we want. There are many possible reasons for this: First, we have to search ourselves for ego-ic or Power Over motivations hidden within our efforts. Next, even with pure motivations, the desired result may not be in alignment within the larger picture, or the timing may not yet be quite right. Sometimes, we have more work to do on ourselves first, or we may need to gather additional support from others. Maybe something even better than what we intend is being co-created by spirit, and we just need to be patient and continue to trust. Remembering our miraculous nature means we also remember that the universe is miraculous too, and we must work in concert *together*. Just as with the need to focus on our vision rather than on chaos, it is important not to let temporary setbacks in miraculous manifestation discourage us from our efforts. I truly believe, and have witnessed in my own life and the lives of many others, that with practice, patience, intention and love, and keeping our moral compass on the point of No Harm, we can and will create miraculous events for the benefit of all.

A Call to Action: Re-Awaken to Our Own Miraculous Nature

"Synchronicity reveals the meaningful connections between the subjective and objective world."

~ DR. CARL JUNG
(Swiss Psychiatrist, 'Collective Unconscious' Explorer)

"A good traveler has no fixed plans and is not intent upon arriving. A good artist lets his intuition lead him wherever it wants. A good scientist has freed himself of concepts and keeps his mind open to what is. Thus the Master is available to all people and doesn't reject anyone. He is ready to use all situations and doesn't waste anything. This is called embodying the light."[29]

~RICHARD TARNAS
(Author, Cultural Historian-Philosopher)

Embrace a Wake-Up Call

Sometimes it's hard for us to see or believe in the miraculousness of our own human nature. We're often so stubborn, blind, self-absorbed, or simply bound to our societal programming, that it takes a wake-up call of one kind or another to get us to see the truth that has been there all along.

Years ago, Joseph Jaworski, the founder and chairman of Generon Consulting and the Global Institute for Responsible Leadership, wrote a book entitled *Synchronicity: The Inner Path of Leadership*. The book recounted Joseph's shift from a leadership style that was based in ego to one that was more integrated, drawing upon both logic and intuition in dynamically balanced ways.

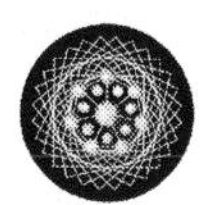

With great vulnerability, Joseph expressed how he had lost everything, especially his wife, by forgetting that he was and is a part of a greater whole. Then he described how he began to remember: By paying attention to everything around him, and learning to see the world anew, with fresh eyes, he "came to see this as the most subtle territory of leadership, creating the conditions for 'predictable miracles.'"[30]

When Joseph finally remembered who he really was, synchronicity became the cornerstone of his life, and thus the title of his book. His story is a transformational "hero's journey" (as delineated in Joseph Campbell's profound work on the mythology of our lives). It's also the story of "everyman." Joseph Jaworski was tested, and he came up against the essential need to break free of limits, both external and self-imposed. When we have the courage to break through our own limiting beliefs, we help release more of our human potential, allowing seemingly unattainable dreams to manifest. Joseph experienced this by learning to surrender to his deeper nature, truly caring about a colleague, and witnessing the impact he had by sharing just the "right" things to say and do. These accurate messages and actions were inspired by his intuition, when logic didn't know how to proceed. He described how, through a dialogue process emphasizing Being versus Doing, his teams repeatedly came up with innovative solutions to seemingly intractable problems.

Like Mr. Jaworski, many of my clients and friends have also experienced miraculous turnings in their lives. They've described rising from bankruptcy to create multi-million dollar businesses, or coming back from a tragedy like the near-suicide of a child to forge new intensely loving family bonds. Others have described the gifts gained from tragic accidents, near-death experiences and terminal illnesses. Many have had visions of angels and guides, and/or dreams that warned them of integrity breaches, or foretold that they would be graced with a new business or life partner. All of these experiences were beyond the reach of logic and our typical cultural norms.

Our brains and nervous systems are far more pliable than we have imagined. This, too, is part of our miraculous nature. Many of our beliefs

appear to be ingrained, but that's merely a product of mechanisms designed to keep us safe and protected. Familiar choices become our defaults, even when they no longer serve us, because the neural pathways were formed when we were very young (typically before the age of five). These are like well-worn trails for hiking, clear and easy to traverse. But they are not the only pathways we can take. We can intentionally re-route; we can learn to opt for roads less traveled — roads that lead us toward the miraculous. As Lynne McTaggart said, our present systems and concepts of leadership are based on outdated models of competition and selfishness; the future of leadership must be based upon connection and healing, allowing for miracles to emerge. If we, as leaders, consciously decide to shift to this worldview, the future could be astounding.

With focus and effort, we have the capability to create new neural pathways in our brains, pathways that represent healthier ways of being. These new pathways can then become our *new* "norm." Just as when a hiking trail in a forest is reconfigured because the human traffic threatens the wildlife, the first few hikes on that new trail may not be so easy; thickets and thistles may be temporarily blocking the way, but the trek is do-able nonetheless, and later travelers will have an easier time. This is the way in which new forms of leadership can be created.

Live in Awareness

"Around us, life bursts with miracles — a glass of water, a ray of sunshine, a leaf, a caterpillar, a flower, laughter, raindrops. If you live in awareness, it is easy to see miracles everywhere. Each human being is a multiplicity of miracles. Eyes that see thousands of colors, shapes, and forms; ears that hear a bee flying or a thunderclap; a brain that ponders a speck of dust as easily as the entire cosmos; a heart that beats in rhythm with the heartbeat of all beings. When we are tired and feel discouraged by life's daily struggles, we may not notice these miracles, but they are always there."

~THICH NHAT HANH
(Buddhist Spiritual Teacher, Peace Activist)

As you might imagine, recognizing our miraculous nature speaks to suspending the weightiness of our gravest concerns, and embracing the joy of being alive and being present in every moment. Living this way can catalyze better relationships, open us to infinitely more possibilities, and save lives — perhaps even our own. Healing begins to occur when we begin to remember our connection to All That Is.

In that place of peace and healthy equilibrium, we begin to see the infinite vastness of our bodies, in equal proportion to the universe: our bodies are not just our physical vessels, but energy fields that stretch outward towards infinity. Many people can actually see these fields, and see how they interact with the fields of all other beings. We can develop that same awareness, if not with our physical eyes, then at least with our "inner eyes" and our somatic feelings. With such awareness, we can also begin to see that our thoughts, actions and subtle ways of being impact both ourselves and the world: first, inwardly, at the cellular level, rippling like radar across the boundaries of our cell walls and skin, and then outwardly expanding beyond the boundaries of bodies, cities, planets, and more.

As we become intimately aware of that impact, we might then choose to take on more responsibility for the consequences of our thoughts upon our own sacred bodies and then, in turn, on other human beings and creatures. As discussed earlier, many researchers have done experiments on the effects of loving versus non-loving thoughts on health and other physical processes: loving thoughts produce positive results, while hate and indifference give rise to systems that become ill, fail to thrive or show below-optimum results.[31] We do this experiment on our own bodies every moment of the day. Imagine how our magnificence would grow if we could stay in grateful and loving thoughts. We can also request, with love, that any foreign substance leave, including cancer or other illnesses. We can even make this request of people who are consuming or depleting our energy instead of relying on their own. We have a right to ask them to leave, with love.

Remember the Time Before We Forgot

When we were small children, before we were conditioned to suppress and forget, we just knew that the world was miraculous, and that magic was everywhere. This is one of the reasons why books and movies about magical events remain so popular with adults. It's not just because they're fun; it's because they trigger our own powerful memories. We need to remind ourselves — and each other — of our early sense of wonderment. This was done for me when I forgot:

When I was in junior high school, one of my teachers noticed that I was becoming a little too serious. One day, she gently pulled me aside, put her arm around my shoulder, and asked, "When you were a little girl what made you laugh? What were some of the things that you did, where you completely lost track of time?"

What immediately came to me was that I had absolutely delighted in communicating with plants and animals, and in imagining what it would be like to be one of them. My imaginings had been so tangible that I could actually feel myself becoming a tree, or a butterfly or an industrious ant. I remembered also feeling the sensation of being a flower, attended to by all the bees and other creatures. I'd expected flowers to have very still, unexciting lives, but when I'd actually experienced the sensation of being one, I was amazed to discover their lives were far from passive!

This recollection still fills me with delight. Imagine what these interactions implied. How much might we learn from Nature if we were willing to empathically merge with the essence, the unique soulprint, of other beings — from our own species or another?

Listen to Guidance

"The breeze at dawn has secrets to tell you. Don't go back to sleep. You must ask for what you really want. Don't go back to sleep. People are going back and forth across the doorsill where the two worlds touch. The door is round and open. Don't go back to sleep."

~RUMI

(Sufi Mystic, Poet "The Breeze at Dawn")

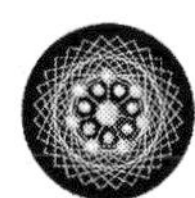

Paying attention to the miraculous magnifies the possibility of miracles coming to and through us. The old expression "ask and you shall receive" is so very true. But this attentiveness is not easy to maintain when challenges mount in our lives, and the lists of things that need to be done read like rulebooks to complicated games. Our consciousness constricts and it becomes difficult for many of us to shift toward openness and curiosity. It takes time and intention. We need to be lovingly patient with ourselves and trust that we *do* know how to do this. As with any skill, the more we practice, the greater our chances of experiencing amazing events.

First, we must discover how the miraculous speaks to each of us. Although we are one with All That Is, we are also each *unique* expressions of that All. This means that our gifts and life paths are uniquely ours, including the methods that will work best to help us access our guidance. For some of us, the miraculous may speak to us through our dreams. This happens to work really well for me, as indicated by many of my personal stories. I know that others are also blessed with this gift, where guidance comes through dreams and visions, often with great clarity. But not everyone receives information this way; some people may not even remember their dreams. Luckily, this is not the only way the miraculous chooses to speak with us.

The most important thing is to *be open* and to pay attention. Guidance may come in a form that seems mundane, yet is actually an indication of deep synchronicity. For example, while wrestling with an issue, we may get an unexpected phone call, perhaps from an old friend we haven't heard from in a while. We might bounce our concern off this caller, and they may have an answer we hadn't considered. Or, the miraculous may show up as an act of kindness offered by a total stranger. As if by magic, we are guided to just the right insight or person needed to assist us.

Guidance may also appear through a feeling in our bodies or an inner "knowing" to do or not do something — like canceling a trip or taking the long route home from work one day, resulting in our avoiding an accident or traffic jam that could have caused us harm or hours of delay. Sometimes we might just have a "hunch" about a prospective employee:

on paper, he or she doesn't seem to have the right skills, but we trust our "gut feeling," and it ends up being just the right choice.

"Gut feelings" reflect how guidance can often come through our bodies, through specific somatic sensations and perceptions. Our bodies are extraordinary vessels, and we can learn a lifetime of wisdom just by tapping into our body's awareness alone. How does your body speak to you? How does it tell you whether something is healthy for you or not? How does it tell you whether or not you resonate with someone else's energy field? Pay attention to your body's signals.

Our bodies may also steer us to the right environment where our guidance can come through. We may be athletic and our intuition or miraculous nature makes itself known through our sport. We may find guidance coming through playing music, driving, or even while taking a shower or a bath. We may receive internal guidance while walking in Nature, or doing yoga, Chi Gong, Tai Chi, etc.

When my clients are baffled by some challenge in their personal or work life, I sometimes invite them to turn those challenges over to Nature. Paying attention to which animals, birds or insects cross our path, or what flowers or stones catch our attention, can be a tremendously insightful way to gain access to inner guidance. Books such as Ted Andrews' *Animal Speak, Animal-Wise*, and *Nature-Speak* can provide assistance in interpreting what these signals from Nature mean. If we are open-minded and open-hearted, and if we are ready to receive, Nature can be one of our greatest spiritual teachers, and its wisdom is there for the asking.

Develop Your Intuitive Side

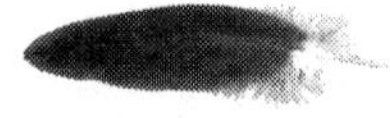

"The intuitive mind is a sacred gift and the rational mind is a faithful servant. We have created a society that honors the servant and has forgotten the gift."

~ALBERT EINSTEIN
(Theoretical Physicist, Philosopher)

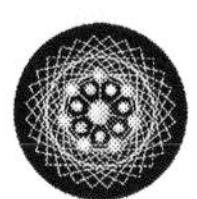

According to the Merriam-Webster Dictionary and the Oxford English Dictionary, "intuition" is generally defined as a natural ability or power that makes it possible to know something without any proof or evidence, or as a thing that one knows or considers likely from instinctive feeling rather than conscious reasoning. All of the methods mentioned above can help us develop our intuition. The miraculous is more likely to speak to us through our intuitive side, but we may not even hear it unless that side is sufficiently developed. Although scientists have studied how the miraculous speaks through dreams, visions, Nature and/or our bodies, etc., the Power Over style of our culture means that these aspects of science have been downplayed in favor of the purely technical. Most of us have been conditioned to rely primarily on our rational minds, and need to learn how to re-open to other channels. By the same token, some very intuitive people may have trouble getting tangible results and putting their guidance into action, so they need to develop their logical side. In response to those potentially challenging imbalances, I suggest the following protocol to develop both sides of our nature:

A. Select a challenge or issue that you would like to work on. Be open to all "signs" as to what path to take; include your intuition so that the hidden is not ignored.

    1. Observe what your default path is: Is it logical or intuitive?

        a. If logical:

            i. Observe the problem/issue/concern.
            ii. Look for the easiest solutions.
            iii. Identify what's blocking the resolution of the concerns.
            iv. If you already tried something, ask what worked and what didn't?
            v. Reflect on steps that might logically work, but be open to examining steps that could include intuition.
            vi. Write down some of the top solutions derived from logic.

        b. If intuitive:

            i. Get really quiet and center through the heart.
            ii. Do a meditation to evoke an intuitive response and/or

solution. What works or doesn't?

iii. With your dominant hand, write a question or state the problem, and then with your non-dominant hand write a response. Do this as if you had a Guardian Angel, a mentor or a wise guide at your disposal (perhaps from other realms) OR

iv. Connect with Nature and pay attention to the signs.

v. If there are blockages in your process, and you have the opportunity to do so, take *3 full days* to observe the natural process that makes its way into each day relative to the issues at hand. If you don't have time, shorten it to a few moments each day.

vi. Reflect on processes that might intuitively work, but be open to examining steps that could include logic.

vii. Write down some of the top solutions derived from intuition.

2. Now, redo the exercise applying your non-default method.
3. Get help from someone whose default is the opposite of yours.

B. Integrate your Logic and Intuition:

1. Have a dialogue with others from your team, or share your result from Part A above (*which was to select a challenge or issue you'd like to work on — being open to both logic and intuition*), with a professional consultant, coach or trusted advisor.
2. Come up with 2 or 3 best solutions from the processes related to logic and intuition. (Steps A1a, vi and A1b, vii — looking at the top solutions generated from both methods, logic and intuition)
3. Try each solution from step B2 above (using the best solutions from each method, logic and intuition), in the real world with your issue. If it is not effective, ask why, and move on to the next solution until an effective one has been discovered, or until you reach a point where none of the solutions have worked.
4. At this point, either re-try the process above, OR Surrender to the Divine. When you reach a point where you have asked yourself,

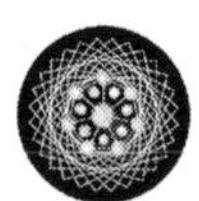

"Have I done everything humanly possible to resolve this issue?" and the answer is "Yes," then surrendering is a welcomed next step.

Surrender was discussed in Vital Key #1 on Power as a way of acknowledging when we can no longer steer the process and need to relinquish trying to control it! If we have done everything we can, then we need to let the issue go. This creates a space into which our miraculous nature can pour new nourishment. Surrender is not always easy, especially the first time we try it, but when it is the right thing to do, we will almost immediately feel release and calm.

Commit to Living Your Miraculous Nature

"A certain power to alter things indwells in the human soul and subordinates the other things to her, particularly when she is swept into great excesses of love or hate or the like ... For a long time I did not believe it ... [but] I found that the emotionality of the human soul is the chief cause of all these things ... "

~**Albertus Magnus**
(Catholic Bishop, Saint 1200-1280)

It is especially important to remember our miraculous nature in the midst of really challenging circumstances. If I had not been reminded of this, I might have missed an amazing opportunity to impact a man suffering from deep despair and a hardened heart. This happened at a time in my life when I, too, was feeling challenged, and it transformed both our lives in significant ways:

In the 1990's, while I was teaching, I was also beginning the emotionally stressful process of divorce. To make the transition financially feasible, I took on two additional part-time jobs. One of these jobs was as a scenic designer, creating sets for Hollywood, Disney and the annual Macy's parade. My shift began at 5:30 a.m.

Several weeks into this uncomfortable life scenario of divorce, three jobs and barely enough sleep, I decided to treat myself to a very early breakfast at a local diner. The place was nearly empty. In silence, I blessed my food and began to eat, when I suddenly became aware of how sad I felt about my situation. I pulled out my journal, and decided to write for a few minutes before heading off to work. Feeling vulnerable, but also resilient, I noticed my words flowing onto the pages along with the occasional tears that fell, smearing portions here and there. I felt guided to simply express gratitude, knowing that I had loved and been loved, and would continue so, no matter what. I wrote that I also felt grateful just to be alive and to have experienced everything I had in life, even my disappointments and heartaches.

The very moment I finished writing that sentence, I thought I heard someone calling my name: "Joyce." I looked around, but no one was there except for a thirty-something gentleman, sitting all the way across the restaurant. It couldn't have been him. I heard my name again: "Joyce." And then a third time: "Joyce, do you see that gentleman over there?"

I answered silently, "Yes?" Then I heard the following insight: "He is very depressed and wants to commit suicide because he believes that no one loves him. He also believes that he is an utter failure in both life and work." As I listened intently, the message continued: "He has no idea that his father, from whom he has been estranged for many years because of a horrible misunderstanding, loves him and wants to reconnect, but doesn't know where he is. His father is very ill and will die soon — within the year."

In silence I asked, "Why are you telling me all this information that I can do nothing about?"

The response was clear, "Oh, but Joyce, you can! That's why we came to you!"

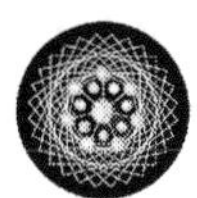

"What can I do?"

"Take a piece of paper from your journal, write down the insights you've just received, and then give it to this man. You can sign it, 'From a Loving Angel across the way.'"

I felt goosebumps all over my body. I knew this to be a somatic signal that what I was hearing was true — the hidden realms lending a helping hand. I also experienced the sensation of time temporarily standing still, and every cell in my being sending love to this man. So, without hesitation, and despite my own time constraints, I tore a page from my journal, wrote a letter to this man and gave it to the waitress, instructing her to please give it to him after I left.

Two months passed, during which I reflected on this experience from time to time. One day, I went back to the diner for breakfast. As I entered, the same waitress ran to the door and greeted me exuberantly: "Do you remember you gave me a note to give to someone the last time you were here?" I said that I did. She continued, "That gentleman came by yesterday and asked me if I knew the 'angel' who had left the note. He asked me to please pass on that the note saved his life, and that it had enabled him to reconcile with his dad who passed away two weeks ago. He said that the note brought joy back into his life, and if there was anything he could ever do to thank that 'angel,' to please let him know."

This news brought tears to my eyes. It validated that heeding this type of guidance is a significant part of my lifework. But that wasn't the end of the message. The waitress continued to explain that she'd told the gentleman that I was working three jobs, and that she wished I didn't have to work so hard. He replied that he was quite influential in the business world and he would ensure that I would either be offered a raise, or he would create a new position for me.

In a stupor of disbelief, I thanked the waitress and drove to work. As I walked in the door, my boss called me into her office and offered me a raise. I remain uncertain whether that gentleman was directly responsible for my salary increase or not (my boss wouldn't say); I've never been able to locate him directly to ask. Since he seemed to have discovered who I was and may have contributed, at least energetically to my raise, I continue to think of him with gratitude, from the bottom of my heart, for that ripple of mutual miraculous action.

Many leaders are not yet aware of the incredible benefit that learning to call on their miraculous nature can bring to them — personally and to their organizations. Having witnessed the impact for years on both personal and professional lives, I testify to its generative power.

Support Others to Live Their Miraculous Nature

"You've gotta dance like there's nobody watching, Love like you'll never be hurt, Sing like there's nobody listening, And live like it's heaven on earth."

~WILLIAM W. PURKEY
(Author, Storyteller, Songwriter)

Sometimes, we are given the opportunity to support others in acknowledging their own miraculous nature, such that they are able to fulfill their life's purpose. I'd like to share one such story:

Nearly 20 years ago, I was co-chair of a college art department in the Southwest. I was charged with teaching and mentoring a group of students who were at different skill levels. I wanted to challenge those who were more advanced, while ensuring that those who had less previous exposure didn't feel intimidated, and to keep everyone engaged and excited — quite a balancing act!

In my class on three-dimensional design, I had a Native American

student named Troy who particularly impressed me. When in class, Troy seemed to have a very solid understanding of many of the materials and processes we used — clay, wood, metal, multimedia, etc. But he was falling behind because he wasn't completing assignments on time or, when he did complete them, they seemed sloppy and thrown together, mismatching the talent and skill level I saw in him in class. Concerned, I asked Troy to take a walk with me one day. I wanted to listen to him to discover if I could better understand what was happening. Very gently, I asked him if anything was going on at home or elsewhere to prevent him from completing his work. He responded nervously, saying that he had chores at home and many classes at school, and that these consumed almost all of his time. I explained that I wanted to be able, in good conscience, to give him a passing grade because I knew my class was a prerequisite for other art classes that he'd expressed a desire to take. I asked him to commit to completing future assignments, and to work together to create a plan for him to catch up on what he'd already missed. I also suggested he remember that his passion was to be an artist, and that the assignments were meant to help him realize that goal.

Troy seemed on board, and said he would commit. We were about to finish our dialogue, when I caught a look on his face that seemed to belie his agreement. He seemed filled with internal conflict and sadness. I asked if he was okay and he said, "yes," so I didn't push it, but I still felt concerned about his wellbeing. I knew in my heart there was something else he didn't feel able to share.

As I often did, I brought the whole class (virtually) into my meditation that evening. In particular, I asked for guidance regarding this bright young man. In response, I was given a remarkable vision:

> *A powerful and handsome Native American elder appeared, with wrinkles engraved on his face, like a beautiful etching. His hair was long, black-peppered-with-gray, and woven into braids. His presence brought me great joy, and I felt a huge tear falling from my right eye — the medicine of gratitude.*

> *The elder looked deeply into my eyes, took both my hands in his, and said, "You, my beloved sister, are a guiding teacher to my grandson. He is on his life quest of which you are a part. He already has learned so much from your engagement with him and his fellow classmates. But, he has a much greater task right now. Come. I will show you." He signaled me toward the direction of the East.*
>
> *Suddenly, everything went black. Then, slowly, the light of the full moon emerged from the darkness, casting a beam like a spotlight on Troy. He was dressed in special ceremonial clothing, and he began to dance a native dance like I'd never witnessed before. As he moved through the darkness, I saw his soul's purpose, undeniably.*
>
> *The dance came to closure, and his grandfather — now more ghostlike in appearance — whispered in my ear: "Troy is destined to be our tribal ceremonial dancer. He must practice daily and pass through initiations. He must leave spontaneously whenever called, even if it means missing classes at school. He* ***must*** *go if he is to fulfill his destiny." The elder quietly added, "Remind him that I love him."*

In silence, I thanked them both, and opened my eyes knowing that I needed to share this vision with Troy. I also knew in my core that Troy would be selected to be the tribal dancer. For this young man, dancing was a spiritual calling, and his life at that point was like a vision quest; he was seeking to fulfill his life's purpose.

The following day, after receiving affirmation from spirit that it was acceptable to share my experience with Troy, I did so in vivid detail, down to the feathers and symbolic beadwork that I had seen him wearing in his ceremonial dance. The expression on Troy's face was ecstatic. Without hesitation, he began excitedly sharing information about the pathway he was following, guided by his grandfather who was now in the Spirit realm. Then he told me he was afraid he might not be chosen for the position. Startled by the ferocity of Spirit speaking

through me, I said, "But you will be! And when you are, we will celebrate!" When I reminded him of his grandfather's love, he wept.

As now expected, Troy missed many classes in subsequent months. I encouraged him to share what he could with his classmates, and we worked out blocks of time when he could complete his assignments, incorporating his love of dance into his artistic expression. He did complete my class.

Months later, after a prolonged absence from school, Troy came to my office to let me know that he had become the primary ceremonial dancer for his tribe. Moved, we hugged each other and cried in recognition of this message from spirit. He also brought me a precious gift. It was a very sacred bundle of hand-selected feathers that remain, to this day, on my ceremonial altar.

Express Gratitude

This can be done through a daily practice of communing with Nature — for example, by such things as taking a moment in time to thank the Earth for a flower emerging out of a crack in the sidewalk, or a sunset spilling over the western sky, or the next breath of air entering our lungs. When leaders I've worked with have consciously begun to express gratitude, or consistently practiced heart coherence exercises such as those popularized by the HeartMath Institute, doorways that previously seemed closed suddenly open.

Seek Additional Sources of Inspiration

Whenever I find myself forgetting my own miraculous nature, I make a point of seeking out activities and practices that stimulate my memory. I also reach out for stories from others. Some of my favorite inspirations include stories from Glenn Aparicio Parry's book, *Original Thinking*, and Stephen Dinan's spiritual and educational curriculum from the Shift

Network, which embraces the miraculous. This includes works such as "Soulful Women's Leadership" by Devaa Haley Mitchell[32] and Elayne "Kalila" Doughty; "Woman Stand's Shining"'s powerful storytelling of the miracles to be gleaned from the Grandmother Lodge; and Victoria Hanchin's *The Seer and the Sayer: Revelations of the New Earth*, a true story carefully documenting miracle after miracle with Mohawk Grandmother Dona, Mayan Grandmother Flordemayo, and Mayan high priest Don Alejandro Oxlaj verifying the Mayan 2012 prophecy of the convergence of an underground river connecting three other sacred rivers in Peaceburgh.

Over the years, I have gained great insights and wisdom regarding our miraculous nature through the writings of Rumi, Madame Blavatsky, Carl Jung (*The Collective Unconscious),* Jane Roberts (the *Seth* books and *Oversoul Seven*), Edgar Cayce (*The Sleeping Prophet*), Gregg Braden (*The Divine Matrix*), the Vatican's publication of the "Secret of Fatima," Richard Bartlett (*The Physics of Miracles*), Barbara Brennan (*Hands of Light*), Barbara Marx Hubbard (*Birth 2012 and Beyond*), Robert Monroe *(Journeys Out of the Body*), books by Paul Elder, Joseph McMoneagle and Skip Atwater, Eckhart Tolle, Anodea Judith, The Findhorn Community, Theodore Esser IV's dissertation (*Lucid Dreaming, Kundalini, The Divine and Non-duality*), Ariel Spilsbury and Michael Bryner (*The Mayan Oracle: Return Path to the Stars*), and many, many others.

As we begin to remember and explore our miraculous nature, we have an opportunity to manifest remarkable solutions for the many problems of our world, creating a much stronger foundation, through our hearts, for extraordinary leadership to unfold. Heart-centered connections, embracing the miraculous, lie at the foundation of our collective dream. Humanity's collective unconscious is calling this dream forth, igniting the spirits of extraordinary leaders to bring it into reality.

Vital Key #7:
Manifesting Dreams and Transforming World Systems through the Heart

"We are at the dawn of an age in which many people feel that extreme political concepts should cease to dominate human affairs. We should use this opportunity to replace them with universal human and spiritual values and ensure that these values become the fiber of the global family that is emerging."

~DALAI LAMA
(Tibetan Spiritual Leader, Global Peace Advocate)

There is a dream stirring in us — a collective dream, a global dream. It is, as Charles Eisenstein writes, a dream of "the more beautiful world our hearts know is possible."[1] I believe this dream is emerging from our collective desire to experience this precious life in very different ways, to champion our gifts as an ever-evolving species, and to manifest the extraordinary leadership that we were born to live. As expressed at the beginning and touched on throughout this book:

The dream is of a world that thrives on every level, where each of us is valued and respected and allowed to contribute our gifts without fear. It is a dream in which all cultures and peoples are honored, and all age groups are cherished and inspired to share their wisdom. The dream acknowledges ways we have gone astray, succumbing to corruption in our actions and our systems, and addresses our need to shift these unhealthy methods of leading. It encourages the removal of instruments of war and aggression, while offering apology and restoration to the people and lands already harmed. The dream reminds us to be people of integrity, discernment, divine creativity and wisdom.

Whenever a visionary leader articulates this dream, as was done in the 2008 presidential election, it stirs us. Hope comes alive, and people all over the globe are galvanized. That is because it is a resonant dream of humanity. Our minds may tell us the dream is impossible; established hierarchy may say it is unrealistic; but our hearts won't let it go. That is why this dream won't die, why it keeps re-surfacing. It is time to listen to our hearts.

We cannot give up on this sacred vision, nor let it be relegated to rhetoric alone — especially rhetoric used to mask underlying agendas that actually undermine the dream. Neither can we let it be lost to the dismantling bipartisan politics and corrupted systems that are currently in place. Instead we must continue to persist with faith, courage and hope, to manifest our collective dream, despite feeling overwhelmed by economic burdens, the daily barrage of challenges and responsibilities, or the sense of not knowing where to begin. Our hearts *do* believe this dream is still possible!

A Call to Manifest Our Dreams and Transform the World

"Changing is not just changing the things outside of us. First of all we need the right view that transcends all notions — including of being and non-being, creator and creature, mind and spirit. That kind of insight is crucial for transformation and healing."

~THICH NHAT HANH
(Buddhist Spiritual Teacher, Peace Activist)

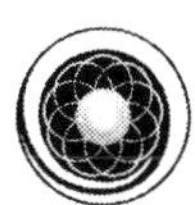

These extraordinary times of crisis and great opportunity set the stage for our initiation into the fullest expression of our collective dream. If we allow ourselves to be fueled by hope and the fervent belief that more beneficent outcomes want to emerge, we can begin to manifest the positive differences we wish to create in our lives, our systems and our world. This requires that each of us Do and Be our part. To manifest our collective dream, there are three intertwined elements of transformation for us to consider:

1. Personal Transformation through the Vital Keys, as discussed throughout this book.
2. World Transformation through the Vital Keys, which includes restructuring existing organizations and systems, as well as creating entirely new organizations, systems and movements.
3. Mutual Transformation through the Intersection of our personal dreams with the collective dream, creating an energetic "sweet spot."

Personal transformation is essential for extraordinary leadership. It alone is powerful, and nothing else is required of us. Our personal change may stimulate and induce change in others, as well as the groups and organizations with which we are associated; we can consciously choose to apply the vital keys to the workings of local and global systems to create external changes. This, too, is powerful. We may also combine the two, exploring and clarifying our personal dreams — which may include identifying our purpose, passions, gifts and worldview — internal to external, small to large — and discover how and where our personal dreams intersect with the greater collective dream. This creates a "sweet spot" for sweeping transformation and the manifestation of extraordinary outcomes to occur.

Our hearts know when this spot is found, because we can feel the resonance of our dreams within them; we feel motivated and inspired to move forward to do whatever is necessary to bring our dreams into reality. So, we can build on personal transformation to bring changes to existing organizations and structures and/or to create new ones, ultimately leading to large-scale transformation of world systems having long-term global impact. Such transformation is the crux of this final Key, which synergistically incorporates all of the other keys within it.

Element #1:

Personal Transformation through the Vital Keys

The best place to begin the process of personal transformation is with the Vital Keys I've presented in this book. This type of transformation requires an increase in conscious attention to the choices we make; these changes alone will have a profound effect on both us and our world. Here are my recommendations for how to begin:

1. Choose the Vital Key that resonates most for you. In order to clarify your own focus, simply start with *one* key at a time — the one that you identify as most needing attention. This may be one that calls for the most significant change.

2. Take a deep dive to explore the various aspects of that key. Work with it and allow it to be your starting place. Think of this Vital Key as your Teacher.

3. Follow your personal transformation work where it leads, and you will begin to see that the key is "magic" — you will start to see your key reflected in larger and larger ripples around you, offering you the possibility of generating an even greater impact beyond your own personal evolution and transformation.

For example, you may notice that your connection to power is unhealthy in that you tend to over-control. Recognizing that this generates oppression and heartache, you become conscious of your need to shift away from Power Over and towards Power With. You select the principles in Vital Key #1 that you want to work with to modify your actions and ways of being. As you begin to understand your personal power, fueled by your deepening love for yourself and others, Power With solutions naturally begin to ripple out into the world. This is because the world reflects back to us what we put out. Power With solutions, fueled by our own divine empowerment, help us to teach by example and lead others, through the heart, to do the same.

As this occurs, natural feedback loops kick in to inspire individuals and groups around us to create new transformational structures and systems — such as new forms of governance, new styles of funding and support, and new methods of interacting with each other and the planet. This is the basis for long-term global transformation, which may include the development of projects, movements, innovations and legislation enhancing the path to the next part of the process — the intersection between our personal dreams and the collective dream. This process applies and extends to all seven Vital Keys, not just Power.

Personal Nuances Of Transformation

"Entelechy is the power that directs an organism toward the fulfillment of its own nature."[2]

~**ARIEL SPILSBURY AND MICHAEL BRYNER**
(Metaphysicians, Authors)

Just as each of us carries a unique soulprint like holographic pieces of a magnificent puzzle, each equally important to the whole, we also occupy a unique place in our own development and evolution as a species. Each of us has different areas that need attention and areas that are already strong. One person may have a deep connection to Spirit and their miraculous nature, but feel separated from their family and community. Another may have great ability to bridge logical and intuitive solutions concretely, yet have difficulty staying in balance. And yet another may feel the need to shift their lack of connection to Nature and spirit, while already being adept at Power With engagement and truth-telling.

Our strengths require less attention than our challenges. Since no one is better than or less than anyone else, the vital keys and their transformations toward extraordinary leadership all carry equal weight.

We each fall somewhere on a spectrum that varies from our general propensities of "this is not something I need to work on now" to "this is my Achilles heel" or "these are my greatest stumbling blocks." What we attend to regarding the vital keys is also reflected in what wants to emerge in our daily moment-by-moment interactions. It is a gift to recognize what transformation is needed and where the call to shift appears in our lives and the ways in which we lead.

No one is expected to master every Vital Key! (Like "perfecting love," working with these keys is a lifelong occupation.) We only need to do our part each day. As our transformation evolves, we may be inspired to do larger work in the world, or we may find we only want to work on ourselves. *Both are hugely transformative to the world as a whole.* Both require courage — to fail or succeed, to look bad or good, to be disliked (or even hated) or to be loved. They also require an increased willingness to take risks and to work for the long haul to benefit generations to come. But remember that working on personal transformation alone is already a beginning to manifesting the dream; the impact ripples through our personal lives and beyond.

We may also discover that our decisions regarding the ways we choose to manifest do not need to be set in stone, but can and will shift. We may start down one path and then find we need to make different choices based upon our readiness, or the necessities and/or circumstances at hand. Our immediate and global environments, as well as historic and ancestral influences, often guide these choices. Our lives become more of an adventure as we discover each "next step."

Once we make the commitment to transformation, we will be given "signposts" along the way. What I and others, including Lynne McTaggart in her "Intention Experiments," have observed is that, when we make conscious choices toward our dreams, it changes our experience of the world. For example, if we make a commitment to shifting from Power Over to Power With, things begin to show up very differently in our

lives — more peacefully, more non-violently, and we feel an ever-strengthening connection to one another and the rest of the world.

Of course there can also be moments of discouragement. When these come, we need to step back and try to see the bigger picture. What might appear to us as having very little impact, may actually be having an extraordinary effect on others; we cannot always know. We must therefore suspend judgment. It is also vitally important that we never give up on our own or another's ability to change. No matter how long someone has been "stuck," it's never hopeless; it's always possible. This includes no matter how *old* we might be. Sometimes we just need to "suspend our disbelief." This, too, is part of the key to transformation.

Whether we determine we'd like to transform ourselves with *each* of the vital keys, or if we only feel a need to address one, it is important to note that there is a constant interplay between and amongst them. This creates additional fields of energy that can connect transformative pathways, like new connective tissues in our brains' neural networks. We must try not to judge or pre-determine how this will look or unfold, but instead ignite our curiosity as to how these vital keys play roles in our lives — seen and unseen, consciously and unconsciously. That curiosity will help us remain open to new discoveries.

The Keys lead us into an incredible network of possibility. This is akin to the matrix of our ever-expanding Internet and telecommunications systems, but this is a matrix of *consciousness*. Within this consciousness matrix we will discover an infinite number of "if/then" expressions leading to an infinite number of potential outcomes and solutions. It is fantastically exciting, because we are each helping to create it. With more awareness, more consciously-made choices, and more *allowing* for decisions to naturally emerge from spirit, we have the potential to impact everything around us in amazing new ways. This is the hope that we thought was lost. This is the sacredly held collective dream of a better future, of a world that thrives, made manifest.

Element #2:

World Transformation through the Vital Keys

"True transformation begins when we start to find appreciation for all people, for all interactions and relationships that cross our paths ... What I have found is when you make a choice to find the gift within the most difficult interactions in relationships within your life, you start to become your own miracle worker. Opening the door to seeing and experiencing from a place of non-judgment and acceptance invites miracles into our lives ... Literally, the world transforms."[3]

~OPRAH WINFREY
(Philanthropist, Talk Show Host)

Extraordinary leadership calls us to connect personal transformation with systemic reform. The vital keys can help us accomplish this. The following is an overview of the beneficial outcomes that can occur when we choose to transform our ways of being and leading relative to the seven Vital Keys, and how these outcomes help to manifest our collective dream.

Key 1: Transforming Our Power Over Paradigm To Power With inherently addresses *our collective dream to honor equality for all beings and our planet, while removing instruments of war and aggression.* Like the stories of Sequoyah, as we transform our dualistic and autocratic "victim/perpetrator" model and approaches, we create hope in place of oppression, empowering people to act, live and lead in healthier ways. As part of our manifestation, we will see improved relationships at every level, with reductions in domestic violence and in conflicts within organizations and teams, ultimately extending to reductions in crime, wars, genocide and ecocide. Such change also encourages the once-shadow leaders and organizations to potentially support the movement to lead by greater wisdom. Consciously choosing such positive approaches stimulates the creation of healthier collaborations and innovative

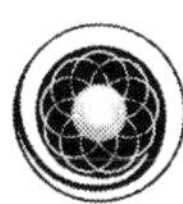

solutions that are not based on competitive, predatory or warring ways, but instead on our mutual desire to resolve our greatest challenges and concerns. We may even see the new paradigm inspiring worldwide environmental and humanitarian projects.

Key 2: Transforming to Timely Truth-Telling addresses *our collective dream to speak truth to power, to call out corruption, to be able to share our gifts without fear, and to own our misdeeds, offering apology and atonement for damages done.* In the wake of stories of truth-seekers, like Snoden, Catherine Austin Fitts and others, this transformation inspires us to take risks in support of the greater good, ultimately creating a culture of ease where "speaking one's truth" becomes the norm. This allows people to feel seen and heard, resulting in more effective solutions being brought to the table. Leading with greater wisdom becomes easier because decisions are no longer based on false premises and deceit, but on increased truth-telling and transparency. This also reduces resentment and retaliatory abuse, and encourages increased truth-seeking behavior in others, clarifying relationships at every level — personal, organizational and global. Our nation may even regain the mutual respect and honoring of other nations by encouraging the same behavior globally. Coupled with the new Power paradigm, speaking Truth allows us to shift from nations based on deceitful rigged systems and manipulative control to ones who wish to put their cards on the table. This includes unveiling long-held secrets (that ultimately tear nations apart), and reconfiguring our systems to reflect healthier, more transparent ways of being. The arc of this change may be long, but as one nation begins to model this behavior, others will follow.

Key 3: Transforming Our Integrity to Walk Our Deeper Talk supports *our collective dream of a world that thrives, where our gifts are shared without fear and our desire to shift away from corruption in our actions and our systems* is satisfied. By realigning with our core allegiance and moral compass, we become more fully ourselves, and bring that congruence to our personal and professional relationships. As reflected in the ceremonial stories of the Mamos of Colombia, with greater integrity, there's no need to hide or separate parts of ourselves; this allows for more effective and authentic communication, including offering apology and atonement when needed. Together, transformed Integrity, Truth, and Power give rise to new governance practices, which, because of their reduced tendency toward corruption, both decrease the need for "whistle blowers" and offer them respect and protection when problems do arise. Leaders with greater integrity are better able to see breaches within our larger (national and global) systems, and to identify where such breaches — especially those that have infiltrated our legislation with corrupted processes — can be shaken up, and changed or replaced with healthier ones. Transforming integrity on the personal, organizational and global levels can turn the tides to create a more unified and congruent world, supplanting that which no longer serves the greater good of humanity and our planet.

Key 4: Transforming Unhealthy Separation and Honoring Uniqueness Within the Whole directly addresses *our collective dream to honor all peoples and cultures, and to value and respect each individual and the gifts they contribute to the whole.* The more connected we feel to our own gifts and contributions, the more we appreciate those of others, and the more motivated we are to collaborate with commitment, flexibility and responsibility. This creates deeper connections in all our relationships, increasing joy, morale and productivity in both our home and work environments. As our leadership approach shifts to embrace shared power, each member is intrinsically valued for the important roles they play. As we recall the story of Raj, we can more easily imagine that as training in empathy, emotional fluency and multicultural awareness become part of our organizations, we *will* shift from conflict, resentment, competition and fear to support, cooperation and non-violent communication. On a larger scale, this transformation reduces race-creed-color prejudice, violence, crime and war, while increasing multicultural collaborations designed to positively improve all areas of our lives; this includes atoning for atrocities against "the other," and committing to greater stewardship of plants, animals, all of Nature, and ultimately our connection to Spirit.

Key 5: Transforming to Dynamic Balance intersects with *our collective dream of honoring all cultures and individuals, and valuing each contribution from youth to elders, feminine and masculine, intuition and*

logic, head and heart. When we transform to a more dynamically balanced life, we naturally lead with greater grace and wisdom, and experience increased health in body, mind and spirit. When many people begin to lead their lives and their work in this way, tremendous integration becomes possible. As reflected in the story of Robert who was not allowed to attend his own mother's funeral due to a workplace desperately out of balance, this key helps each of us to move from environments of extreme and dualistic approaches to those of multiple possibilities and alternative solutions rich with options. Work arenas synergistically shift from reliance on entrenched processes and structures to the flexible consideration of what is actually needed, melding existing elements with innovations. Extending this to our current societal norms (which carry tremendous imbalances), this shift impels intuitive approaches to flourish. It allows for reflection, with the divine feminine dancing alongside the divine masculine, and integrates being and doing, right brain and left brain — like the Eagle and the Condor prophecy — rather than waging battle one against the other. With new balanced paradigms in all sectors, we can replace unhealthy structures in our economy, health, education, governance and other systems throughout the world.

Key 6: Transforming to Remember Our Miraculous Nature addresses *our collective dream of a world that thrives on every level, honoring and cherishing all, and reminding us to be people of discernment, divine creativity and wisdom.* With this shift, we create the opportunity for our higher selves and spirit to move through us, encouraging the best decisions and paths to manifest — for everyone involved. We then can change our most ingrained beliefs and default reactions towards more life-affirming and healthier choices. It also increases our faith in our inner capacities and connection to all life, allowing us to evolve without so much unnecessary struggle. Connected by spirit, we experience greater ease and discernment in intimate and collegial relationships. As with the story of my vision that inspired me to give a man hope rather than leave him to take his own life, we also recognize how each experience can serve us in miraculous ways — including unusual encounters with mentors and teachers who suddenly appear when we need them, or messages from Nature, other creatures, or other-dimensional beings that provide us with insights into the exact solutions that happen to work. As this wisdom multiplies within each leader, and is shared across communities, cultures, society and the world, we will have the opportunity to witness an increase of miracles on this planet, encouraging our collective dream to flourish.

Key 7: Manifesting Dreams and Transforming World Systems through the Heart encompasses all aspects of the collective dream. The very choice to transform, with the hope of becoming better leaders of our own lives, our organizations, our countries, etc., marks our commitment to Extraordinary Leadership, a lifelong process that is ongoing, mutually gifting, and ever-evolving. With passion and divine guidance, we can connect our personal dreams of the life we wish to live with the collective dream of a better world that embraces the honoring of all beings and the principle of No Harm. As we expand our inner transformation out into the world, we create ripples of transformation that encourage others to do the same — to share their passions and visions in inventive ways that allow concrete and integrative solutions to take hold. As transformation synergistically combines and enhances all the other keys, we will witness shifts, both small and large, throughout our lives — addressing issues of poverty, energy, water, healthcare and more — along with the rapid expansion of solutions, inventions and innovative practices that work to positively impact our world.

"A single powerful change of heart can counteract the multitudes of heartless choices from the past and champion transformation on a planetary scale."

~WHISPERS FROM THE HEART OF THE WORLD
(Great Spirit's Messenger)

Here is an example of a world transformation that was made a long time ago, and which applies several (if not all) of the Vital Keys, including Power, Integrity, Balance, Healing Unhealthy Separation, and Transforming through the Heart. In his comprehensive book, *The Land of the Living,* Dr. Steven Borish describes an incredible story of transformation through the heart of a single leader.[4] Although this happened many years ago, I believe this story is still very relevant today.

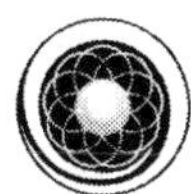

(The names in this story have not been changed.)

> *In late 18th century Denmark, most people were tenant farmers living on rural estates governed by a feudal system: all males between the ages of four and forty were bound to the estate; the landowner appointed all estate officials, including the judge, priest and bailiff; forced labor was required on the landowner's fields; tenant farmers had no inheritance rights; and forms of torture were legally allowed. In summary, a luxurious existence for the few estate owners, who often lived in Paris and Copenhagen, was made possible by the labor of the many — a bound community of subsistence tenant farmers.*
>
> *Led by a single man, a magnificent series of Land Reforms (mid-1700's through 1799) carried out a skillful and non-violent social revolution in which every one of the above feudal features was abolished without a single shot being fired. The acknowledged leader behind these reforms was Christian Ditlev Reventlow (1748-1827), one of the wealthiest of all landowners, a man who had multiple estates.[5] Moreover, Reventlow successfully recruited both the Danish king and a majority of the other wealthy landowners to support him. One piece of the enacted legislation shows its practical wisdom: the law that abolished forced residence on the estate, passed on June 20, 1788, decreed that "forced residence to the estates shall be completely abolished from the first of January, in the year 1800." If the law had abolished forced residence the next day, there would have been chaos! By allowing the intervening twelve years between 1788 and 1800, there was time for local councils to be formed on each estate. Tenant farmers met with the estate owners and their representatives. All the necessary details were peacefully negotiated, and in this way a huge and fundamental transformation of Danish society was accomplished.*

In a contextual framework similar to that of our own current Power Over economic and cultural environments, the Danish people were able to accomplish a series of non-violent cooperative reforms that shifted the balance of power for generations to come. Even more astonishing, this successful land reform movement was initiated by one of the wealthiest, most influential members of the Danish nobility. And it was this man who recruited other members of his own privileged group to collaborate

in the hard work that was required for this groundbreaking social transformation to take place.

Fueled by the European Enlightenment's dream to create more illuminated ways of being and leading, this visionary, Christian Ditlev Reventlow, passionately and effectively championed the interests of the disenfranchised tenant farmers (the equivalent of our current 99%). In our world today, we can look to examples like this to emulate, and use similar synergetic problem-solving methods to transform many of our own failing systems. Imagine if this type of approach could be used to more effectively navigate through issues related to healthy food creation and distribution, the stewardship of water and land, and the preservation of original organic seeds, endangered species and our planet! This was an amazing example of Extraordinary Leadership, in particular what can happen when members of the highest elite of a society become passionately involved in sacred service to the Whole.

New Transformational Governance Structures

"Everything depends on a new spirit breaking through among men. May it be that, after the many centuries of fear, suspicion and hate, more and more a spirit of reconciliation and mutual trust will spread abroad. The constant practice of the art of Sociocracy [Dynamic Governance] and of the education necessary for it, seem to be the best way in which to further this spirit, upon which the real solution of all world problems depends." [6]

~KEES BOEKE

(Dutch Reformist Educator, Pacifist, 1884-1966)

Christian Ditlev Reventlow radically altered the way his world operated. Transformation via the vital keys does the same thing: it implicitly alters the way governments and organizations operate. Such change may seem daunting, but it is essential if the existing order is unhealthy or corrupt — as is the case today. For the most part, our modern organizational structures are oppressive and constrictive — and not working. These

systems frustrate nearly everyone involved, from the lowest to the highest levels of power. See if this exasperated venting from a dedicated hard-working businessman sounds familiar:

> "I am supposed to be living in a democracy ... but I spend much of my life at work in a basic feudal structure. There is the Duke of Operations, an Earl of Administration, a Baroness of Personnel, and so on. Even if those people are called Managers or Vice-Presidents, it amounts to the same thing. I am not at all enfranchised. If I think they aren't doing well, the only vote I have is with my feet, walking out the door."[7]

Most of our current governance structures operate this way: using outmoded, Industrial Age, top-down, command-and-control hierarchical models that almost inevitably default to Power Over. They suppress Truth, promote Separation and squelch our dreams, both personal and collective. Kees Boeke, one of the pioneers of new governance forms, insightfully expressed this:

> "We are so accustomed to majority rule as a necessary part of democracy that it is difficult to imagine any democratic system working without it. It is true that it is better to count heads than to break them, and democracy, even as it is today, has much to recommend it as compared with former practices. But the party system has proved very far from providing the ideal democracy of people's dreams. Its weaknesses have become clear enough: endless debates in Parliament, mass meetings in which the most primitive passions are aroused, the overruling by the majority of all independent views, capricious and unreliable election results, government action rendered inefficient by the minority's persistent opposition. Strange abuses also creep in. Not only can a party obtain votes by deplorably underhanded methods, but, as we all know, a dictator can win an election with an 'astonishing' majority by intimidation."[8]

By contrast, new governance systems are constructed around different assumptions about how people operate in a healthy environment. These new systems assume that organizations, companies, and communities can *self-organize* to solve their own problems, can gracefully adapt to changing conditions, and can address issues that come up in daily operations in ways that honor each individual's contributions. Imagine living and working in environments with exceptional interpersonal alignment, where trust is a natural by-product of the organizational structures, and where checks and balances are already in place to activate fairness and feedback. Imagine organizations where the concerns of *all* stakeholders — investors, donors, workers, the community and the global environment — are taken into account in critical decision-making. In such systems, people are valued, their voices are genuinely heard, and their concerns are addressed and integrated; also, space is provided to resolve issues and explore new ideas and opportunities. What a refreshing and healing transformation it would make for our world if organizations, from small to large, became corruption-resistant while including the best in leadership, performance and decision-making practices!

Such transformations are possible through the exploration of the vital keys as they intersect with new and emerging governance models. These new models seem to naturally support Power With approaches, Truth-telling, and Honoring Uniqueness and Wholeness.[9] I have been exposed to several of these new systems (and their offshoots) over the past seven years, and have come to see governance structures as one of the most significant aspects of transformation — for both their innovators and our planet. From the individual perspective, this work is truly a labor of the heart; it is inspired by a deep motivation to create a better world in which to live, and every person I know who has been involved in the evolution of one of these new systems has spent at least ten years of their lives on it, often without much acknowledgement or remuneration. From the planetary perspective, the rise of these new governance structures signifies another way in which our collective dream is trying to be born: we are seeking foundational processes to assist in our re-emergence as a whole and thriving people, as well as a means by which to bear witness to the positive effects we wish to experience and engender in our world. In the following sections, I will provide a summary of three of these new governance systems — Sociocracy, Holacracy, and an emerging framework under development by Coalescence. I will also present some reflections on "heart-infused" evolutionary models of interaction and positive engagement.

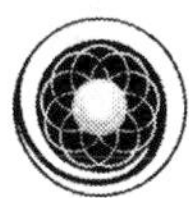

Sociocracy

Sociocracy, also known as "Dynamic Governance" or dynamic self-governance, is the oldest of the new models, and the inspiration for most of the others. It is a method of organizing and governing groups using the principle of *consent*. Sociocracy promotes the values of equality, freedom, and the mutual exchange of each person's unique gifts. Its precepts complement core democratic ideals while introducing new ways to lead, which entail and encourage Power With practices, neutralizing the negative effects of long Power Over dominance. All of this results in clearly-distributed, self-organizing power structures that try to take into account the concerns of all stakeholders and members, enabling organizations to be more sustainable and adaptable. Since its inception, Sociocracy has been adopted (although not always publicly) around the world by hundreds of different public, private, and non-profit businesses, associations, and communities — as well as several local government agencies.

Interestingly, the history of Sociocracy is integrally woven into the development of sociology, which was introduced by the French philosopher, August Comte. Hoping to heal the social malaise created after the French Revolution, Comte extended his long-standing desire to better understand human group dynamics by beginning, in the 1850's, to develop a new organizing system for which he coined the term "Sociocracy." Derived from the Latin word *socius* (*"companion"*) and the Greek word *kratein* (*"to govern"*), Sociocracy defined a *society of equals governed by themselves*. This was done with mutual consent[10] guiding decision-making at every level. This groundbreaking philosophical work deeply influenced Lester Frank Ward, who brought sociology to the United States in the early 1900's. Ward identified the focus of "socios" (i.e., society) not merely as "masses of people," but rather as "people who have a social relationship with each other."[11]

Ward's work, in turn, influenced the Dutch educator and global peace activist Kees Boeke, who then applied Sociocratic concepts to education in the 1920's. Coupled with operational practices implemented by the Quakers, Boeke's work specifically focused on equality and consent-based

decision-making. Boeke founded the Werk Plaat Community School in Holland in 1926 that became nationally known and highly influential for making students co-responsible for both their curricula and the school's support activities (e.g., cooking, cleaning, etc.). Children were treated like adults and were on a first-name basis with their teachers — this even included the children of Holland's royal family. This school is still in operation today.

Although the term "Sociocracy" had been used since the early 1800's, it was attached to sociology as a new way of studying human behavior, akin to anthropology and other sciences. It was therefore used in educational and philosophical environments, but it didn't evolve into an *organized governance system* until the 1970's, when Gerard Endenburg, one of Boeke's students at the Werk Plaat school, envisioned applying it beyond education to all types of organizations. Taking a whole systems approach, Endenburg expanded the original Sociocratic ideals and created a model based upon the following four foundational principles[12], listed here as they are *currently* articulated:

1. **Consent** — This Principle states that policy decisions (e.g., the rules and boundaries in which an organization or group operates) will be made by consent. Consent differs from consensus in that it does not mean everyone agrees; instead, it means that no one objects significantly. Specifically, consent exists when there are no remaining major "risks" (to mission, products, job performances, etc. — expressed as "objections") that are deemed too detrimental for the organization to allow. Consent averts the "Tyranny of Consensus," which can thwart decision-making by demanding full group agreement. In Sociocracy, consent-based decision-making is used for elections (see below), as well as proposals, performance reviews, dismissals, etc.

2. **Circles** — The Principle of Circles states that a Sociocratic organization is made up of circles — semi-autonomous, self-organizing groups (or teams) that each make their own membership decisions, decide on their own working methods, and manage their own budgets. Each circle defines its policy (plus some policies which

apply to other circles reporting to it) by consent, and uses other decision-making methods, as applicable, to perform its operational work.

3. **Double-Linking** — Most conventional organizations have a top-down organizational structure, with managers providing links from one level of the organization down to the one below, but these "single links" often become chokepoints for key information that people on the front lines know but upper management does not, resulting in "the right hand doesn't know what the left hand is doing" situations. "Double-linking," with representation top-to-bottom and bottom-to-top, curbs such problems. Note: Sociocratic organizations use "double-links" to hierarchically connect circles. A "super-circle" provides guidance and prioritization to "sub-circles" below it through an operational Leader role (elected by the super-circle); simultaneously, a Representative role (elected by the sub-circle) provides feedback and guidance from the lower circle back to its super-circle. Representatives (plus the operational Leader) are full members of both circles for the sake of any consent decision-making.

4. **Elections By Consent** — The Principle of Elections by Consent replaces majority-rule voting, which usually obscures the voice of anyone whose opinion is in the minority. This principle states that the selection of important roles, especially the role of Representative, cannot be delegated; instead, they must be chosen by the consent of the circle which they represent. This ensures that the organization is woven together by a web of consent, and that power flows in circles through the entire organization. Note: Sociocracy includes some significant meeting practices to ensure equivalency amongst members. For example, circle meetings start with an opening "round" that allows each member to "check in" and share what's real for them, without reaction or dialogue, including anything that might affect their participation in the meeting. Circle meetings additionally end with a closing round, where valuable feedback about the meeting process becomes part of the permanent meeting record.

Endenburg applied these powerful principles to his family's electrical engineering firm in the Netherlands. Endenburg Electrotechniek was the first Sociocratically-organized modern corporation and, after over four decades, it continues to successfully serve the public as a thriving business. Endenburg and his colleague Annewiek Reijmer also founded the Sociocratic Center in Rotterdam, Netherlands, to assist other organizations in adopting Sociocracy.

Beginning in the 1980's, word spread internationally about Sociocracy's successes, and numerous non-Dutch consultants sought out and earned certifications at Endenburg's Center. One of these consultants, an American businessman named John Buck, co-authored a book titled *We the People: Consenting to a Deeper Democracy* with his colleague Sharon Villines. Based on the authors' years of experience expanding and developing advanced training programs in Sociocracy, the book stirred great interest and helped spread Sociocratic practices in the U.S. and abroad.

"Sociocracy has been extremely beneficial for us at Ternary [Software company]. We're one of the fastest-growing companies in Philadelphia – with revenue growth of 38 percent last year [2005] and an average of 50 percent per year over the last three years. We could never have achieved this under a traditional management system. We plan to find or create other companies ready to adopt our governance model, in hopes of creating a sociocratic collective that would make it easier for our organizations to do business with one another."[13]

~**BRIAN ROBERTSON**
(Software and Governance Entrepreneur)

With any system, there are potential benefits and challenges. For Sociocracy, the benefits include more clearly distributed power (reducing both Power Over and the burden on management), as well as greater organizational alignment, harmony, and exceptional trust. Sociocracy is corruption-resistant, and helps bring to light any implicit or shadow aspects (e.g., worker oppression) that might exist. It is also extremely

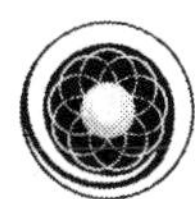

effective in integrating worker perspectives, so much so that the Dutch government has granted Sociocratic businesses exemption from union labor laws. This governance model helps to create more adaptive, efficient, and sustainable organizations, attempting to integrate stakeholder perspectives in critical decision-making (including investors, donors, workers, community, and the environment). Sociocracy also has principles and rules that can be embedded into legal bylaws and charters, and is scalable to very large organizations.

While Sociocracy beautifully articulates four powerful principles, its potential challenges include confusion arising from loosely defined terms, and its lack of a turnkey platform (i.e., no commercially available software) or templates for ease of implementation. There are no detailed guides to track metrics (e.g., structure, roles, accountability, etc.), or to help navigate the nuances of process (such as compensation, hiring and firing, strategic planning, and so on). This results in a steep learning curve, making Sociocracy difficult to back-fit into existing organizations. Similarly, Sociocracy's specifications are presented in the original cybernetic terminology — easily translatable for engineers, but not so easy for other disciplines. For all these reasons, Sociocracy requires a great deal of training to properly implement. Even with training, Sociocracy demands great sensitivity and finesse on the part of facilitators to process information and reach consent, or meetings can bog down, causing delays in critical decision-making and task completion.

Despite these challenges, Sociocracy has paved the way for new forms of governance to take hold in nearly all sectors of society. Several significant institutions who adopted Sociocracy and used it as a springboard to help them move to structures more in alignment with their needs include: the U.S. Green Building Council[14]; the European divisions of Shell, Heineken, Mars, and Pfizer; and Yukon College. Organizations that are currently using Sociocracy include: the Institut Français at the University of Regina (Canada); a division of Woodbury University in California; technology companies such as Storm Integrated Solutions (which provides organizational governance solutions to other organizations); and several cohousing and intentional communities. For additional information, visit http://sociocracyconsulting.com/ or www.sociocracy.biz.[15]

Holacracy

Holacracy defines itself as a "real–world–tested social technology for agile and purposeful organizations. It radically changes how an organization is structured, how decisions are made, and how power is distributed."[16] Originally inspired by Sociocracy and organizational best-practices such as efficiency studies, leadership work, and Ken Wilbur's integral philosophy, Holacracy emerged during the 2000's from the efforts of Brian Robertson and his team at Ternary Software company.

Intended as a comprehensive model for structuring, governing and running organizations, Holacracy utilizes several of the key principles and methods of Sociocracy while attempting to avoid its drawbacks. Like Sociocracy, Holacracy includes consent–based decision-making (i.e., "no objections"), circles, double-linking, and consent-based elections. Unlike Sociocracy, Holacracy defines itself as a *purpose–driven* system with a highly structured set of rules outlining governance processes. These enable organizations to exist with their broader purpose intact, even as the people involved come and go. Roles are defined by purpose, domains of authority, and accountability. In addition, individuals can *create* roles that support the expression of their talents to the fullest. This requires each person to identify and process their "tension," which is defined as "the gap between what actually is and what could be" — encompassing both issues and opportunities. Processing these "tensions" is done to clarify how each role needs to be modified in order to get the job done in the best way possible. In an attempt to alleviate some of the initial implementation challenges (which have also, at times, been experienced by Sociocracy), Holacracy created a 30-page rule–based constitution, and turnkey processes for meetings. Both of these are supported by an online software platform called "Glass Frog," which can record organizational structures, roles, trends, projects, meeting records, etc.

Holacracy has benefits and challenges as well. On a broad scale, its benefits overlap with those of Sociocracy: fairer and more efficient distribution of power, dynamic representation with transparency and inclusivity, and greater organizational alignment, harmony and trust — all due to the same self-organizing circle structures that use consent and

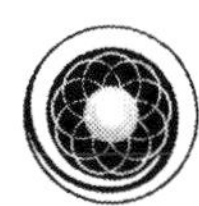

double-linking. Like Sociocracy, Holacracy reduces corruption and encourages Power With. Holacracy's *unique* benefits include its focused design, which helps purpose-driven businesses and professional organizations to more easily adopt it through a turnkey approach (which features a software platform with predefined step-by-step structures and templates). Also, Holacracy's highly-defined shared "language" helps people communicate changes to their role definitions readily and clearly, allowing for autonomy and ease of process. Holacracy also has strongly-defined protocols that simplify meeting facilitation, and it excels at meticulous record-keeping (items-to-complete, metrics and current projects) and clear accountability (public lists of roles).

Even with a compelling business case (Ternary Software), the online software platform "Glass Frog," and impressive marketing and training packages, Holacracy is challenging to implement. First, its constitution is thorough but complex, and is written in legalese, often making the system rules difficult to understand.[17] Next, Holacracy requires extensive (and often repeated) training for both meeting facilitators and participants; for example, "processing tensions" requires very skillful facilitation or people shut down and begin to process in ways that are unhealthy and unproductive. Another issue is that fair compensation and salary distribution (not covered in the constitution) can be difficult to define: Holacracy's framework of dynamically changing role definitions can create imbalances between what's best for the individual and what's best for the organization. This can lead to burnout and resentment ("I'm overworked and underpaid"), even when people have chosen their own roles. In addition, Holacracy is currently a "closed system." That is, its constitution is legally limited in such a way that the community cannot move the system forward, but must rely on Holacracy's developers to draft successive versions of the document (the developers are working on this issue.). Finally, the purpose-driven system, which focuses on roles rather than people, may serve to negate the value of collaborative teams, unintentionally depreciating the holistic aspects of individuals.

Navigating through some of these concerns, Holacracy's popularity has increased dramatically over the past several years, receiving considerable media business coverage from sources like CNN, Forbes Business Week, Business Insider, etc. Even Dilbert published a cartoon about Holacracy. Significant adopters of Holacracy include the David Allen Company, Arca Tech Systems, TalkSpirit (Europe), and Zappos.com — the most publicized due to the size and quality of its culture and product. For more information, visit www.holacracy.org.

Coalescence — Organizational Operating System

There is a newly-emerging governance and organizational operating system called Coalescence. Conceived by J.T. Brown III, Coalescence seeks to integrate, refine, and expand upon the strongest aspects of both Sociocracy (powerful principles) and Holacracy (clear rules and processes), while addressing some of their shortcomings.

Like its predecessors, Coalescence takes a whole systems approach, using circle structures, consent-based decision-making, and the equivalent of double-linking to ensure fair power distribution, dynamic representation, and transparency. It also incorporates structures and practices that facilitate meetings and support meticulous record-keeping and clear accountability. Coalescence differs from other new forms of governance in two significant ways. First, it is designed around a set of "core principles" necessary to support *true* democratic systems — such as non-domination, interconnection, the fundamental equality of individuals, mutual responsibility and other Power With concepts.[18] Because of this orientation, Coalescence is both purpose-driven (like Holacracy) and *principle–driven,* supporting flexibility and helping to ensure that roles do not override human value. Secondly, Coalescence seeks to make it easy for organizations to adopt its approach: it has a unique, full-featured organizational framework; it has a plain-language, open-source organizational standard, which includes legal architecture that can be fully incorporated into bylaws and operating agreements; Coalescence also plans to provide a wide range of implementation support services (including customized software), plus training and certification programs.

As with other systems, Coalescence will have both benefits and challenges. Its anticipated benefits will include those previously listed for Sociocracy

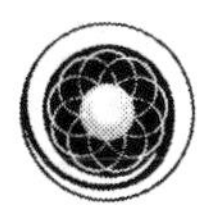

and Holacracy. It will enable the creation of highly-adaptive principle-*and*-purpose-driven organizations that increase performance, efficiency, resiliency, transparency, and trust. Additionally, Coalescence's open-source standard will allow the rapid integration of critical feedback and experience from users, enabling the system to evolve dynamically.

One of the known challenges for Coalescence (as with all new governance systems) is that skillful facilitation of meetings requires considerable training. Although Coalescence is still under development it is a very promising system. As more individuals and organizations become aware of Coalescence, the leaders who adopt and test its organizational operating system will also be able to speak to its benefits and challenges. For more information, visit: http://www.coalescence.global/.

"Heart-Infused" Governance Systems

Many of the new governance systems began because heart was not sufficiently involved in the pre-existing systems. However, I believe that there are still elements missing from even the new methods, and these would be remedied through explicit infusion of the 7 Vital Keys. Most new governance systems do support and demonstrate *some* of the vital keys, such as consciously choosing Power With versus Power Over, speaking Truth, encouraging Integrity and Honoring Uniqueness within the Whole. This can be seen in the following features that are shared by these new systems:

- *Consent-based decision-making and circle structures* (encourage and honor Power With, Truth, Integrity and Uniqueness).
- *Double-linking between circles* (honors Power With, Truth, and Integrity).
- *Elections by consent* (supports Uniqueness, Truth, and Power With; eliminates the "Tyranny of the Majority" which can disenfranchise 49% of the population).
- Some systems also allow for individuals to define their own roles (further supports Uniqueness).

All of these features are certainly beneficial. At the same time, my

personal experiences with several of the new governance models is that they often neglect the need for balance, have challenges with organizational sustainability, and could go farther in both examining power dynamics and incorporating intuitive and extra-ordinary elements (like our miraculous nature). In practical terms, people in the field (including some of my colleagues) are diligently addressing some of these issues by working on the following:

- Creating governance constitutions that are not overly complex and that are written in layman's terms.
- Making the systems more user-friendly without removing important elements.
- Ensuring flexibility within the systems to allow adjustments based on cultural or tribal climates (including dynamic shifts due to cycles of group evolution).
- Addressing issues related to collaboration and the integration of individuals who prefer to work solo.

Some of the issues with new governance systems mirror what can happen to people who become inspired about following spiritual paths but go overboard and become ungrounded and lacking in practicality. Within governance terms, this can play out as meetings that are so oriented toward hearing everyone's voice that no decisions get made, and group issues get bogged down by individual objections. On the other end of the spectrum, some systems are so rule-based that they don't easily allow for individual differences that are not covered within the protocols. Just as spirituality has to be balanced with the needs of physicality, these systems need to inject Dynamic Balance into their structures to deftly blend head with heart, doing with being, and masculine with feminine principles (for example, knowing what issues to continue to discuss within a meeting, and what issues to take offline in separate sessions such as empathy training or conflict resolution). Dynamic Balance is also needed to help organizations to remain financially viable while trying to apply new practices that shift power and communication dynamics.

Balancing head with heart and logic with intuition are especially

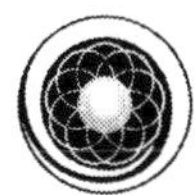

important within governance systems when there is conflict. For example, even within the new systems, dismissal (firing or laying off) is often done unilaterally and privately. This violates the spirit of the circle system, and increases Separation and emotional disconnection. People who are asked to leave usually do so under a "cloud," and people left behind don't get to honor the person for the contributions they actually made. In contrast, I have been involved with organizations that fully empowered circles so that dismissal was group-facilitated, and the result was an amazing outpouring of truth and appreciation. In these situations, the person exiting left with a true understanding of their value and accomplishments, as well as clarity about the job they no longer "fit," while fellow employees got to speak their truth openly without gossip or shame. This cleared the air for everyone and paved the way for healthier future engagements.

I also believe that governance systems need to encompass deeper levels of meaning than those generated from organizational purposes alone. We need to ask: "Why do people seek jobs and careers in the first place?" Yes, we want to get a paycheck, and yes we want to support our organization's goals, but people seek professions that give meaning to their lives, that satisfy their need for personal expression, and that challenge their skills and help them to grow. Governance systems that try to lock these boundless concepts into a set of bounded rules can become stuck and unsatisfying. They can also create situations where people burn out or become confused and chaotic as they try to accurately and thoroughly define all their roles for the governance structure. At the very least, it is important to have a dialogue or check-in on the question: "Does your job utilize your skills to your satisfaction, and is this what you want to be spending 8 hours a day doing?"

Finally, I also feel that new governance systems must incorporate into their core the new world that is coming into being — one in which the intuitive and miraculous are honored and accepted as "normal." One way to do this is to introduce meditation practices (guided or not) into organizational processes such as meetings, especially those in which persistent problems or interpersonal issues are trying to be resolved.

I have used this in my "Divine Leadership" work with executives, including CEOs, and VPs from a broad spectrum of disciplines — spanning healthcare, engineering (electrical, industrial and nuclear, etc.), science, education, the arts and more — and the results have been truly amazing. Even (and sometimes especially) people who are resistant to meditation find that when they relax within sacred space and open to intuitive and extrasensory information, they receive remarkable insights and guidance. When groups are involved in such a process, synergy can create even more extraordinary results — when, for example, multiple people get the same unexpected idea, helping to confirm its validity.

Similarly, organizations can make time in their daily routine for such support mechanisms as: bodywork (yoga, Tai Chi, etc.); emotional techniques (such as empathy training, non-violent communication, or even simple practices like returning focus to loving thoughts or gratitude instead of anger); and communion with the natural world (e.g., going for a walk, holding meetings outdoors, etc.). Our entrenched Separation-based systems label such activities as "frivolous" or "touchy-feely," but organizations who have begun embracing these techniques are already seeing significant positive results — in both organizational goals and employee satisfaction.[19] Dynamically balancing these practices helps to create environments in which inventions, innovations and evolutionary movements have the potential to emerge in a heartbeat.

Since most of these miraculous mechanisms are not well-known within business, and some are highly contingent on the quality of the facilitation, I encourage organizations to *hire an expert* to bring these methods into the work paradigm. I cannot emphasize enough how critical it is for us to reinstate the intuitive element into our work processes. To the best of my knowledge, none of the existing new governance structures incorporate (or even address) this Vital Key, so progressive organizations and groups will have to implement it themselves; again, I encourage hiring a consultant who is well-versed in this area of expertise to facilitate this.

Just as each individual has a unique soulprint, so do organizations. This means that any new form of governance must also be dynamically flexible to support societal and organizational uniqueness. We no longer live in a

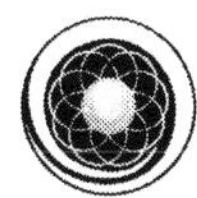

world consisting only of cookie-cutter structures. This is especially true in the United States, where we have been referred to internationally as "the melting pot" of cultures and traditions from all over the world. This diversity doesn't need to be a detriment, but rather can serve as an asset to inform new ways of leading. What this means is that each organization has an opportunity to carefully discern the governance models and practices that are the best fit for their greatest contribution to the Whole.

What is most clear to me is that people want and need change that helps create the world of our collective dream. There is an urgency to re-empower people with the ability to value and share their own unique contributions and voices. As power is redistributed, there is an enlivening of the human spirit, igniting the possibility that all of us can and do make a difference in our world. New governance systems, reflective of processes long held sacred by indigenous tribes, have already demonstrated practices that work and are creating a positive impact. As more organizations, from small to large and private to public, begin to integrate these new systems, our world will shift toward the "more beautiful" version that "our hearts know is possible." Imagine prime ministers, presidents and other heads of states who, after being elected by the people, become *truly accountable* for promises they made — so that when commitments are broken (regardless of the reason), people's voices continue to be heard, valued, and used to help create new alternative solutions that honorably steward humanity and our planet.

Although new governance structures are still evolving, their very existence represents a quantum leap in our journey toward transformation. I believe that their intersection with the vital keys is essential in order to match the best practices and systems with the needs of each unique organization, company and institution. One of the most important elements to include is the rebalancing of heart with head in leadership; remember that empathy is the foundation of all wholistic and healthy relationships, from the personal to the global. It is also useful to remember that different forms of governance have been used in the past by different cultures; I think especially of the circle structures of indigenous councils, Celtic ceremonies, and King Arthur's Round Table.

Element #3: Finding Where Our Personal and Collective Dreams Intersect (the "Sweet Spot")

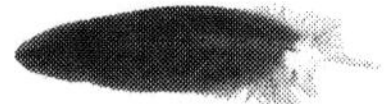

"Love is our true essence. Love has no limitations of caste, religion, race, or nationality. We are all beads strung together on the same thread of love. To awaken this unity — and to spread to others the love that is our inherent nature — is the true goal of human life."

~AMMA
(Spiritual Teacher, The "Hugging Saint")

If we want to be actively involved in manifesting "the more beautiful world," it is important to identify where our personal dreams and transformative shifts intersect with our collective dream. This includes noting which areas in our lives and world systems need the most significant change and which resonate the most with our personal paths. Here, personal and global explorations inform each other, and we cannot always predict what the impact will be. For example, we might start with: "How far can I get in looking at my power issues, and seeing how changing my paradigm affects my family?" and discover that this exploration propels us into: "Hey, I can address power on a larger scale! Maybe I can go into government and make an impact on the world at large."

Identifying Personal Dreams: Consider Purpose, Passion, Gifts and Worldview

We each have gifts, talents, capacities and an overall purpose that we bring into the world — our unique soulprints. But our purpose may remain hidden and unexpressed unless we each ask ourselves evocative questions, such as: *What are my gifts? Why am I here, on this planet at this time? What am I passionate about? What does the world need that I am longing to express?*

By following up on these urgings of our hearts, we will be fulfilling our personal dreams and at least part of our soul's mission in this life. Note that this is not about being "perfect," but about our full expression as people and leaders. Our inspiration can also change over time, and so our purpose or meaning may also transform as we live our lives — or we may stay inspired by a single vision for our entire lifetime. Each of us gets to choose what matters most to us, in each moment and across time, and to choose how we wish to support our heart's callings.

In addition to understanding our purpose, passion and gifts, it is important to understand our personal worldview — the overall perspective from which we see and interpret the world. This overall view is made up of our values and universal beliefs. Our values are what we consider most important as our priorities in life, while universal beliefs are broader beliefs about self, people, and how the world and systems work.

There are most likely as many worldviews as there are people. It is my belief that in order to transform in extraordinary ways, two foundational elements related to worldview are critical to catalyze the greatest positive impact: In all of our thoughts, actions, and ways of being, we (1) honor ourselves, all beings and the planet, and (2) express ourselves with as little harm to ourselves, others and the planet as is humanly possible. Obviously, these two elements guide and support each other, since few of us ever want to harm that which we honor, and one way to honor is to treat with the deference that does no harm.

I also want to express how crucial it is that we believe in others. One of the aspects of being human that I have witnessed as such a tremendous contribution is our capacity to love unconditionally. We also have the ability to remain hopeful despite seemingly untenable circumstances. We are all in this together, and when we support each other — in successful times as well as challenging ones — we can have a significant impact on global transformation. Sometimes this support may take very small forms, like an encouraging smile, an expression of confidence in someone, or lending an unexpected helping hand. Because of my background with intuitive work, I sometimes find myself involved in divine interventions, being drawn by guidance to speak to a total stranger. These interventions are often to tell this person how valuable they really are in a world that might not otherwise tell them so. The responses to the mindful delivery of these comments have invariably been of overwhelming gratitude, a resurgence of hope, and often tears, accompanied by the phrase, "You have no idea what that means to me." I am not talking about "fixing" other people. I am talking about making a heart-felt connection with compassion for our collective state of combined power and vulnerability. Mutual support brings out our divine power, transforming our vulnerability into strength by providing us with motivation and understanding, and by deepening our heart-centered interconnectedness.

"Your ordinary acts of love and hope point to the extraordinary promise that every human life is of inestimable value."

~DESMOND TUTU
(Archbishop, Spiritual Leader)

Another significant human gift is our will-to-live as a species — an extremely powerful instinct, reflected in the even more powerful instinct of a parent to help its offspring — not only to survive, but to thrive. If we could combine these gifts of survival instinct and unconditional love in such a way as to offer them to the *whole* world, not just to our immediate selves, families or species, the purpose of our lives would magnify a million-fold. This is what planetary stewardship really means — feeling that every element of the whole is as important as our own little piece of it, and therefore all must be cherished, protected, honored and loved. Each of us has a role that stirs inside of us, and each action, thought and way of being does indeed impact all other beings, whether we see it or not.

Listening to Crises

Many people who recognize the importance of transformation have a really difficult time actually doing it. The stakes have to be high enough to make the effort of transforming worthwhile in spite of the difficulties. In

fact, the stakes right now are *so* high, that most of us are concerned that transformation may no longer be generated by *conscious* choice, but by the domino effect of corrupted practices and system-to-system collapse *forcing* us into change — changes that will almost assuredly impact us in ways that we do *not* want.

As we witness such unwanted shifts around us, we can seek to be proactive by identifying some of the more pressing personal, organizational and collective dreams we'd like to manifest. Often these dreams become most apparent through *crises* that erupt in the world or in our lives; that is, *crises can actually help to clarify our dreams.* For example, the death in Ferguson, Missouri, in the Autumn of 2014, and the race-related violence it sparked nationally, speaks to our collective dream of *honoring all peoples and cultures.*[20] When we witness what appear to be brutal law enforcement behaviors based on racial profiling, it can trigger core wounds and an array of emotional responses. We might react without thinking, or forget that there are other ways of handling both the immediate and long-term challenges. Large-scale, it may remind us of the need to heal unresolved cultural wounds still festering from slavery, genocide, and any other type of violence due to racial prejudice. Although circumstances like these, seen in the daily news, on YouTube videos, or experienced as live events in our neighborhoods, often do trigger core wounds, we can consciously choose to respond in healing ways.

The critical juncture at which transformative acts can enter is the moment when we find ourselves overwhelmed by an event. We may want to react violently — which will nearly always ignite further violence, often spreading like wildfire across the nation or world. But, we can choose, instead, to use the event as a catalyst for self-examination bringing forth from each of us the commitment to express our emotions non-violently. We can independently research the causes behind the violence rather than to be judgmentally reactive, and perhaps ultimately work to transform our punitive justice system to instead incorporate restorative justice practices. This is one of many examples of how we can personally transform relative to systems in crises that negatively affect us. The collective dream that permeates these events must be addressed first

through personal transformation, and then brought into systemic transformation — in this case, the criminal justice system as a whole.

Our personal dreams may intersect with the collective one through structures we are already involved with, like businesses and social organizations, or we may be inspired to create new systems and structures in the world. The journey is different for each of us. Because life is endlessly creative, there is no "recipe" to tell us how to find our personal intersection with the collective. Curiosity and truthful observation must be our guides. We will know when we have found our personal "sweet spot" by *the way our hearts feel.* We can sense the resonance of our dreams within; we feel galvanized and inspired to move forward to do what is necessary to bring our dreams into reality. The next section presents a series of stories about courageous and resourceful men and women who have made enormous impacts on the world by finding *their* "sweet spots."

Profiles in Transformation

"The stories of past courage ... can teach, they can offer hope, they can provide inspiration, but they cannot supply courage itself. For this, each man must look into his own soul."

~JOHN F. KENNEDY
(35th U.S. President, 1961-1963)

The following story beautifully exemplifies the "sweet spot" intersection of personal and collective dreams. It's about a company that, in fulfilling its purpose in the world, provided an environment in which all the people who worked there could find *their* "sweet spots" too. This refreshing paradigm shift was accomplished primarily through the Vital Keys of Power, Truth, Wholeness, and Balance:

> *The company was called Vickers Metal Works, Inc., of Orlando, Florida. Since I was trained as a fabrication welder, I was encouraged to apply to this company because of their outstanding reputation for high*

quality work and employee satisfaction with little to no turnover. I was hired in November, the only woman on the fabrication floor. I noticed immediately the respect I received from all of my male colleagues and from the owner himself. I was included in all company meetings from the very beginning, and had an equal voice. It was incredibly satisfying to be appreciated, valued and respected in this way.

Due to this collaborative atmosphere, my colleagues also felt comfortable in asking me for my opinion and my support. Then, one day, approximately three weeks after my hiring, the owner called me into his office to tell me he really appreciated my work and that he wanted me to know that typically he gave each of his employees a week's salary as a bonus for Christmas. Because I had just started, he felt that giving me a bonus would be unfair to his other employees, but that he wanted me to know it wasn't because I wasn't doing a great job. I was stunned by this thoughtful gesture. Once again, this company was turning out to be extraordinary!

But the story doesn't end there. Two weeks later, the owner called me into his office for a second time to tell me that he felt, in all fairness, that he needed to run this issue by the rest of his team. He held a meeting with everyone but me, to ask them whether it would be good to give me a bonus too, despite the fact that I would only have been there for approximately five weeks by the time the bonuses were distributed. He told me that it was unanimous: everyone shared with him how much I'd already contributed to the team and that "it would be only fair and reasonable" to give me the bonus too. I was incredibly appreciative. I'd never worked for a company that treated each and every employee with such dignity and equality, while maintaining the highest standards for output with deadlines met.

At a time when so many organizations were ignoring the feminine voice, Vickers demonstrated a wonderful balance by invoking that voice right from the start. This flew in the face of the company's demographic, which was 90% men and 10% women. This amazing experience occurred because one benevolent leader chose to break the default mindset of Power Over and treat all his employees in an extremely positive way. If there were an opportunity to honor Vickers with an award for Extraordinary Leadership, I would support it 100%! I wish all people had the chance to work for a company that advocated such Power With leadership at every turn. This is a form of leading by wisdom that changed the lives of everyone associated with the company, and changed the world just by being present in it.

Becoming the Change You Want to See in the World

"May we each find our way to reclaiming our wholeness. May we find right relationship to ourselves, each other, and Mother Earth. May we rediscover and remember the masculine and the feminine in their magnificent complementary dance that is so life-affirming and so loving. And may we each be messengers in the ways that birds carry seeds in their feathers to re-seed this magnificent home of ours with love and fertility and empathy and compassion and justice and grace. A-men, a-women, and ah-ho." [21]

~NINA SIMONS
(Co-Founder/President Bioneers, Founder Everywoman's Leadership)

For entrepreneurs, their personal dreams often intersect with humanity's path in the creation of new organizations that inspire transformation and manifestation for millions of people. During my Extraordinary Leadership Telesummit Series in 2013, I had the opportunity to dialogue about the creation of one such company — The Shift Network (or just Shift) — with its founder, Stephen Dinan. Shift was created to support the evolution of human consciousness through high-quality, online telesummits and courses, as well as through retreats and live events. Shift's journey from inception to its current incarnation has involved numerous twists and turns — some exciting and satisfying, some overwhelming and challenging. The process required constant attention to stay in Integrity, Wholeness and Dynamic Balance, the primary Vital Keys associated with this transformational "sweet spot." During my interview with him, Stephen described how it all began:

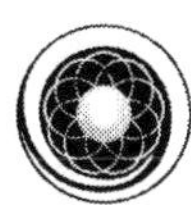

> "I feel like it was a vision that was given to me by a higher plane, a higher source — that there's ultimately a kind of a gameplan for a shift to a new and more enlightened civilization that ... literally tens of thousands of souls have collaborated on ... I was sitting in a meditation retreat in the year 2000 and I got about three days of a very profound download ... [I saw a webwork of awakening consciousness, in the form] of lights turning on around the world, and weaving those together and seeing how the culture of planet Earth is going through what could be the most significant evolutionary shifts in history."[22]

Stephen began by creating programs focused on accelerating the awakening and transforming of individual consciousness. In a short time, Shift had over one hundred courses facilitated by faculty members specializing in leading edge content. Stephen's hope was that if those who participated could experience a more beautiful life filled with connection and vitality, the world could reach a critical mass of transformation for our entire civilization.

With such an elevated sense of purpose, Shift also had to operate as a sustainable business — no small challenge. Some of the issues that arose concerned the timing and roll-out of new projects, team dynamics and the distribution of power. Front and center were decisions about balance relative to the economic exchange: how could Shift make its offerings as accessible and affordable as possible to a global audience while still being able to make payroll, and keeping a keen eye on self-care. Manifesting such a vision in a balanced way meant that many "dots needed to be connected." Stephen expressed that in attempting to support the big picture, he fell out of balance. He kept his focus on the vision, but lost sight of the details, rolled out too many offerings too quickly and ended up "dropping [Shift's] bank accounts close to zero, which was a very, very challenging time."[23]

Additional transformation was needed, but where and how? Although the organization that Stephen and his team had created was providing amazing life-affirming training to millions of people, the venture did not seem sustainable. Because Shift's vision and mission were so compelling and the work so fulfilling, team members were willing to forego portions of their compensation even as they worked extended hours. But they could not keep this up indefinitely.

Over time, it became clear that in order for Shift to survive and thrive, it had to change in multiple ways. Fittingly, an organization leading the way toward transformation needed to go through its own transformation. This had to occur from the inside out, beginning with Stephen himself, as he described:

> "I used to come from what I would call the 'warrior mode': 'I have this heroic destination and I'm just going to use raw will power to force it through,' and that ultimately has cost for body and team and the organization ... I was so attached to the big vision, that I wasn't seeing all the pieces come in ... I've learned this year to really stay attuned to the flow of the river, to not just be listening to my own vision, but stay tuned to listening to those around me."[24]

Stephen recognized that his pushing too hard was a vestige of the old paradigm of the dominant masculine principle, and that he was actually abusing the feminine within him. This was just one of many examples of what wanted to change. Armed with new insights, he and his team chose how to address the issues by mutual consent. They decided to scale back the number of courses they offered as well as some of the larger projects. This enabled them to shorten their work-week to something more humane, and to reduce total costs for the company. Stephen's willingness to change, while fostering a climate that encouraged others to do the same, created the balance needed to retool and reshape Shift. Shift's transformation also shows how incorporating a willingness to open in order to be informed by a higher wisdom helps to evolve extraordinary leadership.

Shift is not the only organization dedicated to supporting global transformation. Many such organizations have already been mentioned in other chapters; a complete list is beyond the scope of this book, but please reference my website, www.leadbywisdom.com, for an ongoing resource list of organizations and companies manifesting extraordinary systems solutions and leadership for our planet.

Answering Calls to Conscience

"Leadership is ultimately about creating a way for people to contribute to making something extraordinary happen."

~ATTRIBUTED TO ALAN KEITH
(Creative Leadership/The Leadership Challenge)

Bioneers is a more established organization than The Shift Network: it has existed for over 25 years, and its process of evolving wise leadership is incredibly rich. Bioneers' founder, Nina Simons, exemplifies an extraordinary leader who has remembered her Miraculous Nature and who seeks Truth and Integrity, with humility and grace. In my 2013 Extraordinary Leadership Telesummit, Nina described three major turning points, or "callings." Each was pivotal to her personal transformation, and helped clarify her "sweet spot(s)."

First, she listened to the calling of her heart, and left her job in the arts to dive into the world of biodiversity. Drawn by an expansive experience of "gardens beyond her wildest dreams," she began to work at "SEEDS of Change," a company started by her husband, Kenny Ausubel and his colleague. One of the intentions of this company was to encourage diversity in our food supply, increasing the abundance of food while minimizing the threat of extinction to our plant species. Feeling the need to expand this effort to connect others with their vision, Nina and Kenny created Bioneers in 1990. Bioneers is a non-profit organization that serves as a hub "for social and scientific innovators with practical and visionary solutions for some of the world's most pressing environmental and social challenges."[25] Through their annual conferences and innovative outreach affiliations, Bioneers connects socially concerned people with breakthrough solutions and with one another. The organization grew rapidly by touching that "sweet spot" at the intersection of personal and collective dreams. By showcasing concrete solutions that are clearly making a difference on our planet, these "bio-pioneers" inspire real hope.

Nina's other two "calls" to transform, which also influenced the evolution of Bioneers, were the need to help re-empower women and the need to shift our justice system.[26] Both of these callings came through intuitive and synchronistic experiences, and Nina was willing to pay attention. The conscious shift to attend to these two very important issues encouraged Nina to author a book called *Moonrise* (a collection of essays on women's leadership) and to develop the "Cultivating Women's Leadership" training series. It also fuels her passion for the fair representation of all voices, regardless of gender, age, race or class. This is Nina's contribution to our collective dream to honor All Our Relations.

World Transformers: Taking on the Big Work

More recently, movements have been created to evoke the greatest transformation possible. One of the most effective of these is the "Thrive Movement," which emerged during the production of the movie "Thrive." It is a global movement, intended to transcend politics and integrate personal spiritual work with informed activism. This movement incorporates and demonstrates *all* of the Vital Key principles. One of the most amazing outcomes is Thrive's website which includes a "Solutions Hub" (www.thrivemovement.com/solutions). This is a public-access, open-source website where people throughout the world can see innovations that are being generated globally in twelve different system sectors, carefully designated by a team of transformational leaders.[27] These sectors include Economics, Science, Education, Justice, Health, Spirituality, Infrastructure, Environment, Media, Governance, Relations (to oneself and to other beings), and the Arts. (Many of these were already discussed at the end of Vital Key #2 on Truth.)

As a result of the Thrive movement, a host of solutions to current issues and problems have already been identified. Thrive's co-founder, Kimberly Carter Gamble, a former *Newsweek International* journalist and social justice activist, believes these solutions confirm the emergence of new paradigms. She has summarized these developments as follows: over 400 inventors have addressed power, water decontamination, and healing technologies; over fifty-five countries have banned or restricted GMO's;

processes have been developed to resist attempts to suppress the Internet; additional processes have been developed to prevent alternative treatments for cancer and other illnesses from being co-opted and suppressed by the pharmaceutical industry and its confederates; twelve UFO research files have been proactively released; and critical news is now being spread through social media and other non-mainstream media sources. These reflect significant transformations "to where we need and want to be."[28]

To take this one step further, the Thrive team has also created a real-time interactive "think-tank" called "Thrive Together." This is a subscription-based online research forum for people who want to engage in more intense and detailed dialogues about the issues, and for those who want to pursue their own investigative research. Thrive Together features webcasts and other interactive projects.

The beauty of the Thrive movement is that it brings together like-minded people from widely-disparate disciplines who then go on to create even more unique and innovative ventures. For example, it stimulated a powerful collaboration between myself and a young spoken-word poet named Jahsiah Abijah Jacobs. This young man has the courage to speak his truth and the passion to manifest his dream for our world. His words carry a "call to action," moving people beyond themselves toward the greater whole in which we live. He shares this with deep appreciation for all sentient beings and with divine inspiration. Here are some of Jahsiah's heart-felt lyrics[29]:

"I Believe in this Generation"

Progressive revelation expands through generations
Advancing civilization with living information of cosmic origination
Although there's some degradation to the message's presentation
Due to the limitations of the mind of its impartation
Conveying inspiration through the imagination
Transforming light pulsations into sound vibrations
Unify with Divine Mind in meditation
Realization from the source of creation

No cessation to the sacred sensation
From this higher elevation we confirm the assertation
All rivers converge at the same location: the Sea of Liberation
With open-minded contemplation we find the permeation
Of the same core truths in every religious organization
Now the dire situation our human race is facing is extinction or elevation
Based on the choices we're collectively making
Greed and material temptation are eating away at the foundation
of our great nation
This is in contraindication to the changes they *say* they are making
Only a corrupt delegation needs classified documentation
With freedom of information we'll see the advent of unsurpassed
technological innovation
Let's overcome the complication through unification
And widespread cultivation of true values, education,
And dedication to harmonious human relations
Let the leaders of nations feel the pain of their population
United in demonstrations of non-cooperation
It's the people that have the power
To financially collapse unjust regimes and corporations
No judgment or condemnation, I believe in this generation!

There are many other organizations besides the Thrive Movement, Bioneers, and Shift, that are involved in global transformation. These include, but are by no means limited to: the Biomimicry Institute[30], the Buckminster Fuller Institute, the Heifer Project, the Rodale Institute, Women for Women, the Seva Foundation, Human Havens, the Pachamama Alliance, and BeeFriendly from FungiPerfecti, as well as thousands of organizations championing organic farming, permaculture, sustainable energy production, sustainable construction and manufacturing methods, alternative medicine, energy transformational work, creative programs and more. In addition, there are millions of *individuals* engaged in this work, some well-known, but many of them private "hidden gurus" who are quietly living their lives well below the radar, but making contributions that are globally-transformative.

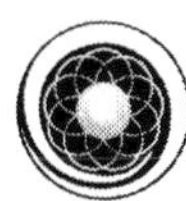

One of the public individuals is architect Jason F. McLennan, founder of the International Living Future Institute. Jason is a recent recipient of the Buckminster Fuller Prize for his innovative and aesthetically intriguing off-the-grid residential and commercial buildings — both in the United States and around the globe.[31] Another public transformer is Sequoyah Trueblood, mentioned in previous vital keys. One of Sequoyah's recent projects was to facilitate a retreat for international oil business executives. The executives engaged in meditation, a sweat lodge, and deep dialogue about what the impact of oil and gas drilling and processing is or potentially will be on current and future generations, as well as the overall effects on our planet.

Each of these "profiles in transformation" illuminates how deeply *courageous* it is to commit to our collective dream. It is the extraordinary leader who recognizes this as their calling! It is the extraordinary leader who goes beyond greed and possessiveness, and who is willing to step beyond their fears to do their part to bring about that dream.

The process of transformation may appear messy and chaotic, and sometimes we will feel alone. But, like caterpillar after caterpillar, each in their respective chrysalises, we will re-emerge. One after the other, like a kaleidoscope of butterflies bringing a multidimensional beauty into being, we will shift as whole systems do, rippling our influence outward into the world.

Navigating the Dark Night: Even Risk is Transformative

"There comes a time when one must take the position that is neither safe, nor political, nor popular. But he must do it because conscience tells him it is right."

~DR. MARTIN LUTHER KING, JR.
(Civil Rights Activist, Spiritual Leader)

As with the other vital keys, sometimes our attempts to implement transformation in support of the collective dream may result in threats to our safety and that of our family and friends. Each of us must weigh the risks and benefits of actions taken to stay aligned with our moral compass. It is very important to consciously and personally make these choices in alignment with Great Spirit and our higher selves. The following is a story that reflects challenging events experienced by several clients and colleagues, each of whom made one of these critical choices — a choice to transform relative to Power, Truth, Integrity, and Our Miraculous Nature, despite the ever-looming risks that threatened to destroy them. May we all have the courage and faith to lead with the wisdom that served to guide them, as represented by Sam's story below.

In most U.S. cities, the government has established departments of fraud detection. These are intended to perform oversight on government projects and programs initiated to benefit communities. Sam, a mid-Western gentleman employed in one of these fraud detection departments, came to me for counsel.

Sam had a top-level security clearance and therefore was privy to a great deal of very secret information. It was his job to detect and expose fraudulent behavior, and he was very good at it. But over time, to his shock and dismay, he began to uncover evidence of fraudulent and illegal activities ***within his own department****. These activities were being carried out against U.S. citizens — the very people the agency was sworn to protect.*

Being a diligent investigator, Sam continued to do his job with integrity, but he grew more and more concerned as evidence of internal fraud mounted. When he was denied a well-earned promotion, Sam discovered that his test results for the promotion had been illegally modified so that another person could get the position — someone his bosses did not perceive as a potential "whistleblower."

When Sam tried to protest his treatment and present his evidence to the department's leaders, he was horrified at what happened. Suddenly, ***he*** *was accused of fraud and cheating. He experienced strong-arming and*

*"the dirty cop syndrome." He tried to tell the truth but got nowhere; he was raked over the coals at every juncture and publicly humiliated. Finally, he was given an ultimatum: "Shut the f*** up or lose everything!"*

Sam felt like he had a gun to his head. He had put his life on the line hundreds of times for our country, and could not believe that this was his reward. As his name and reputation meant everything to him, and he really believed in the importance of his work, he fell into a deep depression. Even the strongest leader can feel like a cornered animal in circumstances this extreme. Unable to make any headway against his corrupt department, Sam's frustration turned inward, and he became suicidal.

Concerned about how much he could reveal, Sam carefully reached out to me for guidance and support. We spoke of his core allegiance, to both his country and his own integrity, his belief in himself and his faith. With vulnerability and trust, he spoke to me through his despair. He wanted to believe that he could be true to himself and that his life was still worth living. He also loved his wife and children and was committed to them, but this was a very challenging time for him. He was experiencing what many have called "the dark night of the soul." I, and many others, believe that it is moments like these — when things seem bleakest and there appears to be no exit — that we can rise up to our greatest expression of courage and humanity. I encouraged Sam to speak his truth, while weighing the risks and potential dangers.

Weeks went by and I did not hear from Sam. I hoped — and felt in my heart — that he would choose life and make decisions that would be empowering and in alignment with his integrity and truth. Happily, my hopes were borne out. One morning Sam contacted me. He told me that sometime after our meeting, he had seen a news report about the punishment systems in Iran and Iraq. He said, "I watched this victim, a distraught mother whose son had been gruesomely slaughtered right in front of her. The perpetrator was about to be hanged. He was standing on a chair with a noose around his neck. The woman said she thought she had known the truth, which was that her son would want her to

exercise retribution by pulling the chair out from under the killer. But then, her eyes welled up with tears. She said that her son had visited her in a dream and said, 'Mom, it's okay. I'm doing great. You don't have to do this.' So she reached up, pulled the rope and the hood from her son's murderer, slapped him on the face, pulled him to her and hugged him."

Sam looked at me with tears in his own eyes and said, "After seeing that, I knew I could never leave this world without fully living my truth and forgiving, no matter what happens." With this divine insight, Sam was reminded of his own miraculous nature and did not commit suicide. By discovering what was truly important to him regarding his core allegiance to greater truth and integrity, he felt more empowered to leave his job. Although this put him at great economic risk and the danger of further retaliation, Sam did indeed quit. He also chose to redirect his time and energy to pursue a new career, one dedicated to fostering truth-telling on a larger scale. Through this experience, Sam became aware of how his own personal dream intersected with the collective dream of living in a world of greater truth, forgiveness and love. He is aware of the courage, patience and faith it will take to turn the system around, and is committed to that transformation through the development of new legislation.

In many stories like this, the risks are external. But in every transformation, there are also *internal* risks within our body and being. We are changing who we are and how we are in the world; that is, we are changing our identity, either whole or in part. Although this carries benefits, it can also, at times, feel like we are dissolving or lost! This can be disturbing and disorienting. We may also find that change in one area of our psyches creates resistance or propulsion in another, blocking, derailing or uncomfortably expanding transformation in those other areas. However, these blocks or expansions will then become the seeds of new projects of transformation. In short, transformation is a life's journey, not a single event. And life, when truly lived, always involves risk. But as this section's title says, the risk itself is also transformative: whichever way we choose to go, we will not be the same again.

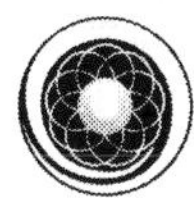

Future Possibilities: A World that Works

"If our children could open the heart-vault to our soul's past, would we make different choices now, for our future?"

~WHISPERS FROM THE HEART OF THE WORLD
(Great Spirit's Messenger)

We are building a new foundation for humanity — it is a foundation of hope to support us in becoming who we are intended to be. As we evolve our extraordinary leadership during these extraordinary times, we have the opportunity to change our lives and our world, but we must each be willing to manifest the greatest expression of who we are in order for it to unfold — and to help others to do the same. I can almost hear the repeated echoes of Dr. Martin Luther King, Jr. reminding us that, "I can never be what I ought to be until you are what you ought to be. And you can never be what you ought to be until I am what I ought to be..."[32]

Global transformation can take many shapes and forms, and it is up to each of us, as leaders, to choose how we will contribute. All choices are equally valuable. For example, I have been guided to engage with transformation on several levels. From sharing new governance models beyond my small sphere, I have also continued to support personal transformation in other leaders, as well as their subsequent organizations and projects that are already established or that they wish to create. Sometimes dreams won't let us go. Sometimes all that is being asked of us is that we say the dream out loud so that others can hear. This gives the dream power. It can then take on a life of its own.

Daring to Dream

Here is one particular large-scale project of transformation that I wish to manifest, if possible. It was presented to me as a vision during a deep meditation inspired by a television news report I saw at the very end of 2013: The news anchor was deftly presenting a history of the conflict

between Israel and Palestine, and nonchalantly stated that (and I paraphrase), "They are at it again in hand-to-hand combat, killing each other in cold blood." The combination of the horrific content of the report, coupled with the cavalier tone of the reporting, catapulted me into a deep sense of grief, coupled with some anger. I felt as if I had a sword slowly piercing my heart. I realized I was experiencing psychic *global* pain.

In that state of being, I made a decision to center myself and connect back to spirit for guidance about what was needed to manifest a different outcome — the collective dream of a more peaceful world, a world in which people seek arms to hug, not arms to kill. In my meditation, I was given a call to action, along with the conceptual details of a project I was guided to name "Habitat for Peaceful Engagement." This vision, gifted from Great Spirit, touched my heart, reminding me that part of my path is in service to peace and the honoring of all nations, all people, all cultures and all creatures. Despite the fact that many people believe this vision may not be possible, I know that I carry the greatest hope in my heart that it *is* possible. The project, as shown to me in that deep meditation, includes the gathering of people from many disciplines to work together in collaboration. It involves land, perhaps near the Gaza Strip, and the building of a group of eco-friendly, self-sustaining, dome-shaped structures on that land. Each structure will be used as duplex housing, with one half inhabited by an Israeli family, and the other half by a Palestinian family — with the intention to create peaceful engagement. The people of the land, those who understand the space and place most intimately, would guide the entire process, introducing the best time for cultural exchange, circle groups of dialogue, and creative projects to emerge over time.

This vision was an invitation for me to discover the transformation that is right, good and whole for my own divine expression and work in the world — despite the risks. I believe that we all are being called to discover what is best for each of us through our own unique expressions, gifts and passions. The more connected we are to how we can transform and how our dreams can become reality, the more we become fully

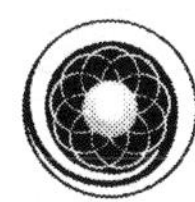

empowered with divine energy — not for accolades or guru status, but for the joy of our divine nature. This is also part of extraordinary leadership: we are compelled by our hearts and our innermost being to do what we can to transform the world. Since we are divinely connected, our courage to transform in whatever ways are best for *us*, will impact all else, through an interwoven matrix that carries messages — like the sounds of a sacred gong calling in a new era of being — one where our willingness to take down unhealthy structures is honored, where choices are made based upon truth and integrity for the betterment of all, and where unconditional love is not the exception, but the rule.

That's the type of love that fuels us to manifest our greatest dreams and hopes for this planet. Like the Eastern spiritual vision of "Indra's net," we become a vast interconnected web — points of light joined by fine lines of energy. The net represents the universe, and each one of the points of light a living being. Every point is unique, irreplaceable and beautiful — like snowflakes. And yet, each point is also a shining jewel that recognizes and reflects all the other jewels and the entire net — a hologram of infinite beauty. *This* is who we are. This is the greater vision for all of us, to keep our eyes on the prize of this universal dream, as we go out into the world to bring extraordinary leadership to these extraordinary times.

Closing Prayer

Dear Loving Universe, All That Is~

What a blessing it has been to create this book in service of humanity and all my relations! My heart is filled with gratitude for the innumerable beings that contributed to its completion.

As I sit in quiet reflection, I am awed by the gift of the preciousness of life on this planet, and filled with a deep peace, love and gratitude for what moved through me from Great Spirit into the world in the form of this book on Extraordinary Leadership.

May all those who read this book be brought to a greater love for themselves, for other brothers and sisters on the beauty way, for Nature and for our planet. May each word carry a seed of hope for those who are touched and moved by it directly through the reading of it or indirectly through the transformation and manifestation witnessed in our fellow human beings.

I have been guided to share that our opportunities are vast and, if our hearts and minds remain receptive, we will receive the guidance we each need to lead ourselves and others to our ever-more extraordinary lives and world. As the gifts of wisdom touch our hearts and ripple out into the universe, the children will giggle with delight.

Endnotes

VITAL KEY #1, PP.1-48

1 JFK coverage 1:30pm-2:40pm 11/22/63 found on YouTube: https://www.-youtube.com/watch?v=pDOojsg62OO (at marker 1:06:43). See also CBS NEWS Live Coverage of the Assassination of President Kennedy, Part 1 (1:30 p.m.-2:30 p.m.): https://www.youtube.com/watch?v=vwtqvuWOV-Wo&list=PLJZPvqeFqoFgB7BJ9k7iy5Cs5oKrmXp&index=1. See also CBS NEWS Live Coverage of the Assassination of President Kennedy, Part 2 (2:30 p.m.-3:30 p.m.): https://www.youtube.com/watch?v=jNTvduZud4U.

2 The National Network to End Domestic Violence put together a valuable Fact Sheet of Statistics: http://nnedv.org/downloads/Census/DVCounts2013-/DVSA_Factsheet.pdf.

3 This quote by Frederick Bastiat, a French economist in the 1800's, was included in the 2012 documentary film, "Four Horsemen": The official version can be found on the RenegadeEconomist You Tube Channel (published September 13, 2013) at https://www.youtube.com/watch?v=5fbvquHSPJU.

4 Louise L. Hay, *Heal Your Body* (Hay House, Inc., Carlsbad, CA, 1988), pp.3-8, 81-83.

5 Craig A. Anderson and Brad J. Bushman, "Effects of Violent Video Games on Aggressive Behavior, Aggressive Cognition, Aggressive Affect, Physiological Arousal, and Prosocial Behavior: A Meta-Analytic Review of the Scientific Literature," American Psychological Society, *Psychological Science*, vol. 12, no. 5, September 2001, pp.353-359. Particularly noteworthy was that the target audience of children (fourth-graders) tended to *prefer* "violent" video games versus non-violent and that "many games involving violence by cartoonlike characters are classified by the industry as appropriate for general audiences, a classification with which adults and youngsters disagree." One additional serious concern involves the lack of parental oversight, with up to 90% of parents never checking the ratings on video games for kids grades 8-12; close to the same percentage reported that their parents never limited time spent playing videos. See also: more recently Craig A. Anderson and Wayne A. Warburton contributed an entire chapter to the book, *Growing Up Fast and Furious: Reviewing the Impacts of Violence and Sexualised Media on Children*, edited by W. Warburton and D. Braunstein (The Federation Press, Annandale, NSW, Australia, 2012), pp.56-84.

6 The National Network to End Domestic Violence Fact Sheet, *op.cit.* Also according to the most recently published statistics from the National Coalition Against Domestic Violence (NCADV):

- One in every four women will experience domestic violence in her lifetime; and only approximately one-quarter of all physical assaults, one-fifth of all rapes, and one-half of all stalkings perpetrated against females by intimate partners are reported to the police. (Information provided by Patricia Tjaden and Nancy Thoennes, National Institute of Justice and the Centers of Disease Control and Prevention, "Extent, Nature and Consequences of Intimate Partner Violence: Findings from the National Violence Against Women Survey," 2000.)

- An estimated 1.3 million women are victims of physical assault by an intimate partner each year. (From: "Costs of Intimate Partner Violence Against Women in the United States," Centers for Disease Control and Prevention, National Centers for Injury Prevention and Control, Atlanta, GA, 2003.)
- Females who are 20-24 years of age are at the greatest risk of nonfatal intimate partner violence. (From: U.S. Department of Justice, Bureau of Justice Statistics, "Intimate Partner Violence in the United States," December, 2006.)

Even more significant, is the impact on our children, on our health and personal economic stability. Here are a few more startling statistics:

- Witnessing violence between one's parents or caretakers is the strongest risk factor of transmitting violent behavior from one generation to the next. See: http://www.breakthecycle.org/html%20files/I_4a_startstatis.htm.
- The cost of intimate partner violence exceeds $5.8 billion each year, $4.1 billion of which is for direct medical and mental health services; and victims of intimate partner violence *lost almost 8 million days of paid work* because of the violence perpetrated against them by current or former husbands, boyfriends and dates. This loss is the equivalent of more than *32,000 full-time jobs* and almost *5.6 million days of household productivity as a result of violence.* (From: "Costs of Intimate Partner Violence Against Women," *loc.cit.*)
- There are 16,800 homicides and $2.2 million (medically treated) injuries due to intimate partner violence annually. (From: "The Cost of Violence in the United States," Centers for Disease Control and Prevention, National Centers for Injury Prevention and Control, Atlanta, GA, 2007.).

7 "Senators Talk Tough on Domestic Violence in Sports," NFL Controversy, NBC News, quoting Mike Bates, "MLB's Record on Domestic Violence Worse than NFL's," *SB Nation*, July 28, 2014: http://www.sbnation.com/mlb/2014/7/28-/5936835/ray-rice-chuck-knoblauch-minnesota-twins-mlb-domestic-abuse-violence.

8 Harvey Mackay, "Reward Workers, then Reap Rewards," On Business, Albany Times Union, November 20, 2012: http://www.timesunion.com/business-/article/Reward-workers-then-reap-rewards-4051445.php. See also: http://harveymackay.com/column/tag/articles-by-harvey-mackay/, and http://harveymackay.com/column/2012/11/. See also Robert Chapman's Blog at: http://www.trulyhumanleadership.com/.

9 David D. Kirkpatrick, "Syrian Children Offer Glimpse of a Future of Reprisals," Middle East (from Zaatari, Jordan), *The New York Times*, September 3, 2012. (Ranya Kadri contributed reporting.).

10 Lucas Kawa, "CHARTS: The US Has Some Of The Worst Health Statistics In The Developed World," Markets, *Business Insider*, January, 10, 2013:

http://www.businessinsider.com/us-health-lags-the-developed-world-2013-1. The New York Times published an article summarizing a study conducted by the Institute of Medicine and the National Research Council on mortality rates and other measures of healthcare. "The panel [of experts] called the pattern of higher rates of disease and shorter lives 'the U.S. health disadvantage,' and said it was responsible for dragging the country to the bottom in terms of life expectancy over the past 30 years. American men ranked last in life expectancy among the 17 countries [developed and undeveloped] in the study, and American women ranked second to last." And when it comes to the health of a pregnant mother or her soon-to-be/newborn child, the U.S. has the highest mortality rate among all developed nations.

11 Reporter Anders Kelto, "From the shacks to the prom a South African girl's night of glamour." PRI's The World, October 2, 2014 (1:45 p.m. EDT). Online at: http://www.pri.org/stories/2013-10-02/shacks-prom-south-african-girl-s-night-glamour.

12 James O'Dea, "Extraordinary Leadership Telesummit #1," September 24, 2013, Joyce Anastasia Interview Transcript, p.4.

13 Harvey Mackay, *loc.cit.*

14 *Ibid.*

15 The following is the last portion of Martin Luther King, Jr.'s "I Have a Dream" Speech (transcript from FoxNews.com and video found at: http://www.ibtimes.com/i-have-dream-speech-full-transcript-video-read-dr-martin-luther-king-jrs-1963-speech-its-50th):

" ... Let us not wallow in the valley of despair. I say to you today my friends — so even though we face the difficulties of today and tomorrow, I still have a dream. It is a dream deeply rooted in the American dream.

I have a dream that one day this nation will rise up and live out the true meaning of its creed: 'We hold these truths to be self-evident, that all men are created equal.'

I have a dream that one day on the red hills of Georgia the sons of former slaves and the sons of former slave owners will be able to sit down together at the table of brotherhood.

I have a dream that one day even the state of Mississippi, a state sweltering with the heat of injustice, sweltering with the heat of oppression, will be transformed into an oasis of freedom and justice.

I have a dream that my four little children will one day live in a nation where they will not be judged by the color of their skin but by the content of their character.

I have a dream today.

I have a dream that one day down in Alabama, with its vicious racists, with its governor having his lips dripping with the words of interposition and nullification -- one day right there in Alabama little black boys and black girls will be able to join hands with little white boys and white girls as sisters and brothers.

I have a dream today.

I have a dream that one day every valley shall be exalted, and every hill and mountain shall be made low, the rough places will be made plain, and the crooked places will be made straight, and the glory of the Lord shall be revealed and all flesh shall see it together.

This is our hope. This is the faith that I go back to the South with. With this faith we will be able to hew out of the mountain of despair a stone of hope. With this faith we will be able to transform the jangling discords of our nation into a beautiful symphony of brotherhood. With this faith we will be able to work together, to pray together, to struggle together, to go to jail together, to stand up for freedom together, knowing that we will be free one day.

This will be the day, this will be the day when all of God's children will be able to sing with new meaning 'My country 'tis of thee, sweet land of liberty, of thee I sing. Land where my fathers died, land of the Pilgrims' pride, from every mountainside, let freedom ring!'

And if America is to be a great nation, this must become true. And so let freedom ring from the prodigious hilltops of New Hampshire. Let freedom ring from the mighty mountains of New York. Let freedom ring from the heightening Alleghenies of Pennsylvania.

Let freedom ring from the snow-capped Rockies of Colorado. Let freedom ring from the curvaceous slopes of California.

But not only that;

Let freedom ring from Stone Mountain of Georgia.

Let freedom ring from Lookout Mountain of Tennessee.

Let freedom ring from every hill and molehill of Mississippi — from every mountainside.

Let freedom ring. And when this happens, and when we allow freedom ring — when we let it ring from every village and every hamlet, from every state and every city, we will be able to speed up that day when all of God's children — black men and white men, Jews and Gentiles, Protestants and Catholics — will be able to join hands and sing in the words of the old Negro spiritual: 'Free at last! Free at last! Thank God Almighty, we are free at last!'"

16 The Nelson Mandela Foundation provides a comprehensive biography of this man, including his personal papers. The website is: https://www.nelsonmandela.org. The History channel also provides a beautiful tribute via video and narrative regarding Mandela's life and humanitarian work at: http://www.history.com/topics/nelson-mandela.

17 For more information regarding the history and spiritual leadership of the Dalai Lama, go to the official website at http://www.dalailama.com.

18 Malala Yousafzai, I Am Malala: *The Girl Who Stood Up for Education and Was Shot By the Taliban* (Orion Publishing Group Ltd., London, 2013). ISBN 978-0-297-87092-0.

19 Immaculeé Ilibagazia, *Left to Tell: Discovering God Amidst the Rwandan Holocaust* (Hay House, Inc., Carlsbad, CA, 2006, 2014). ISBN 978-1-4019-0897-3. For another very moving account of the Rwandan genocide, see: Fergal Keane, "The Rwandan Girl Who Refused to Die," reprinted by PBS online with

permission from the Sunday Times, 1997. (This was also a Frontline Special Report called "Valentine's Nightmare.").

20 James O'Dea, *op.cit.*, p.6.

21 Gregg Braden, *The Divine Matrix: Bridging Time, Space, Miracles and Belief* (Hay House, Inc., Carlsbad, CA, 2007), p.114-115. ISBN 978-1-4019-0573-6.

22 This is the *minimum* number required for a change to register. The more people beyond this minimum that participate, the larger and/or the faster the change that occurs.

23 James O'Dea, *op.cit.*, p.8.

24 Vicki Abadesco, www.soulshoppe.com.

25 John Bradshaw, *Homecoming: Reclaiming and Championing Your Inner Child* (Bantam Books, New York, 1992). ISBN 0-553-35389-6.

VITAL KEY #2, PP.49-90

1 James O'Dea, *op.cit.*, p.7.

2 Geoffrey Nunberg, *Going Nuclear* (Public Affairs, a member of Perseus Books Group, 2004), p.67, quoting "The Second Casualty" from the April 6, 2003, *New York Times Week In Review.* Notably, according to Nunberg, the language used by Hiram Johnson was "in its full euphemistic glory ... the first casualty of war is less often the truth itself than the way we tell it."

3 Jenna McCarthy, "The Truth About Lying," *Real Simple* (online magazine), Time Inc. Lifestyle Group, 2015: http://www.realsimple.com/work-life/life-strategies/truth-about-lying. McCarthy summarized the core themes expressed in Susan Shapiro Barash's *Little White Lies, Deep Dark Secrets: The Truth About Why Women Lie* (identifying 75% of women admit to lying to loved ones about money). Jenna McCarthy also identified Dr. David Smith, Ph.D. research regarding the "six top ways people lie."

4 *Ibid.*

5 **Lying to Protect Someone:** This lie is complex. One form of such a lie is Lying to Protect Someone *Else*. In Nazi Germany, many people hid Jews and others targeted by the Nazis, and then lied about it so the hiding places would not be found. Similarly today, people who reveal truths about a corporate, military or political wrong-doing, may find their lives in danger, and other people may lie about their whereabouts to keep them from being killed. In the same vein, animal lovers might lie to hunters about which way they saw a fox running in a fox hunt. The ones lying may also later lie *about* their lying in order to protect themselves as a corollary to the first lie, since revealing the fact that they're lying would defeat the purpose of the whole exercise. These kinds of lies are motivated by a deep moral conviction about the value of life, and offer the liar no financial or other material gain. I feel that lies like these fall into the same category as Edward Snowden's comment, "Sometimes to do the right thing, you have to break a law" (discussed later in this chapter).

But this concept quickly becomes blurred in today's twisted moral climate. As the list of truth-tellers in the section "Truth-Telling Can Be Dangerous" indicates, many individuals have been asked to lie for the "protection" of

corporate, military, and governmental interests (and no doubt gangs, mafia-type organizations, and countless other self-interested parties), when those organizations were engaged in corrupt activities. What is really being "protected" here is these organizations' continued ability to engage in "Power Over" tactics. In my opinion, acquiescing to such lies does not fall into the same category of "protection" as the first examples. However, telling the truth in these latter situations may then put the truth-teller's life at risk, which *does* go back to the former examples of lying to protect someone — it just happens to be oneself that one is protecting. Or, it may not be life that's on the line, but one's livelihood, or an entire system structure that may cause disaster if it falls. The threat of such disaster was the excuse for many wars, especially in Asia in the last century.

On a smaller scale, "protection" of someone's *feelings* is the underlying rationale for Lying to Be Nice and Lying to Save Face. Although these remain lies, there is a large grey area where communication via words is *so* complicated that we find ourselves in subtle "Have You Stopped Beating Your Wife" situations where, no matter what we say, *some* kind of lie is going to be told. In such situations, do we answer to the "letter of the law" or the "spirit of the law?" The classic and dreaded partner question "do I look fat in this?" really means "do you think I look attractive?" or, more basically, "do you love me?" If the answer is "yes" to all three questions, do we say "yes" or "no" to the first?

In the end, each person has to choose for themselves what they can live with and what they can't. Many people choose to leave organizations and relationships that demand lies in the name of loyalty; this effectively removes the moral dilemma from their lives. This may mean that such organizations continue to engage in behaviors that harm the public and/or the planet, but at least without the complicity of the person who has withdrawn. This is a form of lying by silence, but it may also be a strategic choice to "live to fight another day," and then enter into some other form of activity that *will* eventually bring the wrong-doing to light in a way that can't harm anyone, or that will render the wrong-doer obsolete as a result of societal evolution. Many spiritual teachers throughout history have taught — as this book also advocates — that changing oneself changes the world. Therefore, many people engaged in spiritual practice at the personal and small group level are actively engaged in "changing the ground of being" of all humans on the planet. It is their spiritual hope that such activity will bring Power Over to an end, and will do so without endangering lives in either the short- or the long-term.

6 A. G. Miller (ed.), *The Social Psychology of Good and Evil*, (Guilford Press, New York, 2004), pp.303-326, referencing Chapter 12, "The Many Faces of Lies," by Bella M. DePaulo, PhD. DePaulo noted (p.307) that the contents of everyday lies that were collected in her studies fell into five categories: 1-their feelings and opinions; 2-their actions, plans, and whereabouts; 3-their knowledge, achievements, and failings; 4-explanations for their behaviors; and 5-facts and personal possessions. See also: Pamela Meyer, *Liespotting: Proven Techniques to Detect Deception*, (St. Martin Press, New York, 2011), pp.1-46, (Part I, "Detecting Deception"). ISBN 978-0-312-60187-4. See also Press Release from

EurekAlert, The Global Source for Science News, "UMass researcher finds most people lie in everyday conversation," June 10, 2002.

7 *Ibid* (all).

8 Pamela Meyer, "How to Spot a Liar," TED Talk, July, 2011 (at video marker 5:02-5:36; transcript p.2), published August 9, 2013 on YouTube at: https://www.youtube.com/watch?v=eZ4zlkhdcCw.

9 I have seen some studies in which very young children lie, implying that lying *may* be instinctive. However, if so, I feel that this is only true for a very small percentage of the population. My "gut" tells me that for most of us, it is the result of living in an environment that is energetically bathed in the cultural default that "lying is necessary," and we therefore respond on "automatic" even at an early age. We then believe it is intrinsic, but actually we were "programmed."

10 Dr. Anita Kelly and Dr. Lijuan Wang, "Lying Less Linked to Better Health, New Research Finds," American Psychological Association. This "Science of Honesty" project was funded by a grant from the John Templeton Foundation, and the presentation "A Life Without Lies: How Living Honestly Can Affect Health," was held on August 4, 2012 in Florida; the PowerPoint presentation can be found at: https://cbsphilly.files.wordpress.com/2012/08/kelly-a-life-without-lies.pdf.

11 *Ibid.* See also K. B. Serota, T. R. Levine, and F. J. Boster, "The prevalence of lying in America: Three studies of reported deception," *Human Communication Research*, vol.36 (2010), pp.1-24.

12 Barbara Brennan, *Hands of Light* (Bantam Books, a division of Random House, Inc., New York,1988). ISBN 0-553-34539-7.

13 Louise L. Hay, *loc.cit.*

14 Kathryn Esplin, "Can Lying Affect the Intimacy of a Relationship?", Global Post: America's News World Site: http://everydaylife.globalpost.com/can-lying-affect-intimacy-relationship-33513.html.

15 *Ibid.*

16 The concept of "Satyagraha" as expressed by Gandhi was described to me by my dear friend and colleague Dr. Steve Borish and supported in writing by Prabhakar Kamath in his article called "The Basic Principles of Satyagraha," in the *Nirmukta* online magazine, published on July 29, 2011, at the following website: http://nirmukta.com/2011/07/29/the-basic-principles-of-satyagraha/. "Manjushri" is considered the bodhisattva (enlightened being) of wisdom in Tibetan Buddhism. Images can be viewed online.

17 The following is the list of some of the individuals, spanning nearly a century who have experienced persecution of some form or another for speaking their truth in a non-truth-seeking climate:

- Nikola Tesla — scientist and innovator who discovered/invented brilliant technology including methods of obtaining energy that don't rely on combustion, fossil fuels, radioactivity, or other toxic or unsustainable sources; his career and his life were brought to ruin, and his inventions were co-opted and concealed from the public. (early 1900's)

- Paramahansa Yogananda — spiritual guru who wrote the book *Autobiography of a Yogi* (made into the film "Awake" in October, 2014) and inspired millions to seek spiritual self-realization by connecting to a higher source. His popularity grew to such an extent (during a time when segregation and external submissiveness were the norm) that he became a target of the U.S. government and other organizations: he received death threats and personal harassment, but was eventually publicly exonerated. (early 1900's to his conscious death in 1952)
- J.I. Rodale — health researcher and sustainable agriculture pioneer who was, for decades, ridiculed, vilified, and called a "quack" for saying that what we eat affects our health, and that foods laced with toxic pesticides, food additives and other artificial ingredients are unhealthy and contribute to disease. (1950's and beyond)
- Jim Garrison —New Orleans District Attorney who tried to expose the truth about the JFK assassination; he was villainized, lost his job, had his life threatened, and he and his family were persistently harassed. *Hundreds* of his witnesses experienced premature death, many under suspicious circumstances. Oliver Stone, who made a movie about these events was denounced and labeled a liar, but the movie's assertions were largely vindicated when government documents about the events surrounding the assassination were eventually released. (1966, 1991-movie release)
- Daniel Ellsberg — U.S. military analyst who revealed (via the top-secret "Pentagon Papers") the lies and deceits used by the Johnson administration to prolong and expand the Vietnam war; he was harassed, had his life and family threatened, and was charged with conspiracy, espionage, and theft of government property — all of these charges were eventually dropped when investigators discovered how the administration had engaged people to discredit him. (1971)
- Lois Gibbs — discovered and publicized the presence of illegally-dumped life-threatening toxic chemicals in the water and soil of Love Canal in Niagara Falls, NY; was ridiculed, dismissed, and demonized, but eventually won her case along with numerous environmental awards. (1978)
- Karen Silkwood — attempted to expose the reckless endangerment of workers in a nuclear power plant; was harassed and threatened, and died in a suspicious car accident. (1983)
- Erin Brockovich — engaged in a legal battle against corporate agencies that were covering up vital facts about contaminated ground water from a chemical plant that was causing chronic illnesses; her life was threatened and, even though she won her case, she is still being harassed and discredited years later. (1993)
- Jeffrey Wigand — research chemist who exposed the tobacco industry's illegal insertion of toxic additives to make cigarettes more addictive; he was fired, his life was threatened, lawsuits were levied against him (with the potential loss of all medical insurance), and he, his family and anyone close to him were harassed. (1993)

- Kathryn Bolkovac — American police officer and U.N. peace keeper who exposed U.N. sex trafficking; she was forced out of her job, had her life threatened and lived briefly in hiding. Although she eventually won a lawsuit for wrongful dismissal, she cannot return to police work in either the US or internationally. (1999)
- Joe Wilson and Valerie Plame — Valerie Plame was a CIA operative married to Joe Wilson, the US ambassador to Iraq who publicly accused the White House of manipulating intelligence to make a case for the 2003 Iraq war: Wilson challenged the existence of "weapons of mass destruction" and debunked the Iraq/Niger uranium deal; to shut him up, the White House leaked *his wife's* identity to the press, blowing her cover, endangering her life, and destroying her career. (2003)
- John Perkins — government operative who wrote a memoir called *Confessions of an Economic Hit Man* that exposed international corruption involving the economic colonization of third-world countries on behalf of a "cabal" of corporate banks and the U.S. government — including "drugs for arms" and the buying off of new leaders in other countries — and his own role in it; he was defamed and villainized, and lives under a continuing death threat. (2004)
- Catherine Austin Fitts — former U.S. Assistant Housing Secretary who exposed how international banks and the U.S. government conspired to "implode the U.S. economy" via the mortgage loan debacle and the illegal transfer of trillions of dollars offshore as a means of "sacrificing the American middle class;" she was ridiculed, harassed, and subjected to a fraudulent lawsuit (which she won). (2010).
- Edward Snowden — former CIA, DIA and NSA computer professional who leaked secret information about the extent to which the National Security Agency is spying on Americans; has had to flee the country, can have no contact with his family, has had his life threatened, and has been labeled a traitor and charged with espionage and theft of government property. (2013)

18 **Institutionalized Lying: Cults and Secret Organizations**

Over my three decades of transformational work with people committed to becoming wise leaders, I've noticed a disturbing trend. Many of these leaders have found themselves immersed in organizations that have turned out to be manipulative and dangerous cults. I've also seen paralleling characteristics in the unhealthy elite organizations that are shrouded in secrecy, sometimes deep in the hearts of governments.

Such organizations deliberately seek out influential leaders (including celebrities of one kind or another) to promote their business interests. To accomplish this, they employ a recruitment technique akin to snaring fish (by dangling bait). They recruit by claiming to do things that appeal to the leader's sense of purpose and idealism, but beneath the surface they actually have an entirely different, self-serving agenda.

Through my clients, I've become aware of at least three different organizations like this. Each of these organizations has (eventually) been

accused of, and/or prosecuted for, criminal acts associated with cult abuse, or at best, "organizational deception." It's not my role to name them, but to encourage those who thrive on manipulating others to reconsider their approach. I also consider it my responsibility to train people to be discerning regarding the organizations they become involved with.

Every single person I've known who was deceptively "lured" in this way is highly intelligent, creative and collaborative. They've all served in numerous leadership positions throughout their lives and never suspected they'd be vulnerable to the manipulative control of a cult or secret society.

How exactly were they lured? They were marketed to their values, such as the spiritual aspiration "to become One," the opportunity to learn "self-actualizing" leadership skills or better ways to understand the workings of our world, or offered the joy associated with becoming part of a like-minded, elevated community. They were also flattered, and told they'd make extraordinary members. These all sound like very valid reasons to join a professional or religious/spiritual group. It's what happens *after* people become committed members that reveals the unpleasant truth. From one cult to the next, the telltale signs include:

1. MONEY DEMANDS — The more money/resources/time you provide, the more attention you'll receive and the higher "ranking" you'll achieve. (The signals include "tithing" and/or special training to move into the ranks of the "elite.") Later, it may be found that these monies were misappropriated — i.e., not used to support the poor (or whatever the original stated intention happened to be), but rather used for the material comforts of the designated leader. Ex-members have reported "turning into slaves to the leader and the system."

2. FAVORITISM AND SUPERIORITY/ELITE STANCES — The cult leaders are often brilliant intellectuals who use their knowledge to control people through verbal arguments and manipulative logic. They use sophisticated methods to lure people deeper — i.e. "If you do this or that, you can be part of the *elite* of the elite." Some of the requests may verge on unethical or illegal behavior, but members comply because they cannot find any flaws in the well-crafted "Socratic arguments."

3. SECRECY ABOUT INNER WORKINGS — Since this is one of the primary ways of controlling people, the leaders employ/misuse powerful mind control tools to spin their web. These include satanic rituals, hypnosis, speaking in tongues, channeling or "spiritual downloads," neurolinguistic programming, past life regression, remote viewing, and others. Many of these tools are extremely beneficial in healthy organizations and individual practices; the key warning sign in a cult is that these messages CANNOT BE QUESTIONED.

4. DEMANDS TO RECRUIT NEW MEMBERS/DEMONIZING NON-MEMBERS — Recruiting others is typically required of new members. If they do not "bite the hook," they're automatically categorized as "the lesser ones." Non-members are often demonized — literally. For example, when I refused to join an organization, I was told "The questions you're asking are a signal that you are 'Of the Devil.'" The speaker then turned to one of my closest relatives and shouted at him, "You better denounce her and shout to her face that she is of

the devil!" Thank goodness, when my relative looked into my eyes, he couldn't do it, because he knows me well and I'm not possessed.

5. MEMBERS ENCOURAGED TO LIE AND WITHHOLD TRUTH ABOUT ORGANIZATION'S ACTIVITIES — The organization's activities are "special," and not to be shared with the outside world, except when a potential recruit is received. If that recruit fails to become a member, then they are deemed "no longer worthy," and it becomes commonplace to withhold information from or lie to them. In my case, my relative no longer divulged any information regarding the organization to me, until after he ultimately chose to leave.

6. CONTROL BY ACTS OF SEXUAL MANIPULATION/ABUSE WITH PUNISHMENT FOR NON-COMPLIANCE — Many cult leaders have entourages of followers that others might describe as sex slaves or concubines.

7. DANGEROUS CONSEQUENCES FOR MEMBERS WHO DECIDE TO LEAVE — It is nearly impossible to leave a cult or secret society, or even express a desire to leave, without dire consequences. I've seen a range of repercussions, including verbal harassment, physical/sexual abuse, demotions before departure, broken agreements regarding substantial monetary loans, lawsuits, and death threats.

To complicate the situation, belonging to these organizations often has great benefits, or perhaps the original intention wasn't to be a cult. It may also be true that the teachings have "saved people's lives" or had some other very positive impact. These contradictions can confuse even the most intelligent members, making it very challenging for them to leave, particularly the longer they remain active members. Not until the negative consequences (including all the persistent lies) outweigh the positive, will a member gather the conviction and courage necessary to break away.

19 The film "Citizen Four" is an excellent documentary recounting the risks and care taken by Edward Snowden to unveil his perceived truth: see the trailer at www.citizenfourfilm.com.

20 Brian Williams, NBC Anchor, interviewed Edward Snowden, May 29, 2014. It is online at: http://www.nbcnews.com/feature/edward-snowden-interview. Transcripts were also made available: This quote was spoken in Segment 1 at video marker 10:00-10:40.

21 *Ibid.*, Segment 4, video marker 37:00-38:00.

22 *Ibid.*, Segment 4, video marker 3:00-3:30.

23 See Vital Key #7, Sub-heading "New Transformational Governance Structures."

24 This show can be viewed at: http://thedailyshow.cc.com/

25 See this section's Endnote #5, referring to "Lying to Protect Someone."

26 Foster Gamble, "Extraordinary Leadership Telesummit #3," October 22, 2013, Joyce Anastasia Interview Transcript, p.9.

27 Brian Williams, *op.cit.*, segment 4 at video marker 29:30-30:00, transcripts p.21.

28 *Ibid.*, segment 4 at video marker 11:00-11:50, transcripts p.13.

29 Pamela Meyer, TED Talk, *op.cit.*, at video marker 18:08-18:36; transcript p.7.

30 Foster Gamble, *op.cit.*, p.9-10.

31 The following is the link to the Official website http://www.thrive-movement.com/ and the official Movie "Thrive" on YouTube: https://www.youtube.com/watch?v=lEV5AFFcZ-s.

32 Carl Sagan, *The Demon-Haunted World* (a Ballantine Book, published by The Random House Publishing Group, U.S. and Canada, 1996), p.241.

33 Pamela Meyer, TED Talk, *op.cit.*, at video marker 1:45-3:10; transcript p.1.

34 Foster Gamble, *op.cit.*, p.6.

35 Daniel Estulin, *The True Story of the Bilderberg Group* (published by arrangement with Lennart Sane Agency AB, TrineDay LLC, Walterville, OR, 2009).

36 The official Thrive website, http://www.thrivemovement.com/solutionshub, articulates problems and ways in which to effectively address solutions. In addition, the following are a few of the excellent reporters and writers on the subject of "made-up money": Ellen Brown (Financial Reform advocate), segments of Karl Denniger (Business/Finance blogger), and my two personal favorites, Bill Still (Still Reporting on the Economy) and Charles Hughes-Smith (concise and articulate blogger). These individuals are courageous enough to report as objectively as is humanly possible. Let's continue to explore ways to achieve a more fair and equitable distribution of wealth and resources without defaulting to the unhealthy aspects of communism. See also the following: Ellen Brown, *The Web of Debt* (Third Millennium Press, Baton Rouge, Louisiana, Fifth ed. 2012). ISBN 978-0-9833308-5-1. Ellen's website and blog are at: http://ellenbrown.com/. Michael Hudson is an avid blogger and author of numerous articles and books, including *Global Fractal: The New International Economic Order* (Pluto Press, Ann Arbor, MI, 2005). ISBN 0-07453-2394-4; Bill Still is an avid video-blogger and author, publishing on his YouTube station at https://www.youtube.com/user/bstill3.

37 Lynne McTaggart, *What Doctors Don't Tell You: The Truth about the Dangers of Modern Medicine* (Avon Books, an Imprint of HarperCollins Publishers, New York, 1999). An online magazine is available with same title through her website http://theintentionexperiment.com/.

38 This is not a new phenomenon, but it seems more prevalent today. Content is controlled, and media and individuals who deviate from what they are told to produce, either have to conform or leave their sometimes-"coveted" positions. Threats to them are very real.

I am reminded of Bob Woodward and Carl Bernstein. If it weren't for their renegade reporting and investigative approach, perhaps the 1972 Watergate scandal and cascading lies would never have been sufficiently uncovered. A few days before Nixon resigned, a House committee found proof that Nixon himself had paid money to the Watergate burglars to keep them quiet, and that he had also ordered the CIA to keep the FBI from investigating him and his staff. This made it absolutely certain that he would be impeached (similar to being indicted) by the House and tried and convicted by the Senate. A number of his former supporters called to explain this to him over the next few days. Facing this certainty, he resigned in 1974 (the only President to ever do so) to avoid impeachment and trial. He was not formally impeached or tried. (As a

point of fact: Both Andrew Johnson and Bill Clinton were formally impeached, and both were tried and acquitted. No U.S. president has ever been impeached, tried, and found guilty.)

I believe that this was a huge turning point in governmental oversight via the network news stations. What news sources now can be relied on to share the greater truth? Most have become platforms for propaganda with the split edit to the left or the right politically. Where can we get real news? That really translates for me into, "where can we find those reporters who have chosen truth over abuse of power and who have chosen, at times, to put their lives on the line?" Amy Goodman from Democracy Now has done this, and other respected independent news stations like NPR, Russian TV, etc.

39 The Australia Walk Free Foundation website is at: http://www.walkfree-foundation.org/. See also: Max Fisher, "This map shows where the world's 30 million slaves live. There are 60,000 in the U.S.," *The Washington Post*, October 17, 2013. Online at: http://www.globalresearch.ca/globalhuman-trafficking-a-modern-form-of-slavery/5377853. See other related articles: http://www.washingtonpost.com/blogs/worldviews/wp/2013/10/17/this-map-shows-where-the-worlds-30-million-slaves-live-there-are-60000-in-the-u-s/; http://www.culturaldiplomacy.org/experienceafrica/index.php?en_the-african-diaspora; http://news.sky.com/story/1193503/slavery-should-be-made-essential-reading; http://www.dailykos.com/story/2013/12/27/-1265498/-The-slaves-that-time-forgot.

40 HAARP — the High Frequency Active Auroral Research Program, with a series of 180 antennas (72 feet tall) linked together to function as one steerable antennae, was created in 1992. It is located in Gokona, Alaska, originally a joint effort of the Air Force and Navy in cooperation with a number of academic institutions. It is the most powerful short-wave radio broadcasting station in the world, but it's not designed to broadcast for human ears. It uses unique patented ability to focus the energy coming out of the antenna field and injects that energy into a spot at the top of the atmosphere in a region called the ionosphere. It can aim millions of watts of ELF waves into one tiny patch of the ionosphere. The amount of energy that this requires is 3.6 million watts (for reference, the largest legal a.m. radio station in North America is 50,000 watts; HAARP is 72 times as potent). The public statement regarding the purpose of HAARP is to study the physical and electrical properties and behavior of the ionosphere for both civilian and defense purposes. According to the history.com station, another theory that is being proposed is that HAARP is being used to heat up the atmosphere causing weather changes. The military documents support this theory, but they are still denying it to the public. The theory indicates that by moving the ionosphere, the stratosphere must move and water is shifted to a degree that significantly changes the weather and other planetary phenomena. See the Thrive Movement's website at http://www.thrivemovement.com/human-geo-engineering-chemtrails-and-haarp; see Foster Gamble's article "Danger: HAARP ("High Altitude Active Auroral Research Project [sic]") and the accompanying video "Japan Quake by Project HAARP?" See also: Nick Begich, *Angels Don't Play This HAARP:*

Advances in Tesla Technology (Nicholas J. Begich and Jeane Manning, 1995, 2002). ISBN 978-1-890693-19-0 and the bonnefire coalition: http://www.agriculturedefensecoalition.org/content/welcome-bonnefire-coalition.

41 "Robert McNamara admits Gulf of Tonkin attack did not happen" Video on YouTube, March 7, 2010: https://www.youtube.com/watch?v=5AaGVAipGp0. This is an extract from Errol Morris's film "The Fog of War," interviewing Robert S. McNamara, former Secretary of Defense during the Vietnam War.

42 See the Thrive Movement website at http://www.thrivemovement.com/. See Margaret Cheney and Robert Uth, *Tesla* (Barnes and Noble Books with New Voyager, New York, 1999). ISBN 0-7607-5568-X.

43 As an alternative to the textbook descriptions of "Manifest Destiny," consider the words of Chief Seattle, a Native American mystic who lived at the time of President Washington, and who is known for a controversial speech identified as "Chief Seattle's Thoughts": http://www.ceng.metu.edu.tr/~ucoluk/yazin-/seattle.html.

44 The transcript of Dwight D. Eisenhower "Military-Industrial Complex Speech, 1961" (Public Papers of the President, Dwight D. Eisenhower, 1960, pp.1035-1040) can be found online at: http://coursesa.matrix.msu.edu/~hst306/-documents/indust.html and also (in part) at: https://www.youtube.com/-watch?v=8y06NSBBRtY.

45 For information about UFO non-disclosures, see: http://www.disclosure-project.org/. For information on secret societies, see: JFK's Secret Society Speech (full version) "The President and the Press," presented to the American Newspaper Publishers Association on April 27, 1961: www.jfklibrary.org; for alternative video version, see: https://www.youtube.com/watch?v=8y-06NSBBRtY.

VITAL KEY #3, PP.91-124

1 The mission of the Foundation for Global Humanity (FGH) is to explore and document indigenous and contemporary ways of healing and knowing for our planet. As its former Creative Production Lead, I am deeply grateful for the work they continue to do in the world. Go to FGH's official website to view the projects, videos and educational material they have created: www.f4gh.org or http://www.forndationforglobalhumanity.org

2 "The Dawn of a New Time" was held in the Fall of 2011. The invitation and overview prior to the event can be seen on YouTube at: http://www.youtube.com/watch?v=N1uAotKuZGo.

Here is a summary: "WHAT HUMANITY WAS WAITING FOR ...The Dawn of a New Time. Video presented by the Foundation for Global Humanity (http://www.forndationforglobalhumanity.org).

"For the indigenous peoples living in Colombia's Sierra Nevada de Santa Marta: Kogi, Wiwa, Arhuaco and Kankuamo, sustaining the balance of the spiritual and physical world is their sacred task, they are guardians of the earth and have managed to live in harmony with the planet for hundreds of years ...

It's time to listen and learn from our elder brothers. In their wisdom are ancient records of human history and ancestral memory that remind us how to live in harmony, which contributes to our transformation as a human race and invites us to a new and conscious way of living.

If you feel in your heart the call to participate in this sacred gathering, sign up and be part of 'the dawn of a new time.'"

See http://www.foundationforglobalhumanity.org/dawn-new-time to view the sequence of videos created during the gathering. For more information and videos of the Mamos, see: http://adamdearmon.com/ or http://www.oneheartproductions.net/.

3 ABC NEWS/WASHINGTON POST POLL: Obama and 2014 Politics; 12:01 a.m. Sunday, Jan. 26, 2014. ABC News polls can be found at ABCNEWS.com at http://abcnews.com/pollingunit.

4 *Ibid.* See also: http://www.langerresearch.com/uploads/1158a1Obama-and2014Politics.pdf. Politics 2014: Low Confidence in Leaders and a Dead Heat in Midterm Preferences: http://abcnews.go.com/blogs/politics/2014-/01/politics-2014-low-confidence-in-leaders-and-a-dead-heat-in-midterm-preferences/.

5 Pew Research Center, "Public Sees U.S. Power Declining as Support for Global Engagement Slips: America's Place in the World 2013," December 3, 2013: www.pewresearch.org; referenced in blog: http://smarkos.blogspot.com-/2013/12/public-sees-u.html.

6 Marianne Williamson Announces Candidacy for Congressional Seat — YouTube video at: http://www.youtube.com/watch?v=fz_ijN3kS8s#t=98.

7 A word on *competition*. Part of our current paradigm says that competition is both necessary and that it's "healthy", at least a good portion of the time. Gregg Braden has compiled the results of many research studies, and the truth is that the percentage of interpersonal and inter-organizational competition that's actually healthy is *zero*. See Gregg Braden, *The God Code* (Hay House Inc., Carlsbad, CA, 2004).

8 http://www.oxforddictionaries.com.

9 Nina Simons, "Extraordinary Leadership Telesummit #7," November 19, 2013, Joyce Anastasia Interview Transcript, p.6.

10 C. Jeriel Howard and Richard Francis Tracz, Ed., *The Responsible Person: Essays, Short Stories, Poems* (Canfield Press, a department of Harper and Row, Inc., San Francisco, CA,1975). ISBN 0-06-383901-6.

11 http://en.wikipedia.org/wiki/The_Elders_(organization).

12 http://www.theguardian.com/world/occupy. Wikipedia says: "The Occupy Movement is an international protest movement against social and economic inequality, its primary goal being to make the economic and political relations in all societies less vertically hierarchical and more flatly distributed. Local groups often have different foci, but among the movement's prime concerns is the belief that large corporations and the global financial system control the world in a way that disproportionately benefits a minority, undermines democracy and is unstable. The first Occupy protest to receive widespread attention was Occupy Wall Street in New York City's Zuccotti Park which began

on 17 September 2011. By 9 October, Occupy protests had taken place or were ongoing in over 951 cities across 82 countries, and over 600 communities in the United States." The original "The 99% Declaration" was removed from the original links through the internet. The following is what I had captured as the document had been presented in 2013:

1. The Elimination of the Corporate State — Implementing an immediate ban on all private contributions of money and gifts ... to be replaced by the fair, equal and total public financing of all federal political campaigns.
2. Rejection of the Citizens United Case — " ... We, the People, demand that this institutional bribery and corruption never again be deemed 'protected free speech.'"
3. Elimination of Private Contributions to Politicians.
4. Term Limits.
5. A Fair Tax Code — "...to require ALL citizens to pay a fair share of a progressive, graduated income tax by eliminating loopholes, unfair tax breaks...and ending all other methods of evading taxes."
6. Healthcare for All — "Medicare for all or adoption of a single-payer healthcare system. The Medicaid program will be eliminated."
7. Protection of the Planet.
8. Debt Reduction — "...to reduce the national debt to a sustainable percentage of GDP by 2020..."
9. Jobs for All Americans.
10. Student Loan Forgiveness.
11. Immigration Reform — "... 'Immediate passage of the 'Dream Act'..."
12. Ending of Perpetual War for Profit.
13. Reforming Public Education.
14. End Outsourcing. (Note: this one I do not fully endorse and I encourage further dialogue to explore all avenues of this global piece.)
15. End Currency Manipulation "... implementing immediate legislation and WTO intervention if need be, to encourage China and our other trading partners to end currency manipulation and reduce the trade deficit."
16. Banking and Securities Reform.
17. Foreclosure moratorium.
18. End the Fed (eliminating the privately owned Federal Reserve Bank).
19. Comprehensive Campaign Finance Reform.
20. End the wars in Afghanistan and Iraq.

[13] "The Dawn of a New Time," *loc.cit.*

[14] Dr. Henry Cloud, *Integrity: The Courage to Meet the Demands of Reality* (Harper Collins Publishers, New York, 2006), p.17.

[15] See David M. Kennedy, *The Modern American Military*, (Oxford University Press, New York, 2013). Further writings can be found at: https://friends-ofjustice.wordpress.com/2013/02/08/david-kennedy-how-to-stop-the-killing/.

[16] Mitch Albom, *The Five People You Meet in Heaven* (Hyperion, New York, 2003). See also the thoughtful movie rendition of the same title, directed by Lloyd Kramer in 2004.

17 See all three parts at: http://www.foundationforglobalhumanity.org/sequoyah-trueblood. For alternative direct online access (if website cannot be accessed) see:
1. A Mamo's Gift: The Seed of Peace to All the Hearts of the World: http://www.youtube.com/watch?v=68IvYY6QQKU,
2. A Mamo's Gift Part II: The Law of Origin: http://www.youtube.com/watch?v=g20v1BWfHqQ,
3. A Mamo's Gift Part III: Global Telepathy...Translating The Law of Origin: http://www.youtube.com/watch?v=4r8GoxHiF1g.

VITAL KEY #4, PP.125-172

1 Of course, my use of the expression "every man for himself" is intended to include all genders, with the understanding that we must move away from that way of thinking so that we truly can create the more-inclusive paradigm of a thriving world.

2 Katherine Woodward Thomas, *Conscious Uncoupling: 5 Steps to Living Happily Ever After*, e-book created from Evolving Wisdom course, 2014.

3 As noted in Wikipedia: In chaos theory, the butterfly effect is the sensitive dependency on initial conditions in which a small change at one place in a deterministic nonlinear system can result in large differences in a later state. The name of the effect, coined by Edward Lorenz, is derived from the theoretical example of a hurricane's formation being contingent on whether or not a distant butterfly had flapped its wings several weeks earlier.

4 Polly Higgins was voted one of the "World's Top 10 Visionary Thinkers" by the Ecologist, and proposed Ecocide as the 5th Crime Against Peace to the U.N. in 2010. She is also an author of the award-winning "Eradicating Ecocide" directive — helping to create new laws and governance to prevent the destruction of our planet. I had the honor of interviewing her on the "Extraordinary Leadership" teleseminar, August 22, 2012. For more information,see: http://eradicatingecocide.com/. To see her TEDxEXETER talk on YouTube, see: https://www.youtube.com/watch?v=8EuxYzQ65H4.

5 Joe Wertz, "A Sharp Rise in Earthquakes Puts Oklahomans On Edge" from NPR, has been tracking Earthquake activities and reported on the sharp rise in Oklahoma. The specific report is online at: http://www.npr.org/2014/01/02-/259127792/a-sharp-rise-in-earthquakes-puts-oklahomans-on-edge. More information can be found at: www.npr.org.

6 G.A. Bradshaw, Ph.D, "Elephants, Us, and Other Kin," video presentation was created for "Affect Dysregulation and the Healing of the self," UCLA Annual Interpersonal Neurobiology Conference, March 14-16, 2014. This is an outstanding presentation and well worth watching; the 27 minute video is found on YouTube at: https://www.youtube.com/watch?v=1JB1XCbBJQ-s&feature=youtu.be. For more information, contact The Kerulos Center at: www.kerulos.org.

7 Alzheimer Europe presented research data on "the four main approaches" for Alzheimer's patients at: http://www.alzheimer-europe.org/Research/-

Understanding-dementia-research/Types-of-research/The-four-main-approaches. See also Jen Christensen, from CNN, "Cynicism linked to greater dementia risk, study says," May 29, 2014: http://www.cnn.com/2014-/05/28/health/cynical-dementia/.

8 Amit Goswami is a quantum physicist, professor and author. His latest book is *Quantum Creativity: Think Quantum, Be Creative* (Hay House, Inc., Carlsbad, CA, 2014). Amit spoke of the necessity to bridge the gap between Quantum Theory and "what Quantum Physics is freeing us to do." The concept he identifies as "Quantum Activism" includes the awareness that God has causal efficacy and that with free will, we too can become responsible creators in this world. The conference was presented by the SEED Graduate Institute. I had the honor of interviewing and filming Amit with the Foundation for Global Humanity team: It is a two-part video presented on the FGH website at: http://www.foundationforglobalhumanity.org/amit-goswami.

9 This spoken word film was written, performed and directed by Gary Turk; he published it on YouTube on April 25, 2014: https://www.youtube.com/-watch?v=Z7dLU6fk9QY#t=90. It features Louise Ludlam and Stuart Damley, with sound engineering by Daniel Cobb and the original score by New Desert Blues. For more information, go to: http://www.garyturk.com.

10 Joanne O'Brien-Levin, "Extraordinary Leadership Telesummit #2," October 15, 2013, Joyce Anastasia Interview Transcript, p.8.

11 Gregg Braden, *The Divine Matrix, loc.cit.* See also Alexander Loyd, PhD, ND with Ben Johnson, MD, DO, NMD, *The Healing Code* (Grand Central Life and Style, a Hachette Book Group, New York and Boston, 2010). ISBN 978-1-45550-201-1.

12 Roger Nelson: http://consciousresonance.net/?cat=102 (see also, below). Dean Radin, Ph.D, Experimental Psychologist and Chief Scientist at the Institute of Noetic Sciences; see: http://www.noetic.org/directory/person/dean-radin/. Scientifically, this has been verified by numerous studies on human consciousness, non-locality and precognitive experiments. Dean Radin and his co-investigator Ana Borges conducted studies to determine whether people pre-conceive the impact of emotionally volatile images on their lives. In particular, a study was done with an individual staring at a computer monitor and "most of the time there would be nothing on the screen, but randomly, pictures would appear for a moment." Radin was monitoring the iris of the participant, with a macro video camera looking back at her and recording the dilations of her eye. "Not always, but to a highly significant degree, just before a picture appeared on the monitor, her iris would dilate. And the degree of dilation would correlate with the emotional content, the numinosity, of the picture. Violence or sex, not surprisingly, produced the largest effect. She had a presentiment." Consciousness Researcher, Eva Lohbach, at the University of Amsterdam, did a peer review of research in this area and concluded that, "Past and present research has shown that emotionally arousing stimuli, visual or auditory, produce stronger anticipatory effects than neutral ones. The most important physiological measures used in presentiment studies are heartbeat, EEG, fMRI (BOLD signal), and electrodermal activity (EDA). So far, all of these

have shown evidence of presentiment, so the whole body seems to be involved. Women appear to be somewhat more sensitive to presentiment than men..." (http://consciousresonance.net/?p=3243)

The data is also indicating that this effect is social. Across several decades of research, Roger Nelson, an Experimental Psychologist and Lab Manager for PEAR (Princeton Engineering Anomalies Research), would ask individuals to affect the performance on a random event generator (REGS), with the noted odds to be one in a billion chances. Despite the precision of these instruments to assure random performance, human performance could make them go "non-random". After a dozen studies, Nelson asked the following question, "Could an individual effect produce an objective verifiable collective expression?" To answer this question, he created the Global Consciousness Project (GCP), which has run for over a decade. The study was designed to identify whether it was possible that "a mass of people having an individual, but linked experience, could have an effect on a constantly running coordinated planet-wide network of computer-linked REGS? A measure of consciousness linked non-locally expressing itself as social awareness." Some of the examples given were the socially similar grieving response to Princess Diana's car accident, or the Japanese Tsunami of 2011. Nelson describes it as, "Subtle interactions link us with each other and the Earth. When human consciousness becomes coherent and synchronized, the behavior of random systems may change. Quantum event-based random number generators (RNGs) produce completely unpredictable sequences of zeroes and ones. But when a great event synchronizes the feelings of millions of people, our network of RNGs becomes subtly structured. The probability is less than one in a billion that the effect is due to chance. The evidence suggests an emerging noosphere or the unifying field of consciousness described by sages of all cultures. **Coherent consciousness creates order in the world.**" This information and more on consciousness studies can be found at: http://consciousresonance.net-/?cat=102.

13 Linda Kohanov, *The Tao of Equus: A Woman's Journey of Healing and Transformation through the Way of the Horse* (New World Library, Novato, CA 2001, 2007). ISBN 978-1-57731-420-2.

14 J. Allen Boone, *Kinship With All Life* (Harper, San Francisco CA, 1954). ISBN 0-06-060912-5.

15 G.A. Bradshaw Ph.D, *loc.cit.*

16 From the essay "The Three Seeds": http://charleseisenstein.net/the-three-seeds.

17 Peter Senge, *The Fifth Discipline: The Art and Practice of Learning Organization* (Currency Doubleday, New York, 1990). ISBN 0-385-26094-6. See also Peter Senge and George Roth, *The Dance of Change: The challenges to sustaining momentum in a learning organization*, (Currency Doubleday, New York, 1999). ISBN 0-385-493223.

18 One organization in particular called "Free To Be" addresses bullying head-on, by creating emotive exercises with children gathered in school auditoriums (with administration support and parental permission) — from elementary

and middle education to high school levels. These require great sensitivity and professional facilitation and can be extremely effective in introducing concepts of empathy to young people, while helping to further train teachers in methods that would help to continue such practices. For more information, go to: http://free-to-be.net/.

19 During the "Wisdom of the Origins Conference," (September 13-18, 2012) sponsored by the SEED Graduate Institute (founded by Glenn A. Parry), and with permission from the 13 Indigenous Grandmothers, international Peace Ambassador James O'Dea read, in a powerful oration, the "Declaration of Commitment to the Indigenous Peoples" as transcribed below:

"**Humanity** faces a time in our evolving story when we must harvest our deepest collective wisdom in order to survive and even thrive as a healthy, peaceful and sustainable planetary civilization.

In the course of humanity's journey we have many great achievements to celebrate and honor but we have to acknowledge what has been misguided, damaging to each other and harmful to all life. It is time for healing and a new beginning.

Great skill is now needed to reconnect the bonds of our collective interdependence on behalf of all of Earth's diverse peoples and cultures and to restore an original contract with our planet's eco-system and its intricate design for all life.

We cannot evolve skillfully at this vital juncture in our collective story if we fail to integrate the teachings of our wisdom keepers.

Both reason and conscience require that the precious wisdom of Earth's Indigenous peoples be fully acknowledged. Their skillful ways of living in harmony with Nature and its laws have too often been marginalized and ignored.

Humanity has paid a great price for destructive actions committed against Indigenous peoples. In the name of religion, profit and progress, some of humanity's greatest knowledge about the interrelationship of all life forms has been placed in jeopardy.

Increasing numbers of people now recognize the importance of supporting the transmission of this essential wisdom.

It is in this spirit of deep recognition and appreciation for the value of Indigenous wisdom that we, the signatories to this declaration, hereby proclaim our commitment to the following:

Apology is due to Indigenous peoples for the suppression and violation of their cultures and ways of being. We invite communities, institutions, local authorities and governments to formally and informally offer sincere apology for past actions that resulted in cultural oppression and denigration.

Responsibility for past violations, wounding and discrimination must be expressed in truthful historical narratives and educational materials. We recommend the formation of local and national initiatives to take responsibility for the past and explore the nature of Indigenous wisdom. We encourage support for the production of a wide array of accessible media and curricular materials to set the record straight and ensure the accurate and appropriate transmission of Native wisdom teachings.

Reconciliation must be sought so that healing may occur between Indigenous and non-Indigenous peoples. We call on representatives of public and private institutions to seek ways to engage in meaningful acts and processes of reconciliation through ceremony, presentations and gatherings.

Collaboration in multiple contexts relating to health, environment, sustainable economies and educational opportunities will constitute an essential dimension of expressing sincere apology, acknowledging responsibility and fostering reconciliation. To these ends we encourage collaboration with Indigenous communities and institutions to optimize our collective learning and healing in this pivotal time for all humanity.

We, the undersigned, pledge our commitment to these ideals and the promotion of concrete actions to support respect for Indigenous peoples, a shared partnership for life on Earth and the transmission of our collective wisdom."

The video can be viewed at: https://www.youtube.com/watch?v=sYkTL-xmeaW4. This video was sponsored by The Shift Network, SEED Graduate Institute and the Foundation for Global Humanity, and aired on www.peaceday.tv in 2012. See all the SEED dialogue video interviews (Sequoyah Trueblood, Pat McCabe, Matthew Bronson, David Abram, Amit Goswami, Jerry Honawa, Phil Duran, F. David Peat, Ashok Gangedean, and Leroy Little Bear) on the FGH site: http://www.foundationforglobal-humanity.org/video-highlights.

20 http://www.angelfire.com/ok/TheCherokeeLady/warriorsrainbow.html. One of the interviews and video segments I created was of a young man who was guided by spirit through his shared collective dream of this vision of a "rainbow tribe." The video "Benjamin Hopi Summer Colombia Interview" can be found on the FGH website at: http://www.foundationforglobalhuman-ity.org/dawn-new-time-0.

21 Victoria Hanchin, *The Seer and The Sayer: Revelations of the New Earth* (Balboa Press, Bloomington, IN, 2012). ISBN 978-1-4525-5727-4.

VITAL KEY #5, PP.173-216

1 There are (extremely rare) times when it is actually helpful to be out of balance. Sometimes we need to experience extremes or the chaos created out of imbalance in order to appreciate balance. This may be true for the rare "deltas" of the world who find equanimity "simple": an occasional bout with chaos can help them develop understanding and compassion for the rest of us!

2 The online magazine "Examined Existence," published the article "Lack of Sleep Affects Over 700 Genes," reviewing research emerging from the University of Surrey, England. The original feature story was published by the University of Surrey on March 11, 2013 at the following web address: http://www.sur-rey.ac.uk/features/lack-sleep-alters-human-gene-activity. See also: http://crc.surrey.ac.uk/sleep-and-wake/key-publications. Other studies include: Joseph S. Takahashi, ed., "Effects of insufficient sleep on circadian rhythmicity and expression amplitude of the human blood transcriptome," *The Proceedings of the National Academy of Sciences of the U.S.A.*, vol.110, no.12

(October 3, 2012). Research contributors include Carla S. Moeller-Levet, Simon N. Archer, Giselda Bucca, Emma E. Laing, Ana Slak, Renata Kabiljo, June C.Y. Lo, Nayantara Santhi, Malcolm von Schantz, Colin P. Smith and Derk-Jan Dijk. This report was republished at the Howard Hughes Medical Institute, University of Texas Southwestern Medical Center, Dallas, TX, on January 23, 2013. For details regarding the research, see: http://www.pnas.org/content/110-/12/E1132.abstract and http://www.alphagalileo.org/ViewItem.aspx?Item-Id=128841&CultureCode=en. See also: Ines Wilhelm, Michael Rose, Kathrin I. Imhof, Björn Rasch, Christian Büchel, Jan Born, "The sleeping child outplays the adult's capacity to convert implicit into explicit knowledge," *Nature Neuroscience*, doi: 10.1038/nn.3343 (2013). See also research conducted by the National Institute of Neurological Disorders and Stroke, "Brain Basics: Understanding Sleep": http://www.ninds.nih.gov/disorders/brain_basics/understanding_sleep.htm. See also: http://www.bloomberg.com/news/-articles/2013-02-25/sleep-loss-alters-genes-while-raising-risk-of-disease (online article by Elizabeth Lopatto published February 25, 2013).

3 Similarly, I happen to be allergic to garlic, which is considered to be one of the healthiest antioxidants that people can easily ingest, but not me. One of the best ways to find out if certain foods are good for you is to keep a journal and record what happens after you eat specific items. Ask yourself what your energy level was like during the day. You will begin to notice what foods have a draining effect on your body and which ones make you feel incredibly vital. Follow your body's wisdom, and take the time to learn your own food signals; it will help to keep you at an optimal weight, with energy and focus, and it will rarely fail you.

4 James O'Dea, *Creative Stress: A path for evolving souls living through personal and planetary upheaval* (www.jamesodea.com/Pioneer Imprints, Ross, CA, 2010). ISBN 978-1-4499-9590-4.

5 Glenn A. Parry, "Extraordinary Leadership Telesummit #2," October 15, 2013, Joyce Anastasia Interview Transcript, p.7.

6 Stephen Larsen, in the forward to the book *Forest of Visions: Ayahuasca, Amazonian Spirituality, and the Santo Daime Tradition* written by Alex Polari de Alverga (Park Street Press, Rochester, VT, 1999), pp. ix-x: Larsen eloquently describes the prophecy of the Eagle and the Condor as follows: "Exactly five hundred years had passed since the coming of the European conquerors to the New World, and an Incan prophecy was asking for fulfillment. The white men's arrival had been prophecied before they ever set foot on this continent. The white brother, forgetful of many things, would enact awful cruelties on the native peoples during the first five hundred years. There would be disrespect of the most fundamental rules of the proper human relationship to the earth, and the resulting catastrophes would affect Pachamama, the Great Earth Mother. But after five hundred years, a great turnabout would occur. The white brother would awaken, like a sleepwalker, from his violent trance. There would be an amazing healing that would affect the entire world, helping with the purging catastrophes that were coming. The spirit of the Condor (South America) was asking to dance with the Eagle (North America). From

their flight would emerge great joy and brotherhood between the peoples of North and South America and a new understanding between the children of the white brother and of the traditional peoples. A new relationship between the earth and all of humanity would ensue."

See also: http://www.pachamama.org/blog/the-eagle-and-the-condor-prophecy. The Pachamama Alliance, a global community that "offers people the opportunity to learn, connect, engage, travel and cherish life for the purpose of creating a sustainable future that works for all, devoted a web page specifically to the understanding of the "The Eagle and the Condor" prophecy.

During the FGH journey to Colombia for "The Dawn of a New Time," a sacred ceremony unexpectedly took place: on the 4th day, an Ancient Mayan, Pedro Pablo Chuc Pech and the Incan Sun Priest, Naupany Puma introduced the "Sacred Solar Ceremony with the Sun-Rainbow." This sacred and ancient ceremony was intended to be inclusive of all tribes, to express deep reverence for all sentient beings, to bridge and unify the masculine and the feminine and to give homage to our sacred planet, the sun, the moon and the universe itself. To view the video, go to: https://www.youtube.com/watch?v=tIy2xmSp-Auo#t=2.

7 Dr. Jill Bolte Taylor, "Stroke of Insight," TED Talk, March 13, 2008. Watch the entire video at: https://www.youtube.com/watch?v=UyyjU8fzEYU. As the You Tube site describes, "As it happened — as she felt her brain functions slip away one by one, speech, movement, understanding — she studied and remembered every moment." This is a powerful story about dynamic balance even within one organ of our body: our brain.

8 Dr. Jill Bolte Taylor, *Ibid.*

9 Louise Hay and others have identified that issues with feminine principles often show up as imbalances and illnesses on the left sides of our bodies, while issues with masculine show up on the right side (remember that there is a cross-over in our systems so that left brain associates with the right side of the body, and the right brain with the left side of the body). Thus, being angry with our father or with men in general, or being fearful of our power, or being over-identified with yang action and results, might show up as weakness or illness in our right arm, right leg, or organs on the right side of our body. Similarly, being angry with our mother or with women, or fearful of our feelings and our yin side, might show up as weakness in organs or limbs on the left side of our body. These correspondences are the same for both men and woman.

10 Pat McCabe ("Woman Stands Shining"), "Extraordinary Leadership Telesummit #4," October 29, 2013, Joyce Anastasia Interview Transcript, p.6. See also the video the Foundation for Global Humanity produced in collaboration with the SEED Graduate Institute: http://www.foundationforglobalhumanity.org/pat-mccabe.

11 Ram Dass with Stephen Levine, *Grist for the Mill: Awakening to Oneness* (HarperCollins and HarperOne publishing, New York, 2013), p.151.ISBN 978-0-06-223591-6. This quote was Ram Dass' response to the question, "You say every situation is a perfect lesson. How is that so?"

12 This quote was noted in http://my-head.gaia.com/blog/2007-/6/sense_of_place, and is originally from Fritjof Capra's *The Tao of Physics* (Shambhala Publications, Inc., Boston, MA, 1999), p.307. ISBN 1-57062-519-0.

13 Many educational programs are offered at Evolving Wisdom (http://evolvingwisdom.com/). Some of the course work presented by Katherine Woodward Thomas and Clair Zammit encourages the examination of false beliefs that might include the following: "I'm alone, I'm bad, I don't belong, I'm a burden, I'm crazy, I'm different, I'm not enough, I'm a failure, I don't have, I'm not important, I'm inferior, I'm invisible, I'm not loved, I don't matter, I'm powerless, I'm not safe, I'm too much, I'm unworthy, I'm not wanted, I'm worthless, I'm wrong." Course teachings include how people show up with these false beliefs, their affect on others, their belief about others, their belief about life, ways of acting or being that validate the false identity, and skills and capacities to cultivate in order to evolve beyond that (including affirmations), plus gifts, deeper truth statements and true identity.

14 In her 2013 "Extraordinary Leadership Telesummit" interview, JoAnne O'Brien-Levin said: "Is leadership really follow-ship? It's listening for what is really wanting to unfold through nature, and in the process of working together."

15 Aspects of this think-tank/heart-tank format are described in Vital Key #7, "Manifesting Dreams and Transforming World Systems through the Heart," in the section called "Heart-Infused Governance Systems."

16 Stephen Dinan, "Extraordinary Leadership Telesummit #6," November 12, 2013, Joyce Anastasia Interview Transcript, p.8.

VITAL KEY #6, PP.217-252

1 There are many books on animal, plant and nature communication, such as: David Abram, *The Spell of the Sensuous: Perception and Language in a More-Than-Human World* (Vintage Books, a division of Random House, New York, 1996). ISBN 0-679-77639-7. See also the two-part video created through the Foundation for Global Humanity at: http://www.foundationforglobal-humanity.org/david-abram. See: Jeremy Narby, *The Cosmic Serpent: DNA and the Origins of Knowledge* (Jeremy P. Tarcher/Putnam, a member of Penguin Putnam, New York, 1999). ISBN 0-87477-964-2. See also: J. Allen Boone, *Kinship With All Life* (Harper, San Francisco, CA, 1954). ISBN 0-06-060912-5. See also (refer to the Bibliography) the work of people such as Stephen Buhner, Marco Pogacnik, John Milton, Machaelle Small-Wright, Eileen and Peter Caddy and Dorothy Maclean (founders of Findhorn), etc. Also see experiments by IONS and others, such as: Dean Radin, PhD, *Entangled Minds: Extrasensory Experiences in a Quantum Reality* (Paraview Pocket Books, New York, 2006). ISBN: 978-1-4165-1677-4. Bruce H. Lipton, *The Biology of Belief: Unleashing the Power of Consciousness, Matter, and Miracles* (Hay House, Inc., Mountains of Love Productions, Carlsbad, CA, 2008,). ISBN: 0-9759914-7-7. Joseph McMoneagle, *Remote Viewing Secrets* (Hampton Roads, Charlottesville, VA, 2013). ISBN: 1-57174-159-3. Laila del Monte, *Psychic Communication*

with Animals for Health and Healing (Bear and Company, Rochester, VT, 2010). ISBN: 978-1-59143-100-8.

2 Dean Radin, PhD, *Supernormal* (Deepak Chopra Books, New York, 2013). ISBN 978-0-307-98690-0. See also the Theta DNA Activation group: http://www.thetadnaactivation.com/medical3.html.

3 Michael Murphy, *The Future of the Body: Explorations Into the Further Evolution of Human Nature* (Jeremy P. Tarcher/Putnam, a member of Penguin Putnam, New York,1992). ISBN 0-87477-730-5.

4 Joseph McMoneagle, *loc.cit.* See also Lyn Buchanan, *The Seventh Sense: The Secrets of Remote Viewing as Told by a "Psychic Spy" for the U.S. Military* (Paraview and Pocket Books, a division of Simon and Schuster, New York, 2003). ISBN: 0-7434-6268-8.

5 This is specifically mentioned in *The Cosmic Serpent* by Jeremy Narby; many other books also talk about healers learning the power of plants by communicating with the plants themselves. For example: Stephen Harrod Buhner, *The Secret Teachings of Plants: The Intelligence of the Heart in the Direct Perception of Nature* (Bear & Company, Rochester, VT, 2004). ISBN 978-1-59143-035-3; Pam Montgomery, *Plant Spirit Healing: A Guide to Working With Plant Consciousness* (Bear & Company, Rochester, VT, 2008), ISBN 978-1-59143-077-3; J.P. Harpignies (ed.), *Visionary Plant Consciousness: The Shamanic Teachings of the Plant World* (Park Street Press, Rochester, VT, 2007). Additional fascinating research is the work of Paul Stamets, his team and other significant collaborators, like the well-known time-lapse filmmaker, Louie Schwartzberg. Paul Stamets has written numerous books, including *Mycelium Running: How Mushrooms Can Help Save the World* (Ten Speed Press, Berkeley, CA, 2005). ISBN 978-1-58008-579-3.

6 Thomas Sugrue, *There Is a River: The Story of Edgar Cayce* (A.R.E. Press, Virginia Beach, VA, 1942, 1996, 1997). There are numerous books written about Edgar Cayce's life, and this is one of the most comprehensive.

7 Jane Roberts (with Robert F. Butts Commentary), *Seth Speaks: The External Validity of the Soul* (Amber-Allen Publishing Inc., San Rafael, CA, 1972, 1994, 2012). ISBN 978-1-878424-07-5. Jane Roberts was a prolific writer and I have personally enjoyed many of her books, especially those exploring our miraculous capacities as loving human beings. There are many other researchers who also channeled information, including the following: Helena Blavatsky, Alice Bailey, Benjamin Creme, Laura Horst, Barbara Marciniak, Barbara Hand Clow, Elisabeth Kűbler-Ross and others.

8 Walter Semkiw and Jim Tucker, MD, presented the research of Dr. Ian Stevenson and others in a YouTube video dated May 21, 2013: https://www.youtube.com/watch?v=9w2MCpzE8u0. This includes footage about a very young girl who appeared to be the reincarnation of Anne Frank: the girl knew personal details of Anne's life that were not publicly known. Similarly the video https://www.youtube.com/watch?v=SF3KqGpxXvo is about a family whose child appears to be the reincarnated soul of a dead World War II fighter; again, the young boy actually remembers details of his past life.

9 Dr. Michael Newton, *Journey of Souls* (Llewellyn Publications, St. Paul, MN, 1994, 2003). ISBN 1-56718-485-5. Dr. Michael Newton, *Destiny of Souls* (Llewellyn Publications, St. Paul, MN, 2001). ISBN 1-56718-499-5. Many of Dr. Newton's hypnotherapy clients found themselves exploring not just former lives, but the time *between* lifetimes. The information they obtained often helped then to heal from physical and psychological issues in their current lifetime, and gave extraordinary insights into our paths as human beings. Dr. Newton is also the founder of The Newton Institute for Life Between Lives Hypnotherapy.

10 The former MatterPsyche.net organization held an event called "Synchronicity: Matter & Psyche Symposium" at Joshua Tree, CA on September 12-14, 2014. It was created with the intention of gathering visionary leaders "whose work has pioneered our understanding of the unity of psyche and matter." This symposium brought together people involved in the arts, psychology, science and other embodied heart-centered practices to share ideas and visions for our world. The following quote from *"Synchronicity: the phenomenon"* was listed on the website used for this event (and since has been removed):
"Pauli pursued the symmetries. The Chinese spoke of the Yin and the Receptive in the Tao. The ancient Egyptians honoured the goddess Maat as an extended grid against which all could be measured and balanced. The Navajo imagine Changing Woman, who, with her bundles re-creates Creation in space-time. Modern mathematicians write, 'Yes, God is a geometer.' But never forget: She's better at it than we are." – B. Zabriskie

11 *Ibid., C. G. Jung, CW 8, par. 982.* These referenced quotes were also listed on the website which has been removed from the internet because the event has already taken place.

12 Louie Schwartzberg is one of my favorite filmmakers, capturing life through his moving art in ways that I have rarely witnessed. His work helps to shed light on many unseen elements in our world, reminding us of our integral interconnectedness, and how important it is to hold sacred each sentient being and our truly miraculous lives! For examples of his extraordinary work, go to: Movingart.com/louie-schwartzberg/.

13 György Doczi, *The Power of Limits — Proportional Harmonies in Nature, Art, and Architecture* (Shambhala Publications Inc., Boston, MA, 1981, 1994), p.5. ISBN 0-87773-193-4.

14 See , for example, Dean Radin, PhD, *Entangled Minds: Extrasensory Experiences in a Quantum Reality* (Paraview Pocket Books, New York, 2006). See also The Global Consciousness Project (GCP) or EGG Project: http://noosphee.princeton.edu/.

15 See the Bibliography for details on the following: See, for example, the works of Dr. Russell Targ (physicist) and Dr. Harold Puthoff (physicist and electrical engineer who worked for the NSA) who led SRI International (Stanford Research Institute) experiments; Dr. Targ has written many books and lectured worldwide on remote viewing; Dr. Puthoff has also founded the Institute for Advanced Studies and EarthTech International, dedicated to exploring new frontiers in physics. See also works by Robert Jahn (aerospace

engineer), Brenda Dunne (psychologist), and Dr. Roger Nelson (psychologist and physicist) from the PEAR (Princeton Engineering Anomalies Research) Labs, now at the International Consciousness Research Laboratories (ICRL). See work by Lian Sidorov at EmergentMind.org (an open venture between scientists, scholars and others exploring the relationship between physics, physiology, and consciousness) and at the Mind Matter Mapping Project. See also work by Dr. Charles Tart (psychologist and parapsychologist), also worked at SRI, now at the Institute for the Scientific Study of Consciousness (ISSC). See also the Foundation for Mind Being Research. See also the Institute for Neuroscience and Consciousness Studies (INACS), See also the work of Dr. William Tiller, and Lynne McTaggert.

16 Dr. William A. Tiller, Dr. Walter E. Dibble, J. Gregory Fandel, *Some Science Adventures with Real Magic* (Pavior Publishing, Walnut Creek, CA, 2005). ISBN 1-929331-11-8.

17 See: http://eng.wavegenetics.ru/

18 See: http://www.biologyreference.com/Fo-Gr/Genomics.html and Sara L. Crowston's report, "The Human Genome Project" (1999) at: http://www.-ndsu.edu/pubweb/~mcclean/plsc431/students99/crowston.htm.

19 See, for example, Lipton, Dr. Bruce, *Ibid.* See also: Church, Dawson, *The Genie in Your Genes: Epigenetic Medicine and the New Biology of Intention* (Energy Psychology Press, Santa Rosa, CA, 2007). See also the HeartMath Institute: www.heartmath.org, the Phoenix Center for Regenetics: www.phoenixregenetics.org, and others.

20 See, for example (reference the Bibliography), works by Dr. David Bohm, Dr. Amit Goswami, Dr. Fred Alan Wolf, Dr. Ronald Bryan, and others.

21 See, for example: Rupert Sheldake, *The Rebirth of Nature: the Greening of Science and God* (Park Street Press, Rochester, VT, 2009), and other works by him in the Bibliography

22 Lynne McTaggart, "Extraordinary Leadership Telesummit #5," November 5, 2013, Joyce Anastasia Interview Transcript, p.3.

23 A second healing intention experiment was scheduled for mid-year; however, the following message was posted on the QuantumWorldTV website (http://quantumworld.tv/experiment/):

"Dear Participants,

The "Post Intention Experiments Panel" with Lynne McTaggart, scheduled for June 29th, 2014, has been canceled. The experience of joining together to heal as a group was positive, even transformational, for all who participated – intenders and healing targets alike. However, some issues with the study design preclude us from discussing the study further in support of previous scientific evidence concerning the power of intention.

For more information, please read the article from Lynne McTaggart about the "Results of the First Healing Intention Experiment." She welcomes your comments.

Quantum University wants to thank everyone who participated in the First and Second Healing Intention Experiments on QuantumWorld.TV.

QuantumWorld.TV will continue to educate, entertain, and enlighten through live interactive video classrooms with innovative lectures from renowned speakers.

Thank you. QuantumWorld TV".

24 Brennan, Barbara, *Hands of Light* (Bantam Books, New York, 1988).

25 The Monroe Institute has provided consciousness training for well over sixty years, initially under the direction of Robert Monroe, the founder. Through his own life journey, Robert became consciously aware that "we are more than our physical bodies," and created trainings, with the use of his patented system Hemi-Sync, assisting millions of people throughout the world to explore regions (within our mind's consciousness) beyond the physical. Robert also wrote several books, the first of which sold over 300,000 copies, titled *Journeys Out of the Body*, (Broadway Books, New York, 1992). ISBN 0-385-00861-9. Dr. Joe Gallenberger studied under Monroe and created a program with complementary exercises to ground some of the learning into our daily lives. Joe calls his offshoot program "Sync Creation." I also studied at the Monroe Institute and became a certified Outreach trainer, as well as completing training in Remote Viewing and Joe's "Sync Creation." They have provided both invaluable experiences and tools in my life and leadership work. For additional information, go to https://www.monroeinstitute.org/ and http://synccreation.com/. See also Paul Elder, an author on related subject matter, who currently facilitates Monroe trainings in Canada and the U.S., and who was also filmed through the Foundation for Global Humanity; see the video at: http://www.foundationforglobalhumanity.org/our-dinner-paul.

26 For information on Dr. Emoto's water experiments, go to: http://www.high-existence.com/water-experiment. Dr. Emoto has also written numerous books on his experimental work, including *The Miracle of Water*. (Atria Books/Beyond Words Publishing, Hillsboro, OR, 2007,2011). ISBN 978-1-58270-162-2.

27 Lynne McTaggart, telesummit, *op.cit.*, p.2.

28 Peter Tompkins and Christopher Bird, *The Secret Life of Plants* (Harper and Row Publishers, New York, 1972). ISBN 0-06-091587-0. See also Lyall Watson, *The Secret Life of Inanimate Objects* (Destiny Books, Merrimac, MA, 1992). ISBN 978-0-89281-408-4. See also Dr. David Hawkins, *Power vs. Force: The Hidden Determinants of Human Behavior* (Hay House Inc., Carlsbad, CA 1995, 2012), ISBN 978-1-4019-4507-7.

29 Richard Tarnas spoke at the MatterPsyche.net Symposium on Synchronicity, (mentioned in this section's Endnote #10), above, and made this paraphrase from the *Tao Te Ching 27*.

30 Joseph Jaworski, *Synchronicity: The Inner Path of Leadership* (Berrett-Koehler Publishers, Inc., San Francisco, CA, 2011), preface to the First Edition, p.*xi.* ISBN: 978-1-60994-017-1.

31 Dr. Emoto, *loc.cit.* (this section's Endnote #26 above).

32 Devaa Haley Mitchell also composes and performs soulful music which often alludes to our miraculous nature and invites both our evolution and rebirth to begin now. She invited me to film one of my favorites of her inspired musical expressions; to view this music video, published on December 17, 2012

through the Shift Network, go to: https://www.youtube.com/watch?v=-AUQbZZL70kc.

VITAL KEY #7, PP.253-301

1 Charles Eisenstein, *The More Beautiful World Our Hearts Know is Possible* (North Atlantic Books, Berkeley, CA, 2013).

2 Ariel Spilsbury and Michael Bryner, *The Mayan Oracle: Return Path to the Stars* (Bear & Company, Rochester, VT, 1992, 2011), p.293. ISBN 978-1-59143-123-7.

3 This quote was transcribed from the August 2013, global online 21-day Meditation Challenge facilitated by Oprah Winfrey and Deepak Chopra, Day 11.

4 Dr. Steven Borish, *The Land of the Living*, (Blue Dolphin Publishing, Inc., Nevada City, CA, 2004). ISBN: 1-57733-108-7.

5 Note that Reventlow began these reforms when he was still only a very young man.

6 From Beatrice C. Boeke's summary of her husdand's work, "Democracy as it might be; first published in May 1945 by Kees Boeke (1884-1966)," published in Holland: http://worldteacher.faithweb.com/sociocracy.htm.

7 John Buck and Sharon Villines, *We the People: Consenting to a Deeper Democracy, A Guide to Sociocratic Principles and Methods* (Sociocracy.info Press, Washington, DC, 2007), p.17. ISBN: 978-0-9792827-0-6.

8 From Beatrice C. Boeke, *loc.cit.*

9 Sometimes, a phenomenon occurs such as the Occupy Movement which, although not a governance structure (or indeed a formal organization), nonetheless has a tremendous impact on existing governments. In the Occupy Movement, the focus has been on everyone's voice being heard, not just the 1% who have Power Over. This is consistent with the Vital Keys of Power, Truth, and Honoring Uniqueness.

10 John Buck and Sharon Villines, *op.cit.*, pp.31-32. Note that the formal definition of "consent" within Sociocracy has changed from "agreement" in Comte's time to "no objections" today. This is due to practicalities of implementing Sociocracy within real systems. See also: http://www.bolenderinitiatives.com/sociology/auguste-comte-1798-1857.

11 Lester F. Ward, *The Psychic Factors of Civilization.* (Ginn & Co, Boston, 1893), Chapter 38 ("Sociocracy"). This was an expansion of the original ideas presented in his book *Dynamic Sociology* (1883). See John Buck and Sharon Villines. *op.cit.*, pp.32-34.

12 John Buck and Sharon Villines, *op.cit.*,pp.38-47. See also: Gerard Endenburg, *Dictatuur, Democratie, Sociocratie* (Endenburg Elektrotechniek , Rotterdam, 1998). ISBN 978-9014030616. See also Gerard Endenburg, *Sociocracy As Social Design.* (Eburon, Delft, Netherlands, 1998). ISBN 90-5166-604-7.

13 Brian Robertson, "The Sociocratic Method," *Strategy+Business* (online magazine), Issue 44, August 28, 2006: http://www.strategy-business.com-/article/06314?pg=all.

14 Kris Prendergast, http://www.asaecenter.org/Resources/ANow-Detail.cfm?ItemNumber=18309.

15 For an ongoing list of the organization utilizing the principles and practices of Sociocracy, go to: http://www.sociocracy.info/sociocratic-organizations.

16 http://holacracy.org/. (The definition of Holacracy is located on this home page). Brian Robertson also created a video overview at: https://www.youtube.com/watch?v=s1GvHZDOM8g.

17 This has been addressed by producing a more layman-friendly version of the constitution at: http://holacracy.org/constitution.

18 http://joelgetz.com/principles/democratic.htm. The following is a summary of Joel Getzendanner's principles; Coalescence actually has additional ones:

Democratic Principles

"First, the principles relating to the initial conditions of democratic systems:

- *Self-determination (or Autonomy):* This principle suggests the freedom of an individual (or group of individuals) to define themselves and determine their own course of action, without compulsion. People of various religious viewpoints might argue with the *fact* of this principle as it relates to a divine plan or power, but in democratic institutions where there is a separation of church and state, it is accepted as a matter of political *practice.*
- *Fundamental equality of individuals:* Although there are distressingly frequent "exceptions" made to this principle in the historical record, it is generally recognized as foundational to a healthy and principled democracy. A democratic system should not create an intrinsic advantage for one set of citizens over any others. Democracies are supposed to be "peer-to-peer" systems at their core.

Second, principles relating to the formation of the parts of democratic systems, as well as the system as a whole:

- *Voluntary agreement among participants:* Most clearly seen in the formation of unprecedented democratic institutions, such as the European Union or the United States, the potential participants come together, negotiate, and eventually bind themselves to a common agreement or constitution. And, abiding by the autonomy principle above, no one should be coerced into participating. However, if they don't choose to participate under the common agreement, then they have no claim on the benefits resulting from that agreement. The source of authority of a democratic system is the agreement among those who have inherent authority, and who use it to create something new.
- *Self-organization:* A corollary to the principles of voluntary agreement and self-determination is that democratic institutions set their own boundaries, no matter how arbitrary they may seem from the outside. Canada does not have a "right" to join the US; India does not have a "right" to join the EU, and so on. People and entities work with whom and how they want when they form democratic institutions. There is also the question of who or what are the "selves" that do the forming. In the EU, it was nation-states; in the US, it was citizens and their respective states.

- *Granting of sufficient and necessary authority:* The formation of a democratic institution is meaningless unless it is entrusted with sufficient authority to undertake actions on behalf of the participants or enforce the agreement(s) that created the institution in the first place. No one trusts a system that can't enforce its own rules. On the other hand, no more authority than is necessary should be granted. The "and" in this principle is that an authority should be both sufficient and necessary before it is granted by participants.
- *Solidarity:* Solidarity refers to the union of interests, purposes or sympathies among members of a group. Unlike most of the other democratic principles, the precise notion of solidarity can differ greatly, depending on the interests, purposes, etc., that bring a group together. For example, the purpose of forming the United States included it being a sovereign state, an equal actor among the other nations of the world. This required the highest level of solidarity — it takes an act of the whole community to create it, and that it takes an act of the whole community to dissolve it. The US civil war was fought over whether the latter half of this principle was strongly enough present in the US Constitution. Other entities allow very easy entry and exit, where solidarity is a choice that is renewed at every step along the way. (Note: In the Pope's most recent encyclical, he uses the term "solidarity" to refer to the religious principle that each person in a community (or world) is responsible for the well being of every person in that community. I refer to this principle as "mutual responsibility", below.)
- *Mutual responsibility:* A close cousin to solidarity, this principle defines the degree to which participants are responsible for or accountable to each other within the system, and for what. Tight knit communities have a high degree of mutual responsibility at many levels. Computers on the Internet only have high mutual responsibility for operating consistently with the Internet protocol. Users on the Internet have no explicit mutual responsibility (and the system may have suffered because of that lack).

Third, principles regarding the way in which democratic systems operate internally:

- *Subsidiarity:* This political principle suggests that matters ought to be handled by the smallest, lowest or least centralized competent authority. It's intent is to limit the circumstances in which it is appropriate for a more centralized or more complex body to interfere with decisions that can reasonably be made more locally. It is one of the key principles adopted by the European Union, and is present in the US Constitution and Bill of Rights, most expressly in the 10th Amendment.
- *Protecting freedoms:* A political principle for those circumstances in which a more central body feels compelled to act. As it considers various forms of intervention available to it, it should, if the effect is the same, opt for the approach that leaves the greatest freedom to more local bodies or individuals. Again, both the EU and US constitutions embody this principle. (Note: In some EU documents, this principle is described as

"proportionality." But since I use that term for another principle, I chose to not use it here.)

Fourth, principles about decision-making that mostly can be derived from the above principles, but often are useful to have stated explicitly:

- *Non-domination:* No participant, or group of participants should be able to dominate discussions or control decisions. This doesn't mean that all decisions need to be made by consensus or that everyone will be happy with the decisions that are made, it merely suggests that the process should be fair and unbiased.
- *Among relevant and affected parties:* Not everyone needs to be involved in all decision, that is, there is no requirement for "death by democracy." Individuals who are bound by a decision are definitely both relevant and affected. But beyond that, it is a matter of judgment. My personal inclination is to interpret this principle quite narrowly. Other people prefer to interpret it very broadly...
- *The Economic Principle of Proportionality:* There is a general sense that fairness requires that those who contribute more to a system should have proportionally more influence in decision-making, up to a point... Bigger investors tend to have more voting rights than smaller investors, for example. Few people would characterize this as "unfair." However, democratic networks need to balance this principle with the non-domination and fundamental equality principles to establish their structures and processes.

19 Peter Goodman, "Why Companies Are Turning to Meditation and Yoga to Boost the Bottom Line," www.huffingtonpost.com, posted July 11, 2013 and updated Nov. 4, 2014. Notably, the employees also are exposed to Emotional Intelligence training.

20 The New York Times presented the article "What Happened in Ferguson" outlining the violent events in Missouri and across the nation, and the call to address race-related issues; to review, go to: http://www.nytimes.com/interactive/2014/08/13/us/ferguson-missouri-town-under-siege-after-police-shooting.html?_r=0.

21 Nina Simons, Telesummit, *op.cit.*, p.16.

22 Stephen Dinan, Telesummit, *op.cit.,*, pp.2-3.

23 *Ibid.*

24 *Ibid.*, p.6.

25 The Bioneers website is filled with valuable information about their conferences as well as the evolutionary and innovative work being done globally, including video clips of Paul Hawkins, Jane Goodall, John Powell and others; go to: http://www.bioneers.org/.

26 Nina Simons, Telesummit, *op.cit.*, pp.1-16.

27 This team includes Stephen Dinan, Foster Gamble and others, and is led by Barbara Marx Hubbard to help structure her own transformational work in Conscious Evolution.

28 Kimberly Carter Gamble, "Extraordinary Leadership Telesummit #9," December 10, 2013, Joyce Anastasia Interview Transcript, pp.1-23. See also: http://www.thrivemovement.com/.

29 To view the video of Jahsiah Abijah Jacobs performing "I Believe in this Generation," see: https://youtu.be/AHAt1dsv4ZE (now under the name "Message 2 Humanity (A Music Video)." For more information, contact: joyceanastasia@gmail.com.

30 Janine Benyus, founder of the Biomimicry Institute, was invited to do a TED Talk entitled "Janine Benyus:12 sustainable design ideas from nature": https://www.youtube.com/watch?v=n77BfxnVlyc. The official website for Biomimicry is: http://biomimicry.org/ . See also her groundbreaking book: Janine Benyus, *Biomimicry: Innovation Inspired by Nature* (Perennial, an Imprint of HarperCollins Publishers, New York, 2002). ISBN 0-06-053322.

31 The details related to International Living Future Institute can be found at: http://living-future.org/. For more information regarding the Buckminster Fuller Institute, see: http://bfi.org/.

32 This Rev. Martin Luther King, Jr. quote was part of a Commencement Address for Oberlin College (Ohio) "Remaining Awake Through a Great Revolution," June 1965.

Bibliography

Abadesco, Vicki. See Free To Be organization.

Abram, David. *The Spell of the Sensuous: Perception and Language in a More-Than-Human World.* New York: Vintage Books, a division of Random House, 1996.

Albom, Mitch. *The Five People You Meet in Heaven.* New York: Hyperion, 2003.

Alliance for Wild Ethics: www.wildethics.org.

Alzheimer Europe. "The Four Main Approaches." http://www.alzheimer-europe.org/Research/Understanding-dementia-research/Types-of-research/The-four-main-approaches.

Anderson, Craig A. and Brad J. Bushman. "Effects of Violent Video Games on Aggressive Behavior, Aggressive Cognition, Aggressive Affect, Physiological Arousal, and Prosocial Behavior..." American Psychological Society, *Psychological Science,* vol. 12, no. 5, Sept. 2001.
— edited by Warburton, W. & D. Braunstein. *Growing Up Fast and Furious: Reviewing the Impacts of Violence and Sexualized Media on Children.* Annandale, NSW, Australia: The Federation Press, 2012.

Anderson, Lelanie Fuller. "The Warriors of the Rainbow." 1990: http://www.angelfire.com/ok/TheCherokeeLady/warriorsrainbow.html.

Andrews, Ted. *Animal Speak.* St. Paul, MN: Llewellyn Publications, 1993.
— *Animal-Wise.* Jackson, TN: Dragon-Hawk Publishing, 1999.
— *Nature-Speak.* Holt, MI: Partners Publishing Group, 2004.

Atwater, F. Holmes ("Skip"). *Captain of My Ship — Master of My Soul.* Charlottesville, VA: Hampton Roads, 2001.

Bailey, Alice. *Esoteric Psychology Series.* NY: Lucis Trust, 1936-1953.

Barash, Susan Shapiro. *Little White Lies, Deep Dark Secrets: The Truth About Why Women Lie.* New York: St. Martin's Press, 2009.

Bartlett, Richard. *The Physics of Miracles.* New York: Atria Books, a division of Simon & Schuster, Inc., 2009.

Bates, Mike. "MLB's Record on Domestic Violence Worse than NFL's." *SB Nation,* July 28, 2014: http://www.sbnation.com/mlb/2014/7/28/5936835/ray-rice-chuck-knoblauch-minnesota-twins-mlb-domestic-abuse-violence.

BeeFriendly: http://beefriendly.ca/

Begich, Nick. *Angels Don't Play This HAARP: Advances in Tesla Technology.* Anchorage, AL: Earth Pulse Press, Inc., 1995,2002.

Benyus, Janine. *Biomimicry: Innovation Inspired by Nature.* New York: Perennial, an Imprint of HarperCollins, 2002.
— http://biomimicry.org/
— "Janine Benyus: 12 sustainable design ideas from nature," *TED Talk,* July, 2009: https://www.youtube.com/watch?v=n77BfxnVlyc.

Blavatsky, Helena P. (ed. by Boris de Zirkoff). *The Secret Doctrine.* London: Theosophical Publishing House, 1888,1978,1993.

Boeke, Beatrice C. "Democracy as it might be; first published in May 1945 by Kees Boeke (1884-1966)." Holland: http://worldteacher.faithweb.com/sociocracy.htm.

Bohm, Dr. David. *Wholeness and the Implicate Order.* New York: Routledge, 1980.
— See also references in: www.implicity.org/bohm.htm.
— See also Interview with David Bohm on Perception: https://www.youtube.com/watch?v=Mst3fOl5vH0.

Bonnefire Coalition (HAARP, etc.): www.agriculturedefensecoalition.org/content/welcome-bonnefire-coalition.

Boone, J. Allen. *Kinship With All Life.* San Francisco, CA: Harper, 1954.

Borish, Dr. Steven. *The Land of the Living.* Nevada City, CA: Blue Dolphin Publishing, Inc., 2004.

Braden, Gregg. *The God Code.* Carlsbad, CA: Hay House, Inc., 2004.
— *The Divine Matrix: Bridging Time, Space, Miracles, and Belief.* Carlsbad, CA: Hay House, Inc., 2007.

Bradshaw, G.A., PhD. "Elephants, Us, and Other Kin." Video presentation created for "Affect Dysregulation and the Healing of the self," UCLA Annual Interpersonal Neurobiology Conference, Los Angeles, March 14-16, 2014: https://www.youtube.com/watch?v=1JB1XCbBJQs&feature=youtu.be,
— The Kerulos Center: http://www.kerulos.org.

Bradshaw, John. *Homecoming: Reclaiming and Championing Your Inner Child.* New York: Bantam Books, 1992.

Brennan, Barbara. *Hands of Light.* New York: Bantam Books, a division of Random House, Inc., 1988.

Brown, Ellen. *The Web of Debt.* Baton Rouge, LA: Third Millennium Press, 2012.
— http://ellenbrown.com.

Brown, James T., III. Coalescence: http://www.coalescence.global/.

Bryan, Dr. Ronald: http://people.physics.tamu.edu/bryan.

Buchanan, Lyn. *The Seventh Sense: The Secrets of Remote Viewing as Told by A "Psychic Spy" for the U.S. Military.* New York: Paraview and Pocket Books, a division of Simon and Schuster, 2003.

Buck, John and Sharon Villines. *We the People: Consenting to a Deeper Democracy, A Guide to Sociocratic Principles and Methods.* Washington, DC: Sociocracy.info Press, 2007.

Buhner, Stephen Harrod. *The Secret Teachings of Plants: The Intelligence of the Heart in the Direct Perception of Nature.* Rochester, VT: Bear & Company, 2004.

Caddy, Eileen and Peter, and Dorothy Maclean (The Findhorn Community). *The Findhorn Garden.* New York: Perennial, a division of HarperCollins, 1976.

Capra, Fritjof. *The Tao of Physics.* Boston, MA: Shambhala Publications, Inc., 1999. See also: http://my-head.gaia.com/blog/2007/6/sense_of_place.

Center for the Advancement of Human Potential: www.ian-asheville.com.

Cheney, Margaret and Robert Uth. *Tesla.* New York: Barnes and Noble, 1999.

Christensen, Jen. "Cynicism linked to greater dementia risk, study says." *CNN*, May 29, 2014.

Church, Dawson. *The Genie in Your Genes: Epigenetic Medicine and the New Biology of Intention.* Santa Rosa, CA: Energy Psychology Press, 2007.

Cloud, Dr. Henry. *Integrity: The courage to meet the demands of reality.* New York: Harper Collins Publishers, 2006.

Clow, Barbara Hand. *The Mayan Code.* Rochester, VT: Bear & Company, 2007.

Coast to Coast: www.coasttocoastam.com.

Continuum Movement (Emily Conrad): http://continuummovement.com/.

Covey, Steven R.: www.myspeedoftrust.com.

Creativity for Peace: http://www.creativityforpeace.com.

Creme, Benjamin. *The Awakening of Humanity.* London: Share International Foundation, 2008.

Cronkite, Walter. "Live Coverage of the Assassination of President Kennedy" Part 1 (1:30 p.m.-2:30 p.m.) and Part 2 (2:30 p.m.-3:30 p.m.). Dallas, New York, Washington DC, *CBS NEWS*, November 22, 1963: https://www.youtube.com/watch?v=pDOojsg62OO, (At marker 1:06:43), https://www.youtube.com/watch?v=vwtqvuWOVWo&list=PLJZPvqeFqoFgB7_7BJ9k7iy5Cs5oKrmXp&index=1 and https://www.youtube.com-/watch?v=jNTvduZud4U.

Crowston, Sara L. "The Human Genome Project." 1999: www.ndsu.edu/pubweb/~mcclean/plsc431/students99/crowston.htm.

Dalai Lama: http://www.dalailama.com.

Dass, Ram and Stephen Levine. *Grist for the Mill: Awakening to Oneness.* New York: HarperCollins and HarperOne Publishing, 2013.

del Monte, Laila. *Psychic Communication with Animals for Health and Healing.* Rochester, VT: Bear and Company, 2010.

Democracy Now: www.democracynow.org.

Denninger, Karl: http://market-ticker.org/.

Dinan, Stephen. "Extraordinary Leadership Telesummit #6," November 12, 2013. Mill Valley, CA: Joyce Anastasia Interview Transcript.

Doczi, György. *The Power of Limits — Proportional Harmonies in Nature, Art, and Architecture.* Boston, MA: Shambhala Publications Inc., 1981,1994.

Eisenhower, Dwight D. "Military-Industrial Complex Speech, 1961." *Public Papers on the President, Dwight D. Eisenhower*, Washington, DC, 1960.
— http://coursesa.matrix.msu.edu/~hst306/documents/indust.html.
— https://www.youtube.com/watch?v=8y06NSBBRtY.

Eisenstein, Charles. *The More Beautiful World Our Hearts Know is Possible.* Berkeley, CA: North Atlantic Books, 2013.
— "The Three Seeds" essay: http://charleseisenstein.net/the-three-seeds.
— *Sacred Economics.* Berkeley, CA: Evolver Editions, 2011.

Elder, Paul. *Eyes of an Angel.* Charlottesville, VA: Hampton Roads, 2005.

Emoto, Masaru Dr. *The Miracle of Water.* Hillsboro, OR: Atria Books/Beyond Words Publishing, 2007,2011.
— http://www.highexistence.com/water-experiment.

Endenburg, Gerard. *Dictatuur, Democratie, Sociocratie.* Rotterdam, Netherlands: Endenburg Elektrotechniek, 1998.
— *Sociocracy As Social Design.* Delft, Netherlands: Eburon, 1998.

Esplin, Kathryn. "Can Lying Affect the Intimacy of a Relationship?" *Global Post: America's News World Site* (online site): http://everydaylife.globalpost.com/can-lying-affect-intimacy-relationship-33513.html.

Esser, Theodore, IV. *Lucid Dreaming, Kundalini, The Divine and Non-duality.* Dissertation, 2014 (to be published).

Estulin, Daniel. *The True Story of the Bilderberg Group.* Walterville, OR: Lennart Sane Agency AB, TrineDay LLC, 2009.

Feldman, Robert. "UMass researcher finds most people lie in everyday conversation." Amherst, MA: *EurekAlert: The Global Source for Science News,* June 10, 2002.

Findhorn: www.findhorn.org.

Fisher, Max. "This map shows where the world's 30 million slaves live. There are 60,000 in the U.S.." Washington, DC: *The Washington Post,* October 17, 2013: www.washingtonpost.com/blogs/worldviews/wp/2013/10/17/this-map-shows-where-the-worlds-30-million-slaves-live-there-are-60000-in-the-u-s/.

Fitts, Catherine Austin: https://solari.com/blog/.

Foundation for Global Humanity (FGH: Connie Cummings, Joyce Anastasia, Matt and Mary Page): www.foundationforglobalhumanity.org.
— http://www.youtube.com/watch?v=N1uAotKuZGo, Dawn of a New Time.
— http://www.youtube.com/watch?v=68IvYY6QQKU, A Mamo's Gift, Pt.1.
— http://www.youtube.com/watch?v=g20v1BWfHqQ, A Mamo's Gift, Pt.2.
— http://www.youtube.com/watch?v=4r8GoxHiF1g, A Mamo's Gift, Pt.3.
— http://www.foundationforglobalhumanity.org/ashok-gangadean.
— http://www.foundationforglobalhumanity.org/amit-goswami.
— http://www.foundationforglobalhumanity.org/pat-mccabe.
— http://www.foundationforglobalhumanity.org/david-abram.
— http://www.foundationforglobalhumanity.org/our-dinner-paul.

Foundation for Inner Peace. *A Course in Miracles.* Mill Valley, CA: Foundation for Inner Peace, 1975,2007.

Foundation for Mind Being Research: www.fmbr.org.

Free To Be organization (to stop bullying): http://free-to-be.net/.

Fuller, Buckminster. The Buckminster Fuller Institute: http://bfi.org.

FungiPerfecti: www.fungi.com.

Gallenberger, Dr. Joe. "Sync Creation": http://synccreation.com/.

Gamble, Foster. "Extraordinary Leadership Telesummit #3," October 22, 2013. Mill Valley, CA: Joyce Anastasia Interview Transcript.
— http://www.thrivemovement.com/.

Gamble, Kimberly Carter. "Extraordinary Leadership Telesummit #9," December 10, 2013. Mill Valley, CA: Joyce Anastasia Interview Transcript.
— http://www.thrivemovement.com/.

Gangadean, Ashok. Global Dialogue Institute: http://www.awakeningmind.org.

Gariaev, Dr. Peter: http://eng.wavegenetics.ru/.

Getzendanner, Joel. "Democratic principles." joelgetz.com: http://joelgetz.com/principles/democratic.htm%5B4/7/2011 7:47:06 PM%5D.

Global Consciousness Project: http://noosphee.princeton.edu/ (or EGG Project).

Goodman, Peter. "Why Companies Are Turning to Meditation and Yoga to Boost the Bottom Line." *The Huffington Post*, Nov. 4, 2014: www.huffingtonpost.com.

Goswami, Amit, PhD. *Quantum Creativity: Think Quantum, Be Creative*. Carlsbad, CA: Hay House, Inc., 2014.
— www.amitgoswami.org.
— *God Is Not Dead: What Quantum Physics Tells Us About Our Origins and How We Live*. Charlottesville, VA: Hampton Roads, 2008.
— with Richard E. Reed and Maggie Goswami. *The Self-Aware Universe: How Consciousness Creates the Material World*. New York: Putnum, 1995.

Greer, Steven. http://www.disclosureproject.org/.

Hagopian, Joachim. "Global Human Trafficking, A Modern Form of Slavery." *Centre for Research on globalization*: http://www.globalresearch.ca/global-human-trafficking-a-modern-form-of-slavery/5377853.

Hanchin, Victoria. *The Seer and The Sayer: Revelations of the New Earth*. Bloomington, IN: Balboa Press, 2012.

Harpignies, J.P., ed. *Visionary Plant Consciousness: The Shamanic Teachings of the Plant World*. Rochester, VT: Park Street Press, 2007.

Hawkins, Dr. David. *Power vs. Force: The Hidden Determinants of Human Behavior*. Carlsbad, CA: Hay House, Inc., 1995,2012.

Hay, Louise L. *Heal Your Body*. Carlsbad, CA: Hay House, Inc., 1988.

Heifer Project: http://www.heifer.org.

Higgins, Polly. "Extraordinary Leadership Telesummit," (pre-summit) August 22, 2013. Mill Valley, CA: Joyce Anastasia Interview Transcript.
— http://eradicatingecocide.com/.
— *Your Guide to Making Ecocide a Crime*. London: Polly Higgins, 2012.
— You Tube video of TEDxEXETER Talk: https://www.youtube.com/watch?v=8EuxYzQ65H4.

Holacracy — see Robertson, Brian.

Hopi, Benjamin. "Benjamin Hopi Summer Colombia Interview," August 18-22, 2011: http://www.foundationforglobalhumanity.org/dawn-new-time-0.

Horst, Laura. *Astonishing Messages from the Cosmos.* Houston, TX: Palmer Publishers, 1986.

Houston, Jean. *The Wizard of Us.* Hillsboro, OR: Beyond Words, 2012.

— www.jeanhouston.org.

Howard, C. Jeriel and Richard Francis Tracz (eds). *The Responsible Person: Essays, Short Stories, Poems.* San Francisco, CA: Canfield Press, a department of Harper and Row, Inc., 1975.

Hubbard, Barbara Marx. *Birth 2012 and Beyond.* Petaluma, CA: Shift Books, 2012.

Hudson, Michael. *Global Fractal: The New International Economic Order.* Ann Arbor, MI: Pluto Press, 2005.

Hughes-Smith, Charles: www.oftwominds.com/blog.html.

Ilibagazia, Immaculeé. *Left to Tell: Discovering God Amidst the Rwandan Holocaust.* Carlsbad, CA: Hay House, Inc., 2006,2014.

Institute for Cultural Diplomacy, Berlin. "The African Diaspora." http://www.culturaldiplomacy.org/experienceafrica/index.php?en_the-african-diaspora.

Institute of HeartMath: www.heartmath.org.

Institute for Neuroscience and Consciousness Studies (INACS): www.inacs.net.

Institute of Noetic Sciences (IONS): http://noetic.org/.

Institute for the Scientific Study of Consciousness (ISSC): www.issc-taste.org.

Institutes for the Achievement of Human Potential (IAHP): www.iahp.org.

International Consciousness Research Laboratories (ICRL): www.icrl.org.

Jahn, Robert G., and Brenda J. Dunne. *Consciousness and the Source of Reality: The PEAR Odyssey.* Princeton, NJ: ICRL Press, 2011.
— International Consciousness Research Laboratories: www.icrl.org.

Jaworski, Joseph. *Synchronicity: The Inner Path of Leadership.* San Francisco, CA: Berrett-Koehler Publishers, Inc., 2011.

Jondean. "Documents For: The 99 Declaration." New York: Occupy Wall Street, January 13, 2012: http://www.theguardian.com/world/occupy. http://www.nycga.net/group-document-categories/the-99-declaration.

Judith, Dr. Anodea. *Waking the Global Heart.* Santa Rosa, CA: Elite Books, 2006.

Jung, Carl. *The Collective Unconscious.* New York: Princeton University Press/Bollingen Foundation, 1959.

Kamath, Prabhakar. "The Basic Principles of Satyagraha." *Nirmukta* online magazine, July 29, 2011: http://nirmukta.com/2011/07/29/the-basic-principles-of-satyagraha.

Kawa, Lucas. "CHARTS: The US Has Some Of The Worst Health Statistics In The Developed World." *Business Insider*, January, 10, 2013: www.businessinsider.com/us-health-lags-the-developed-world-2013-1.

Keane, Fergal. "The Rwandan Girl Who Refused to Die." *Frontline Special Report (BBC)*, April 1994; reprinted *New York Sunday Times*, 1997.

Kelly, Dr. Anita and Dr. Lijuan Wang. "Lying Less Linked to Better Health, New Research Finds." *American Psychological Association and John Templeton Foundation*, "Science of Honesty" project, August 4, 2012: https://cbsphilly.files.wordpress.com/2012/08/kelly-a-life-without-lies.pdf.

Kelto, Anders. "From the shacks to the prom, a South African girl's night of glamour." *PRI The World*, October 2, 2014 (1:45 p.m. EDT): http://www.pri.org/stories/2013-10-02/shacks-prom-south-african-girl-s-night-glamour.

Kennedy, David M. *The Modern American Military*. New York: Oxford University Press, New York, 2013.
— https://friendsofjustice.wordpress.com/2013/02/08/david-kennedy-how-to-stop-the-killing/.

Kennedy, John F. "The President and the Press: JFK Secret Society" talk. *American Newspaper Publishers Association*, April 27, 1961: www.jfklibrary.org and https://www.youtube.com/watch?v=8y06NSBBRtY.

Kerulos Center: http://www.kerulos.org. (See also: Bradshaw, G.A.)

King, Martin Luther, Jr. "Remaining Awake Through a Great Revolution." (Address for Oberlin College graduation), Oberlin, Ohio, June 1965.
— "I Have a Dream" speech, 1963. FoxNews.com, http://www.ibtimes.com/i-have-dream-speech-full-transcript-video-read-dr-martin-luther-king-jrs-1963-speech-its-50th.

Kirkpatrick, David D. "Syrian Children Offer Glimpse of a Future of Reprisals." Zaatari, Jordan, *The New York Times*, September 3, 2012.

Kohanov, Linda. *The Tao of Equus: A Woman's Journey of Healing and Transformation through the Way of the Horse*. Novato, CA: New World Library, 2001,2007.

Kübler-Ross, Elisabeth. *On Death and Dying*. London: MacMillan, 1977.

Langer, Gary. "Politics 2014: Low Confidence in Leaders and a Dead Heat in Midterm Preference." Washington DC, ABC NEWS/WASHINGTON POST POLL, January 26, 2014: http://www.langerresearch.com/uploads-/1158a1Obamaand2014Politics.pdf.

Lead By Wisdom (Joyce Anastasia): http://www.leadbywisdom.com.

Leonard, George. www.itp-international.org/

Lipton, Bruce H. *The Biology of Belief: Unleashing the Power of Consciousness, Matter, and Miracles*. Carlsbad, CA: Hay House, Inc./Mountains of Love Productions, 2008.

Lohbach, Eva. http://consciousresonance.net/?p=3243.

Lopatto, Elizabeth. "Sleep Loss Alters Genes While Raising Risk of Disease." *Bloomberg online*, February 25, 2013: http://www.bloomberg.com/news/articles/2013-02-25/sleep-loss-alters-genes-while-raising-risk-of-disease.

Loyd, Alexander, PhD, ND, with Ben Johnson, MD, DO, NMD. *The Healing Code.* New York and Boston: Grand Central Life and Style, a Hachette Book Group, 2010.

Mackay, Harvey. "Reward Workers, then Reap Rewards." On Business, *Albany Times Union*, November 20, 2012: http://www.timesunion.com/business/article/Reward-workers-then-reap-rewards-4051445.php.
— http://harveymackay.com/column/tag/articles-by-harvey-mackay/.
— http://harveymackay.com/column/2012/11/.

Macy, Joanna. *Pass it On.* Berkeley, CA: Parallax Press, 2010.
— http://www.joannamacy.net/

Mandela, Nelson. Foundation: https://www.nelsonmandela.org.
— http://www.history.com/topics/nelson-mandela.

Marciniak, Barbara. *The Pleiadian* Series. Novato, CA: New World Library, 1992-2004.

Martin, Nick. "Slavery Should Be Made Essential Reading," *Sky News*, January 11, 2014: http://news.sky.com/story/1193503/slavery-should-be-made-essential-reading.
— http://www.dailykos.com/story/2013/12/27/1265498/-The-slaves-that-time-forgot.

MatterPsyche.net. "Synchronicity: Matter & Psyche Symposium." Joshua Tree, CA: September 12-14, 2014.

McCabe, Pat ("Woman Stands Shining"). "Extraordinary Leadership Telesummit #4," October 29, 2013. Mill Valley, CA: Joyce Anastasia Interview Transcript.

McCarthy, Jenna. "The Truth About Lying." *Real Simple* (on-line magazine), Time Inc. Lifestyle Group, 2015: http://www.realsimple.com/work-life/life-strategies/truth-about-lying.

McGraugh, Susan, and Richard Rosenfeld, Larry Buchanan, Ford Fessenden, K.K. Rebecca Lai, Haeyoun Park, Alicia Parlapiano, Archie Tse, Tim Wallace, Derek Watkins and Karen Yourish (and Missouri State Highway Patrol). "What Happened in Ferguson." *The New York Times*, July 13, 2014: http://www.nytimes.com/interactive/2014/08/13/us/ferguson-missouri-town-under-siege-after-police-shooting.html?_r=0.

McLennan, Jason F. International Living Future Institute: http://living-future.org.

McMoneagle, Joseph. *Remote Viewing Secrets.* Charlottesville, VA: Hampton Roads, 2013.

McTaggart, Lynne. "Extraordinary Leadership Telesummit #5," November 5, 2013. Mill Valley, CA: Joyce Anastasia Interview Transcript.
— *What Doctors Don't Tell You: The Truth about the Dangers of Modern Medicine.* New York: Avon Books, an Imprint of HarperCollins, 1999.

— *The Field.* New York: HarperCollins, 2002.
— *The Bond.* New York: Free Press, a division of Simon & Schuster, Inc., 2011.
— *The Intention Experiment.* New York: Atria Paperbacks, a division of Simon & Schuster, Inc., 2007.
— http://theintentionexperiment.com/.
— "Results of the First Healing Intention Experiment." *QuantumWorld.TV,* June 29th, 2014: http://quantumworld.tv/experiment/.

Meyer, Pamela. *Liespotting: Proven Techniques to Detect Deception.* New York: St. Martin Press, 2011.
— "How to Spot a Liar." *TED Talk,* July 2011, published August 9, 2013 on You tube: https://www.youtube.com/watch?v=eZ4zlkhdcCw.

Miller, A.G. (ed). *The Social Psychology of Good and Evil.* New York: Guilford Press, 2004.

Milton, John: http://sacredpassage.com/

Mitchell, Devaa Haley. "The Birth of a New Way." *The Shift Network,* December 17, 2012: https://www.youtube.com/watch?v=AUQbZZL70kc.

Monroe, Robert. *Journeys Out of the Body.* New York: Broadway Books, 1992.
— https://www.monroeinstitute.org/.

Montgomery, Pam. *Plant Spirit Healing: A Guide to Working with Plant Consciousness.* Rochester, VT: Bear & Company, 2008.

Morris, Errol. "Robert McNamara admits Gulf of Tonkin attack did not happen," from the film "The Fog of War." Presented on YouTube, March 7, 2010: https://www.youtube.com/watch?v=5AaGVAipGp0.

Murphy, Michael. *The Future of the Body: Explorations Into the Further Evolution of Human Nature.* New York: Jeremy P. Tarcher/Putnam, a member of Penguin Putnam, 1992.

Narby, Jeremy. *The Cosmic Serpent: DNA and the Origins of Knowledge.* New York: Jeremy P. Tarcher/Putnam, a member of Penguin Putnam, Inc., 1998.

National Coalition Against Domestic Violence (NCADV): http://nnedv.org/-downloads/Census/DVCounts2013/DVSA_Factsheet.pdf.

National Institute of Neurological Disorders and Stroke. "Brain Basics: Understanding Sleep." February 26, 2013: http://www.ninds.nih.gov-/disorders/brain_basics/understanding_sleep.htm.

National Public Radio (NPR): www.npr.org.

Nelson, Dr. Roger. http://consciousresonance.net/.
— Global Consciousness Project: http://noosphee.princeton.edu/.
— See also: International Consciousness Research Laboratories (ICRL).

Newton, Dr. Michael. *Journey of Souls.* St. Paul, MN: Llewellyn Publications, 1994,2003.
— *Destiny of Souls.* St. Paul, MN: Llewellyn Publications, 2001.
— Institute for Life Between Lives Hypnotherapy: http://newtoninstitute.org/.

Noë, Alva, PhD. Varieties of Presence. Cambridge, MA: President and Fellows of Harvard College, 2012.

Nunberg, Geoffrey. *Going Nuclear: Language, Politics, and Culture in Confrontational Times.* New York: Public Affairs, a member of Perseus Books, 2005.

O'Brien-Levin, Joanne (interviewed with Glenn A. Parry). "Extraordinary Leadership Telesummit #2," October 15, 2013. Mill Valley, CA: Joyce Anastasia Interview Transcript.

O'Dea, James. "Extraordinary Leadership Telesummit #1," September 24, 2013. Mill Valley, CA: Joyce Anastasia Interview Transcript.
— *Creative Stress: A path for evolving souls living through personal and planetary upheaval.* Ross, CA: Pioneer Imprints/www.jamesodea.com, 2010.

Oxford Dictionary online: http://www.oxforddictionaries.com/.

Pachamama Alliance. "The Eagle and the Condor prophecy." February 2015: http://www.pachamama.org/blog/the-eagle-and-the-condor-prophecy.

Parry, Glenn A. (interviewed with Joanne O'Brien-Levin). "Extraordinary Leadership Telesummit #2," October 15, 2013. Mill Valley, CA: Joyce Anastasia Interview Transcript.
— *Original Thinking: A Radical Revisioning of Time, Humanity, and Nature.* (to be published)

Pew Research Center. "Public Sees U.S. Power Declining as Support for Global Engagement Slips: America's Place in the World 2013." www.pewresearch.org: December 4, 2013:
http://smarkos.blogspot.com/search?q="AMERICA'S+PLACE+IN+THE+WORLD+2013.

Phoenix Center for Regenetics: www.phoenixregenetics.org.

Pogacnik, Marco. *Nature Spirits and Elemental Beings: Working with the Intelligence in Nature.* Tallahassee, FL: Findhorn Press, 1995.
— *Touching the Breath of Gaia: 59 Foundation Stones for a Peaceful Civilisation.* Findhorn, Forres, Scotland: Findhorn Press, 2007.
— http://www.marcopogacnik.com/

Poitras, Laura and Edward Snowden (his story). Film "Citizen Four." www.citizenfourfilm.com: 2014.

Polari de Alverga, Alex and Stephen Larsen. *Forest of Visions: Ayahuasca, Amazonian Spirituality, and the Santo Daime Tradition.* Rochester, VT: Park Street Press, 1999.

Prendergast, Kris. "Dynamic Governance, Dynamite Component." Center for Associated Leadership, *Associations Now*, June 2006: http://www.asaecenter.org/Resources/ANowDetail.cfm?ItemNumber=18309.

Pribram, Dr. Karl H. *The Form Within.* Westport, CT: Prospecta Press, 2013.
--TV/DVD Series: "The Holographic Brain," www.thinkingallowed.com.

Princeton Engineering Anomalies Research (PEAR) Labs: www.princeton.edu/~pear/.

Puma, Naupany and Pedro Pable Chuc Pech. "Sacred Solar Ceremony with the Sun-Rainbow" video: https://www.youtube.com/watch?v=tIy2xmSpAuo#t=2.

Puthoff, Dr. Harold. *CIA-Initiated Remote-Viewing at Stanford Research Institute*: http://www.biomindsuperpowers.com/P/CIA-InitiatedRV.html.
— Institute for Advanced Studies: www.researchgate.net/profile/H_Puthoff
— EarthTech International: http://earthtech.org/

Radin, Dean, PhD. www.noetic.org/directory/person/dean-radin.
— *Supernormal.* New York: Deepak Chopra Books, 2013.
— *Entangled Minds: Extrasensory Experiences in a Quantum Reality.* New York: Paraview Pocket Books, 2006.
— http://www.thetadnaactivation.com/medical3.html.
— http://consciousresonance.net/?cat=102.

Roberts, Jane (and Robert F. Butts Commentary). *Seth Speaks: The External Validity of the Soul.* San Rafael, CA: Amber-Allen Publishing Inc., 1972,1994,2012.
— *The Nature of Personal Reality.* San Rafael, CA: Amber-Allen Publishing, Inc., 1994.
— *Oversoul Seven* (trilogy). San Rafael, CA: Amber-Allen Publishing, Inc., 1987,1995.

Robertson, Brian. "Overview of Holacracy." http://holacracy.org/.
— On You Tube: https://www.youtube.com/watch?v=s1GvHZDOM8g.
— "The Sociocratic Method," written for *Strategy+Business on-line magazine*, Issue 44, August 28, 2006: http://www.strategy-business.com/article/06314?pg=all.

Rodale Institute: http://rodaleinstitute.org/.

Rumi (translated by Coleman Barks with John Moyne). *The Essential Rumi.* New York: Harper, 1995.

Sagan, Carl. *The Demon-Haunted World.* New York: Ballantine Books, 1996.

Schwartzberg, Louie. http://Movingart.com/louie-scwartzberg/

Seattle, Chief. http://www.ceng.metu.edu.tr/~ucoluk/yazin/seattle.html.

SEED Graduate Institute. "Wisdom of the Origins Conference." Albuquerque, NM: September 13-18, 2012: https://www.youtube.com/watch?v=sYkTLxmeaW4.
— http://www.foundationforglobalhumanity.org/video-highlights.

Semkiw, Walter and Jim Tucker, MD. "Evidence of Reincarnation." You Tube, May 21, 2013: https://www.youtube.com/watch?v=9w2MCpzE8u0.

Senge, Peter. *The Fifth Discipline: The Art and Practice of Learning Organization.* New York: Currency Doubletree, 1990.
— Peter Senge and George Roth. *The Dance of Change: The challenges to sustaining momentum in a learning organization.* New York: Currency Doubletree, 1999.

Serota, K.B., T.R. Levine and F.J. Boster. "The prevalence of lying in America: Three studies of reported deception." *Human Communication Research*, Vol. 36, 2010.

Seva Foundation: http://www.seva.org.

Sheldrake, Rupert: www.sheldrake.org.
— *The Presence of the Past: Morphic Resonance and the Habits of Nature.* London: Icon Books, 1988,2011.
— *Morphic Resonance: The Nature of Formative Causation.* Rochester, VT: Park Street Press, 2009.
— *The Rebirth of Nature: the Greening of Science and God.* Rochester, VT: Park Street Press, 1991,1994.

Sidorov, Lian: www.emergentmind.org.
— The Mind Matter Mapping Project: www.mindmattermapping.org.

Simons, Nina. "Extraordinary Leadership Telesummit #7," November 19, 2013. Mill Valley, CA: Joyce Anastasia Interview Transcript.
— with Anneke Campbell. *Moonrise.* VT: Park Street Press, 2010.
— Bioneers: www.bioneers.org.

Snowden, Edward — see under Poitras; see under Williams.

Sociocracy: http://www.sociocracy.info/sociocratic-organizations.
— http://www.bolenderinitiatives.com/sociology/auguste-comte.
— http://sociocracyconsulting.com/.
— www.sociocracy.biz.

Soulshoppe: www.soulshoppe.com

Small-Wright, Machaelle. *Co-creative Science: A Revolution in Science Providing Real Solutions for Today's Health and Environment*: Warrenton, VA: Perelandra, LTD, 1997.
— *Behaving as if the God in All Life Mattered.* Warrenton, VA: Perelandra, LTD, 1997.
— The Center for Nature Research: www.perelandra-ltd.com.

Smith, Dr. David. See under McCarthy, Jenna.

Spilsbury, Ariel and Michael Bryner. *The Mayan Oracle: Return Path to the Stars.* Rochester, VT: Bear & Company, 1992.

Stamets, Paul. *Mycelium Running: How Mushrooms Can Help Save the World.* Berkeley, CA: Ten Speed Press, 2005.

Stewart, Jon. http://thedailyshow.cc.com.

Still, Bill. https://www.youtube.com/user/bstill3.

Sugrue, Thomas. *There Is a River: The Story of Edgar Cayce.* Virginia Beach, VA: A.R.E. Press, 1942,1945,1970,1973,1997.

Takahashi, Joseph S. (ed), Carla S. Moeller-Levet, Simon N. Archer, Giselda Bucca, Emma E. Laing, Ana Slak, Renata Kabiljo, June C.Y. Lo, Nayantara Santhi, Malcolm von Schantz, Colin P. Smith and Derk-Jan Dijk. "Effects of insufficient sleep on circadian rhythmicity and expression amplitude of the human blood transcriptome." *The Proceedings of the National Academy of Sciences of the U.S.A.*, Dallas, TX, Howard Hughes Medical Institute, University of Texas Southwestern Medical Center, October 3, 2012, vol.110, no.12: www.pnas.org/content/110/12/E1132.abstract.0

Targ, Dr. Russell. *The Reality of ESP: A Physicist's Proof of Psychic Ability.* Wheaton, IL: Quest Books (Theosophical Publishing House), 2012.
— *Do You See What I See? Memoirs of a Blind Biker.* Charlottesville, VA: Hampton Roads, 2008,2010.
— with Dr. Jane Katra. *Miracles of Mind: Exploring Non-Local Consciousness and Spiritual Healing.* Novato, CA: New World Library, 1998.
— www.noetic.org/directory/person/russel-targ/

Tart, Dr. Charles. *The End of Materialism: How Evidence of the Paranormal is Bringing Science and Spirit Together.* Oakland, CA: New Harbinger Publication, Inc., 2009.
— *Altered States of Consciousness.* New York: Harper, 1990.
— www.paradigm-sys.com
— See also Institute for the Scientific Study of Consciousness (ICCS).

Taylor, Dr. Jill Bolte. *My Stroke of Insight: A Brain Scientist's Personal Journey.* New York: Penguin Group, 2006.
— *TED Talk,* February, 2008. On You Tube: https://www.youtube.com/watch?v=UyyjU8fzEYU.

Thomas, Katherine Woodward. *Conscious Uncoupling: 5 Steps to Living Happily Ever After.* e-book created from the Evolving Wisdom course, 2014.
— with Clair Zammit. "Transformation of Identity Matrix": http://evolvingwisdom.com/.

Thrive movie and movement: www.thrivemovement.com.

Tiller, Dr. William A., Dr. Walter E. Dibble and J. Gregory Fandel. *Some Science Adventures with Real Magic.* Walnut Creek, CA: Pavior Publishing, 2005.

Tolle, Eckhart. *A New Earth.* New York: Penguin Group, Inc., 2005.
— *The Power of Now.* Novato, CA: New World Library, 1999,2004.

Tompkins, Peter and Christopher Bird. *The Secret Life of Plants.* New York: Harper and Row, 1972.

Turk, Gary. http://www.garyturk.com,
— You Tube, April 25, 2014: https://www.youtube.com/watch?v=Z7-dLU6fk9QY#t=90.

Twist, Lynne with Teresa Barker. *The Soul of Money.* New York: W.W. Norton & Company, 2003.

University of Surrey. "Lack of Sleep Affects Over 700 Genes." *Examined Existence,* Surrey, England: March 11, 2013: http://www.surrey.ac.uk/features/lack-sleep-alters-human-gene-activity
— http://crc.surrey.ac.uk/sleep-and-wake/key-publications.

Vatican's publication of the "Secret of Fatima": www.vatican.va/roman_curia/congregations/cfaith/documents/rc_con_cfaith_doc_20000626_message-fatima_en.html.

Walk Free Foundation: http://www.walkfreefoundation.org/.

Ward, Lester F. *The Psychic Factors of Civilization.* Boston, MA: Ginn & Co, 1893.

Watson, Lyall. *The Secret Life of Inanimate Objects.* Merrimac, MA: Destiny Books, 1992.

Wertz, Joe. "A Sharp Rise in Earthquakes Puts Oklahomans On Edge." *NPR's All Things Considered,* January 2, 2014: http://www.npr.org/2014/01/02/259127792/a-sharp-rise-in-earthquakes-puts-oklahomans-on-edge.

Wikipedia: www.wikipedia.org.

Wilheim, Ines, Michael Rose, Kathrin I. Imhof, Björn Rasch, Christian Büchel, Jan Born. "The sleeping child outplays the adult's capacity to convert implicit into explicit knowledge." *Nature Neuroscience,* doi: 10.1038/nn.3343, 2013: www.alphagalileo.org/ViewItem.aspx?ItemId=128841&CultureCode=en.

Jacobs, Jahsiah Abijah and Joyce Anastasia. "Message 2 Humanity" (previous title: "I Believe in this Generation") — music video: https://www.youtube.com/watch?v=d3kyj_KxbiA.

Williams, Brian. "Edward Snowden Interview," May 29, 2014: http://www.nbcnews.com/feature/edward-snowden-interview.

Williamson, Marianne. *A Return to Love: Reflections on the Principles of "A Course in Miracles."* New York: HarperCollins, 1992,2012.
— "Announces Candidacy for Congressional Seat." You Tube, November 19, 2013: https://www.youtube.com/watch?v=fz_ijN3kS8s.

Wiser.org: http://wiser.org/.

Wolf, Dr. Fred Alan. *Mind Into Matter: A New Alchemy of Science and Spirit.* Portsmouth, NH: Moment Point Press, Inc., 2001.
— *Mind into Feeling: A New Alchemy of Science and Spirit.* Portsmouth, NH: Moment Point Press, Inc., 2002.
— www.fredalanwolf.com.

Women for Women: http://www.womenforwomen.org/

Yousafzai, Malala. *I Am Malala: The Girl Who Stood Up for Education and Was Shot By the Taliban.* London: Orion Publishing Group Ltd., a Hachette Livre Company, 2013.

Index

C

H

I

J

N

About the Author

Joyce Anastasia, MA/MFA, is a transformational leadership consultant, multicultural counselor, educator, writer and visionary activist whose lifelong passion is to inspire new ways to lead by wisdom, co-creating a more peaceful, resilient and loving world.

Joyce is the founder of LeadByWisdom.com, an organization whose mission is to develop and expand leadership training that encourages people to explore their relationships to Power, Truth, Integrity, Wholeness, Balance, Miracles, and heart-centered Manifestation and Transformation — for themselves and the world. Deeply connected to All That Is, Joyce has been guided throughout her life to serve humanity for the greatest good, to honor all beings and to assist others to evoke their greatest gifts, to communicate with deep respect and gratitude with all others, allowing the mysteries of life to naturally emerge.

Although Joyce has received two advanced degrees and numerous certifications, her greatest understanding comes from her exposure and life experiences with wisdom keepers and beautiful "ordinary" people throughout the world. Joyce travels internationally as a transformational leadership consultant for individuals and groups, providing teaching, training, and facilitation to invite "Extraordinary Leadership During Extraordinary Times."

For more information, contact Joyce at www.LeadByWisdom.com or joyceanastasia@gmail.com.

[Book Cover, Interior Graphic Design, co-created with Andrew Howansky © Joyce Anastasia; Back Cover Portrait provided by Janelle Maguire (With Permission).]